AF181506

Islands of Law

Studies in Modern European History

Frank J. Coppa
General Editor

Vol. 40

PETER LANG
New York • Washington, D.C./Baltimore • Boston • Bern
Frankfurt am Main • Berlin • Brussels • Vienna • Oxford

Richard S. Tompson

Islands of Law

A Legal History of the British Isles

PETER LANG
New York • Washington, D.C./Baltimore • Boston • Bern
Frankfurt am Main • Berlin • Brussels • Vienna • Oxford

Library of Congress Cataloging-in-Publication Data

Tompson, Richard S.
Islands of law: a legal history of the British Isles / Richard S. Tompson.
p. cm. — (Studies in modern European history; vol. 40)
Includes bibliographical references and index.
1. Law—British Isles—History. I. Title. II. Series.
KD532.T66 349.41—dc21 99-056142
ISBN 0-8204-4898-2
ISSN 0893-6897

Die Deutsche Bibliothek-CIP-Einheitsaufnahme

Tompson, Richard S.:
Islands of law: a legal history of the British Isles / Richard S. Tompson.
–New York; Washington, D.C./Baltimore; Boston; Bern;
Frankfurt am Main; Berlin; Brussels; Vienna; Oxford: Lang.
(Studies in modern European history; Vol. 40)
ISBN 0-8204-4898-2

Cover design by Mark Wickersham

© 2000 Peter Lang Publishing, Inc., New York

All rights reserved.
Reprint or reproduction, even partially, in all forms such as microfilm,
xerography, microfiche, microcard, and offset strictly prohibited.

Table of Contents

Preface

My interest in legal history dates from early encounters with the documents of grammar school foundations. The unearthing of these dry formulations by Charity Commissioners opened a window for me into the world of some nineteenth-century barristers. Meanwhile, I had developed a parallel interest in the multilateral histories of the British Isles, and these two came together in considering the striking preservation of so many separate legal systems in the archipelago. At the outset, my efforts to explore the wider context were frustrated by the absence of any general historical accounts. This more than anything made me decide to try my hand at a political survey of *The Atlantic Archipelago*, by way of self-education. But all along it was my aim to explore the several legal systems and their histories.

I have three goals in this work: first, to make legal history more accessible to general historians; second, to explain the links between the legal histories of England, Scotland, and Ireland; and third, to provide a framework for more specialized studies in legal interaction. As one without formal legal training who has come late to the field of legal history, I have the greatest debts to the published work and private assistance of many others. For their generous help I am truly grateful.

I am pleased to acknowledge the support of the University Research Committee and the College of Humanities of the University of Utah, whose assistance made the research for this book possible.

Richard S. Tompson
Salt Lake City

Abbreviations

A.C.	Appeal Cases, 1891–
All E.R.	All England Law Reports, 1936–
App. Cas.	Appeal Cases, 1875–1890
A.P.S.	Acts of the Parliaments of Scotland, 1124–1707
B.W.C.C.	Butterworths' Workmen's Compensation Cases, 1908–47
Ch.	Chancery Reports, 1891–
C.M.L.R.	Common Market Law Reports, 1962–
D.	Dunlop, Bell, and Murray Session Cases, 1838–62
E.C.R.	European Court Reports, 1954–
E.R.	English Reports (reprints of reports to 1865)
F.	Fraser Session Cases, 1898–1906
H.C.J.	House of Commons Journal
H.L.J.	House of Lords Journal
H.L.R.O.	House of Lords Record Office
H.M.C.	Historical Manuscripts Commission Reports
I.H.L.J.	Irish House of Lords Journal
I.R.	Irish Reports, 1894–
Irv.	Irvine's Justiciary Reports, 1851–68

M.	MacPherson's Session Cases, 1862–1873
MacQ.	MacQueen's Scottish Appeal Cases, 1851–65
P.D.	Parliamentary Debates
R.	Rettie's Session Cases, 1873–98
S.C.	Session Cases, 1906–
S.L.T.	Scots Law Times (Reports), 1950–
S. O.	Standing Orders
S.P.	Sessional Papers (year. volume. page)
S.T.	State Trials, ed. T. B. Howell.
W.L.R.	Weekly Law Reports, 1953–

NOTE: conventional legal citation is used for works in series, giving volume, title and page number, *e.g.*, 23 E.R. 133 is volume 23 of English Reports, page 133.

Introduction

Insularity and Interaction

A comprehensive legal history of the British Isles has never been written. Two roadblocks appear to stand in the way: first there is the separation between legal and general history. Historians of the law prefer their own sphere, and general historians afford the law little space in their surveys. In recent years this avoidance has been overcome by some ambitious efforts which survey history and law in tandem.[1]

The second impediment is the anglocentric treatment of British history. Here there has been substantial progress in the last twenty-five years.[2] Recent research and writing have moved toward a more comprehensive view of the British Isles as the essential unit of historical explanation. But in legal history there is little evidence of this kind of movement. English law has long been the principal focus of the legal historian. The quantity of records, the size of reading publics, and the traditions of scholarship have dictated this orientation. To remedy the detachment of legal history, and to challenge the segmented study of the British Isles, this book charts a course with which to begin the journey.[3]

The law—any law or legal system—inhabits and informs the life of a community: its relations of power, status, wealth, and culture. The essential qualities of law are formed by and help to shape the elementary character of that society. Therefore, it is of no small consequence when law and legal systems are not treated as vital parts of the history of a tribe, folk, kingdom, or nation. The historian's challenge is to find a suitable method for integral presentation. Here we will adopt a simple format: the major themes of each period discussed will be viewed in and through stages or episodes of legal history—that is, the legal history of the British Isles as a whole. Each chapter will begin with a sketch of historical events and some of their legal connections. This will be followed by a multipart analysis of interaction between the legal systems of the British Isles in that period.

To begin to characterize the institutions of law we will be studying, our first observation is that there has never been a single, unified legal system which served the whole of the British Isles. In the jurisdictional sense, there are royal, ecclesiastical, commercial, and administrative laws. In the territorial sense, there are still distinct systems of public and private law for England and Wales, for Scotland, for Ireland (North and South), and for the Channel Islands and the Isle of Man. The variety is daunting, and there is no simple way toward comprehensive treatment.

Systems of law are by nature insular. The rules they follow are guarded in order to maintain the integrity of the system. Thus no system in the British Isles fully accepts the original jurisdiction of another; the decisions in one system may not be binding precedents in the others; lawyers seldom practice in more than one jurisdiction, and doing so requires additional training and certification.[4] However, the insulation of professional requirements need not dictate the shape of legal historiography. To be an "island of law" was not to be isolated historically. To look within for rules and precedents did not prevent interaction. There have always been situations which produced contact; and when two systems came together the event could have very important consequences for all involved. The nature, extent, and effects of these encounters changed markedly from the earliest times to the seventeenth century, in the prelude to the modern age of interaction which is the subject of this book. The key point here is that insular systems were not isolated systems: interaction was abundant, and it shaped and preserved the lasting legal identities in the British Isles.

Legal interaction is the convergence or collision of two systems of law through the agency of any of their constituent parts: litigants or lawyers, lawmakers, judges, or rulers. The thesis of this book is that such activity has been a constant feature of the history of the British Isles. But where once the result was either survival or subjugation, in modern times the effect of interaction became less severe, if no less important. Since 1660 the systems which cohabited in the archipelago have been constantly engaged, but they have steadily moved toward more benign contact.[5] This book will concentrate on the laws and legal systems of England, Scotland, and Ireland. The small island jurisdictions do offer some interesting examples of interaction, but the Isle of Man and the Channel Islands do not present the complex and connected and richly documented legal histories which are found in England's larger neighbors. There will be points at which the smaller systems will be cited to illustrate larger interactive themes; but on grounds of size and significance, it seems right to concentrate on the three major areas. Those regions and their laws offer a challenging setting for combining legal and general history.

Islands of Law Before 1066

Successive migrations into the British Isles—Celtic, Roman, Christian, Saxon, and Scandinavian—brought with them many different legal customs and institutions. These imports had in common the elementary connection between law and the society's power, property, and beliefs. Celtic tribal ideas of kingship, custodial relation to land, and the worship of particular deities were passed down by learned priests and lawmen, members of the bardic class. With no written materials, law was custom based on memory. Roman occupation after the first century brought contact with a massive political empire and a civilized society. Romanized Celts were introduced to written law, not only that of Rome, but later Christian mission transcriptions of the old native laws as well. Contact with Rome brought social and economic change to many parts, but not to the North of Britain or to Ireland. In the wake of Roman withdrawal in the fifth century, Germanic migration introduced another customary society, one which would also encounter missions and comprehensive change: an international church helped to establish written Saxon law, more advanced monarchies, property-based elites, and, of course, a powerful clerical order. This structure was threatened and then replicated by the fearsome Scandinavian assaults of the ninth and tenth centuries. In the same era, the "Norman" community on the continent was born, and it would lead a late and emphatic invasion of the British Isles in the eleventh century.

As products of oral traditions, the early customary laws can never be known to us without the mediation of their earliest transcribers. The tribal laws were probably not immune to interaction before the arrival of Roman and Christian influence. If impossible to recreate, it is plausible to imagine tribal law being shared by an over-king with his Celtic clients. With Roman occupation of Britain from the first to fourth centuries, there was a different sort of contact: written and oral systems collided; Roman acceptance of mixed laws allowed the preservation of Celtic customs; mixing of populations brought new laws for federated tribes and hybrid communities. In the latter part of the Roman occupation the advent of Christian missions brought not only spiritual conversion but also a new kind of legal interaction. A passage in the Irish law tracts suggests the blending of sources.[6]

> The joint memory of the ancients, transmission from ear to ear, the chanting of the poets, its being augmented by the law of Scripture, its being founded on the law of nature...That which is contrary to [Christian] conscience has been made forfeit by ink.

The monk in royal service was in fact an agent of interaction in both a combining and a correcting capacity.

The committal of oral laws to writing was evident in Saxon communities also. The mission of Augustine to Kent may have produced the first written publication of Anglo-Saxon dooms. This first Saxon "code" was the beginning of a tradition, and successive kings produced their own versions, each time providing an opportunity for modifying custom as it was committed to written form. The laws of Ine and Offa continued the Saxon tradition, and with the reign of Alfred in the ninth century there was more extensive engagement with the church and restatement of the laws. These laws were only one part of the system: courts in hundreds, shires, and boroughs embodied the communal jurisdictions; royal sheriffs presided, with bishops; writs were used to start proceedings, charters were made to record transactions. These elements were apt to be found in each of the Anglo-Saxon kingdoms. But in the ninth century, the coming of the Danes radically altered the picture.

The Scandinavian assaults brought new laws, and there were different forms of interaction. In Shetland and Man, Norse laws were introduced and lasted for centuries. In Irish coastal towns and in the Five Boroughs in England there were temporarily dominant Danish systems, later assimilated by local laws. In the tenth and early eleventh centuries, kings of England were forced to acknowledge limits on their authority.[7]

> The Danes live very much under their own laws...The Norsemen of York have perhaps a yet larger measure of independence under their own earl. To a lesser degree this is true also of Mercia and East Anglia, to whose ealdorman copies of Edgar's legislation are sent in order that it may be made known generally in their provinces. Edgar is not the direct lord of all England and he himself distinguishes between legislation applying to the English and legislation applying to the whole nation, English, Danes and Britons, as he puts it. English

administration and English law have as yet proceeded only a few steps toward unification.

The most successful Danish ruler, King Cnut, adapted the laws of the English kingdom and issued a new version composed by Archbishop Wulfstan, one which bore the marks of the laws of the church. The return of a Saxon, in the person of Edward the Confessor in 1042, interrupted the exposure to the Scandinavian orbit. On the other hand, Edward's exile in Normandy assured that he would bring royal servants, and perhaps legal advisers, from that province.

England's neighbors included many varied polities: Scottish kings, Irish high-kings, Welsh princes, and other overlords, each ruled by means of customary and sometimes written laws, composed and collected by their lawmen and clergy. Laws were preserved by rulers, used by them, and upheld as a communal bond. There was little or no sense of lords as lawgivers or innovators. The societies of the eleventh century depended for their security or survival—as had their ancestors—on a class of armed and wealthy warriors. That wealth was derived from the land and its produce, and governments found ways to assess and tax that wealth; to monitor and punish malefactors; and to settle disputes between its members. All of these functions were common enough; the many discrete units in which they were performed meant, of course, innumerable opportunities for interaction.

Feudal Law and Common Law, 1066–1307

The essential character of medieval England and of the archipelago was reshaped by the arrival of William of Normandy in 1066. A central rule imagined by the descendants of Alfred and foreshadowed by Cnut was initiated by the agency of feudalized laws and institutions. These dominated the rather wealthy English economy, now controlled by the king's mostly French vassals. The conquest directly affected England, while Scotland and Wales were treated as hostile neighbors; Ireland did not host the Anglo-Normans until a century later. A new kind of lordship was enabled by the act of conquest: the king claimed ownership of the land, which was distributed on various tenures to his earls and barons, his archbishops and bishops. Knight service was provided in exchange for property and the lord and vassal accepted terms which embodied legal rights and obligations. The knight's fee (*feodum*, hence feudal) was a contractual unit which represented a new legal concept and a new level of legal sophistication.

The feudal order engendered stronger central institutions: the Norman *curia regis* and the office of justiciar were powerful administrative innovations. In addition, King William shrewdly preserved the written laws of the English as well as their traditional Saxon writs and their sheriffs. Thus there was a certain amount of blending in matters of law. Finally, the process of settling disputes meant further mixing of laws, as Norman and English parties sought the judgments of royal and baronial courts. The story of this combination was recorded in early twelfth century collections such as the so-called Laws of William the Conqueror, the Laws of Henry I, the *Les Williame*, and the Laws of Edward the Confessor. These collections offer a properly confusing picture of shifting legal ideas and rules in a period of transformation and assimilation. It was also a period of major institutional development, occasioned by the need to accommodate Norman practices: private jurisdiction, separate church courts, trial by battle, and the Frankish (royal) inquest were unknown to Saxon law, and their introduction entailed more interaction.

In the early twelfth century there were further innovations in the machinery of the royal court, with the formation of the exchequer to audit royal revenue and the dispatch of itinerant justices to try offenses against the king's peace. The system of frankpledge (like the Anglo-Saxon tithing) was a local grouping for the purpose of law enforcement. By the reign of Henry I (1100–1135) the English legal system made very significant departures from its eleventh-century predecessors. The English experience was in some measure emulated by marcher lords in Chester, Montgomery, and Hereford; it became known to the Scots by way of migration and borrowing (including the exile and marriage of David I). For the moment, Irish kings (and French barons) were outside this English legal orbit.[8]

After the death of Henry I there was a disputed succession, and between 1135 and 1154 England was preoccupied with internal warfare and deteriorating royal legal authority. It was in response to that disruption that the new Angevin ruler Henry II took the vigorous steps which mark the origin of the English common law. This new departure built upon Saxon and Norman foundations with several elements enhancing the capacity of royal courts: possessory writs which gave parties access to royal courts for property claims; other royal writs to order subjects to do right; more itinerant justices and meetings of local courts under their supervision; and evolution of the central courts (the exchequer, common bench, and those judges who were in the king's company, in the King's Bench. By the late 1180s the workings of the royal courts were described in a *Treatise on the Laws and Customs of England.* [9]

The political character of the reign of Henry II had a great deal to do with the role of the common law in the British Isles. Henry extended his lordship, and in so doing he brought the legal systems into a series of engagements with striking and varied results. We should not expect him to have sought to impose a uniform system. After all, this was a French ruler with extensive continental holdings, whose English and British lordships were the branches of a major European federation. There was a wide array of relationships, driven largely by local circumstances. In Wales, Henry tried to use his legal authority to control the marcher lords. In Scotland, the migration of Anglo-Normans helped to encourage introduction of English legal customs: "a process which took place over many generations, the result not of imposition from without, but of willing borrowing and adaptation."[10] In Ireland, the first visit in 1171 to assert royal control was followed by King John's visits, especially that of 1210 which marked the importation of common law (for the English in Ireland).[11] When the Duchy of Normandy was lost in 1204, the English crown retained authority over the Channel Islands and they kept their customary laws; later in the century the first and only native Prince of Wales was removed to make way for an English principality; in Ireland there was the notable episode where several Irish bishops offered to purchase access to the king's courts for the native Irish in the late 1270s.[12]

By that point English legal development had reached another stage: the famous tract known as "Bracton" had been composed by the middle of the century *(De Legibus et Consuetudinibus Angliae)*[13] and was the first systematic statement of English law. It was aimed at compiling cases and commenting on court procedure, and whether Henry de Bracton was author or more likely compiler or editor, the work stood as a mark of maturing law. From about 1270 decided cases were being recorded for future reference in the *Year Books*, which perhaps originated in private notes of apprentices, lawyers, and judges.

Edward I had succeeded in restoring the power of the English Crown after a disastrous rebellion in the 1260s. The young king summoned his nobles and knights and burgesses to meet with him in parliaments, further formalizing earlier councils, and widening the political nation. This was a phenomenon being seen all over Europe. Such bodies served as sources of advice and consent for royal policy and action—especially for raising revenue. Early English parliaments did not legislate; rather they approved (re)statements of law, often in response to collected petitions from the king's subjects. The creation of Magna Carta in 1215 was regarded as a prototype for statute, and the reissue of the charter many times over the next three centuries reinforced that idea. Of course the ordinary statute seldom rose to such lofty levels or touched upon the fundamental laws of the realm. All the same, the appearance of parliaments (also in Scotland, Ireland, and Man) provided a new agency for statements of law.

Edward made extensive use of statutes to reshape the rules governing landholding as the feudal system became outmoded. Laws were enacted to limit gifts of land to the church, to remove some restraints on sale of land and to aid the preservation of family estates. While his parliaments were ratifying these renovations, Edward I was making the strongest medieval assertion of English political power in the British Isles. His conquest of Wales was incomplete, but the Statute of 1284 made expansive claims for English royal law; his plans for Scotland promised legal centralization there, but Scotland soon regained its independence;[14] his plan, if any, for Ireland is not known. But in spite of these efforts, Edward's death was followed by a reversal of the anglocentric trends in legal interaction.

Late Medieval Islands, 1307–1485

The fourteenth and fifteenth centuries were a period of serious political and economic and social turmoil. Simply put, this was an age marked by conflict. Most notable were the Hundred Years' War with France (1337–1453); the Scottish War of Independence (1307–1328); the invasions of Ireland (Bruce in 1315; Richard II in 1394 and 1399);

rebellion in Wales (1400–1410); and baronial "Wars of the Roses" in England (1455–1485). While it is often observed that these conflicts were not sustained campaigns in the manner of modern warfare, it is clear that the fighting left a deep imprint on the political and social order. Parallel with political and military distress, these two centuries were a time of sharp economic fluctuations, as trade patterns, employment, and taxation were affected by plague and famine as well as periodic warfare. High taxes, labor shortages, and military campaigns were some of the impulses which undermined traditional legal relations, creating such aberrations as "bastard feudalism," a loose term for monetary payment in lieu of knight service. Such forces were felt in England and beyond in varied degrees—little noticed in Gaelic areas, but vital influences on manorial and urban communities.

In this climate of conflict, English legal authority declined in the archipelago in the fourteenth and fifteenth centuries. That decline took several forms: a mixing of laws in Scotland, native revival in Ireland, and rebellion in Wales. Meanwhile, in its own territory, English common law continued its independent evolution. Scottish legal historians have disputed the extent and nature of English influence on Scots law, and they have wrestled with Lord Cooper's concept of a "Dark Age"—the idea that for two centuries after the wars of independence Scotland rejected English models, turned to France and elsewhere, only emerging in the sixteenth (or seventeenth) century with a new system of Scots law. This view has been decisively rejected in favor of one that sees continuing English influence alongside the entry of continental influence from France in the shaping of the estates of parliament, the formation of royal courts, and the schooling of Scottish lawyers.[15] James I (1406–1437) spent time in English captivity, and when he came to the Scottish throne he tried to renovate judicial administration by appointing as judges a chancellor and several delegates from each estate plus a clerk register to form the "session" (1426–1470). He also named a commission to examine books of law (1425). In the sixteenth century this experimentation culminated in the establishment of the College of Justice, the first enduring and effective central court in Scotland. This does not seem like a "dark" age, even if no institution established an unalloyed tradition. Law and legal development continued; varied influences (clergy, civilians, feudatories, clansmen) interacted with the sheriffs, justiciars, procurators, and other officials. There was both a strong anglicized foundation and a period of eclectic development. The product would be unique to Scotland.

The Irish story was clearly different. The English lordship cohabited with a Celtic society; the Anglo-Irish lords yearned for English legal parity, while every day they fought battles with their Gaelic neighbors.[16] In the fourteenth century the tide seemed to turn in favor of the older inhabitants. There were several attempts to shore up the colonial administration, especially under Richard II. But part of the Gaelic revival in Ireland in the fourteenth century was the increased power of native courts. The *brehons* had experienced a sort of eclipse in the thirteenth century, but revived in the next. Moreover, the use of Irish law began to spread from the march into the English lordship in the fourteenth century. The angry denunciations of Irish law in the Statute of Kilkenny (1366) reflected the fear that its influence was growing. The *brehons* were responsible for supervising arbitrators and their sessions; enforcing the awards of arbitration was imperfect and depended on kin-groups. At the same time, there was evidence of interaction in the opposite direction. Steven Ellis has given an arresting picture of other kinds of late medieval mixing:[17]

> During the period 1350–1500 Gaelic law was evidently transformed, much as Welsh law had been, by the introduction of the pledge as a means of alienating land, by the jury, and common law concepts .... The precise impact of all this is not yet clear, but it seems that common law ideas were adapted to strengthen seigneurial control at the same time as Gaelic law was being modified in accordance with changing structures in Gaelic society.

Fifteenth century Ireland saw a continued decline of English power, typified by the shrinkage of the Pale around Dublin. The famous statement by the Irish parliament in 1460 that it alone could make laws for Ireland was partially true; the English parliament had lost that power; the crown might still appoint deputies; cases still could go to King's Bench in London; but the Lord Deputy, like Kildare, relied on networks of native or old settler property in order to function. There was, until the 1530s, a kind of mixed society and mixed authority in Ireland. There was no question that the English crown was the highest authority, but there was no way to exercise that authority in and through the old feudal colonial structure by itself.

There was yet another story in Wales. After Edward's conquest, there was relative peace in the fourteenth century, and there was increased prosperity. Davies writes of "gradual adoption of English law" facilitated by these conditions; there was also a decline in the strict racial divisions between Welsh and English.[18] But the revolt of Owain Glyndwr abruptly changed all this in 1400. Growing resentment from the later fourteenth century spilled over in a decade of rebellion. There was even a threat to form a rebel alliance reaching across the North of England. These events, including the fleeting presence of a Welsh Parliament, only succeeded in feeding a deep fear and distrust on the part of the English. The reaction to the rebellion was embodied in a string of restrictive laws, in the revival of the severe racial divisions, and in repressive measures of various kinds.[19] This must have retarded the desire to embrace English law, but it may not have been able to slow down the kind of mixing going on at the everyday level in civil and criminal process.

What was happening in the English legal system while these signs of autonomy were appearing? The late thirteenth and early fourteenth centuries were, in fact, an important time for the maturing of the English system. The lawyers were now a secular profession; the use of law French as the language of the courts may have aided the division into a two-tier profession of pleader in court (barrister) and agent at law (solicitor). In the Common Pleas the former were serjeants, a select guild which controlled the business of that court. They and others organized common quarters for living and studying—the Inns of Court—in the course of the fourteenth century in London.

The English courts remained the same with one major exception: by the fifteenth century the lord chancellor, who received the bulk of the petitions to the crown and granted writs to suitors, began to hear bills, in a court free of the procedural rules of the common law. Thus the Court of Chancery was born, a court of conscience which heard cases in which legal remedy was unobtainable at common law. The timing of the equity court's appearance is ironic, for the fifteenth century in England was not noted for law and order. In the political and social turmoil which marked the middle decades, courts and judges were not able to function properly; livery and maintenance meant the surrender of power to warlords, especially when the crown itself was the prize of factions in the Wars of the Roses. By the 1470s, Edward IV launched a revival of monarchical government with stronger councils, more intervention, and a restoration of order. About the same time, John Fortescue wrote *de Laudibus Legum Angliae*, a classic tribute to the late medieval English law (composed in exile in France).

By the time of Fortescue, the common law was nearly three centuries old. In that time, Wales had moved well into the English orbit; Scotland had shared English law but developed its own centralized system; while Ireland was divided into an anglicized pale and zones of mixed laws. The Middle Ages had seen these different interactions, all of which defined the national laws, none of which had the power to fuse them. The Tudor dynasty would make a pronounced effort to achieve greater control. Would it attempt to forge a unified system? Could it possibly succeed?

English Legal Reformation

In the sixteenth century the further development of English law was paralleled by the evolution of the unitary state and the royal supremacy in the church. The net effect was to weld English legal supremacy to the English constitution, but it was not clear that this would in fact change the nature or the identity of the subordinate systems. As it worked out, Wales was amalgamated, Scotland was alienated, and Ireland was colonized.

The English legal system was revived by the Tudors. The old common law courts had suffered during the fifteenth century, and they were revitalized by "a revolution produced largely from within" by "counsel and judges anxious to accommodate outdated concepts to a changing society."[20] The setting up of conciliar courts, that is, bodies constituted by members of the royal council, was at once an effective use of royal power and an effective stimulant to the old common law courts to restore themselves. If there was a danger, it was in the Tudors' tendency to multiply jurisdictions. Henry VII had the revived privy council which spawned Star Chamber, the Council of Wales, and courts of requests; Henry VIII (with Wolsey and Thomas Cromwell) invented courts for augmentations, wardships, and church governance; Queen Elizabeth created the Court of High Commission (1580) which traced its authority back to earlier commissions. The Court of Exchequer Chamber (1585) was a revival of an old court in the exchequer, where all the high court judges decided points of law. These events were overshadowed by the dramatic confrontation between the English Crown and the papacy. In that process, the English parliament was used by Henry VIII to ratify major steps in the secession from the church of Rome. Scholars debate the exact meaning of the constitutional change, but it is clear in our context that such an enhanced legislative power brought a new dimension to the relations between the islands of law.

In Wales native laws had lost ground steadily. There had been competing legal rules since the earliest times; there had been outside intervention on a large scale since the Normans; and there had been an English royal presence since the conquest of Edward I. The contrasting patterns of the fourteenth century (gradual anglicizing) and the fifteenth century (violent nationalist resistance) neither destroyed nor consolidated native courts and laws. So when the Tudor house, with its Welsh patrimony, pushed for closer constitutional ties, the issue came to a head. In 1536 the marcher lordships were merged with the principality to form new counties with representation in the English parliament; English law and the English language were to be used in all courts. Further reforms were made in 1543, with new counties plus provision for English-style county courts and officers, and a unique regional structure, the Court of Great Sessions. The measures were predicated on lawless conditions in Wales, but the crown's agent, Bishop Reginald Lee, had been vigorously dispatching felons before the acts of union, and he had little use for reform. The assimilation of England and Wales concluded the conscious absorption of one of the archaic legal systems in the British Isles and disposed of the ungainly march. The relative ease of this accomplishment, owing to the lack of a central native Welsh legal authority, stood in marked contrast to the relations with Scotland and Ireland.

The Scottish legal system was being revived in the fifteenth century, as Scottish kings attempted to strengthen central control of their dominion. The role of the crown was pivotal, even though at the end of the Middle Ages its legal authority was replicated in many "regalities" and its central power was thus diluted. Over the course of the fifteenth century and into the sixteenth, the Scottish kings used royal councillors and members of the estates to sit in session as judges, and they were joined there by a number of ecclesiastical lawyers. This central court was formalized in 1532 as the College of Justice, encompassing both judges and advocates. The court had fifteen judges who were to be supported by a levy on the Scottish church. This novel central legal institution would give a distinctive character to the development of Scottish law. The new court was not given a mandate to reform the law, but the legal business that came to it, plus active royal interest, plus the impact of religious reform, all combined to produce significant changes by the end of the sixteenth century. A new commission was set up in 1560 to examine the records of parliament and to compile a list of acts. This was done again in 1574 and 1592. By about 1579, Sir James Balfour's *Practicks* (decisions) had been composed. This and other manuscript records of cases were an important step toward a literate judicial system. The formation of advocates and writers into professional groups was another step, though legal education developed more slowly. In the 1590s provisions were made to examine candidates for the bench, to require a property qualification, and to reduce nepotism, though some of these steps met with only limited success.[21]

The legal development of Tudor Ireland was tied to the shifting position of the English Crown: from the Kildare Ascendancy to Henry VIII's assumption of the Irish kingship, to the final conquest of Ireland by Elizabeth. There were strong assertions of royal authority at each of these stages; there was continuing Irish resistance also, and it was only in the seventeenth century that Gaelic law would be decisively restricted. The reciprocal extension of English law was obviously not an undiluted transfer. The concentration of power in the lord deputy at the end of the fifteenth century brought periods of royal pressure to limit or retrieve power. In 1495, the deputy Edward Poynings introduced measures which adopted English laws and required English approval for new Irish legislation. By this date, the Dublin courts had become sedentary. Their practice was more in line with English common law, perhaps because there was access to English courts for appeals. But there was never apt to be a true reflection of the courts of Westminster Hall in Dublin, because the setting, the personnel, and the business were so different.[22]

This underlying dissimilarity was especially clear when Henry VIII assumed the title of King of Ireland in 1541. This extension of Crown authority surely was meant to strengthen the royal supremacy, improve secular authority, and facilitate legal change in Ireland. The Crown adopted an ambitious policy of "surrender and regrant," designed to coax gaelic lords into converting their traditional titles into English ones, thus gaining royal endorsement. The policy failed, due to native hostility and the program's inherent legal complexities. In the last half of the century the Tudors turned to more forceful ways to alter and extend legal authority. Areas outside Dublin were hard to govern, and at times commissions were sent out to try cases and assert royal power. In some cases, resident commissioners were used. This model was the pattern for the presidencies of Munster and Connaught, both of which were *ad hoc* extensions of royal authority, similar to medieval palatine jurisdictions in England, or the Tudor councils in Wales or in the North of England.[23]

There were also innovations at the center of the Irish legal structure. When Henry's kingship was proclaimed, a group of Dublin lawyers banded together to found the King's Inns on an old monastic property in the city. This lawyers' club never attained the same status as its namesakes in London; indeed, there was soon a law requiring Irish barristers to reside for a number of terms in a London Inn in order to qualify to practice in Dublin; this was seen as a sure way to bond two legal communities. There were other structural changes: the Court of Castle Chamber was created in the 1560s, the Court of High Commission in 1564. These prerogative courts took over the legal business of the privy council, as had their English equivalents. But neither these new courts, nor their older common law partners, were freestanding. Most Irish courts stood in the shadow of their English counterparts; indeed, they sometimes had personnel sent over for apprenticeships. They were small, ill-funded, with limited records and procedural powers. There was a definite subordination:[24]

> The English King's Bench still occasionally reviewed Irish cases, Irish business came before the English privy council and Star Chamber, and orders and patents were still authenticated by the English seals.

Ireland might have sheriffs, justices of the peace, and grand juries, but no one in the sixteeenth century would be likely to confuse these with their English models. What existed in Tudor Ireland was an English pattern stretched over a turbulent colony, with an alien culture, an outlawed church, and a pastoral economy. The pattern of judicial machinery was beset with too little local support and too much London supervision. But in the wake of a military victory in 1603, an energetic campaign would begin to assimilate the Irish to the English common law structure.

Seventeenth Century Collisions

When James VI of Scotland came to the English throne in 1603, there were major collisions of legal authority. There were battles over jurisdiction between several courts in England, important legal interventions in Ireland, and significant legal discussions between England and Scotland. In each case, fundamental legal ideas were challenged. After a long gestation, the War of the Three Kingdoms began in 1638, and behind this conflict were questions regarding the Crown and its judges; the Crown and its courts (including the parliaments); the place of bishops and other ministers; the power of taxation; and the power of military command. The English common lawyers strenuously defended their odd, ahistorical insular tradition; authors of the Scottish National Covenant composed a remarkable book of documents on the history of the reformed kirk; the Confederation of Kilkenny called on Irish royalists to support the Magna Carta and a radical provisional government. All of these national legal traditions collapsed in the face of an English army, serving an English republic, doubtless the most challenging interaction to date. But after a period of military occupation and legal experimentation, the old laws were restored. What these decades of confrontation seemed to produce was more fear of legal tyranny and a fervent desire not to assimilate.

The defeat of Hugh O'Neill shortly after Elizabeth died, opened the way for a new chapter in English rule in Ireland. The native "Irish enemies" were subdued, and they abdicated in the "flight of the earls"—the departure of Tyrone and Tyrconnel and their followers for the continent in 1607. In the ranks of the new regime, the English barrister John Davies was made solicitor general (1603) and later attorney general (1606–19). Davies became the central figure in a campaign to abolish native legal customs, a campaign which drew legal authority from a blend of common law and civilian sources: [25]

> The application of [civilian] conquest right vested England with a public law title to Ireland....Davies invoked the now familiar powers of conquest to justify the eradication of domestic Irish law as little more than a barbarous and lewd custom, with an eye to eliminating all competing claims to Irish dominion, foreign and Gaelic, that were contingent either upon the political authority accorded to Gaelic chieftains, or upon the papal donation of Ireland to Henry II in 1154.

In other words, the English lawyer used a mixture of legal concepts to impose English authority over native Irish law, or to justify the conquest retroactively. Several of the most important "cases" which bore the weight of the new direction were in fact judicial *resolutions*, that is, judgments made outside of the regular course of legal proceedings. It was these "decisions" which made up the bulk of John Davies's *Reports* (the first and, until the eighteenth century, the only published law reports in Ireland).[26] In our context, Davies's overall contribution was to put the final touches on a long history of English legal interaction: once the native system lost its political force, there was nothing to hold Davies back from imposing a system of English common law on the Irish; but it was a seventeenth-century Irish version of English common law, a new, compound product.

At his royal court meanwhile, the new king supported a formal attempt to join the legal systems of England and Scotland.[27] The failure of this effort and its political fallout are well known. But the significance of the event for legal interaction requires further study. This first serious project to join two legal systems was unique in the history of the British Isles. Actually, the king's project had three elements: the first, which aroused the most hostility, was the notion of merging English and Scottish laws. English MPs feared a hostile takeover, but James denied a preference for civil law, saying "as King I have least cause of any man to dislike the common law," for he saw in it a support for the royal prerogative.[28] The next element of the project was the practical matter of eliminating the special border laws (on the ground that the border had lost its significance) and those Scottish and English laws which were hostile to the other country (on the ground that the two countries were now one). Here the sovereign was able to enact the desired settlement. The third element was maintenance of concurrent operation of both systems. In this aspect of the project, James did have some success in achieving a closer relationship.

The best example of the influence of joint operation was the famous instance of Calvin's Case. A collusive suit put before the English judges the issue of the legal status of a *post-natus*, a Scottish subject born after the king's accession to the English throne. By arranging a challenge to an inheritance, the case presented a serious (though surely rare) case.[29] It was in some ways no less a judicial show trial than the Irish resolutions of about the same date. In its specific terms, also, Calvin's Case relied on civil law doctrines of conquest and it accidentally demonstrated an unwonted flexibility in English law.

Scottish law had its own unique experience in the first half of the seventeenth century. In the period of union debate, the works of Sir Thomas Craig and Sir John Skene presented the first attempts at systematic analysis of Scots law, triggered by the threat or possibility of its amalgamation with the English system. Craig, in fact, composed a tract in which he noted that "at the present day there are no nations whose laws and institutions more closely correspond than England and Scotland." However "it was by no means imperative that the two kingdoms should submit to identical laws and systems," as that could be "a source of trouble."[30] The faltering of the union project was followed by the king's aggressive administration, in a sense merely a continuation of his earlier pattern as king of Scotland. He added more layers to the already thick local government: justices of the peace were created in 1587, again in 1609; commissions of justiciary were employed, that is, judges of the Court of Session sent on circuit; a king's guard was established to act as an enforcement arm. In two areas especially James exerted his authority: in reducing Highland disturbance and in extending episcopal authority. One measure which had no parallel was the establishment of the Register of Sasines in 1617, a national system of land registration which eluded England and Wales until the twentieth century.

The early seventeenth century was a period of self-conscious English legal insularity. The consensus of legal and constitutional historians has been that English lawyers laid the claim to superiority of the common law upon immemorial English custom. So every document, every decision, every statute embodied this mystical power, which allowed of no taint of foreign influence.[31] The immemorial law was a vital shield for men opposing the royal will. Edward Coke had extensive experience in the English law, and he was composing his famous *Reports* even before being raised to the bench. He surely felt that his Scottish royal master was not well informed and that it was his responsibility to educate the king in the common law. Coke and the other common lawyers were certain that they had to defend their practice against other jurisdictions. But King James saw their acts as simple attempts to grab larger areas of jurisdiction (and fees) for their courts.[32] Coke's judicial tenure ended in disputes with the king over some critical cases, but the judge's removal from the bench was less a severe punishment than a demonstration of royal power to dispose of servants. Coke was put on the Privy Council and continued to work in the royal court, until he went into opposition in the parliaments of the 1620s. There he became a leader of resistance to the crown. The questions raised in the Five Knights' Case (1627), the Petition of Right (1628), and the Ship Money Case (*R. v. Hampden* 1637) all had to do with limits on royal authority. It is no surprise that the king's judges found it right (or expedient) to rule in favor of the crown. It was more surprising that resistance, much of it led by lawyers, helped to galvanize opposition to royal policy.

While a crisis brewed in England, there were serious strains elsewhere, and the powers of lawmaking and enforcement were central to them as well. In 1622 a special commission was sent to investigate the Irish courts. The recommendations of the commission were only partly implemented, and this episode joined a long list of English interventions. When Thomas Wentworth went to Ireland in the 1630s, he brought some coordination to the main tribunals: Castle Chamber, High Commission, the Court of Wards and Liveries, and the newest of these, the Commission on Defective Titles. The new administration set out to increase revenues and reinforce royal authority. In one episode, the Lord Deputy offered a series of concessions—the "graces"—in exchange for money voted by parliament. The articles agreed included promises to put the army under civil law, several changes in the Court of Wards, and a number of reforms in the process of the ordinary courts.[33] When the money had been voted, the reforms were withdrawn!

Legal interaction was an important factor in the advent of the English civil war (or War of the Three Kingdoms). King Charles was the "fount of justice," who by many acts was able to generate hostility to his lawful government. In the several kingdoms there were different central issues; around these the lawyers helped to draft formal statements of opposition: the Scottish National Covenant came first (1638), followed by the English "Grand Remonstrance" of 1641 and the Irish Confederation in 1642. In each case a statement of fundamental law and established practice underscored the basic argument with the Crown, and their separate formulation demonstrated the lack of formal connections between the systems.

The Scottish flashpoint was the king's apparent plan to introduce the Anglican rite into the Presbyterian kirk. The proclamation of a new

Prayer Book in Edinburgh in 1637 brought a violent reply. The rioting in St. Giles Cathedral was probably not spontaneous. Petitions poured in protesting against the liturgy, and soon a covenant was drafted. According to one historian, "the hand of shrewd lawyers is plain in it." By citing a long list of statutes, as well as the coronation oath, there was an appeal to law; but it was "something new in Scottish history" and "reflects English influence."[34] For Scottish acts had not had the permanence of English ones, nor had Scots imbibed the notion of the ability of legislation to inhibit the crown. This habit was learned over the next few years, and in fact the organization of a provisional government showed that the Scots had gone well beyond any feeble English example. Hereafter Scottish leaders pursued an aggressive strategy, allying with English rebels in the Westminster Assembly and the Solemn League and Covenant (1643).

Irish legal resentments had been stoked by Wentworth. His recall in 1639 gave an opening to his adversaries in the Irish parliament. There was a complex division there, for Catholic and Protestant lines crossed over the groups of royalists and their opponents. What emerged at this point was a "patriot" identity, that is, a voice for Irish independence of some sort. One of its spokesmen was the lawyer and politician Patrick Darcy. "In Patrick Darcy's *Argument* (1641) we find an attempt to base the liberties of Ireland upon the Ancient Constitution of England."[35] Darcy asked rhetorically "Whether the subjects of this Kingdom be a free people...to be governed onely by the common lawes and statutes of force in this Kingdom." Darcy was one of the Old English Catholics (about 20 per cent in this Parliament). Sir Richard Bolton, who had served in several courts under Wentworth and who became lord chancellor in 1639, was a more traditional defender of the common law. He said "there is no humane law, within the circuite of the whole world...so apt and profitable, for the honourable, peaceable and prosperous government of the kingdomes of England and Ireland."[36] Profitable it may have been for Ireland, but Bolton's comment is taken from his manual for Justices of the Peace, a tract written because of the *differences* in English and Irish statute law on the subject. In one other ironic comparative episode, Bolton, as the king's man in Dublin, was the target of articles of impeachment which he himself received while presiding in parliament and which he ruled out of order, on the ground that the Irish Commons was not competent to proceed in such a manner. Needless to say, King

Charles upheld his ruling. In October 1641 a rebellion broke out in which Catholic rebels killed a large number of Protestant settlers in Ulster. There were severe reprisals, and there was panic in London. The state of war in Ireland contributed to the deteriorating political situation in Westminster. There was a stalemate over the dispatch of an English force, but parliament did hire Col. Robert Munro to lead his Scottish army to relieve the Ulster protestants.

The English crisis had been outlined by John Pym when Parliament met in April 1640.[37] He listed grievances in the areas of parliamentary privilege, matters of religion, and matters of property. In each area there were legal grounds, but there were also specific grievances about the law and the judges: "the judges presume to question the proceedings of the House," and members were punished "for speaking freely in parliament"; the High Commission "takes upon it to fine and imprison men," and diverse clergy "make and ordain constitutions" with no authority; the ship money judgment was "against all former precedents and laws," and "extrajudicial judgements and impositions of the judges" were a denial of due process. This Short Parliament was dissolved, but Charles soon had to summon another. The Long Parliament met in the fall of 1640, to last until the eve of the Restoration. The momentum of events swept the debates into stormier waters. By 1641, the Courts of Star Chamber and High Commission were abolished, with the assent of the king—as a tactical concession. These prerogative courts were overthrown because the power of the common law was held to be above such arbitrary power. But in short order the parliament assumed executive power itself and began to base its orders on "fundamental law." Legal process and legal personnel continued to function throughout the period of war and revolution, but they had to be affected by the strains of the hostilities.

The legal extremity of the rebellion came with the establishment of the English High Court of Justice which tried the king in January 1649. That body, a combination of army officers and members of the "rump" of the Long Parliament, charged Charles I with treason and, to no one's surprise, found him guilty. After the king's execution, formal steps were taken to establish an English republic: the monarchy was abolished, the House of Lords was abolished and "King's Bench" was changed to the "upper bench." The royal prerogative died with the king, and that void opened the door to legal reforms during the lifetime of the commonwealth. The void also made way for legal change in Ireland and Scotland.

There was no coherent or deliberate plan of legal reform.[38] In England, there were numerous ideas put forward, most of them in the turbulent medium of the ubiquitous pamphlets of the day. Matthew Hale was a lonely judicial advocate, joined by a handful of barristers. There were some measures with real potential: the Hale Commission (1652); the Chancery reform movement (1653); and the new constitutions (Instrument of Government, 1653, and Humble Petition and Advice, 1657). But there was to be no thorough overhaul. One contemporary voiced the general frustration with law and lawyers:[39]

> Our pretending deliverers have been our destroyers and indeed it was irrational to expect better things. Who will expect grapes from thorns or figs from thistles? Who will expect ease from oppression, from masters of oppression, the lawyers? If you will have clean streams flow from the fountain you must be sure to cleanse the fountain itself.

But the apocalyptic cleansing was never done and was never likely to be done. Too few reformers and too little time and too many distractions were the reasons.

The law reforms which came to Ireland and Scotland came in the baggage train of English armies. A few of the army leaders going to Ireland had been engaged in law reform efforts in England. A few had other credentials: John Cook had been commonwealth solicitor (and the main prosecutor) at the trial of Charles I. When he was made chief justice of Munster he was intent on using Ireland as a laboratory for legal reform:[40]

> Ireland was like a white paper, apt to receive any good impression, and in regard that ye Lord hath given a *supersedeas* to the old courts here, it was hoped that...such an expedient for speedie and sure justice might have been settled, that though Ireland be but the younger sister, yet England might have been the learner and gainer by her.

The Four Courts were out of business, and the Cromwellian governors used commissions for the administration of justice and the collection of revenue until in 1655 the Four Courts were restored, and the system as it had operated before 1641 was revived.

Commissioners were also dispatched to Scotland, but in this case Scots were included. Their orders were to see that "lawes of England as to matters of government be put in execution in Scotland." This ambiguous instruction was probably intended to support the many specific assignments in the area of religious practice and other public activity. In any case, there was no significant progress on legal union. The Council was to pursue union according to instructions of 1655. But by 1657 it was clear that "the idea of assimilating...had been quietly abandoned."[41]

Thus the picture of the Cromwellian period is one of contrasts. The most powerful assertion of English authority, and presumably the greatest opportunity for legal assimilation, resulted instead in the preservation of national laws and systems, and it also helped to promote their restoration in 1660. The seventeenth century collisions bring home the main point in the most forceful way: the islands of law cannot be isolated; and though their interactions may produce alterations, they will also reinforce legal identities. Their insular natures will respond to crises; any collision with another system will insure that neither one is the same afterward; but the self-consciousness of each will press for preservation.

The wars of the three kingdoms were a watershed experience in all ways. No future political or religious or social or legal question could be unaffected by that memory. No amount of goodwill could truly restore the situation of 1640. Indeed, all efforts to do so seemed to create or renew hostility. But the restoration also represented the beginning of a new adventure for the three kingdoms: the story of modern legal interaction. At the base of the new legal orientation was the memory of the regicide. We can hardly imagine the depth of feeling generated by the trial and execution of Charles I, but we ought to understand its profound effect in legal terms. The sovereign was the embodiment of law; his prerogative was its manifestation; the blows against that power might be justified by later constitutional history, but in the seventeenth century, especially in the waning days of the republic, a return to a familiar symbol and source of legal authority was desperately needed. That need was vividly displayed in the flood of petitions for royal grace and favor in 1660. Where they would go, who would address them, and what effect they would have on the law and legal systems were central issues in the restoration: they were also the issues around which the story of modern legal interaction began to unfold.

Modern Legal Interaction

The "islands of law" had been formed over a period of many centuries. Thus the modern British Isles inherited well-established and firmly separated legal systems. Nevertheless, their continued autonomy seems out of place in the context of the modern unitary state where most older institutions have declined, a democratically elected Parliament is supreme, and an urban industrial society has so many forms of central control. How did the separate legal systems survive? The answer would seem to lie in three principal facts. The first is that there has been no modern Oliver Cromwell to impose a uniform system. There have been no serious moves, or even proposals, to combine the legal systems since the seventeenth century. The only plausible source for such a move would have been the English system, and its lawyers' notorious combination of a sense of uniqueness and of imperial superiority would thwart any project of archipelago unification. The second fact is the natural insularity of the legal systems. As a system depends upon its internal integrity, it continuously cultivates its identity through the maintenance of a separate constitution, an independent tradition, a separate program of education and training, and the consent of its constituents. These elements were always evident in England and Scotland; they were less apparent in Ireland, until the Republic clearly acquired these traits in the twentieth century. The third principal fact is the subject of this book. The systems have maintained their integrity by developing instruments of and interest in positive and effective interaction. This was not planned. Political, economic, and social factors have dictated the course and the rate of change; just as those factors pushed the political unification and the progressive economic and social development of the modern era, they altered the setting of the legal systems and forced them to adapt. The adaptation might conceivably have produced a federated or centralized law. Indeed, this did occur in a few areas of modern social legislation like workmen's compensation, social insurance, and public housing. But without a powerful political revolution or some other external drive, the traditional legal systems retained their basic form and function through three centuries of rather substantial renovation.

A brief overview of the coming chapters may be in order. The first step in effective interaction was when the several islands forced the channelling of appeals into the English (later British) House of Lords, forming that peculiar ultimate jurisdiction. The lords were a natural agent for traditional petitions; they also were a convenient surrogate for the royal council, though such a role for the peers posed a threat to the privilege of members of the House of Commons. Also at the end of the seventeenth century, the English Parliament (the king, lords, and commons) was recognized as the repository of supreme constitutional power. At that time, it was situated in a crowd of similar bodies: an Irish replica under a separate Irish crown; a Scottish unicameral body with special adjuncts (the General Assembly and the Convention of Royal Burghs); and an array of colonial councils and assemblies. As legislation assumed a more critical role in the eighteenth century, the imperial parliament naturally became the central lawmaking body. But the many impediments to this kind of centralization meant that legislation remained local until much later. This was a critical factor in preserving the separate legal systems.

There were strong motives for assimilation in the revolutionary years of the late eighteenth century, but the rapid and dangerous events of that era brought English political coercion to America, Scotland, and Ireland. That coercion in turn generated different degrees of legal separatism. The American War of Independence vetoed the idea of Parliament's sovereignty. English trials for Scottish treason and Anglo-Scottish debates on the definition of sedition were frustrating examples of inept interaction. English emergency powers to combat Irish rebellion shook the foundations of English law enforcement, helping to accelerate police and penal reforms in the early nineteenth century. The revolutionary years also energized manifold efforts for reform. Those efforts were probably facilitated by the absence of a revolution in the United Kingdom. A desire for change, resisted and shaped by the establishments, entered the legal systems, and entered them all at about the same time. At first fees, then courts, and then laws all came under the microscope of inquiry. In search of "evils" and "abuses," these efforts promoted several kinds of interaction: dispassionate comparison between systems, discussion of alterations by outsiders, and detailed measures of "consolidation."

There was a good deal of legal consolidation, mostly within systems. Much work was needed to modernize and to streamline each; there was not much time for federating or merging the English, Scottish, and Irish systems. One of the ubiquitous royal commissions of the nineteenth century helped to construct a new English supreme court, but that court was never meant to be an instrument of unification. Irish and Scottish appeals were dropped and then restored, and then special judges were added from each of those jurisdictions. This did not look like a plan for unification. In general, patterns of legislation did show more broad United Kingdom activity after 1870. One area affected was the franchise, which was becoming more democratic. Along with changes in electoral law, newly empowered groups of litigants were brought into a widening system with new, specialized courts. Broadly speaking, these changes reflected less threatening and more ameliorating types of interaction.

In the latter decades of the nineteenth century the unwritten British constitution was described in a Victorian canon: supreme Parliament, responsible ministers, rule of law, and an independent judiciary. Each of these terms was about to be challenged or changed by contemporary constitutional revolutions: the advent of administrative law, the separation of Ireland, and the decline of colonial jurisdiction. Together these shifts radically reoriented English law, helping to expose it to more outside influence. In the years since 1950 legal interaction has become much more frequent and accepted. New forms have appeared, ranging from adaptations of Scottish legal practice and principles, to a dangerous extension of emergency law in Ulster and the United Kingdom, to the entry into the European community and accommodation with European law. In general, interaction is no longer combative, at least not in the ways of the seventeenth century. It has become established as an integral part of the multiple, still autonomous legal systems of the British Isles.

Chapter 1

Making Appeals 1660–1720

The Stuart monarchy was restored in its three kingdoms in 1660. An irregular English convention Parliament invited Charles Stuart to return to London. In May he assumed the throne there and was recognized about the same time by a convention in Dublin. His Scottish coronation had been conducted in 1651, and a new Parliament was elected in 1660 to mark the Scottish restoration. The settlements of the three kingdoms were connected in the person of the king but quite separate in their operations and legal consequences.

Charles II returned to his thrones sure of recovering power, and intent upon not losing it again. He reinstituted the monarchies, the peerages, the established churches, and the royal courts. In all three kingdoms he had to deal with institutional problems and individual expectations. The return of royalists and the removal of the usurpers were neither straightforward nor simple. First of all, a number of former enemies of the Crown were instrumental in its restoration: the Cromwellian general George Monk led the army which secured London in 1660; the Earl of Lauderdale, former commissioner to the Westminster Assembly, was now the leading royal councillor in Scotland; the men in power in Ireland (Sir Charles Coote and Roger Boyle, Lord Broghill) were allowed to remain. The major act of the early restoration was an Act of Free and General Pardon, Indemnity, and Oblivion—designed to put all disputes to rest, and to extend a general pardon, excepting a limited number of regicides and rebels for exemplary punishment.

The English courts of law were the only institutions to come through the revolution relatively unscathed. The Convention Parliament preserved judicial continuity with the Act for Confirmation of Judicial Proceedings which endorsed the formal decisions of the courts during the interregnum. But the courts of law were also the one area where the king had to make a major institutional concession. The prerogative courts of Star Chamber and High Commission were not revived. The Cavalier Parliament debated restoring the prerogative courts, but only the Council of Wales was renewed. Thus the champions of the English common law could claim the main residual victory of the rebellion. Of course the king had resumed his place as the fount of justice. In all his kingdoms he restored his councils, he appointed the judges "during pleasure," and he remained in control of the three legal systems.

In the 1660s and 1670s disputes over property, foreign policy, religion, and royal authority were revived in new forms, and in a new European context. Charles II was the ally of Louis XIV and enemy of the Dutch trading republic. This alliance brought the king periodic financial aid and continuing suspicion as to his support for the Catholic cause. Arguments over the king's foreign policy, his finances, and his religion once again built a strong parliamentary opposition. This opposition became even more dangerous when the House of Commons debated a series of bills meant to exclude the king's Roman Catholic brother James from the royal succession (1679–1681).

The exclusion crisis was ignited by a bizarre story of a "Popish Plot" to kill the king and place his brother on the throne. Charles decided to dissolve Parliament and not to summon it again (1681–1685). But this shadow of the 1630s was followed by a different kind of revolution. James II came to the throne in 1685, welcomed at first, and given generous financial support by Parliament. But his efforts to remodel government and prepare for a Catholic restoration cost him most of this support. His son-in-law William of Orange invaded England in 1688 and James was forced to abdicate. The Dutch prince assumed the English throne with his wife, Mary, the daughter of the former king. This "Glorious Revolution" was a bloodless coup in England, but it triggered violence in Scotland and some heavy fighting in Ireland.

William's coup was the centerpiece of a European diplomatic revolution, moving England from the French to the Dutch camp. At home, the Convention Parliament meeting William and Mary obtained their assent to an English "Bill of Rights," a set of constitutional terms amounting to a contract with the Crown. The Crown's power to suspend or dispense with laws was denied; power to raise courts or revenues outside normal channels was forbidden; subjects' rights to bear arms, hold regular elections, and speak freely in Parliament were stated, as were limits on bail, fines, and punishments. In short, a new framework for constitutional law began to emerge. In Scotland, William and Mary were recognized on the terms of the Claim of Right in May 1689. This was an even clearer statement of limited monarchy. Ireland, where James was leading an army against William, did not partake of this kind of contractual settlement. Meanwhile, in all of the kingdoms, from 1689, there were potential allies for the exiled Stuart king and his family—the Jacobites. That claim to the thrones was not extinguished until the later eighteenth century, during which time it was the pretext for rebellion.

After the restoration, the king's judges presided over courts apparently little changed since 1500. There was a small elite of high court judges who, with the law officers, were about forty-five in number for the three kingdoms.[1] These jurists presided over the most important cases, and below them a large group of unpaid magistrates (perhaps 3,000) sat in borough and county sessions of the peace and other local courts. This judicial corps was joined by another large group of specialized judges in ecclesiastical, admiralty, and other civil courts plus a wide range of ancient jurisdictions in manors and county and borough governments. In 1688 the tabulation of the pioneer statistician Gregory King counted 10,000 "persons in the law" in England and Wales, a number which would have included barristers, attorneys, and others.

Senior judges were chosen (by king and councillors) from the higher ranks of the legal profession. These barristers (or the advocates in Scotland) made up a small elite, defined by their right to plead before the high courts. To attain this level, they had completed an apprenticeship as members of an Inn, or in the Scottish case, as graduates of a law faculty. A much larger group of attornies and solicitors (in Scotland "Writers to the Signet") formed the base of the profession (perhaps 6,000). For all of the courts there was a legion of clerks—the scribes and their supervisors who handled the stacks of paper and parchment in this document-laden enterprise.

However much continuity there was in 1660, the legal problems which came with the restoration fostered innovation in law and in legal interaction, readily seen in the body which we will study in this chapter—the English House of Lords.[2] The peerage which was restored in 1660 was diversified. It included Presbyterian members who had fought against the king, old royalists who had returned from exile, and a new generation with no knowledge of the world of the 1630s. And it was part of a larger aristocracy in which owners of land were joined by the captains of commerce and finance. They were largely responsible for the rapid expansion of the imperial economy. There were many elements involved in this expansion, one of which was governmental intervention on various levels, in trade regulation, taxation, and other policy decisions. Another area which evoked legal action concerned the sectarian divisions between and within the three kingdoms. This was still an age when law was used to define and persecute on the basis of belief; it was also an age in which toleration was invoked as public policy. In each of these areas the law was central to the course of history; legal interactions were a vital part of the changing laws; and the House of Lords played a sometimes critical role in the process of interaction.

Our first example of legal change and interaction comes from the area most vital to any landed elite: the law of succession. Once restored to their holdings, the landowners of each kingdom worked to assure continuity, with some extra incentive in the light of recent events. How could the law assure the landowner that his estate would pass to his heirs? There were important differences debated between English and Scots law over the best means of preserving an inheritance: the Scots adopted a strict law of entail to assure the continuity of an estate. The English courts on the other hand upheld a law against perpetuities (e.g. entails). In Ireland, land ownership was buffeted by wartime confiscation, contorted by successive "restoration" measures, and later subjected to the penal laws against the dwindling number of Catholic owners. In these circumstances, the Irish device of the "perpetual lease," or a lease for a number of lives, was a widely used form of tenancy.

These different legal practices would only have been a matter of curiosity if the legal systems had somehow been sealed off and unable to interact. But of course that was not the case. The restoration was a time of unusually large land transfers, and buyers and sellers were not confined to any given legal jurisdiction. In most cases, a disputed settlement would be treated under the rules of the local jurisdiction: but foreign litigants who were aggrieved would try to find satisfaction in a higher court, and this was one source of appeals to the House of Lords.

In our second illustration, the economies of the British Isles were engaged in growing overseas commerce in the seventeenth century. Probably the best-known legal feature, and one which had important consequences in the archipelago and the empire, was the development of the English Navigation Laws. The first of these was enacted in Cromwell's regime, in order to strengthen the national trading system against powerful rivals in Spain, Portugal, and Holland. English ships were granted access to the ports of the archipelago; others were restricted or barred. The Restoration Parliament saw the desirability of retaining this legislation. The main purpose was to protect and support English commerce: the Scots and the Irish were at a disadvantage. In addition to this kind of discrimination, English lawmakers directly interfered with trade, as in the case of a ban on Irish wool in 1699, or in the case of the ill-fated Company of Scotland, which encountered English opposition to its trade with the Americas. The Parliaments of Ireland and Scotland tried to resist, and each made some attempts to legislate on matters economic. However, they continually ran into the superior legislative authority of England, and that authority included the English House of Lords.

Another interactive illustration comes from the realm of religion. The established churches were restored in 1660, but not without difficulty. The Anglican Church turned away from accepting a Presbyterian union; the Scottish Kirk endured a period of violent dissent; and the Church of Ireland resumed its minority establishment in an 80 per cent Catholic nation. In terms of law, each of these bodies was supported by a continuing stream of legislative acts: prescribed oaths, restrictions, and penalties. There was nominal Anglican governance of the whole archipelago, but in reality Dissenters, Catholics, and Presbyterians assured that there was no chance of enforcing general uniformity.[3]

Indeed, one of the important features of this period is that the government began in various ways to intervene on behalf of toleration. Royal declarations of indulgence were crafted as a way of promising Dissenters and Catholics that the Crown would moderate the force of laws against them. For James and Charles this was a way to use toleration for Protestant Dissenters as a screen to lift restrictions on Catholics. A more sincere (but only Protestant) Toleration Act was passed in 1689 which provided relief for Dissenters in exchange for oaths of loyalty. The apparent contradiction in this realm of the law was evidence of the declining efficacy of persecution: that a new age was dawning. In this area of law, the most vigorous action was in the anti-Catholic penal laws of all three Parliaments, which are discussed below (chapter 2).

The laws of the three kingdoms (legislation and litigation) could hardly be kept apart, and their mutual involvement left traces in the society, economy, and culture of the years before 1720. The most vivid example came from the evolving nature of the legal work of the English (later British) House of Lords. The first stage of modern legal interaction was the formation of the appellate jurisdiction in the upper house. By 1720 the peers were taking appeals from England, Scotland, and Ireland, and a body of rules for that enlarged jurisdiction had been developed. This chapter of legal history has never been written, and indeed its English element has just begun to be properly explored.[4]

The decisions of courts of law and equity were meant to be final. On the other hand, the subjects of the Crown were entitled to petition for redress of any grievances, indeed, the petition was at the root of litigation and legislation. In the seventeenth century, the common law courts did not recognize an appeal in the way of rehearing. A party might petition for a writ of error on a point of law, the case then being reviewed by a higher court. In a difficult case, the judges might "reserve" a point for discussion by the whole bench. There was no appeal at law until the nineteenth century in civil cases, and the twentieth in criminal cases. In equity, a "bill of review" was available, but only after the judgment of the court had been carried out.

English petitions to the House of Lords came in a wide variety, only a fraction of them on matters before the courts. Petitions were an ancient part of the business of the house, and though the practice fell into disuse in the sixteenth century, it revived in the 1620s and 1640s. For Irish petitioners, the access to their House of Lords was intermittent, and there were plausible claims of authority by English courts in Irish appeals and errors.[5] Scottish practice was different in yet another way. There was a well-developed form of appeal to the Court of Session, but on decisions in that court, there was no consensus on the right of appeal. While Balfour's *Practicks* (c. 1580) said a protest "for remeid of law" to Parliament was valid, the early seventeenth century jurists doubted the propriety of such appeals. The right to petition was recognized, and the seventeenth century gave ample motives to claimants. The large numbers of petitions in 1660 were witness to the dislocation of the preceding decades. Many points on appeals were unsettled, and in the years after the Restoration, the search for a solution would help to write a major new chapter in legal interaction.

English Appeals

The English House of Lords had old and established powers as a court of judicature: to try cases involving individual peers; to assess peerage claims; to sit as judges in cases of impeachment; and to receive petitions for judicial remedy, by way of a writ of error. The latter category showed impressive growth in the 1620s and 1640s. And as peers heard more cases, they made rules in order to deal with them more efficiently, while their clerks compiled manuals of procedure. With these, and with the voluminous records of the House, we can reconstruct the birth of a comprehensive appellate jurisdiction in the late seventeenth century.[6]

Petitions began to arrive as soon as the Lords assembled in May 1660. A committee for petitions was formed on the 2nd, and it was expected, in the customary manner, to screen petitions, sending some to the courts of law and providing internal procedures for handling the rest.[7] In early July, a subcommittee undertook the screening, while the committee for petitions heard evidence and made recommendations to the whole house.[8] In the session late in the year, the Lords named "receivers" and "triers" of petitions, adopting the old style of medieval Parliaments.

When the Convention Parliament was replaced by the newly-elected "Cavalier" Parliament in May 1661, the Lords appointed five "receavours des petitions d'Angleterre, d'Escoce, et d'Ireland" plus five more for Gascony "et des autres terres et pais de par le mere et les Isles." In addition, thirteen Lords were named as "triours des petitions" for each. The designation of all royal dominions was certainly premature as a statement of the actual business of the house, but it showed the ancient forms which the Lords, or their clerks, clearly had not forgotten. The committee on petitions was re-formed, the Lords saying that it "shall hereby have power to retain and consider of petitions and make report to this house and to reject such as are not fit and proper for the cognizance of this house."[9]

The flood of petitions contained varying numbers for review of cases in court. The committee only accepted those which it judged to be appropriate. However, the process was always one which the judges distrusted. Matthew Hale said[10]

> persons concerned in suits meet with some that are their kindred, friends, favourers, landlords, tenants or relations. And it is grown a fashion in the Lords' House for Lords to patronize petitions, a course that if it were used by the judges of Westminster Hall, would be looked upon, even by the Parliament itself, as undecent, and carrying a probable imputation or temptation at least to partiality.

Others made the same charges in more direct language. Thomas Bevan noted that the Earl of Shaftesbury cited "committee dinners" and the "droves of ladies that attended all causes," and the habit of using "handsome sisters or daughters to deliver their petitions." More damning still was the account of the gossipy Bishop Gilbert Burnet, who wrote later about the visits of Charles II to the House of Lords. "He became a common solicitor, not only in public affairs but even in private matters of justice. He would in a very little time have gone round the house and spoke to every man he thought worth speaking to."[11] How many cases were influenced by the king, or for that matter by "handsome sisters or daughters," was not recorded. Lawyers and judges complained, but laymen found it a useful alternative, perhaps more useful in the restoration period than it had been before the civil wars.

One indication we have that the Lords' business was indeed businesslike is that from the Restoration onward there were rules being composed for these proceedings. Not that rules prove that matters were in order; indeed, the records of the Lords have many directives—so many that we might surmise that enforcement was a continuing problem. The most important of the commands of the house were made into standing orders, and these were kept by the clerk and read out as the occasion required.

In 1661 an order was made which prescribed the procedure for writs of error, noticing that "plaintiffs therein often desire to delay justice, rather than to come to the determination of the right of the cause."[12] Therefore, plaintiffs were to "speedily repair to the Clerk of the Parliament" and pay their fees within eight days or forfeit their cause; and if the plaintiff sued a writ of *certiorari* he had ten days. This was not too exacting, and the procedure was still without serious check against abuse. This order, and all others prior to 1678, dealt specifically with writs of error, not with appeals. But the records show that the house was indeed hearing appeals all along.

The story we have from older legal historians is very different. In that version, the Lords' jurisdiction was only recognized after a set of battles with the House of Commons had drawn the lines. Cases in the 1660s and 1670s pitted Members of Parliament against the Lords' judicial power. In the conventional view, the peers were checked by the Commons and the jurisdiction of the House of Lords was limited.[13] This interpretation has numerous flaws: the foremost is that it ignores the long history of appeals, charted by Hart. Equally important is the fact that the Lords did not initiate the leading cases, but only responded to challenges from the Commons. Finally, none of the cases came to a final decision: in each major case the result was a standoff.

The real issue behind the litigation was the privilege of MPs, or rather, perceived threats to that privilege. Members of both houses were keenly aware of any intrusions and were prone to cast them as breaches of privilege. Any service with legal process or interference with property rights of individual MPs could arouse this cry.[14] The most serious instances were of course those which resulted in full-scale confrontations of the two houses. But it is important to understand that those cases came out of a setting in which anxious MPs were always ready to use privilege as a legal shield.

In the serious cases, members discerned an apparent revival of efforts by the king and his council to supersede the common law courts. The first major privilege confrontation actually began before the Restoration. Thomas Skinner claimed that the East India Company had illegally seized his property in Sumatra in 1659. He tried for six years to gain a hearing, and the king finally referred his case to a special committee of privy councillors. The recommendation of the committee was rejected by the company, and in 1667 the king referred Skinner's petition to the House of Lords. The peers took over a year to decide and in April 1668 awarded Skinner £5,000 in damages.

Since several members of the House of Commons were directors of the East India Company, it was no surprise when the lower house demanded a conference with the Lords to discuss the ruling. The Commons also passed three resolutions. The first said that the Lords' hearing of Skinner's petition and their overruling of that of the company, "being a common plea, is not agreeable to the laws of the land." The second resolution said that "taking cognizance" of the property in the island in question, and "giving damages thereupon...is not warranted by the laws of this kingdom." The third resolution said that the whole proceeding, "wherein several members of this house are parties" amounted to "a breach of the privilege of this House."[15]

The two houses conferred on May 5 and May 8. At the first session the peers heard a long lecture, and they gave their response at the second meeting. Both sides had collected numerous precedents, and there was no sign of compromise. Indeed, on May 9 the Commons resolved

> that whosoever shall be aiding or assisting in putting the order or sentence of the House of Lords, in the case of Thomas Skinner against the East India Company, in execution shall be deemed a betrayer of the rights and liberties of the Commons of England and an infringer of the privileges of this House.

The threat of trial and imprisonment was clear; just as clear was the echo of the revolutionary era in the last phrase. The Commons had reached the limit in defense of their privilege; they would not retreat. With the stalemate, the king prorogued Parliament. It proved impossible to reconcile the parties. In October the Commons passed more resolutions; in November both houses passed bills. In February 1670, King Charles informed both houses that he was ordering his council to "raze" all entries relating to this case, and he suggested that the Lords and Commons do likewise. Both agreed to do so in March.[16]

What then was the import of the Skinner case? Historians have accepted the verdict that the Commons succeeded in challenging and terminating the Lords' original jurisdiction. But since the Skinner petition had been heard and ruled on by a council committee and then was referred to the Lords, there was some semblance of an appeal; and there was some doubt whether any other English court had jurisdiction. What was most disturbing to MPs was the thought that the peers could hear and judge a petition to the Crown, involving the legal rights of its members. This raised fearful legal prospects for members who might oppose the Crown.

Even before Charles made his radical proposal to erase the journals, more petitions had been filed which would further test the appellate jurisdiction. Again members of Parliament were involved. Two appellants petitioned the peers, one in December 1669 and another in February 1670. Both were appealing chancery verdicts won by MPs. During the hearings the Lords resolved that [17]

> their proceedings had been acording to the course of Parliament and former precedents; the Lords do assert it to be their undoubted right in judicature to receive and determine in time of Parliament appeals from inferior courts, though a member of either house be concerned, that there may be no failure of justice in the land.

Dr. Shirley's case against Sir John Fagg in 1675 raised the issue of privilege once more. Shirley was the king's physician, but even before his petition could be heard, the Commons sent a message to the Lords to observe their privilege. This received a chilly reply, after which the sergeant at arms of the House of Commons attempted to arrest Shirley in the lobby of the Lords. Eventually he, his counsel, and even Sir John were taken into custody, because by merely receiving orders from the Lords, they were held to have committed a breach of Commons' privilege. A conference was called for May 20, 1675, and the Commons said:

> That by the laws and usage of Parliament, privilege of Parliament belongs to every member of the House of Commons in all cases except treason, felony, and breach of the peace, which hath often been declared in Parliament, without any exception of appeals before the Lords.

The second point of the Commons' argument was that since members could not attend the Lords' house, it was unjust for trials of members to be conducted there. Then they returned to the shape and tone of the Skinner argument:

> Whereas this house hath been informed of several appeals depending in the House of Lords from courts of equity, to the great violation of the rights and liberties of the Commons of England, it is this day resolved and declared, that whosoever shall solicit, plead or prosecute any appeal against any commoner of England from any court of equity before the House of Lords shall be deemed and taken a betrayer of the rights and liberties of the Commons of England, and shall be proceeded against accordingly.

While some have read this simply as a denunciation of all Chancery appeals, it seems clearly directed against the violation of privilege. It is hard to suppose that the wider reading was understood or intended.[18]

In the Shirley case, the houses threatened each other, and they both arrested persons involved and denounced the powers of the other body. The king tried a compromising speech but had to prorogue Parliament on

June 9. Meeting again in October and November, the two houses fell out once more, and this time Parliament was prorogued for fifteen months. When the next meeting occurred, the Lords waited a year before entertaining some Chancery appeals. As Hart says, "in truth, the dispute had always been more about privilege than jurisdiction" and so long as the Lords did not press their power to hear MPs' cases, the issue could subside.[19]

It was ironic that at this point the appellate power of the peers was ably defended by Denzil Holles, one of the century's best-known MPs. He was one of the five ringleaders whom Charles I tried to arrrest in January 1642. As Lord Holles of Ifield, he wrote a tract on *The Grand Question concerning the Judicature of the House of Peers* during the Skinner case. Later, when an old conviction of 1630 was reversed on a writ of error in 1668, Holles returned to the fray with *The Case Stated Concerning the Judicature of the House of Peers in the Point of Appeals* (1675). At the same time, other peers opposed the Lords' jurisdiction, and many major figures in the legal profession disapproved of the growing role of the peers as a court of appeal. If the debate had been truly centered on that question, it seems unlikely that the peers would have withstood the opposition of such figures as Sir Matthew Hale, Sir John Vaughan, and John Holt.[20]

Another adversary of the peers' judicature was Sir Robert Atkyns. He had been a judge in the Court of Common Pleas from 1672 until his resignation in 1679. He was made chief baron of the Court of Exchequer in 1689, and was speaker of the House of Lords when the Great Seal was in commission, 1689–93. He retired from the bench in 1694, and his *Treatise of the True and Ancient Jurisdiction of the House of Peers* was published in 1699. He supported the Commons' position in the controversies and cast doubt on the Lords' jurisdiction, citing their lack of precedents in the 1620s. While the arguments were not impressive, Atkyns's tract was a useful reminder of the resistance and reluctance to acknowledge the emerging appellate jurisdiction.

However much the judges disapproved, petitions for appeal continued to pour in, and the procedure continued to evolve. When the Lords next convened after the Shirley affair in May 1678, they approved a committee report which held that cases from "the last Parliament" (i.e. 1675) "are still in force to be proceeded on."[21] The house ruled that appeals could carry over to the next session, an important procedural step in establishing the Lords' judicial role. There were other rules adopted about this time which added to the picture of development. In 1678 a new standing order was adopted on time limits. This was also the first instance of a standing order specifically referring to appeals. It was "Ordered by the Lords Spiritual and Temporal in Parliament assembled, That all persons, who shall have any writs of error, or petitions of appeal from any court of equity to be exhibited to this house" should present them within fourteen days of the beginning of the session, after which time no petitions would be received, "unless upon a judgment given in any of his Majesty's courts of judicature, or decree had in any of the courts of equity, whilst the Parliament is actually sitting," in which case the appellant had fourteen days from the date of judgment to file a petition.[22]

An even more important order was made in 1680, but only entered as a standing order in 1710. The house directed that in all appeals brought in to the clerk, appellants had to give security that they would pay defendants' costs if their appeal failed.[23] As it happened, the house in the 1680s did not sit regularly enough to give much continuity to proceedings. It was the 1690s which would see the beginning of regular annual sessions. But throughout this period, there was a great deal of work on rules and orders and the refinement of proceedings, even as the Lords began to work more closely with jurisdictions outside England and Wales.

In 1691 it was decided that the question should be put for reversing in cases of appeal or error (S.O. 78); in 1695 it was ruled that petitions for rehearing could not be taken up on the day delivered (S.O. 82); in 1697 attorneys and solicitors could not be allowed privilege "though employed by any peer or lord of this house" (S.O. 86). In 1698 a very important change was made, requiring that all appeals be signed by two counsel.

> That no person whatsoever do presume as counsel to sign any appeal to be brought into this house for the future unless such person hath been of counsel in the same cause in the courts below or shall attend as counsel at the bar of this house when the said appeal shall come in to be heard. And it is farther ordered that this order shall be added to the roll of standing orders and affixed on the doors of this house and the courts in Westminster Hall.

Several more orders in the next year further outlined the procedure of the house. Proxies were disallowed in "any judicial cause." (S.O. 88) The order on signed appeals was amended somewhat, when "several scandalous and frivolous printed cases" were presented. S.O. 89 required printed cases to be signed by two counsel in April 1698. Not long after that, the submission of printed cases became the rule; at least the continuous collection of printed cases dates from 1702 in the papers of the house. On the other hand, the peers were not willing to have their proceedings printed. In 1703, S.O. 92 said it was a breach of privilege to "print or publish in print any thing related to the proceedings of this house without the leave of this house."[24]

The order restricting printing was made in the midst of the last great confrontation between the Lords and Commons on appellate jurisdiction. In 1701 Matthew Ashby was prevented from casting his vote in a general election by the mayor of Aylesbury, William White. Ashby sued for damages and won his case at the assizes. The mayor took his appeal to Queen's Bench, where the judges held (3–1) that no action could lie, since only the House of Commons could oversee elections. Chief Justice Holt dissented, and his view was upheld in the ensuing hearing on a writ of error in the House of Lords in 1704. That result encouraged other electors to protest the conduct of the Aylesbury authorities.[25] The Commons found these suitors guilty of breach of privilege and ordered them committed to Newgate. When this action was appealed to the Lords, the struggle between the houses could only be settled by prorogation. The jurisdiction of the peers was not curtailed, but the power of the Commons over elections was upheld.

Despite the parliamentary infighting, or perhaps because of it, by the early eighteenth century the House of Lords was a court of appeal, sought after by petitioners, with developing rules and a regular calendar. It may well be that judges didn't like it, that MPs were suspicious, and that lawyers had misgivings. But it was working, and soon it was extending its authority to Scotland and Ireland.

Scottish Appeals

It was not clear in 1660 whether appeals from the lords of session to the Scottish Parliament were still allowed. In 1663 that Parliament was asked to review the case of Nathaniel Eldred, "an Englishman," against Sir Thomas Hamilton of Preston, Member of Parliament for Haddington. Eldred was a judge in a commissary court, and a verdict against him in Scotland had led to seizure of his property. The lords of the articles replied to the king that[26]

> howsoever they did forbear in ane judiciall way to proceid to ane review of that decree given upon the heareing of the parties interessed especially upon the reasons alreadie debated and determined by the Lords of the Session as never done by any Parliament authorized be your Majestie or any of your Majesties so numerous progenitors Seing the reversing of any such decree must needs be upon the iniquitie of the Judges of the supream Judicator of this kingdom in maters civill from whom ther is no appeal be the lawes of this nation.

Eldred went to the English House of Lords in 1667, complaining "that there is no appeal to His Majesty by the laws of that nation." The Lords' committee on petitions dismissed his appeal on a tie vote (4–4) "on the ground that it related to a judgment given in Scotland."[27] The efforts to bring Scottish cases into English courts were few and far between; and any attempt to appeal had first to deal with serious internal resistance.

The degree of resistance was evidenced on the next occasion when a Scottish appeal broke the surface. In 1674 advocates attempted to appeal the decision in *Callendar v. Dunfermline* to the Scots Parliament "for remeid of law." The session of the Scottish Parliament was a noisy one which lasted from November 1673 to May 1674, in which time period there were three prorogations! The judges complained to the king, and he denounced the practice and ordered the advocates to disown the appeals. When the advocates refused, they were suspended and banished from Edinburgh in September 1674. They later submitted to the king and were allowed to return in May 1675.[28]

In the works of the major jurists of the period, James Dalrymple (Lord Stair) and Sir George MacKenzie, there is some ambiguity on the matter of appeals. In his *Institutions of the Law of Scotland*, Stair said "though the narrowest inquiry were made both by the records of Parliament and Sessions" he could find no custom of bringing causes into Parliament. There was "extraordinar remeid" for cases of judicial misconduct, but that was another matter.[29]

In 1689 the basic right of appeal was established in Scotland. The Claim of Right said "that it is the right and privilege of subjects to protest for remeed of law to the king and Parliament against sentences pronounced by the Lords of Session, providing the samen do not stop execution of these sentences." In the wake of this rule, there was considerable activity in the area of "protests." The Parliament of 1690 recorded a large number of acts variously labelled "Act and Decreit" "Act and Remit" or "Decreit in favours of" one party over another.[30] In 1693 a Commission for the Regulation of Judicatories was appointed (c. 72) and a number of acts were passed to revise procedures. In 1695 we find a Committee for Privat Bills and Protests for Remead of Law, plus other acts to regulate procedure (cc. 2, 4). From 1695 there were numerous entries which had the appearance of protests.[31]

Thus there was a developing procedure of appeal from the Court of Session to the Scottish Parliament in the years before the union. When the Scottish and English Parliaments were united, there would obviously have to be some reconsideration.[32] The momentum for union built up after 1703. At that time, when the Scottish Parliament enacted its own laws on the royal succession and on the declaration of war, it was clear (to Englishmen) that some form of legislative union was imperative. The Crown appointed commissioners from both England and Scotland, and negotiation went fairly quickly.[33] The main provision on Scottish courts (art. xix) said their decisions were not

> cognoscible by the Courts of Chancery, Queen's Bench, Common Pleas, or any other court in Westminster Hall; and that the said courts, or any other of the like nature after the union shall have no power to cognosce, review or alter the acts or sentences of the judicatures within Scotland or stop execution of the same.

In the debate on this article, questions were raised in the House of Lords,[34]

> whether after the union the House of Lords of Great Britain will have right to hear and determine causes which shall be brought before them by appeal, writ of error or otherwise from judicatories of Scotland and whether the suitors of Scotland will have right to bring any such causes before the House of Lords of Great Britain to be heard and determined by them?

The motion to debate this question was voted down and the article was passed. This would seem to put to rest the idea that the negotiators had overlooked the future possibility of appeals coming to the Lords. By referring to "any other court in Westminster Hall," the article had carefully sidestepped the Lords' role, since they sat elsewhere in the palace of Westminster.

It is unlikely that the commissioners were in any doubt as to the intent of the article. Their number included senior members of the respective legal professions. They were well aware of the intricacy of the issues and, moreover, they were prepared, in other areas, to provide steps toward legal unification. A new English-style exchequer was provided for Scotland; the two admiralty jurisdictions were to be combined, public law was to be made uniform, and private law was alterable by the new Parliament "for the evident utility of the Scottish people." This was a recipe for English interference, which was not long in coming. The Scottish Privy Council was terminated in 1708, the English law of treason was extended to Scotland in 1709 ("An Act for Improving the Union of the Two Kingdoms") and it was not long before some details of Scottish procedure were altered by statute.[35]

While the Treaty of Union was silent on Scottish appeals to the House of Lords, the same could not be said for Scottish litigants. Before the first British Parliament met in 1707 at least two appeals were recorded.[36] The first formal petition heard from Scotland was that of Lord Rosebery, a union commissioner, against a decree of 1695. The clerk of the Court of Session refused to give Rosebery the documents on the case, and the House of Lords had to order him to comply (March 6, 1708). The peers thereupon formed a committee concerning appeals from Scotland (March 24) and ordered that respondents in Scottish cases "do put in their answers as in cases of appeals from the courts in England" (March 27). Parliament dissolved before the petition of Rosebery could be answered, and there were no further proceedings. But the Scottish appeal had arrived.

The first case which was taken up by the Lords in which the Court of Session was reversed was that of *Sir James Gray v. the Duke of Hamilton* in which an interlocutor of July 31, 1708, was reversed on March 10, 1709. In the next month, a Scottish exchequer decree was appealed, and the House of Lords ordered that[37]

> after an appeal shall be received by this house, from any sentence or decree given or pronounced in any court in Scotland, and an order made by this house for the respondent to answer the said appeal, and notice of such order duly

> served on the respondent, the sentence or decree so appealed against, from such time, ought not to be carried into execution by any process whatsoever.

Quite in contrast to the old procedure for Scotland, in which protest had no impact on execution, there was now a very effective stalling device. Lord Fountainhall took note of this.[38]

> I have marked no less than ten protests this Winter session [1710–11]; they are turned more frequent and numerous since the union than they were before, though access now is both more difficult and expensive than the discussing them before our own Parliaments were. The reason may be, 1st to concuss the victor to a composition rather than undertake a tedious uncertain journey to London; 2nd, they have this advantage now, that how soon it is tabled in the house of Peers, all execution is stopt, whereas with us they were not suspensive of the sentence, but only devolutive.

Fountainhall was concerned about the feature, which came to be a marked contrast between the several appeal proceedings, for the English and Irish process only gave a stay upon petition to the house. By the end of the eighteenth century, the stay seldom operated in England and Ireland, but it was still in effect in Scotland.

When Fountainhall made his lament, the House of Lords was about to decide one of the most colorful cases of this early period of Scottish appeals. The Greenshields case did not establish "the right of the House of Lords to hear appeals from the Court of Session."[39] But the case was important for other reasons, and it demonstrated how the appellate relationship had developed by 1710.

James Greenshields was a native Scot who was ordained by the deposed Bishop of Ross and served in Ireland for twelve years before coming to preach in Edinburgh in 1709. He defied a ban on Episcopal services and was sentenced by the Presbytery and jailed by the magistrates in September. Daniel Defoe insisted that Greenshields had been paid to stir up trouble, and whether paid or not, that is what he did. A pamphlet campaign paralleled the legal efforts to release the clergyman. By November a bill of suspension was put in to the Court of Session and rejected (on grounds of Greenshields' invalid ordination). A revised bill was also rejected, whereupon Greenshields "gave in a protest for remied of law to the Queen and House of Peers in England."[40]

In the debate on Greenshields' petition (February 6, 1710), a motion to send for proceedings asked for the personal attendance of the appellant and some of the magistrates. This would have been a major innovation in appellate procedure, but it was not adopted. By the time the papers in the case arrived in March, the house had to put off the Greenshields case until "the proceedings on the impeachment of Dr. Sacheverell now depending are finished." The house also said that respondent's counsel "shall be at liberty, upon the hearing of this cause, to argue, in the first place, whether the said appeal be regularly and properly before this house, or not."[41]

In the event, the hearing did not take place for another year, because after the Sacheverell case there was a dissolution and a general election. The magistrates took until January to reply, while Greenshields enlisted support from the English hierarchy, especially from the Bishop of Carlisle, William Nicolson. In the bishop's diary and correspondence there were illuminating comments on the strategy used by the appellant and his handlers.[42] They chose to deflect discussion from "the authority of the kirk" and were successful. The Edinburgh magistrates were fixed upon as the guilty parties, although their counsel, Peter King, tried to argue that this appeal was really from the church court, not the magistrates:[43]

> the Presbytery was only a subordinate ecclesiastic judicatory, from which appeals in course lie to the superior judicatories of the provincial synod and the general assembly; and if the appellant thought himself grieved by the sentence of the Presbytery, and omitted this known and proper remedy, he could not in law, or good order, appeal from the Presbytery to the Lords.

The Lords brushed aside this argument and without division they ruled that the house had jurisdiction. After further debate, the judgment was made "That the sentence of the magistrates of Edinburgh, and the decree of the Lords of Session in North Britain, made against the said James Greenshields, be reversed."

Although the decree of the Court of Session was included in the judgment, there was no discussion of that court or its actions in any of the surviving records of the case. That court was similarly reticent: no reports of the appeal were printed, and David Robertson suggested why silence was to be expected at this period:[44]

> Many cases have been appealed which are not to be found among the decisions of the Court of Session hitherto published. In sundry instances, also, where judgments of the Court of Session have been reversed in Parliament, the

> original decisions still remain as precedents (and these in some questions of much moment) in the Collections of Decided Cases, in the Dictionary of Decisions, and in the works of law writers of authority. The instances where such reversals are properly stated in this period [1707–1727] are so few as only to form exceptions to the general practice.

Whatever the Lords of Session felt about the judgment, Scottish officials continued to prosecute episcopal clergy. And some lawyers advised them that the Greenshields verdict had no lasting significance. An anonymous Scottish author, claiming to be a member of Parliament, said that the General Assembly was the "sovereign judicature" of the Church of Scotland "in which the Queen being always present by her commissioner, matters are determined without any appeal, except to the bar of heaven." As for the legal niceties:[45]

> the peers of Great Britain having considered the commitment of Greenshields and reverst it does not at all disable and consequently ought not to discourage any magistrate from acting in their station according to law, it only extends to this particular case in which, whether some omission, some slip or some illegal step has been made is not for me to examine here, their Lordships not suffering their proceedings to be printed or examined in print by anybody: but if in another case which may come before them, such slip or omission or illegal step cannot be found, such other case will receive no prejudice from this.

The Lords' order against printing was thus invoked against their appellate power. The attitude expressed here certainly explains the behavior of Scottish lawyers and judges in continuing to pursue the episcopal clergy. In any event, Scottish appeals were established as part of the Lords' jurisdiction, and a part which would grow to considerable proportions.

Irish Appeals

Irish litigants were able to appeal decisions of their courts to their own House of Lords, at least when it was in session.[46] Also there was a traditional course for a writ of error from the Irish King's Bench to the English. From the 1660s an increasing number of cases can be located. While Irish law reports do not exist for this period, we can piece together records from the journals of Parliaments, from the printed reports of appeals to the English King's Bench and from various manuscript records. There is documentation for at least 98 Irish cases which came to England on appeal between 1660 and 1720, and there were probably more.[47]

The Irish Lords were developing their procedures in the 1660s and they resumed the task in the 1690s. At the same time, they were duelling with the Irish House of Commons and otherwise testing their powers of review. When the Irish Parliament was not sitting, there was a tendency for Irish cases to move toward the courts which were open in England. Some of this tendency was even augmented by Irish peers.[48] The English House of Lords saw a steady trickle of Irish cases between 1660 and 1690. While the Irish Lords were in session (1662–66) there were no appeals, only petitions of a nonjudicial character. The first judicial appeal was in *Nugent v. Talbot*, when proceedings in Ireland were stayed in 1670 while the appellant was allowed to bring in a bill of review. In 1671 Cusack petitioned against an appeal from the Court of Claims to the Court of Chancery in Ireland. Judgment was suspended against Cusack and the order "settled." In the case of *Barrett v. St Leger*, heard in 1679 and in 1685, there was an appeal against a decree of the Irish chancery and the latter was reversed. The Irish appeal cases were outnumbered by writs of error.[49] Some of these cases came to the English courts on procedural points, and sometimes English rules were followed; sometimes the writ itself was defective, ending the process; just as often the reports noted that process was valid in Ireland; about an equal number of cases were upheld and overruled.

In addition to appeals and writs of error, there were many other varieties of interaction between the English and Irish systems. In 1675 Sir George Carteret brought a bill in Chancery in London against William Petty over partition of lands in Ireland. The court said he might have relief there, "but 'tis not proper to be determined here [London], especially upon an original bill." In Tregunnell's Case in 1677, a lost recovery from the Cromwellian era was proven, and "the question was whether the court might cause an original to be put upon the file." The Irish judges had sent "to search for precedents, for which they were much blamed by the Chancellor."[50]

In the same year, a motion was granted for a writ of prohibition, to remove a case from the Court of Admiralty in regard to a ship forced to make port in Ireland (*Pidgeon v. Trent*). In another case, Sir William

Turner of Middle Temple ("an Irish knight") asked if he could deliver a fine to a judge in Ireland without an oath, as an English knight was allowed. Citing Calvin's Case, the court said yes, noting that "the highest and lowest dignities are universal." In the waning days of the popish plot the unfortunate Oliver Plunket, Roman Catholic Archbishop of Ireland, was brought to London and tried and executed for alleged complicity in promoting a French invasion of Ireland.[51]

Some other cases were heard in England, with little or no regard for Irish jurisdiction; Muschamp pleaded for an English decree on Irish lands, and though Lord Keeper North was unsure, "a commission for taking defendant's answer beyond sea granted" (*Earl of Arglasse v. Muschamp*, 1682). Done's son was the captain of a company in Ireland, and Berrisford offered to buy his command, but the deal was blocked, and led to an English Chancery case (*Berrisford v. Done*, 1682). Lord Ranelagh (the notorious farmer of Irish revenue) assigned shares of the Irish excise to Hayes, but later tried to alter the agreement, and took the case to Chancery in England (*Ranelaugh v. Hayes,* 1683). An Irish freeholder gave a lease in London, rent to be paid there; did the heir of the owner have to sue in Ireland for nonpayment? This was argued in *Barker v. Damer* in the English King's Bench in 1689, with an interesting discussion of jurisdiction of Irish courts.[52]

A more important stage of interaction came in the 1690s. Jacobite Ireland had been defeated in battle, and the Treaty of Limerick of 1691 had promised a moderate settlement. The next few years would see the reversal of that policy and the building of the Protestant Ascendancy upon a sturdy anti-Catholic base. The administration of justice would be completely caught up in this process, but there was no intention of submitting to English authority. In fact, the Irish House of Lords and the Irish courts of law were adamant about preserving their powers.

When the Irish Lords convened in October 1692 for the first time after the Williamite conquest, they set about making rules. A committee was appointed to peruse English statutes and decide "which of them may be fit and necessary to be enacted into laws in this kingdom." Meanwhile the rules committee returned its report on November 2 with a number of suggestions on judicial procedure: fines, trial, counsel, and time limits for writs of error. The timing for appeals (either the first fourteen days of session, or when the house and court were both in session) was also debated.[53]

The Irish House of Lords next sat in 1695. The house heard a number of appeals in this session, two of which were destined to provoke serious discussion of the appellate powers of the Irish peers. In the case of *Ward v. Meath*, an English peer, Edward, Lord Ward petitioned against a decree of a lower Irish court. The house appointed a committee to search for precedents, and when it found none, his petition was rejected. The respondents, the Earl and Countess of Meath, were put in possession of the disputed estates, and a perpetual injunction stayed all future proceedings. Ward later appealed to the English House of Lords and the Irish peers' ruling was reversed.[54]

Meanwhile the other major case had begun. The Bishop of Derry (William King, 1691–1703) had a dispute with Londonderry officials over land title and fishing rights. They battled through the Irish courts, and the Irish House of Lords gave the bishop a victory, but that decision was appealed to the English House of Lords in January 1698. The Lords appointed a committee to study their jurisdiction in appeals from Ireland.[55] In May, the Lords decided that the appeal to the Irish house was invalid and the proceedings there were null and void. When the Bishop ignored this decision, the English peers asked the king to have him brought before them on charges of contempt, but he was able to plead ill health. Bishop King was translated to Dublin in 1703, and in 1704 a private act of Parliament compromised the issue.

When the Irish House of Lords reconvened in 1704, there was no private act to smooth the waters in the case of *Ward v. Meath*. The Irish peers were angry at the rejection of their authority and drafted a set of resolutions, saying[56]

> that by the ancient and known laws of this kingdom, her majesty hath an undoubted jurisdiction and prerogative of judging in this her high court of Parliament, in all appeals and causes within this her majesty's realm of Ireland.

and further that those judgments were final, and if any subject remove such a cause, they were "betrayers" of the prerogative, the privileges of the house, and the "rights and liberties of the subjects of this kingdom." At the very least, the constitutional codewords were clearly transmitted. The Lords' resolutions barred any officers from executing such illegal orders, and they put the Earl and Countess of Meath in possession again. The English peers had failed (for the moment) to assert their superiority.

The Irish jurisdiction was settled emphatically by the case of *Sherlock v. Annesley.* Indeed, the turbulence from this case spilled over into the realm of legislative power, as it culminated with the passage of the Declaratory Act in 1720.[57] In 1709 a dispute over an estate in Kildare was settled in favor of Maurice Annesley. The land had once belonged to Christopher Sherlock, who was condemned as a traitor. Annesley became the tenant of the estate and the guardian of the Sherlock children. He claimed that he paid Hester Sherlock £500 for her share of the estate in 1699, and that claim was upheld in the Irish Court of Exchequer. Sherlock appealed to the Irish House of Lords in 1716, and part of the exchequer decree was set aside. She was to receive the deeds to the estate and Annesley was to be compensated. But he was not satisfied and he appealed to the British House of Lords in 1717. That body denied the authority of the Irish peers and ordered Sherlock to put in her answer to Annesley's petition.

When the Irish Lords reconvened in September 1717, they ordered the Sheriff of Kildare to put Sherlock in possession just before they adjourned for eighteen months. The British peers ordered Annesley restored, and under this instruction, in March 1718 the Irish Exchequer issued an injunction to the Sheriff of Kildare. This direct interference in Irish government stung the Irish Lords into a powerful statement of their position, the Humble Representation of October 1719, in which they defended their appellate authority. After acknowledging some earlier appeals to the English House of Lords, they said "such appeals...were never supposed to preclude the king's majesty from his right of giving redress to his subjects of Ireland, in his Parliament when assembled here."[58] They noted that in Meath and Derry "no pleadings to the jurisdiction of the Parliament of Ireland had been offered or mentioned, by either party, on hearing the said causes here."

The Irish Lords warned that "these proceedings of the Lords of England have greatly embarrassed your Parliament and disquieted the generality of your most loyal protestant subjects of this your kingdom." In their view, the British peers had made "great encroachments...upon your majesty's prerogative." But this view was not shared by King George. The Irish Lords were prorogued in November 1719, not to return until September 1721. In the interval the British peers concluded the case firmly with the passage of the Declaratory Act of 1720. In it the appellate power was removed from the Irish Lords:[59]

> Whereas the House of Lords of Ireland have of late, against law, assumed to themselves a power and jurisdiction to examine, correct and amend the judgments and decrees of the courts of justice in the kingdom of Ireland....the House of Lords of Ireland have not, nor of right ought to have, any jurisdiction to judge of, or reverse any judgment...made in any court within the said kingdom.

It is perhaps fitting that the Declaratory Act made no explicit provision for the appellate power of the House of Lords in Westminster with regard to Irish appeals, for while that body remained the only likely venue, the power being developed was as yet unfinished.

By 1720 the British House of Lords exercised a variegated superior power of review, with no certain body of law behind it, with only its own *ad hoc* rules to govern it, with no tradition of publishing the rationale for its judgments, and with no special instruments to enforce its decisions—particularly when it reversed lower courts. The loose arrangement was the product of the separate acts which went into the construction of the jurisdiction. That meant that some central provisions were confused and varied. For example, Scots lawyers made a distinction between appeal and protest: the latter did not stop execution but the former did. This was an important distinction, but one which has not gotten much notice. John MacQueen made the point that English and Irish appeals did stay proceedings circa 1700; the Scots did not, at least until 1709. Then in the course of the eighteenth century, the English and Irish practice was reversed: proceedings were not stayed, while in Scotland the rule of 1709 remained.[60]

One thing the Lords did provide, as perhaps no other venue could: an arena for legal interaction, both judicial and legislative. This arena would see growing activity in the eighteenth century as the communities of the British Isles grew and sometimes prospered, but always took their petitions to the most promising courts of law. If the courts were wary of appeals and seemed to stumble into a formal arrangement, the reverse was true with legislation. At least on the surface, the statute book appeared to be a whole different thing: formal, settled, and clear. Of course it was nothing of the kind, and in blending the many legislatures of the empire, the next important phase of legal interaction played out in the early eighteenth century.

Chapter 2

Imperial Legislation 1689–1766

The English imperial state at the end of the seventeenth century was a powerful newcomer to an old European fraternity, and the empire it managed was a very new creation. England had been a minor European power in the 1640s, but that was totally changed sixty years later. The diplomatic shift of 1689 reduced Dutch imperial rivalry and committed England to war with France. The resulting heavy expenditures accelerated a financial revolution. Royal finance became public finance with a national debt, national banks, parliamentary oversight of accounts, all dependent upon revenue from land tax, customs, and excise. The navy which had begun to grow under Cromwell was brought to the first rank by 1700. A handful of colonial outposts became a bustling imperial enterprise, a collection of variously constituted settlements, governed by Crown officials and local elites.

The conjunction of imperial expansion and diplomatic revolution meant a fundamental transformation of the English state. This was not as readily visible as the massive change in economy and finance. However, the alteration in law and legislation was as profound as the changes in economic structure. The essential alteration can be seen in several legal dimensions: in foundational thought and its instruments (charters, grants, proclamations, etc.); in legal proceedings (decisions of the House of Lords, the Privy Council, and the high courts); and in the legislative acts of the various Parliaments and assemblies. We will focus on the last of these, a story which is bound up with the emergence of the idea of parliamentary sovereignty.

The constitutional position of the English Parliament, the House of Commons in particular, was transformed by its role in producing war-related revenues, and doing so at regular annual intervals. This role, more than anything, settled the key issue of the seventeenth century—the sharing of executive power with Lords and Commons. The change also made the management of the lower house a central concern for the king and his ministers. Political parties, elections, and parliamentary management had barely begun to move toward a modern configuration. Today a party winning a general election will form a government and enact a program of legislation. Three centuries ago, the king selected ministers and they conducted an election, usually obtaining a majority. The legislative acts which followed were less a program than a series of *ad hoc* legal remedies. In the eighteenth century the business of government was not the business of the people, it was the concern of a small group of oligarchs. These men represented the social elites, the peers, gentry, and other persons of wealth and status.

The oligarchy was divided along lines of region, religion, occupation, and relation to the Crown (in office or out). The invitation to William of Orange and Mary in 1688 was one moment when an uncommon unity appeared, as leaders of Whigs and Tories were alarmed by the policies of King James II. Their action in urging William to invade, and his response, set the stage for the Declaration of Rights in 1689. This document stated the case for William's coup and its form was the equivalent of a parliamentary constitution. It effectively renounced the position of the high Tories who had said the Crown must not be resisted under any circumstances. The declaration set conditions for royal government which clearly implied the necessity of parliamentary approval. This concept was made unequivocal in 1701 in the Act of Settlement. Queen Mary had died and her sister Anne was the sole surviving heir standing between the throne and a Jacobite restoration. The act settled the Crown, failing any heirs of Anne, on the electress of Hanover. It prohibited a Catholic succession and required the sovereign to conform to the Anglican faith. The act also nervously insisted on the confirmation of all laws "securing the established religion." There were several other clauses which affected the advisers of the king, but the essential achievement was the assertion of the authority of the king, lords, and commons to regulate the succession. No other monarch in Europe in 1701 would have tolerated this kind of formal legal interference.

The arms of England and the United Provinces had been employed against Louis XIV in the 1690s. After a respite, fighting resumed in 1702. The French king had hopes of controlling the succession to the throne of Spain, and thus its extensive European and colonial holdings. English armies were deployed in the Low Countries and the fleet allied with Dutch forces to patrol the Atlantic and the Mediterranean to thwart the French. After a series of allied victories under John Churchill, Duke of Marlborough, the allies fell out, the English made a truce and agreed to terms with France, which were accepted in the Peace of Utrecht in 1713. Under the terms agreed upon, the Spanish empire was partitioned; Britain received Minorca and Gibraltar from Spain and St Kitts, Newfoundland, Nova Scotia, and Hudson Bay territories from France. Louis XIV also agreed to recognize the Protestant succession in Britain. In addition to new territories, the peace brought concessions in the Spanish slave trade which were vested in a new chartered company, the South Sea Company.

In 1714 Queen Anne died, and George, the elector of Hanover, aged fifty-four, became King of England, Scotland, and Ireland. He was naturally anxious to guard the interests of his native state, and he was inclined to consult familiar advisers. Among the English politicians the king favored the Whigs, and that tendency was fortified when a Jacobite rebellion erupted in September 1715. The most serious threat was in Scotland, where an army of 5,000 was raised at Perth. Another force in northern England was assembled, but both were defeated by November. The rebellion was put down easily, the Tories were discredited, and the estates of the rebels were forfeited. With the Jacobite defeat and an alliance with France, there was a quarter of a century of peace which spanned the 1720s and 1730s.

In the wake of the wars, the financial world did not return to the status quo. Government revenues and government offices retained their newfound expanded size and significance. In the new entrepreneurial economy, speculation fed one especially sordid episode: the South Sea "Bubble" was the result of a plan to have that Company take over the national debt by creating £31 million in new shares of stock. The share prices rose rapidly, tripling in the first months of 1720 and again in the course of the summer. The scheme collapsed in September amid many tales of misconduct, some involving members of the royal court. Robert Walpole, one of the Whig leaders, took the lead in salvaging the government and earned the place as the king's first minister, which he held from 1721 to 1742. His long tenure rested in equal measure on skills as a financial manager and as a manager of Whig factions.

In the late 1730s, politicians were embroiled in disputes over new taxes introduced by Walpole, adding molassses and gin to the growing list of excise targets. Beside his domestic problems, Walpole faced mounting opposition from varied colonial interests, especially with regard to his policies toward Spain. Opposition groups demanded war, and war came in the winter of 1739–1740. Indeed, the better part of the next twenty-five years would see fighting in one area or another. And in the same period, the end of Walpole's long term of successful management of Parliament was followed by a progression of ministers struggling to hold together the warring factions of politicians.

In the first half of the eighteenth century the British government went through a major transformation. Two key forces brought the change: with an active quasi-executive role for the Lords and Commons, their work was no longer occasional but was on a permanent footing; with an expanding colonial empire, the cost of governing multiplied, the cost of fighting skyrocketed, and the overall size of official operations expanded. Beside this growth, some important changes in law were evident. There was a striking increase in the volume of legislation, public and private. In the period 1660–1688 there were 17 sessions, producing on average 17 pieces of public legislation. In the next four decades the average was 28 and in the next four it reached 58. This is but a crude measure, but the simple tally marks an obvious and important phenomenon. The business of the legislature expanded rapidly, enough to suggest a qualitative as well as a quantitative change.[1]

Legislative solutions were eagerly sought in the new imperial economy. Expanding economic activity brought new risks and new legal remedies. The spirit of the entrepreneur, the improving landlord, the provincial banker, or the merchant was abroad in most of the king's dominions, and because of the entrepreneur, the lawyer, magistrate, and MP found themselves involved in a new and wider range of activity. The enterprise of the eighteenth century, with its collateral migration, necessarily produced innumerable interactions. The colonial sphere required new legal machinery and revival of old: the latter in the Privy Council's jurisdiction; the former with colonial courts and agents of London governing boards.

Through most of the situations we have seen here, the theme of parliamentary sovereignty appears: the idea that ultimate power rested with the king, lords, and commons. This concept was English, and its meaning for the other legislatures was not clearly defined at the beginning of the century. What was clear was that Scottish and Irish Parliaments and colonial assemblies were all bound to interact with "that very English beast, the king in Parliament."[2] The actual results in terms of legislation and legal interaction were a bit of a surprise. For if the supreme Parliament of England was able to enact the highest law, subsequent legal interaction with its imperial dependencies produced many instances where the lesser assemblies could oppose and sometimes subvert it. There might be what some called an "imperial parliament" but there were many obstacles to "imperial legislation."[3]

Bills and Acts

Such an essential matter as the history of legislation has been studied seriously by a small number of scholars.[4] That may be because historians have an irresistible penchant for taking enacted law at face value. But as we all know, the words in the statute book are only a small part of the story. This becomes abundantly clear when we look at the lawmaking which went on in the first half of the eighteenth century, and the clarity only increases when we examine in detail what some of the legislation actually accomplished.

Recent writers have noted that the modern idea of a statute (as the command of the sovereign) was not established until the nineteenth century. In the eighteenth century, the idea lingered that statute was supposed to embody custom more than innovation. This was a holdover from much earlier times when legislative acts originated in petitions, themselves designed to call attention to neglected custom. Bills were drafted by various persons, official and unofficial; there were no established rules for drafting. There were both public and private acts, the line between them being very fuzzy. Public bills would come through the council; private measures might be drafted by any legal professional. The series of oral readings in both houses and the committee debates which followed were the machinery of an age when printing was limited.

Statute law was taken to be the highest authority because it contained the deliberate decisions of the peers and Commons endorsed by the royal assent. But the relation of acts to custom or common law was not settled. Did the priority of statute mean that only a literal interpretation of the words of an act was acceptable? That question was debated well into the nineteenth century. Meanwhile judges construed lawmakers' language as best they could, and with as little interference as possible. These general terms apply best to the work of the English Parliament. They obscure some substantial differences within the dominions of the Crown. In the case of colonial legislatures, the lawmaking function was totally different. By royal charter or other means, colonies had assemblies and councils which were given limited legislative powers. The basic rule was that they might enact laws necessary for colonial affairs, provided those laws were not repugnant to the acts of the English Parliament. There was never a clear and completely reliable guide to "repugnance," and assemblies had to make their way independently.

The Scottish Parliament was the creature of an independent constitution under the Scottish Crown. The Scottish unicameral body had three estates (nobles, clergy, and burgesses). Parliament had both judicial and legislative functions; it also had conciliar rivals in older general councils and later conventions of estates; in the General Assembly of the reformed kirk; and in the convention of royal burghs. For some time the agenda of Parliament was tightly controlled by a committee, the Lords of the Articles, which agency was terminated in 1690. Connection to the English Parliament was proposed in 1604, in 1652, 1670, 1689, 1700, 1702, and 1705. In the latter year, commissioners were appointed who drafted the treaty which united the English and Scottish Parliaments.

Irish legislation was enacted by an Irish Parliament which was almost as old as the English but was usually under the latter's influence, or that of the councillors in England. This position was affirmed by Poynings' Laws (1495). These measures had applied English laws to Ireland and required the prior approval of Irish legislation by the English council. After the victory of William III secured the Protestant ascendancy, there was a *de facto* shift in the Poynings procedure. Heads of bills were voted on before the English council gave its approval.[5] All the same, Irish legislation was mainly composed or vetted in England before it could pass. In 1692, in the first Williamite Parliament, the Irish legislators formed a committee to review English statutes to determine "which of them may be fit and necessary to be enacted into laws in this kingdom."[6] But the Irish Parliament did not control its legislative destiny. That fact was underscored by the printing in 1698 of a famous critique written by William Molyneux: *The Case of Ireland's being bound by acts of parliament in England, stated.* The tract became a nationalist landmark, but it did nothing to change the basic position of the Irish Parliament, and it may even have stimulated its further repression.[7] The Irish Parliament was subordinated to the English and it had to chafe at that limitation, especially in any cases where particular Irish interests were affected.

The imperial Parliament assumed the authority to enact laws for all of the king's subjects, but the fundamental legislative relationship was unsettled as the eighteenth century began. Some Crown attempts to muzzle colonial legislatures had failed in the late seventeenth century (Jamaica, 1681; Dominion of New England, 1686). The first major parliamentary alteration came in 1707 with the merger of the English and Scottish Parliaments. The next important step was the formal subordination of the Irish Parliament in the Declaratory Act of 1720. There it was stated that the Parliament of Great Britain "had, hath, and of right ought to have full power and authority to make laws and statutes of sufficient force and validity to bind the kingdom and people of Ireland." This act bore a striking resemblance to one a half century later in the American colonies, where the question of legislative authority was about to be settled by force of arms.

These efforts all seemed to centralize legislative authority, leaving in place a token Irish Parliament and an assortment of remote colonial assemblies. However, each of these bodies challenged the imperial Parliament, and they won legislative independence in the 1780s. Those heroic stories dominate political histories, but the story of legal interaction is more mundane and more complex. By a closer look at some attempts to exercise imperial legislative power in the eighteenth century, we can get a much better idea of the complex character of legal interaction in imperial legislation.

"For the Further Preventing the Growth of Popery"

Ireland should have been a prime area for English imperial lawmaking at the end of the seventeenth century. Defeat in 1691 and the Treaty of Limerick had left the Catholic cause in disarray and the way seemed open to the erection of a powerful colonial regime. We can gain some insight into the hollow realm of imperial legislation from one of the most notorious chapters of eighteenth century lawmaking: the penal laws against Roman Catholics. These laws were enacted for all parts of the British Isles, at different periods and apparently without any general plan, except "preventing the growth of popery."[8] The Irish versions were intended to shore up the Protestant minority by denying religious, political, and economic rights to the Catholic majority. On their face, the laws created a system of persecution, which feature was the main focus of older interpreters. But beneath the surface there was evidence in Ireland of widespread resistance, collusion, and evasion of the laws. Those responses have been the focus of more recent scholarship, which sheds some interesting light on our search for interaction in the realm of imperial law.[9] Our task is to examine the laws, to see how Irish Catholics responded to them, and finally, to look at some of the ways that the penal laws left their mark on the legal systems.

The Irish Parliament met for the first time under William III in 1692. It followed the traumatic "Patriot Parliament" of 1689, and the defeat of James II and the Treaty of Limerick. By an English Act, members had been required to make a declaration which assured a completely Protestant body. Although the king wanted a moderate settlement, by 1695 bills had been passed for disarming papists and prohibiting the foreign education of their children. In 1697, Catholic bishops and regular clergy were banished.[10] Acts against Roman Catholics were certainly not new to Ireland, nor were they unfamiliar elsewhere. In England there were similar laws on the books by 1690: disarming papists, removing papists from the vicinity of London, and allowing universities to confiscate benefices from papists. In 1700 a comprehensive English act passed "for the further preventing the growth of popery." It gave a £100 reward for the conviction of papists saying mass, prison terms for teaching Catholic schools, and finally, loss of rights to inherit land, or have land held in trust, and priority given to any Protestant in the line of succession. This English legislation was followed in 1702 by a new type of measure "for the relief of Protestant purchasers of forfeited estates in Ireland." There were many other measures connected to the handling of forfeited estates, itself a process largely based upon an alleged Catholic conspiracy to alter the royal succession. There were of course measures designed to protect the Protestant churches, such as the Scottish "Act for Secureing the True Protestant Religion" in 1703 in which her Majesty "perpetually confirms all laws statutes and Acts of Parliament made against popery and papists."[11]

Most of these laws were enacted before the principal Irish penal law was passed in 1704. J. G. Simms studied "The Making of a Penal Law" and detailed the steps taken, back and forth across St. George's Channel, to enact the pivotal measure.[12] This act put limits on Catholic inheritance but did not abolish it altogether. The heir was allowed six months to conform (s. 7); one who failed to act might lose the estate to a conforming eldest son (s. 3); and in the absence of conformity, the Catholic estate was to be divided among all male heirs (s. 10). By 1709, this act was seen to be inadequate and an amended version was adopted. This was the infamous act which banned Catholic inheritance (as did the law in England since 1700). Many other pieces of legislation followed, some very specific, most of them in response to a particular scare or crisis. In 1708 Catholics were forbidden to become solicitors; in 1716 they were forbidden to become constables; in 1723 priests were forbidden to officiate at marriages; in 1727 the right to practice law was denied, as was the parliamentary franchise; in 1733 converts were not allowed to become justices of the peace.

In spite of apparent thoroughness, the legislative campaign against the "growth of popery" was countered by successful underground resistance in Ireland. The present generation of Irish eighteenth-century historians has pieced together a convincing picture of Catholic resistance. The picture has several connected elements, each of which puts the matter of "imperial legislation" in a new and different light. In the first place, many "converts" had no desire to conform. Secondly, many "discoveries" of papist landowners were in collusive suits. Finally, Catholics engaged in the legal business designed to reduce their numbers. Bartlett shows in *The Fall and Rise of the Irish Nation* (1992) that the Irish Catholic community not only resisted shrinking, but that some significant "growth of popery" occurred in the first half of the eighteenth century. By 1760 Irish Catholics were manifesting a new political spirit and a sense of victory. By the 1770s, the British government was ready to give up on the penal laws.

In addition to the direct experience of Catholics and their determined resistance, one other aspect of these laws deserves our attention. There were several important legal developments which were tied, more or less closely, to the penal laws. First, the Irish Registry of Deeds was set up in 1709 as a voluntary means of monitoring landholding.[13] Also, the interest in the penal laws, or more precisely in the debate over their repeal, prompted the first printed modern Irish law reports. Gorges Edmund Howard was a prolific writer in Dublin, who had for several years been publishing tracts, such as "*Observations and queries on the present laws of this kingdom relative to papists*" in 1761 "*by a true Church of England man.*" In successive versions, Howard added more and more complaints and suggestions for legal reforms. But what was probably his biggest contribution was the publication, in 1775, of *Several Special Cases on the Laws against the further growth of Popery in Ireland*. Howard collected a series of Irish (and a few English) cases in order to demonstrate the legal consequences of the popery laws. His work was a pioneering effort in the publication of modern Irish law reports.

There is some irony in the fact that from 1720 until 1782, the Irish legislature had its hands tied in terms of legislation. And yet in this same period of time, the story of the demise of the penal regime was unfolding. The Declaratory Act of 1720 did not require the British Parliament to legislate *for* Ireland, it only said it had the ultimate power to do so; meanwhile the English council exercised real authority. Thus Parliament had less control than it did in Scotland via the Act of Union of 1707. Ministers had more control. But as the "growth of popery" clearly demonstrates, the meaning of "control" by means of legislation needs to be examined carefully.

"For Improving the Union of the Two Kingdoms"

The union of Scottish and English Parliaments was made by treaty. But it was prompted, qualified, and ratified by statutes. This conjunction has nurtured a luxuriant debate on the legal nature of union.[14] What is wanted here is a close look at the role of statutes in the unification process and some further study of the provisions for statute-making in the union treaty. The rest of this section will turn to the "Scottish" statutes made under the union. Statutes both English and Scottish played key roles in the unification process. Whereas royal initiatives were responsible in 1604 and 1669 and 1689, the parliamentary role appeared to expand, as in 1700 the Lords passed a bill to appoint commissioners which was defeated in the Commons; in 1702, William addressed Parliament proposing union talks; and after his death Anne in the same year asked the English Parliament to study the method of union, and she appointed commissioners who met between November 1702 and February 1703.[15]

The Scottish Parliament was meanwhile alienated by its exclusion from the succession question and from diplomatic decisions. Thus in 1703 the Act Anent Peace and War claimed authority to declare war for Scotland; the Act of Security stated the authority of the Scottish Parliament to confirm the successor to the Scottish throne.[16] These posed a major threat which the English Parliament countered with the Alien Act, whose central clause said that Scots would lose their rights as subjects and their trade to England would be cut off as of Christmas Day 1705 if the Scottish acts were not repealed.[17] In June 1705 Queen Anne recommended succession measures and union negotiations to the Scottish Parliament, and in July a draft act for a treaty was passed. In September the English Parliament voted to leave nomination of commissioners with the queen. Between April and July of 1706, the Queen's English and Scottish Commissioners treated on the union. Was the result a genuine treaty—that is, an instrument of fundamental law? Or was it a composite of articles and statutes— in other words, a unique piece of legislation? One is drawn toward the latter conclusion by the acts which qualified the union and the acts which ratified it.

In the first place, commissioners agreed that there should be separate acts of security for the Kirk of Scotland and the Church of England. These acts were intended to shield the churches from any future action by the United Kingdom Parliament, and in so doing they abridged the new Parliament's powers, or claimed to do so. As for ratification, both the Scottish and English Parliaments passed legislation which contained the language of the treaty articles. However, the Scottish act added provisions for the election of Scots peers and MPs (which additions had been proposed but not framed by the commissioners). This amending procedure reinforced the view that the union was the product of a piece of legislation.

Next, the union necessarily involved acts of implementation. One such step was the Regency Act of 1707, passed by the new United Kingdom Parliament.[18] This act harmonized the succession practice of the two kingdoms, precluding an embarrassing dissolution of Parliament upon the demise of the sovereign. Another act of implementation was the Exchequer Act (Scotland) of 1707.[19] This carried out the provisions of article 19 that a court of exchequer be erected in Scotland "having the same power and authority...as the Court of Exchequer has in England."

After implementing the treaty, what were the provisions for making statutes in the new regime? Article 3 provided "That the United Kingdom of Great Britain be represented by one and the same Parliament, to be styled the Parliament of Great Britain." This was the entire clause, the shortest of the treaty. There was no mention of the process of legislating; there were no reservations or stipulations as to the legislative power or procedure of the new body, and this silence ensured that the English model would prevail in the new institution.

Some other articles required specific future legislation: to reconcile the two governments' finances, the laws for the "equivalents" were projected (art. 9); a goal of assimilation of trade laws was stated (art. 18); existing Scots acts consistent with the treaty were retained (*ibid.*); the proviso was made that "all laws and statutes in either kingdom" would be void if contrary to or inconsistent with the articles (art. 25); and a restriction was added that matters of "private right" in Scots law should not be altered "except for the evident utility of the subjects within Scotland" (art. 18). With all of these particulars, the treaty still did not address the process of making statute law. Provision for Scottish peers showed that the basic English bicameral model would be adopted, though only a small number of representative peers would sit for Scotland. Beyond that, there was little to suggest what the framers of the union thought about the role of Scottish legislators.

Once the union was formed, what did it mean in terms of Scottish statute law? There were three kinds of "Scottish" acts from 1707 on: (1) existing Scots acts, not repealed or repugnant; (2) exclusively "Scottish" acts made by the Parliament of the United Kingdom (including private and local acts); and (3) Scottish sections of general legislation.[20] The great bulk of the Scottish statute book remained in force after 1707; but it is fair to add that only in the next century would the project of statute book revision get underway. And by that time, the old Scottish acts were being outnumbered by their modern successors. It is notable however, that the *Chronological Table of the Statutes* maintained a list of the Scottish Acts from 1424 to 1707 into the later twentieth century.[21]

The class of specifically Scottish acts passed in the new Parliament numbered 84 pieces of legislation in the first half century after 1707. The largest single category were local acts providing for beer duties in different localities (26); the next largest was legislation for administration of justice: crimes, courts, and officers (23); there were also some improvement acts for roads and bridges (14); and in this period, a special category of laws made in response to the threat (or reality) of Jacobite rebellion (18).

For a broader view of the legal interaction involved in the Anglo-Scottish union, we may look at several large categories of legislation in order to assess the impact of union, and to decide what, if any, imperial legislation was at work, in the areas of constitutional, criminal, and civil law. The alterations in the structure of Scotland's government after the union look like English imperial interference. Certainly these constitutional acts have been so interpreted in the past. Prior to the Regency Act, there was a measure "for rendering the union of the two kingdoms more entire and complete."[22] This act abolished the Scottish Privy Council by merging it with the English. It also provided for Scottish justices of the peace and circuit courts and it made regulations for parliamentary elections.

The new Parliament also intervened in the order and government of the Kirk. There were laws defending Scottish Episcopalians and restoring rights of patronage.[23] A number of early laws altered the operation of the separate Scottish legal system: terms for the Court of Exchequer were changed; oaths for "practisers of law" were required as well as oaths for lawyers and judges. The frequency of judicial circuits was modified (to once a year).[24] These constitutional acts were passed to confirm ministerial control over Scottish government, especially when there was a threat of revolt. These were not merely English measures, and it doesn't appear that they were part of some larger plan for imperial subjection of the Scots.

In the realm of criminal law, the union seemed to promise Scottish independence. Ironically, the Treason Act of 1709 was entitled "An Act for Improving the Union of the Two Kingdoms."[25] The meaning was made clear in the preamble: "The laws of both parts of Great Britain should agree as near as may be...to the end that said union may be more effectually improved." This meant the importation of the English law of treason and of English trial procedure. Commissions of oyer and terminer, including three lords of justiciary "in such manner as is used in England" (s. 2); a grand jury ("oaths of twelve or more good and lawful men of the county" s. 4); and "the same corruption of blood, pains, penalties and forfeitures as persons convicted...in England" (s. 5). The act also proscribed torture of persons accused of capital crimes, excepting the English treatment of persons refusing to plead (s. 8). The statute was used on four occasions: 1715, 1746, 1794, and 1820. It was a clear invasion of the otherwise separate Scottish criminal jurisdiction. The treatment of Scottish traitors was surely not thought to be too lenient. This act was inspired by the Jacobite threat, as several sections make clear. This uniformity was expected to give ministers in London more control over prosecution and a better guarantee of convictions.

Similarly, in the related area of forfeitures there were efforts to exert English influence and apply English procedures. After the rising of 1715, there were commissioners of forfeited estates whose verdicts were anticipated by sequestrations which were appealed to the Court of Session and thence to the House of Lords. The eventual results were disappointing in terms of discipline and penalty. The most intriguing outcome however, was the exploitation of some of the forfeited estates by a London company. The estates were taken over by The "Company of Undertakers for raising the Thames water in York Buildings."[26] The company had been acquired at the same time that forfeited estates were being disposed under an act of Parliament. The new owners partook of the speculative fever of the day in promoting their plan to acquire Scottish property and sell annuities on that capital. They did manage to inflate share values from £10 to £305 in a few months. And their holdings became a source of litigation (and fees) throughout the eighteenth century. But beside its curious joint-stock character, this was not an imperial measure, and it did not affect Scots law.

A more direct impact was felt in the structure of criminal law. Article 20 of the Treaty of Union had promised that

> all heritable offices, superiorities, heritable jurisdictions, offices for life and jurisdictions for life be reserved to the owners thereof as rights of property, in the same manner as they are now enjoyed by the laws of Scotland, notwithstanding this treaty.

In the wake of the 1745 rebellion, this clause was discarded, and in the Heritable Jurisdictions Act of 1747 all of these were abolished. Once again, the purpose was "for rendering the union more complete."[27] The following year the Scottish Sheriff Depute was created. But this office was not an English imitation. It was a new departure, a paid, qualified lawyer who would be included in the commission of the peace.[28] These changes in relation to criminal law in Scotland suggest a mixed picture of intervention and innovation, but not one which was truly aimed at or ever very successful in "improving the union of the two kingdoms."

In matters of private law the treaty provided that Parliament would enact laws only for the "evident utility" of the people of Scotland. Yet it was obvious that a Parliament with a vast majority of English members would be the arbiter of that utility. The large number of local acts on beer duties suggest that there may have been one area of local government not covered by the extensive clauses of the treaty on customs and excise.

There were many other areas of potential friction, where Scottish legislation was involved. In 1712 the Toleration Act and the Patronage Act, passed in the wake of the Greenshields affair, restored some Episcopal influence, especially the revival of lay patronage by the latter act. There was wider debate over the malt tax. When imposed in 1713, it was regarded as a severe infringement on the treaty, one which led to a movement to revoke the union, and a motion in the House of Lords to that effect was defeated by only four votes.

That the acts of the United Kingdom Parliament were of value in "improving the union of the two kingdoms" may be doubted. For every strong measure to achieve that end, much resistance was generated. For any of the more innovative acts, older interests were injured. And in most cases, the intent of ministers was more likely to be ease of government rather than forced legal assimilation. But whatever the motives and outcomes of legislation, it does seem that the Scottish legal community was more closely aligned to the English after a half century of union; maybe in spite of a half century of union! For when we examine what leading Scottish lawyers were writing in the 1750s, and allowing for some amount of postrebellion sycophancy, there is a clear impression of convergence.

There was paradox enough in the midcentury Scot's situation. The conjunction produced by the union built a new polity beside the separated legal systems. The improvement of the union seemed to call for the assimilation of laws; the imperial appearance of moves such as this would surely arouse political hostility: but at the same time, assimilation of laws found some support among lawyers. An early instance was James Innes, who wrote *Idea juris scotici: or a summary view of the laws of Scotland* in 1733. He directed his work to English lawyers, because "it is to be expected that British subjects ought to understand the constitution of North, as well as of South Britain." Innes tried to write a combined essay, relating the two systems. He organized it in sections on "persons," "rights," and "actions." There was a fair amount of comparative comment throughout; one point germane to our subject was his view on the legislation of the Parliament of Great Britain, which "doth more properly appertain to the English than to the Scotch-Laws."

In the wake of the '45, Lord President Duncan Forbes and Lord Chancellor Hardwicke "agreed in thinking that the legal systems of England and Scotland should be assimilated, as far as was compatible with their national characters and traditions."[29] Thus stated, the point was rather ambiguous, and this kind of assimilating was what the two had been doing since 1707. By this point, the relation was being more openly acknowledged, and the correspondents were probably thinking of going beyond such limited convergence.

Andrew McDowall, Lord Bankton, wrote a more substantial work which aimed in the same general direction as Innes. *An Institute of the Laws of Scotland in Civil Rights* appeared in three volumes between 1751 and 1753. The subtitle promised "observations upon the agreement or diversity between them and the laws of England." Bankton meant "civil" in the sense of personal and property rights. As for his British theme, he said

> I have subjoined at the end of each title of the first three books, and in divers titles of the fourth, a kind of parallel between our laws and those of England, in relation to the subject of such title, shewing the conformity or disconformity betwixt the one and the other.

Bankton compared the task of his age with that of Stair:

> The Lord Stair had no occasion to observe anything of this kind, nor was it of great use in his time; but now, since the union of the two kingdoms, there is such intercourse between the subjects of South and North Britain, that it must be of great moment, that the laws of both be generally understood, and their agreement or diversity attended to; so that people, in their mutual correspondence, may regulate themselves accordingly; and the respective laws and usages may likewise receive some light from the comparison.

Bankton often cited imperial legislation, with observations on current practice. For example, he noted that when a criminal statute stipulated that a trial was to be held in Westminster, it also implied that Scottish cases would be heard in the High Court of Justiciary.[30]

In distinct fields of law, controversial issues were apt to be discussed in an Anglo-Scottish framework. The much-debated matter of entails, for example, was the topic of Sir John Dalrymple in *An Essay Towards a General History of Feudal Property in Great Britain* in 1757. The postrebellion climate favored frank suggestions that the Scottish system of entails, which had been authorized by the Scottish Act of 1685, be terminated in favor of an English-style "rule against perpetuities." But in this work, and in his later *Considerations upon the policy of entails in Great Britain* (1764), Dalrymple argued that the true complaint against entails was their perceived obstruction of commercial enterprise.

On this question and others, perhaps the strongest voice for assimilation in this period was that of Henry Home, Lord Kames. In his *Historical Law-Tracts* (1758) and his *Elucidations respecting the common and statute law of Scotland* (1777), plus his *Statute Law of Scotland abridged* (1757) Kames showed a keen interest in assimilation. He corresponded with Lord Hardwicke, the English Chancellor, but no substantial project of assimilation was attempted.

There is some irony that these writers, who were among the authors who produced the Scottish Enlightenment, were also members of an apparently colonial school of legal writing. But the perception is wrong; merely advocating a closer approximation of laws is not the same as accepting imperial control; it may just as well reflect a sense of sharing power and dominion, that of a union which in their eyes was indeed improved. Assimilation, whatever each author meant by it, was not likely to happen in the eighteenth century. There were simply too many complications. And soon there were too many disruptions as the end of the century teetered on the brink of political and constitutional revolution.

"Full Power and Authority in all Cases Whatsoever"

The clearest case of imperial legislation came naturally enough in the American colonies. There the power of Parliament was confronted by the lawmaking of the colonial assemblies. There was no chance of a union like Scotland's. There was instead an overbearing Declaratory Act suspiciously similar to the Irish Act of 1720. The Declaratory Act of 1766 laid claim to full legislative sovereignty, but this was a new departure. The history of colonial legislation has been studied at great length. The delegated powers and the imperial lawmaking were parallel processes which had a complex history.[31] Early colonies had little time or need for legislation. But in the first half of the eighteenth century colonial assemblies became more active, while the occasional attention of Parliament was aimed at commercial regulation. An anonymous writer in Virginia said in 1701,[32]

> great doubts have been raised, how far the Legislative Authority is in the Assemblies of the several colonies; whether they have the power to make certain acts or ordinances in the nature of byelaws only; or, whether they can make acts of attainder, naturalisation, for settling or disposing of titles to lands within their jurisdiction, or other things of the like nature; and where necessity requires, make such acts as best suit the circumstances and constitution of the country, even tho' in some particulars, they plainly differ from the Laws of England.

Colonial assemblies were worried at this stage about prerogative power, or its local imitation in the governor and his council. But soon the Virginia burgesses and other colonial legislators increased their power. In Pennsylvania, the Penn family battled with the legislative assembly after 1701; the Massachusetts assembly tried to exercise direct control of money grants in the 1720s.

In the 1760s there was an ongoing battle between executive and legislative forces in New York, in which legal powers were at stake: the matter of judicial tenure and the question of appellate power over jury verdicts were argued at some length. The Massachusetts colony saw slower maturing of the power of the assembly, and "it was only as late as 1766 that the Assembly gained definitive leadership over the Council." Along the way, there had been bitter struggles over power, such as the 1762 battle between Governor Bernard and the lawmakers over his assumed power to spend public funds.[33] During these debates some strong positions had evolved on questions of colonial lawmaking. Here was what Thomas Pownall, former governor of Massachusetts, reported about colonial views in 1764:[34]

> The people of the colonies say that the inhabitants of the colonies are entitled to all the privileges of Englishmen, that they have a right to participate in the legislative power; and that no commands of the Crown...are binding upon them further than they please to acquiesce under such, and conform their own actions thereto; that they hold this right of legislature, not derived from the grace and will of the Crown...that this right is inherent and essential to the community, as a community of Englishmen: and that therefore they must have all the rights, privileges, and full and free exercise of their own will and liberty in making laws which are necessary to that act of legislation, uncontrolled by any power of the Crown, or of the governor, preventing or suspending that act; and that the clause in the commission directing the governor to call together a legislature by his writs, is declarative and not creative, and therefore he is directed to act conformably to a right actually already existing in the people.

The author's brother, John Pownall, was the longtime secretary to the Board of Trade, and probably the most influential subminister in colonial affairs. But as they both knew, the administrative structure for colonial business was bewildering and without any central control. This lack of imperial direction contributed to the degeneration of colonial policy in the 1760s.

We are interested in more than the political story behind the Stamp Act.[35] Its importance spilled over into a number of areas of the law, which have naturally been overshadowed by the political and constitutional drama. Yet for the student of legal interaction, those more obscure elements were highly significant. British policy dictated a change in colonial finance after 1763. Victory in the French and Indian War yielded large new North American territories, and heavy new expenditures needed to be offset by new revenues. Experience suggested that the colonial governments would not be apt to shoulder those costs. George Grenville took office in 1763 with a new policy of colonial finance. A Sugar Act in 1764 began the collection of new revenue from trade, and planning was begun for a new stamp tax. The new revenue was to be committed to the support of armed forces in the colonies. The idea of parliamentary taxation for colonial government was not new, as many of its opponents asserted. That is not to say that it was prudent, or that it was practicable.

Was the Stamp Act a measure of legal consequence? Any colonial lawyer would respond affirmatively, for the act imposed a tax on "every skin or piece of vellum or parchment, or sheet or piece of paper, on which shall be ingrossed, written or printed" the whole range of legal transactions. Lawyers were warned that all records should be kept in accustomed form (s. 62). The act provided for enforcement and for the punishment of forgery in colonial courts (s. 58). It also indemnified the officials engaged in this enforcement. None of these clauses have received much attention, because the act was repealed soon after it was greeted with widespread hostility throughout the colonies. But the prospective effects were plain, at least to colonial merchants, printers, and lawyers.

At the same time, the majority of the British public and members of Parliament were not sympathetic to colonial complaints. Stamps had been part of public life since the 1680s, and the measure for the colonies was adjusted from English levels and coverage to take account of the different economy of America. The merchant Henry McCulloh had pioneered the measure and submitted a scheme to the Board of Trade in 1757. It was a bill very much like this which Grenville adopted in 1764, and the familiarity of stamp duties explains why the British Parliament gave its approval quickly and with little fuss. The fuss made by the colonists was substantial. They engaged in economic warfare; they physically attacked the stamp officers and prevented them from following their instructions; and they met in illegal assemblies to denounce the act. It was soon evident that the Stamp Act could not be enforced, at least not without a major armed initiative.

The colonists' success in resisting the Stamp Act forced a repeal, but members of Parliament would only contemplate such a reversal after they asserted their power in the Declaratory Act. This step of course perpetuated and underscored the fundamental disagreement. Parliament's sovereignty was becoming a recognized part of the British constitution, but it was not so readily recognized in colonies which had their own legislative bodies. The explanation was simple. While the new concept was being accepted at home, the course of events in the colonies had been different. Legislation was not being constantly foisted on the dominions, and in fact, it was just because of this inattention that Grenville's policy was invented.

Late in 1765, Grenville resigned as the king's chief minister. The ministry of Lord Rockingham was left to deal with the American situation. Its plan was to repeal the Stamp Act, but first to mollify parliamentary opinion by passing a declaration of Parliament's authority over the colonies. The Declaratory Act's preamble said the colonial legislatures "have of late, against law, claimed" the "sole and exclusive right of imposing duties and taxes" in the colonies. The votes taken in the colonies were "derogatory" to the "legislative authority of Parliament" and were inconsistent with their "dependency" upon the Crown. Therefore, the colonies and plantations were declared

> subordinate unto and dependent upon the imperial Crown and Parliament of Great Britain; and that the King's Majesty, by and with the consent of the Lords Spiritual and Temporal, and Commons of Great Britain, in Parliament assembled, had, hath, and of right ought to have, full power and authority to make laws and statutes of sufficient force and validity to bind the colonies and people of America, subjects of the Crown of Great Britain, in all cases whatsoever.

The second and last section of the act declared the offending resolutions of the colonial assemblies "utterly null and void to all intents and purposes whatsoever."

The first consequence of the Declaratory Act in terms of legal interaction was that imperial legislation was now an established fact. However necessary the Declaratory Act was politically, it served to make the issue of sovereignty prominent and inescapable. From this time on every colonial law contained the seeds of constitutional crisis. By the same token, colonial assemblies, still smarting from the Stamp Act experience, and overconfident from the success of repeal, found themselves in deepening difficulty. New York and New Jersey opposed the Mutiny Act of 1765. The Massachusetts Assembly found itself in a dispute over the pardon power. Continuing confrontation led to suspension of assemblies in some cases.

On its face, the Declaratory Act seemed to be a copy of the Irish Act of 1720. The MPs of 1766 may have recalled the Irish Act, but if they did, it was probably in order to alter the new one: the American act asserted dependency upon "the imperial Crown and Parliament" and it was more expansive in adding the phrase "to make laws and statutes of sufficient force and validity to bind...in all cases whatsoever." The differences here represent the distinction between the older view of Parliament's legislative power as one which restricted action and the newer view of that power as one which commands.

The mood of Parliament in 1766 was reflected in the proposal by Lord Shelburne that resistance to laws be deemed high treason; that public expression to that effect be misprision of treason; that offenders should be tried in the colonies or in Britain, and that the act should be enforced with arms! The Declaratory Act of 1766 was a case of politically driven legal interaction. The colonial rejection of imperial legislation had been too successful; the assertion of parliamentary sovereignty was categorical. Interaction was soon transformed into rebellion. As Reid said, "it was Parliament's use of the authority to legislate that took the constitutional quarrel to the point of armed conflict." [36]

Imperial legislation was a form of lawmaking which was confounded by the circumstances of empire. Neither a united British legislature nor separated Irish and colonial bodies could completely satisfy the needs of the imperial governors and their subjects. But this was by no means evident in the 1760s. William Blackstone was publishing his famous *Commentaries on the Laws of England* just as the Declaratory Act crisis occurred. To him, there was no question as to the efficacy of imperial legislation by the omnicompetent Parliament. Yet our examples show clearly that the legal and political reality of imperial law had many points where the practical authority of the legislature fell short. As it happened, no amount of legislative competence would have been able to deal with the turbulent events which awaited in the last quarter of the eighteenth century.

Chapter 3

Revolution and Law 1760–1801

An educated Englishman in 1760 knew of revolution in a particular sense—namely his country's experience in the seventeenth century, and especially in 1689. He also knew of rebellion, most vividly and recently in the defeat of the Jacobite uprising of 1745. Moreover, in the eighteenth century, as the social historians remind us, he had to be aware of mobs and riots, though they might be more ritualistic than revolutionary. When the young George III came to the throne in 1760, and the country was engaged in far-flung battles with France, the new ruler expected to bring stability to British politics. That world would be shattered in the next four decades by American rebellion, French Revolution, and general European wars, all of which made a significant imprint on laws and legal institutions in the archipelago and the empire.

The main theme which links the law with the general history of this period is the matter of sovereignty. The fundamental power of government had been vested in the king, lords, and commons since the Glorious Revolution. This parliamentary sovereignty was resisted by the American colonists; it was challenged by John Wilkes and a growing number of other political radicals; it was asserted with novel force against real or apparent rebels. But for a variety of reasons, the seventeenth century constitutional solution was no longer adequate: it rested on a patchwork electoral law which was wildly out of date; it was operated with a system of patronage which was ridiculed as "Old Corruption"; and the partnership of king and ministers which was charged with managing affairs was itself a work in progress. In other words, there were disparities throughout, and with the crises of government from the 1770s through the 1790s, the question of sovereignty was always close to the center of affairs.

The sovereign ruler for this entire period was King George III. He came to the throne in 1760 on the death of his grandfather, his father Frederick having died in 1751. The new king did not share his predecessors' concern for Hanover; rather he seemed to relish his Englishness. Surely one of the most analyzed of English (British) rulers, George very much wished to exercise the powers and fulfill the duties of a sovereign head of state. Thus on a personal level it may be the more poignant that he encountered so many difficulties. As the head of a victorious empire in 1763, he soon found his government struggling to raise revenues in America and in the process inciting a revolutionary resistance.

As a constitutional ruler, in circumstances far more liberal than any other European monarchy, George was bedevilled by radicals like John Wilkes, who denounced legal methods such as the use of general warrants (a warrant with no specific charge). He was only one of many political figures who were bold enough by the 1760s to engage in organized opposition "out of doors" (i.e., outside the confines of Parliament). In an earlier day, these acts would surely have been condemned as treasonable; by the later eighteenth century they still shocked respectable political circles, as they flirted with legal retribution.

When a terrible revolution broke out in Paris in 1789, George III encountered even more formidable and forthright challenges to his sovereign capacity. Many groups of radicals were encouraged by the events in France (1789–1791) to agitate for reforms in government. With the execution of Louis XVI in 1793, the progressive revolution devolved into a fearsome spectacle of popular repression, with a French national army bent on defeating its monarchical neighbors. In this climate, radical opinion became even less tolerable and loyalist support for the Crown grew significantly in Britain.

In the actual governing process there were important collateral changes. The king was expected to select ministers to serve him, men who could manage the Lords and the Commons and the departments of state. These ministers were given the tools of royal patronage to assist in that management. This process came under increasing scrutiny and criticism at the same time that external affairs increased the pressure on the king to meet the several crises. In an especially graphic episode, in 1788 George was afflicted with a temporary loss of sanity. A modern diagnosis suggests that he suffered from the degenerative nervous disorder known as porphyria; at the time there was no medical certainty and abundant political uncertainty. Should the king still "govern"? Should his chosen ministers continue to hold power? Should the king's son be declared the new king, bringing his set of ministerial advisers into office? The point which concerns us is that no one had these answers, and George's early (though not permanent) recovery put these troublesome questions aside.

The first minister (the term "prime minister" still insinuated an improper degree of power or control) was William Pitt, whose famous father, the Earl of Chatham, had been a heroic figure in the 1750s. The younger Pitt was equally important in political history, for he unknowingly began the transition to a more modern form of government. He helped to diminish the pool of patronage, standing out as the hero of a nation at war and the elected leader of a ministry, precursor of the modern prime minister. This analysis would have been anathema to the lawyers who were contemporaries of William Blackstone. His classic analysis of English law summarized the state of the law at the middle of the eighteenth century. Naturally, that summary could not see, and would not predict the cascade of revolutionary events about to occur.

Blackstone's Law

William Blackstone's great work was written on the eve of the revolutions which fundamentally altered the political, constitutional, and legal order in England and the dominions of the English Crown. In the 1760s, Blackstone saw a settled scheme, based on what his contemporaries called "revolution principles," that is, the legacy of the revolution of 1689. The new revolutions fostered a set of paradoxical interactions which firmly established the modern separation of the legal systems, in total contrast to Blackstone's view of imperial English law.

The famous *Commentaries* were the printed form of Blackstone's Oxford lectures, the first edition appearing between 1765 and 1769. There is no work more widely quoted and discussed in the legal literature of the eighteenth century. While Blackstone was not the first English author to attempt a summary account of the law, his version was by all measures the most popular. His latest editor called it "the most important legal treatise ever written in the English language." According to a leading social historian, "Lord Bute, in charge of Prince George's education after 1755, read in manuscript the Oxford lectures of William Blackstone, and taught his royal pupil doctrines" from that source. The dean of colonial historians said that "to the powerful legal fraternities among the English-speaking peoples on both sides of the Atlantic, the most important repository of knowledge, apart from the Bible, was Sir William Blackstone's *Commentaries on the Laws of England*."[1] Even if these assessments were excessive, we know that writers ever since have put Blackstone at the center of description and discussion of eighteenth century English law.[2]

Blackstone described the Glorious Revolution as "an entirely new case in politics, which had never before happened in our history; the abdication of the reigning monarch, and the vacancy of the throne thereupon... it was the act of the nation alone, upon an apprehension that there was no king in being." The ultimate tribunal, "the voice of society itself" had spoken; though one should not deduce a democratic course from this, "it is now become our duty...to acquiesce in their determination."[3]

To Blackstone, Parliament was of great antiquity. In his brief historical sketch he made clear that the convention of 1689 was an aberration, if an essential one. In the wake of the revolution, Parliament met with new regularity, so that the division between executive and legislative authority was made meaningful. Blackstone made an extensive survey of the foreign and domestic powers of the king. In this list, Blackstone conventionally noted the king as "the fountain of justice" and the "conservator of the peace of the kingdom." He carefully qualified his statement: the king is the "distributor" or "steward" of justice; "he is not the spring but the reservoir."[4]

All the same, the king "has alone the right of erecting courts of judicature" and thus all proceedings were in his name, "pass under his seal and are executed by his officers." The king delegated power to the judges, and in two senses they were "independent." First, they were only subject to removal for misconduct (by address of both houses) and their salaries were secured, as was their tenure, on demise of the Crown. In the second place, the judges were independent in the sense of separation of powers, which Blackstone called "one main preservative of the public liberty."[5]

A number of factors operated against this "independence." Blackstone himself noted the "ubiquity" of the king in legal process, either real or theoretical. He was the author of writs and the executor of decisions; he was the fount of honors and offices and privileges. Beside the judicial prerogative, and overlapping it, the king was what Blackstone called the "arbiter of commerce" and of course the "supreme head" of the church. An even greater limiting factor for the judges was the growth of statute law, which Blackstone appreciated as an early student of the "science of legislation."[6]

Blackstone devoted one section of his introduction to "countries subject to the laws of England." Wales had been "gradually conquered into the enjoyment of true liberty." Scotland, having once had the same government, he thought, "still retained a very great resemblance, though far from an identity, in their laws." But as those laws "continue in full force," the discussion of English law would have "very little occasion to mention" them. Ireland was a separate but dependent kingdom, but as that dependence was forgotten "and ready to be disputed by the Irish nation," it was necessary to pass the Declaratory Act. The laws of Ireland "communicate" with those of England—that is, appeals lay to the House of Lords. This relationship was essential, because otherwise the law "might be insensibly changed" or judgments might be given "to the disadvantage or diminution of the superiority."[7]

The Isle of Man had been a "little subordinate royalty" but its jurisdiction was deemed "inconvenient for the purposes of public justice" (and also a haven for smugglers). The Crown had therefore just purchased the island and it had been vested in the Crown by statute. British excise and customs laws would apply. The Channel Islands had been royal dominions for centuries, but no acts of Parliament applied and legal cases were handled locally, with an appeal to the king in council.

The colonies were either planted or conquered—at least in the minds of jurists. Blackstone saw the American colonies in the latter category, having driven out the natives or made treaties with them. "Therefore the common law of England, as such, has no allowance or authority there." The colonies "are subject however to the control of the Parliament." And any of their laws repugnant to those of Parliament "shall be utterly void and of none effect." Blackstone's circuit of the dominions of the Crown delineated a wide range of relations; there was a general sense of assimilation, past, present, or future. The essence of his account was one of imperial domination, of subservience to Crown and Parliament. We saw already that Parliament's domination had real limits. The revolutions which lay ahead would alter the picture still more.

Blackstone's account of the laws of England was a successful work, but not universally admired. His critics were numerous.[8] They were, of course, a tribute to his influence. The most notable of them was Jeremy Bentham, who attacked another sort of judicial "independence," what he saw as the inherent whimsy of the common law. Bentham would have the whole structure reduced to a statutory code and thus made "independent" of the judges' power to "find" the precedent. Bentham's criticism began in 1776 with his *Fragment on Government, or Comment on the Commentaries*. Shortly before that, the American James Wilson wrote a tract *On the Nature and Extent of the Legislative Authority of the British Parliament* in 1774. He took issue with Blackstone's definition of the "absolute" power of Parliament, particularly his account of the government of the colonies. Wilson's work may have influenced a more prominent adversary, the Virginian Thomas Jefferson.[9]

English Law in America

Jefferson's view of the "supreme" legislature was in direct conflict with the *Commentaries*. Jefferson wrote "A Summary View of the Rights of British America" in 1774 to instruct Virginia delegates to the First Continental Congress.[10] The tone was extreme—one can imagine that it was composed to contradict Blackstone: the king "is no more than the chief officer of the people"; the colonies were made by independent enterprise, but Parliament "assumed upon themselves the power of prohibiting their trade," showing "that bodies of men as well as individuals, are susceptible of the spirit of tyranny." Listing many acts against colonial interests, Jefferson asked:

> Shall these governments be dissolved, their property annihilated, and their people reduced to a state of nature, at the imperious breath of a body of men whom they never saw, in whom they never confided, and over whom they have no powers of punishment or removal, let their crimes against the American public be ever so great?

Jefferson saw "the basis or groundwork of the common law" in feudal tenures, arbitrarily imposed upon the property of Saxon England. The "fictitious principle" that all land was held from the king was transplanted to the colonies. The king also sent alien "armed forces" and gave them power over civilians, which was "criminal against our laws." Jefferson's *Summary* was too strong for the Virginia legislators in 1774, but its sentiments soon became central to colonial resistance. The revolution in the mainland colonies was against a sovereign king in Parliament. It was not against the English legal system, which in fact the colonists tried to sustain, at least in a remodelled form. Their revolt did, however, mean serious and lasting change for that system. Such was the paradox of the complex legal interaction of this shattering event.

The Continental Congress passed an independence resolution in June 1776. Jefferson's famous declaration was adopted to justify and explain the resolution. The declaration was a powerful indictment of King George III.[11] The "true bill" as returned by the grand jury in Philadelphia cited four main areas of crime making up the general charge of tyranny—that the king had refused his assent to colonial laws; that he had "obstructed the administration of justice," that he had imposed standing armies, and that he had endorsed the "pretended legislation" of Parliament. Under the last head, a list of specific complaints included many of a legal nature:

- protecting British soldiers from punishment by "mock trial";
- "depriving us in many cases of the benefits of trial by jury";
- "transporting us beyond seas to be tried for pretended offences";
- "abolishing...English laws in a neighbouring province";
- "taking away our charters, abolishing our most valuable laws";
- "suspending our own legislature"; and
- "waging war against us."

Under the last item, the king had "constrained our fellow citizens" by the press gang, "excited domestic insurrections," and engaged "Indian Savages" in the cause. Therefore the colonies "are and of right ought to be free and independent states" and "absolved from all allegiance to the British Crown." As such they "have full power to levy war, conclude peace, contract alliances, establish commerce."

At the same time that the independence of the colonies was declared, the rights of the colonists were being proclaimed. In the Congress, a Declaration of Rights was adopted which said "the respective colonies are entitled to the common law of England...they are entitled to the benefit of such of the English statutes...[as are] applicable to their several local and other circumstances."[12] The individual states also made their own claims of rights. Virginia was the first (June 12, 1776). It proclaimed a new, republican government, but one that used many terms and provisions which echoed English tradition: elections "ought to be free" (art. 6); "power of suspending laws" ought not to be exercised (art. 7); one cannot be "deprived of his liberty, except by the law of the land or the judgment of his peers." There were also proscriptions of "excessive bail," "general warrants," and standing armies.

The questions involving legal interaction in the revolution are as numerous and varied as the complaints in the Declaration of Independence. As one example, we will focus on the administration of justice during the American Revolution.[13] The subject was one of crucial importance, and this space can only offer a preliminary sketch. The rebelling colonists, only latterly declaring an end to their allegiance to the king, were still professing their adherence to English law. Yet almost all their actions contradicted that position; and those actions had an impact yet unmeasured in the administration of justice in the British Isles. Our sketch can take in several key elements: the compromise or closing of civilian courts; the exercise of military law; and the making of new constitutions.

The courts in the colonies were replicas of their English equivalents: justices of the peace in petty sessions, county courts, and superior (or supreme) courts.[14] There were, of course, many variations between colonies, reflecting different local circumstances. Procedure in these courts was vastly simplified over the English manner; divisions of function (civil-criminal; law-equity) were blurred, and rights of appeal were expanded.

In the early eighteenth century the colonial systems were brought more into line with the English than had been the case in the earliest colonial period. But there were also some disruptive tendencies: a litigation explosion (c. 1710–1730); weakening of older communal bonds in the expanding commercial society; and a surge in colonial law making all fostered increased colonial judicial autonomy.

These matters paled beside the elemental problem of keeping courts open. In Virginia the county courts had been seriously disrupted after 1750.[15] In the 1760s, the protests against the Stamp Act encouraged a wide range of extralegal and illegal acts. The self-proclaimed "regulators" in the Carolinas displaced the ordinary courts and laws. By the early 1770s the imperial government became involved in the disruption of colonial courts. The Administration of Justice Act, May 1774, allowed removal of Massachusetts trials to other colonies or to Great Britain. The Massachusetts courts ceased functioning in February 1775. After hostilities began, there were still more interruptions of legal proceedings.

There were several aspects of the outbreak of violence which had legal significance on both sides of the Atlantic. The first and foremost, from the point of view of colonists, was the formation of an armed force for their defense; for both governors and rebels, there had to be means of dealing with traitors; and special powers were needed to arrest and detain suspects. The formation of an army was a legal question in the sense that it touched upon one of the central "revolution principles"—the aversion to standing armies.[16] In its original form, the idea was to prevent the Crown from having access to a permanent armed force with which to overawe Parliament. But since 1660, the king did have an army, however small that establishment might be. The Bill of Rights in 1689 required parliamentary approval of an army in peacetime, and the instrument of control was the annual Mutiny Act, which enabled the Crown to exercise military law over the regiments. In each annual renewal, the supply for the forces would be subject to review, as would other terms of military law or operation. This complex arrangement was represented by the slogan "no standing armies," which was obviously not literally true, and, moreover, was erroneous in its implications. The Crown had, and had to have, an armed force at its command.

Treason in the colonies was based, like most legal definitions, upon English tradition—in this case, the fourteenth century Statute of Treason as later amended. On a number of occasions in the prerevolutionary period, officials had unsuccessfully attempted to convict colonial protestors on charges of treason; while not "levying war against the king," the wider net of "constructive" treasons might have caught those persons. But before 1776 [17]

> Ministerial attempts to apply the English law of treason to America failed dismally. Efforts to bring persons to trial in the colonies were frustrated by American unwillingness to participate in the proceedings. The idea of bringing Americans to England for trial aroused colonial hostility....Fear of retaliation put an emphatic period to all attempts to try individuals.

It was only when war was indeed being made against the king that the charge became usable. In the new circumstances, the Americans had to develop their own definition. Since treason had been defined as acts against the king, clearly a revision was in order. The Articles of War of the Continental Army (June 30, 1775) had provisions for mutiny, sedition, and aiding the enemy. It was also the army which forced civil society to reckon with acts which constituted treason. The Congress resolved (June 24, 1776)[18]

> That all persons, members of, or owing allegiance to any of the United Colonies...who shall levy war against any of the said colonies within the same, or be adherent to the King of Great Britain, or others the enemies of the said colonies, or any of them, within the same, giving to him or them aid and comfort, are guilty of treason against such colony.

The similarity of the wording to the English statute was unmistakable, but the alteration was equally clear.

The imperial authorities had proclaimed the colonies in a state of rebellion ("traitorously preparing, ordering and levying war against us") in August 1775. Ethan Allen was captured in Canada and sent to England for trial in December 1775. He was able to gain release on a writ of *habeas corpus* and returned to America.[19] It was not until 1777 that the British Parliament suspended *habeas corpus* in the colonies (17 George III c. 9). The full title called it

> An Act to impower his Majesty to secure and detain persons charged with, or suspected of, the crime of high treason, committed in any of his Majesty's colonies or plantations in America, or on the high seas, or the crime of piracy.

The Act was to be in effect until January 1, 1778, and it was continued four times, until 1782. It was designed to grant further authority to colonial governors and army officers to detain suspects.

The process of reforming American governments began before the shots rang out, and it continued long after. Both federal and state governments were being constructed simultaneously, and much was done while the population was engaged in rebellion and war. At this point, our concern is with the early stages: how Americans used English models, and what the early English reactions to constitution-writing were like. There could of course be no true English model since there was no written English or British constitution. However, the eighteenth century had seen many examinations of forms of government. From these and from the vast store of writing and tradition on the common law, the lawyers had enough building materials. With all of these, they were able to build systems of courts and collections of laws.

According to George Chalmers, "We shall find by no long research, that the revolted colonists have interwoven the laws of England into the very texture of their fundamental constitutions, while their animosities were the most warm and rancorous." There were apparent exceptions:[20]

> Georgia adopted into her fundamental constitution nothing more than the Habeas Corpus Act: but if we may believe the affirmation of her Chief Justice [George] Walton, 'the law of England has been studded into the Georgian system.' And thus have we found, that the often refined laws of England have been studded into all the American systems.

This view assumed a priority of English forms and ideas, but this has not been accepted by scholars. In making constitutions for the new states, Americans necessarily drew on their colonial experience.[21]

> Between 1578 and 1725 the constitutional theory evolving in British North America was a concatenation or interpenetration of charters and rules made in England, political ideas and instruments generated by the colonists themselves, English common law, and a developing theory of the colonies' place in the British political system.

Colonial constitutional writers had accumulated a great deal of experience over the period of settlement, composing various compacts, covenants, and codes. This was put to work in drafting the state constitutions which suddenly became necessary in 1776.[22]

The states wrote some seventeen constitutions before 1789. Ten of them composed such documents in 1776, with New Hampshire first (January), then South Carolina (March), and Virginia (June). From these early projects to the federal constitution efforts in the 1780s, the Americans became adept in the art of written constitutional government. They drew upon their own colonial tradition, which contained elements of English law and political ideas, plus a wealth of practical experience of government. The American constitutions were thus another paradox: a rejection of imperial power within a context of colonial experience.

The Treaty of Paris of 1783 marked the arrival of the new United States of America on the international stage, and it was primarily in international law that the treaty was significant. But the peace settlement involved other areas of law which were important. The main legal issue was the settlement of loyalist claims, which was a long and difficult legal process. Lord Shelburne negotiated an extremely generous treaty with the Americans, giving them full rights to inland territories. He hoped that there would be a parallel agreement on open trade between Britain and America, but that was not realized. Peace was declared, boundaries were stated, debts were to be honored on both sides, restitution made of confiscated property (for those not in arms against the states), and exchange of prisoners completed. There were some legal questions not resolved by the treaty. One of the more interesting was raised by Chalmers: were the Americans now aliens in English law?[23] As Chalmers correctly noted, the treaty dealt with the states, not the individual Americans; it evaded any discussion of rebels and/or loyalists (though the use of the phrase "real subjects" in article V caused some debate). Were loyalists still British subjects? Were American "aliens" still entitled to any privileges under English law, and particularly, what did the new statutes mean to merchants and others who came to England? Chalmers was hoping (as had Lord Shelburne) for a new commercial treaty and an expanding flow of trade between Britain and America. He was thus concerned to remove whatever limitations and hindrances might arise out of these unattended legal technicalities.

There were other serious legal issues involving the property of loyalists. Those who resisted the revolution and continued to support the British government had been harrassed and in many cases driven out of their homes with the loss of their property. Chalmers was one of them; a Scot and a lawyer, he was engaged in business in Maryland and he returned to England in late 1775.[24] He was one of the more fortunate, for he found employment as chief clerk for the Board of Trade. Chalmers was active in his own and others' behalf pursuing just settlements for loyalists who, like himself, had lost property in America. Several committees, and ultimately, a Commission of Inquiry looked into loyalist claims. Compensation was granted by Parliament in 1785 and 1788, an estimated £3.3 million was paid out, but of course there was no way in which the total losses could ever be met, if only because of the many cases of contested titles and lost documents.[25]

The process of inquiry was also used in other cases of unsettled legal claims. Again, the basis of inquiry was the contention that rights of property were infringed during a state of war, and outside the realm. Thus the proper court was Parliament (the "grand inquest") and not admiralty, chancery, or common law courts. As we shall see in the next chapter, this expanding concept of parliamentary inquiry would be very important in the political and legal future. As a consequence of rebellion, the only solution for some of the disputes would have to be found in statute.

In the wake of the revolution and the peace treaty, the new American States had to deal with the rupture and to arrange for new legal conditions. Continuity and simplicity argued for use of the old laws with minor alterations. "Between 1776 and 1784, eleven out of the thirteen original states made, either directly or indirectly, some provision for the use of the common law and British statutes."[26] Whether a collection of statutes and law reports would be readily available, and how far these were applicable to the American setting, were serious questions. Some colonies had earlier made selections of pertinent acts (South Carolina in 1712, Rhode Island, and North Carolina in 1746, and New York in 1767—the last two disallowed by the Privy Council), and in the generation after 1783, a number of states adopted this practice. Another approach, used by New York (1788), Virginia (1792), Vermont (1797), and New Jersey (1799) was to revise colonial laws (including those English laws found desirable) and repeal all other English statutes.

The matter of review and revision was a subject which had already risen in England. There was a long history of concern and anxiety about the way that Parliament added, willy nilly, to the statute book. The resulting jumble of laws seemed to require a filtering and consolidating process: Daines Barrington, *Observations on the More Ancient Statutes* (1766) had a reform proposal.[27] Richard Burn's *History of the Poor Law* (1764) and Francis Hargrave's 1787 publication of Matthew Hale, *Considerations Touching the Amendment or Alteration of Laws*, also gave their support to the idea of statute consolidation.

As noted earlier, the volume of English statute law had increased during the early eighteenth century, and growth accelerated in the 1770s and 1780s. The increase came from many sources, mainly economic: roads, canals, and trade, plus the expanded activity in connection with control of the East India Company. It was in this context of growing legislative action (whatever its debt to the revolution) that the next point was important.

There were many areas where the fallout from the American rebellion was visible. Trade regulation, particularly by the navigation acts of the seventeenth century, was challenged on the policy level. Adam Smith's famous book, *The Wealth of Nations*, was in the forefront; the war in America was a brutal endorsement of his arguments.[28] The postwar period saw many more commercial and legal developments. America had been the debarkation point for transported convicts since the seventeenth century. That traffic was halted abruptly by the war and the American victory. The Australian route was opened up by 1788.[29] Another form of human commerce, the slave trade, lost critical support with the independence of the southern colonies. Already being challenged in the North, the voice of the Evangelicals was soon to be heard through the Abolition Society formed in 1787.[30] Thus there were numerous avenues of impact which were affected by the revolution and its legal consequences.

In summary, the revolt in America was a profound shock to the Anglo-American legal community: the nicely balanced law of Blackstone was roughly handled (if partially retained) by the rude Americans; their independence sent a disturbing signal around the empire. In an odd twist, the Americans' most valuable ally in Europe would feel the most powerful reaction. France experienced a major financial crisis after the war, one which precipitated the greatest revolution Europe had ever seen. That revolution inspired British subjects to further challenge their king and Parliament, and one of the legal consequences was a remarkable episode of interaction.

Sedition in Scotland

The French Revolution precipitated an unprecedented political crisis for the British government. A quarter of a century of war and upheaval wrought a great many changes in society and politics, most of them thoroughly chronicled. The legal impact was readily visible in the rash of sedition and treason trials in the 1790s, but those have usually been treated as political subjects. Our concern is with the trials as a chapter in legal interaction between England and Scotland.[31]

The overthrow of the French monarchy was a source of inspiration to British radicals, and a source of horror to the establishment. In May of

1792, endorsement of French radical views was proscribed by royal proclamation.[32] The offending "seditious writings" were chiefly the work of Tom Paine, whose *Rights of Man* appeared in two parts, in 1791 and 1792. Paine's work was written to rebut the *Reflections on the Revolution in France* by Edmund Burke. Paine denied the common boasts of "revolution principles"—the validity of William's title, the power of the houses of Parliament, and the prescriptive authority of the hereditary aristocracy.

Riots and reform societies at home and military and revolutionary events abroad in 1791 and 1792 caused alarm in government ranks. In the autumn of 1792 it was decided to prosecute Paine for seditious libel. His trial in absentia in December was an easy victory for the government. The jury asked to conclude without the government's summation and quickly brought a guilty verdict, a blow to Paine's counsel, Thomas Erskine.[33]

It was clear to government that Paine, the radical London Corresponding Society, and the sprouting supporters in all dominions were a source of danger. Seen against the background of a French republic, and the execution of Louis XVI in January 1793, there was reason for concern. When that republic declared war on England in February, there was even more reason for insecurity. Ironically, the danger probably seemed greater because there was a broad spectrum of support for the establishment. Recent works show us that the Crown, Parliament, and other institutions were secure in the support of the people.[34] When Frenchmen attacked their government, their acts soon went beyond the limits accepted by Englishmen. Thus the purveyors of the sedition of the 1790s may be heroes in modern histories, but they had a much smaller following in their own time.

When the crisis of the 1790s began, English and Scottish law had the same definition for treason, thanks to the Act of 1709. For sedition, there was no such statutory rule in England, and there was no statute or common law definition in Scotland. In the famous English Act of 1351, the outline of treason was laid down in detail. To "compass or imagine" the death of the king, to have intercourse with the queen, to "levy war" against the king, or to "adhere to the king's enemies" each constituted the crime of treason. There was no similar definition in Scotland at that time, and without definition the number of eligible acts was able to grow. In the seventeenth century, Lord Stair's definition included raising a fray, impugning the dignity of Parliament, and procuring innovation or diminution of their power.[35] At least in this sense the 1709 Act brought narrower limits to Scots law.

The definition of sedition was more difficult. In Scotland, there were evidently no sedition trials *per se* before 1793. First it was relatively easy to use the charge of treason before 1709. Second, it was possible to charge the old Scottish offense of "leasing-making,"—that is, a slander upon the person of the sovereign. With this perspective, we understand why Henry Cockburn said (in 1853), "Trials for sedition are the remedies of a somewhat orderly age [where]...political intemperance may be a mere excess in the exercise of constitutional liberty."[36] For England, sedition was not a crime in and of itself. It was a characteristic of another offense: seditious publication, seditious meeting, or seditious conspiracy all had the nature of "tending to bring into hatred or contempt" the king, the government, or the laws and institutions duly established.

In addition to their varied definitions, the English and Scottish systems had a mixed relationship in criminal law. The Treason Act established the option of an English treason trial in Scotland, an option which was used in 1715 and 1746 and again in 1794. On the other hand, ordinary crime in Scotland had been under the ultimate authority of the Scottish courts.[37] That relation was challenged in the 1780s and again in the course of the 1790s. In short, there was separation and some amount of tension between the two, even before the stress of the revolutionary era arrived.

The earliest sedition trials were held in Scotland, where severe penalties were levied in 1793. Then after revelations in a secret parliamentary committee in 1794, a treason trial was conducted in English style in Edinburgh, with the conviction and execution of Robert Watt. Two months later, the London trials of Thomas Hardy and others resulted in acquittals. A year later, when the king's coach was stoned in London in October 1795, the legal definitions of treason and sedition were speedily amended and extended by Parliament. These new prescriptions reflected the recent interaction and the continuing anxiety.

The series of prosecutions for sedition in Scotland began in early 1793. Several journeyman printers were convicted in January for making a toast in the presence of soldiers in Edinburgh Castle ("George the Third and last, and damnation to all crowned heads"). These "seditious speeches" presumably tended to "seduce" the soldiers from their duty, and the sentence was nine months imprisonment. Soon after, Walter Berry and James Robertson were arrested for "wickedly and feloniously printing and publishing" a pamphlet called "The Political Progress of Britain." The two were found guilty, though the jury only decided the fact of printing and publication, not the character of the writing. As Henry Cockburn pointed out, the Scottish jury should have decided both, as Scotland's law had not been like the English law of libel, itself just reformed by Fox's Libel Act of 1792.[38]

There were several English trials in June and July for seditious libel. Daniel Eaton was Paine's publisher. On trial for publishing *The Rights of Man*, the jury at the Old Bailey found him guilty of publishing only, "not with criminal intention." The case went to the twelve judges "but the result was that they gave no decision, and that no sentence ever followed." Eaton was arrested and tried weeks later on the charge of printing a letter from Paine, but the result was the same. There were several other trials in July for seditious libel or seditious words.[39]

Thomas Muir, a young advocate, had been a leader of the convention of Friends of the People in 1792 and read a declaration of the United Irish which caused a stir in the meeting and was eventually rejected by it. Muir had failed to appear for trial in March 1793, and he was removed from the roll of advocates. Muir travelled to Ireland and France before his trial, conduct which suggested a man whose opposition was dangerous. But the evidence against him was not especially powerful. The trial was notable for the arbitrary behavior of the lord justice-clerk, Robert MacQueen, Lord Braxfield. His blunt and hostile language and obvious bias were far below modern standards, if not those of the late eighteenth century. They were also used to stigmatize the Scottish bench when, indeed, the English could boast judges of equally fierce temper. The guilty verdict on Muir was no surprise, but his sentence of fourteen years' transportation was excessive. First, the crime of sedition was not capital; second, the analogous Scottish sentence of banishment (for "leasing-making") was not the same as transportation; nor could it be excused by the introduction of English treason in 1709, which Hume said "abolishes the peculiar treasons of the law of Scotland" though they remain "acts of sedition at common law." [40]

Some sense of English opinion at the time, granted of a radical view, was given in a letter from Samuel Romilly to Jeremy Bentham. Romilly was in Edinburgh, and he wrote:[41]

> I doubt whether this would be a very safe country, just at this moment, for you to be found in; for I heard the judges of the Justiciary Court, the other day, declare, with very great solemnity, upon the trial of Mr. Muir, that to say the courts of justice needed reform was seditious, highly criminal and betrayed a most hostile disposition towards the Constitution.

After Muir's trial, an English clergyman, Thomas Fyshe Palmer, was tried for seditious practices. He had resigned a fellowship at Queen's College, Cambridge, became a Unitarian, and had settled, and preached, in Dundee. His trial in September 1793 also ended in a sentence of transportation.[42]

Plans were underway for another Scottish convention in 1793, and a meeting in London to elect delegates led to more trials. There were still more charges and trials after the convention met. A Scotsman, William Skirving, was sentenced to fourteen years transportation; two English delegates, Maurice Margarot and Joseph Gerrald, were also transported. Their crime was participating in an organized discussion of political reform, chiefly annual Parliaments and universal suffrage. If indeed the convention was the threat that the authorities claimed, the charges should have been treason and not sedition, but the lesser charge was easier to prove, at least in Scotland.

This series of trials raised many comparative questions at the time and later. During February and March 1794, an interesting exchange occurred in the House of Commons. William Adam, a Scottish MP and one of the remaining Whigs, moved to amend Scottish criminal law; he was asking for intervention in the cases of Berry and Robertson, basically suggesting that appeals be allowed from the High Court of Justiciary to the House of Lords.[43] Both the specific and general requests were denied. On March 10, Adam raised questions on the cases of Muir and Palmer. He made the argument that Scottish sedition was equivalent to leasing-making and so ineligible for a sentence of transportation. He also moved to bring up the records of Muir's trail. These attempts to involve the legislature in defining the crime were successfully resisted. The Lord Advocate defended the use of transportation as banishment, though there seemed to be no support for the interpretation in the acts applied to Scottish transportation. The debate also gave Charles Fox a chance to make one of his characteristic remarks: the Scots wanted to impose "the tyrannical laws of Scotland" on the English, but his vigilance was going to protect against such an assault.

That sort of English thinking lay behind the next development. In May the House of Commons formed a Committee of Secrecy to investigate the recent events and to examine documents procured by the government. One of its purposes was to lend credence to the planned suspension of *habeas corpus*. This Committee met in May and June and its reports provide some useful information. While it was beginning its work, news reached the committee from Edinburgh of a discovery of pikes and plans for a revolt.

This alarming report shifted the process onto a new heading. The presence of arms and plans proved treasonable acts. The conviction of one traitor would bring down the whole conspiracy. The key figure here was the unlikely one of the wine merchant Robert Watt. He had been a spy for the government, and his services were at the disposal of the Lord Advocate in 1792 and 1793. He evidently was attracted to the cause of the reformers, and it was only a fortuitous sheriff's search of his property for other contraband that uncovered the infamous pikeheads and plans.

What is of most interest to us is that Watt's trial for treason in Edinburgh in August 1794 was held in the manner of an English treason trial. Due to the provisions of the Act of 1709, it was possible to send a commission to the Scottish authorities, directing them to summon a grand jury and to hear charges of treason under English rules. The court could include Scottish judges, it might be addressed by Scottish and/or English counsel, but it would proceed in the same manner as a trial in England, with the same fearful results. Watt was found guilty and was executed.[44] On September 5 his alleged partner David Downie was put on trial in the same manner. But after conviction Downie was granted a pardon. The interactive significance of the Watt and Downie trials was in the escalation from sedition to treason and the success of the 1709 procedure. The traitors could have been tried in the High Court of Justiciary, whence there would have been no appeal, no involvement of English lawyers, and the risk of another trial by Braxfield. The last may have been the chief motive for using the English procedure. In any case, the focus of events was already shifting to London.

The main event, from the English viewpoint, was the opening of Thomas Hardy's treason trial in October 1794. As secretary of the London Corresponding Society, Hardy was involved with most of the

English and Scottish prisoners tried so far. The records of the society and of their associated groups had been displayed for the Secret Committee, and there was a certain confidence in bringing the highest criminal charges.

Attorney General John Scott opened the main part of the trial with a nine-hour speech. This was a portent, for the trial went on at great length, the evidence presented on both sides being of the greatest extent, and the judge's summation taking almost two whole days. On November 5 Hardy was acquitted by the jury. Next, John Horne Tooke was tried and acquitted. Two weeks later proceedings were dropped against four other defendants. After John Thelwall's trial also led to acquittal, process was halted against the last two prisoners on December 15.[45]

In these trials much credit was given to Erskine's defense and discredit to Scott's prosecution. In fact, the charge of treason was a mistake; convictions on seditious conspiracy would have been readily obtained, and only the sentences would have been in doubt. The attorney general was perhaps encouraged by the results of the Scottish trials, but he later claimed that the evidence required a charge of high treason. Whatever the reason, Hardy and his companions and their counsel were far more formidable than Robert Watt and David Downie. Thus the law of sedition was eschewed when it might have rendered service.

The next year saw another effort to redefine the law of sedition and treason. After an assault on the royal coach, and no doubt mindful of much more serious attacks in recent years in Paris, the legislators quickly passed new laws with a much wider definition of treason and seditious meetings. The Treasonable and Seditious Practices Act incorporated the 1351 Act, but also made it treason to[46]

> compass, imagine, invent, devise, or intend death or destruction...or to levy war against his Majesty...in order, by force or constraint, to compel him or them to change his or their measures or counsels

and if anyone

> by writing, printing, preaching, or other speaking, express, publish, utter or declare any words or sentences to excite or stir up the people to hatred or contempt of the person of his Majesty...[or] of the government and constitution of this realm...[they] shall be liable to such punishment as may by law be inflicted in cases of high misdemeanours

and on a second offense may be punished as for high misdemeanor, or banished, or transported for up to seven years. The Seditious Meetings Act passed later in the same session. In the debate on this law, Fox made a familiar complaint that "the pretended law of Scotland regarding sedition" was being introduced into England. The Act required prior approval for political meetings and gave justices of the peace authority to disperse them and stipulated the powers and measures to be had and used. The seditious meeting was defined as one[47]

> for the purpose or on the pretext of considering of or preparing any petition, complaint, remonstrance, or declaration, or other address to the king, or to both houses, or either house of Parliament, for alteration of matters established in church or state, or for the purpose or on the pretext of deliberating upon any grievance in church or state.

And that in case such meeting "incite or stir up the people" (s. 6) it could be dispersed, and if twelve or more present continued "for an hour thereafter, they shall suffer death as felons."

Soon after the new acts, David Hume published his *Commentaries on the Law of Scotland respecting the description and punishment of crimes*, which became the major institutional work for Scottish criminal law. Hume's comment on the treason and sedition acts was that [48]

> in the end, on the increase of this alarming evil [sedition], to which the powers of the common law of England were found unequal, recourse was had to the legislature; who by statute 36 Geo. III, c. 7 authorised the inflicting of the same punishments, that are competent in Scotland according to the common law; and by means of which, duly and steadily applied, the judges in Scotland had in great measure repressed the growing audacity of the licentious in this quarter of the kingdom.

Hume was enjoying this twist on the usual criticism of Scottish severity; it was, of course, correct to say that the "English common law" in the matter of the late trials, had not been able to dampen the zeal of radicals; whether the 1795 acts were Scottish imports was another matter, but the use of the punishment of transportation was indeed legitimized.[49] The year 1797 actually saw the most threatening actions on the domestic front: militia riots and naval mutinies were far more serious than any of the plans or acts of the people tried for sedition. These events drew even stronger legislative action.[50]

The trials of 1790s began to import the English common law definition of sedition into Scotland; but the experience of 1793 and 1794 in Scotland and England pushed the statutes of 1795 into a new formula. The crime of sedition was to be further refined in the first half of the nineteenth century. The authorities learned from the experience of the 1790s that other tools were needed to control public hostility to the government. In English law, sedition had been confounded with treason in early times. At the beginning of the nineteenth century, Sir Edward East said it was marked off from treason. According to East, sedition[51]

> is now understood in a more general sense, and extends to other offences, not capital, of like tendency, but without any actual design against the king in contemplation.

The clarification was in part a product of the interaction of the 1790s. In that period, enforcement was capricious, not only because of inherent difficulty of definition, but because of the climate of domestic turmoil and foreign war. Another period of similar character came on at the end of the French wars. The "Peterloo" era (1819–20) was notorious for the "Six Acts" regulating meetings and public protest. Later acts amended "leasing-making" in 1826 and invented "treason felony" in 1848, providing a considerably broader definition of treason which enabled felony conviction and life imprisonment—that is, more flexible sentencing than the old treason law.

After the trials of the 1790s, statute became the primary means of definition. There were fewer sedition cases and a proliferation of acts banning conventions, oaths, and societies, plus special acts for insurrection, mutiny, and other public order offenses.[52] At the end of the eighteenth century one other very powerful force pushed in this direction: Irish rebellion in 1798. But in order to understand the place of that event in lawmaking and law enforcement, we must review the special circumstances of Ireland beginning with the period of the American revolt.

Assimilation in Ireland

It would be fair to say that the Irish legal system achieved *de facto* independence by 1780. As Robert McDowell observes, the period

1760–1800 saw thirty-six judicial appointments: one lord chancellor and two chief justices were English, and they were appointed between 1761 and 1767. The other thirty-three were Irishmen, all Protestant, and most from wealthy families.[53] But appointments only told part of the story. On the major issues of penal laws, trade regulation, and political organization, it was clear that a new era had dawned in Ireland before the last shots were fired in North America. These important shifts were clear signs that legal direction was not a mere reflection of decision-making in London. At the same time, these were but temporary alterations: to be affirmed in the "constitution" of 1782, and then to be imperilled by radicalism and reversed by the reaction to rebellion in 1798.

The independent direction originated in the appearance of volunteers in the 1770s. Traces of such local initiative were found earlier, but it was the crisis of 1777–78 which produced a dramatic new development. The government had withdrawn military forces because of the events in America; a militia bill was passed but could not be funded; local groups formed corps of volunteers, particularly in Ulster. Even a Lawyers' Corps was formed in Dublin; local and occupational groups were common; the members supplied uniforms, elected officers, and performed elementary drills. This paramilitary action was tolerated by the authorities, probably because it was dominated by the higher orders, those who owned property and would otherwise pay taxes for soldiers; but when these units began to engage in politics, it was fair for Dr. Johnson to call it rebellion, even though the British authorities made no effort to suppress the movement, as they would do in different circumstances in 1792.[54] Another turn in the late 1770s had been the repeal of penal laws against Roman Catholics. The land law restrictions were annulled in 1778, and a Roman Catholic relief measure was passed in 1780. In Ireland at the time, the leaders of the Protestant Ascendancy, seeing themselves as Irish patriots and seeing English intervention and control as the chief evil, were more inclined to end the disabilities of their Catholic neighbors.

Finally, another link in English control had been the subjection of Ireland to English trade regulation. This had been at the root of the turmoil at the beginning of the century, around the Wool Act of 1699 and the contemporary publication of Molyneux's *Case of Ireland*. The English Parliament had been induced to open the question of Irish trade in 1778. At first the debates there ran against Irish interests, and inflamed opinion in Ireland, stirring plans of nonimportation. At the end of 1779, Lord North announced a plan for reducing most of the restrictions on Irish trade. It is likely that he was moved to do this to avert further discussion of constitutional questions, which discussion nevertheless occurred. This early independence was a tender plant, particularly in its legal branches. Irish law was nominally the same as English, and all outward signs seemed to confirm that. But a closer look showed some important differences.

First, the laws on the statute books were similar but separate; English authority controlled the Irish, but different features persisted. Common law in Ireland followed English, especially since printed Irish reports were rare before this period. But distinctive Irish precedents were abundant, for example, in special fields like penal legislation, or in land law or other ancient areas in which Irish tradition had developed.[55]

Second, procedure was often borrowed from English courts, but seldom without modification. If the outline of the courts appeared identical, that appearance masked differences, sometimes large ones. In civil cases there were many distinctive Irish features such as the civil bill procedure[56] and the perpetual lease. In Irish criminal law, there were provisions for public prosecutors,[57] different rules for jury challenge, and some differences in the law of evidence. There was a writ but no act for *habeas corpus* until 1782.

Finally, in the area of personnel, the requirement that barristers spend a number of terms in an English Inn may have created a legal community for some, but certainly not for all Irishmen.[58] For one thing, an Irish attorney had no such conditioning; for another, one's career was also shaped by a lawyer's Irish experience, including the King's Inns, Irish education, and working in the special conditions of Irish society. In short, there were many grounds of difference, some of which were becoming more pronounced in this period. There was always enough variation, assuming one was not devoted to English superiority, to sustain an independent-minded Irish legal practitioner.

The atmosphere around the volunteers had created a new political climate in Ireland. All eyes were on Henry Grattan's motion that "the kingdom of Ireland is a distinct kingdom with a Parliament of her own, the sole legislature thereof." This motion was defeated, but it was apparent that legislative independence was only a matter of time. Poynings' Law was repealed, the main arguments being over new procedures for sending measures for royal assent. The Declaratory Act of 1720 was also repealed, accompanied by a debate over whether the British government should more formally renounce its power.

In fact, British power remained quite strong: the executive was not altered, nor was the judiciary, and both were subject to London's oversight. Appointments were made under the British Great Seal, as was the assent to legislative acts. A new Catholic Relief bill was introduced in 1782 which signalled a reformist mood consistent with the new constitution, and it was a harbinger of a number of legal reforms. An Irish *habeas corpus* bill had been proposed in 1765, and one finally succeeded in 1782. It was quite different from its English ancestor, and an analysis of these differences highlights the changes over the previous century, as well as the differences on either side of St George's Channel.[59] The main point for us is that this was not an assimilating measure.

The Irish courts were reformed in the 1780s. In 1783 a fourth judge was added to each of the common law courts, thus alleviating the shortage created when the nine judges had had to conduct five circuits twice a year. Between 1784 and 1786, there were grand jury reforms related to the provision of local constables; these may have been inspired by the more ambitious Dublin reform of the magistracy which began in 1778, and which saw a major step taken in 1786 (after English defeat of a similar measure for London in 1785). A paid and professional magistracy was slowly being created.[60] In tandem with this, the office of assistant barrister was created in 1787, a novel attempt, connected with police reform, to provide trained lawyers in local court sessions. In these acts, Irish law was moving more decisively than English into modern alignments.

But some things never change. Agrarian unrest, including tithe protests, marked the 1780s as earlier decades. There were no brilliant new answers to these problems, and when those disturbances were connected to a revival of sectarian violence, they would prove to be a lethal obstacle to the promising direction of legal changes in the 80s. The United Irishmen, formed in 1791, were an extension of the volunteers, an extension of the Protestant patriots and, to some, an extension of the moves for Catholic relief. Unfortunately for all of these assumed relations, the United men were also inspired, in various ways, by the recent terrible events in France.[61] United Irish groups had a large contingent of lawyers, many of whose acts and adventures were widely publicized in their trials. These acts brought prompt intervention by the British government, and its Dublin agents, and the resulting legal clashes were part of the background to insurrection from 1796 to 1798.

McDowell counted a fair-sized contingent of attorneys and barristers in the ranks of the United Irishmen.[62] We would do well to remind ourselves that there were many more on the side of the establishment.[63] Nevertheless, the prominent parts played by Wolfe Tone, Napper Tandy, Hamilton Rowan, and others, as well as the extensive use of the courts and their unavoidable taint of English service were important features which probably added to legal separatism in the years before rebellion and union.

There were many highly publicized cases involving barristers as defendants, an interesting and symbolic reversal for these officers of the court. Tandy was engaged in a series of trials in 1792 which ultimately challenged the validity of the lord lieutenant's patent, as it was issued under the Great Seal of Great Britain.[64] More serious confrontations grew out of the banning of volunteers in the same year, and the trials of Rowan and Drennan for seditious libel in connection with their actions in behalf of the United Irishmen. Rowan was tried for distributing an address from the United Irishmen to the volunteers; William Drennan was tried as the author of the address; the first was sentenced to two years in gaol, the second was acquitted.[65] These trials came after a period (1792–94) of rapid and confusing changes: there was increasing violence of sectarian character; there was a relief act which allowed Roman Catholics to vote in parliamentary elections; and there were several restrictive measures in 1793, reflecting government alarm at deteriorating public order: a militia act, with predictable riots; a gunpowder act; and a convention act limiting the right to hold meetings.

Simon Butler, chair of the Dublin Society of United Irishmen, and Oliver Bond, the secretary, were tried at the bar of the House of Lords for issuing resolutions critical of a Lords committee: they were each fined £500 and given a six-month gaol sentence. Soon after, Tandy fled into exile in America, and the next year a much more serious affair occurred when Rev. William Jackson discussed French invasion with Tone in Rowan's gaol apartment. Tone also left for America; Jackson was later tried and took poison in the dock after being convicted.

The level of tension grew and with it the serious organizing of the Orange Order and its nemesis, the Catholic Defenders. With a series of incidents in the country, the London government expanded the powers of magistrates with an indemnity act and an insurrection act: administering unlawful oaths was punishable by death; taking them punishable by transportation; justices of the peace could ask the lord lieutenant to proclaim their areas, which allowed them to search for weapons, enforce curfews, and round up disorderly persons and send them to military service. All of these provisions would have been very effective in the hands of energetic magistrates, confident of the support of their neighbors: the situation in the more restless parts of Ireland seldom met these criteria.

Many areas were proclaimed, but the enhanced powers of law enforcement were not enough to prevent insurrection. A French invasion had been narrowly averted by bad weather in 1796. By the beginning of 1798, there was an active and dangerous conspiracy afoot. Arthur O'Connor and others were apprehended at Margate in February (and tried for treason in Maidstone in May);[66] a large number of arrests were made in Dublin in March; and still the long-feared rebellion, divided and disorganized, began in the south in late May, and ended in the north in September. The authorities made full use of the legal system to punish rebels, but the picture of repression was full of complicated interactions.

Proclamations of pardon were issued in June and again in September, to encourage defections and submission; they were of variable effect in different areas; specific acts of attainder were employed and in one case a Banishment Act expelled a number of leaders who gave guilty pleas and evidence in exchange for escaping treason trials. These actions occurred beside a large number of courts-martial, convened while civilian courts were in session. The latter were never suspended for more than a matter of weeks, and then only in counties actually in revolt.

The most visible episode was the trial of Wolfe Tone. While awaiting sentence of a court-martial, Tone was granted a writ of *habeas corpus*, which his military gaolers ignored: but Tone had already attempted to cut his throat, and so his release was said to be impossible because of his condition. He died eight days later. After this event, the military seem to have chosen to use civilian courts more often. But only in the Rebellion Act of 1799 was it clearly stated that a court-martial might sit, under orders from the lord lieutenant, even though civilian courts were in session. McDowell estimated that some 1,450 rebels were convicted, which he called "measured severity."

Rebellion on such a scale, with the landing of a French force in County Mayo, was alarming enough to move Pitt to frame a plan for union. At the beginning he included a provision for emancipating Catholics and bonding a largely loyal Ireland to the king. English politics and French war combined to prevent that reasonable solution: George III genuinely believed that he would fail to do his Anglican duty with such a measure, but he might have been persuaded—had other conditions been more favorable.

The Act of Union of 1800 has been an attractive target for study. That study has been overwhelmingly political, for obvious reasons.[67] Our interest is in the act and its consequences in an Irish legal context. In December, 1798, there was a debate among members of the Irish bar on the question of union in which there was a substantial majority against the idea.[68] This set the stage for a debate in the Irish Commons in January, when a union resolution was defeated. For the remainder of that year, Pitt and his colleagues worked on a union act, while Castlereagh and others worked on buying votes for union. Resolutions in favor of union passed in March, 1800. The Irish bill was introduced in May and received the royal assent on August 1.[69] The main clause relating to the legal systems said

> That it be the eighth article of union, that all laws in force at the time of the union, and all the courts of civil and ecclesiastical jurisdiction within the respective kingdoms, shall remain as now by law established within the same, subject only to such alterations and regulations from time to time as circumstances may appear to the Parliament of the united kingdom to require, provided that all writs of error and appeals depending at the time of the union, or hereafter to be brought, and which might now be finally decided by the house of Lords of either kingdom, shall from and after the union be finally decided by the house of Lords of the united kingdom, and provided that from and after the union there shall remain in Ireland an instance court of admiralty for the determination of causes civil and maritime, and that the appeal from sentences of the said court shall be to His Majesty's delegates in his court of chancery in that part of the united kingdom called Ireland; and that all laws at present in force in either kingdom, which shall be contrary to any of the provisions which may be enacted by any act for carrying these articles into effect, be from and after the union repealed.

The first proviso said appeals and errors from Ireland would be heard in the House of Lords of the United Kingdom.[70] In fact, at the same time, the Irish Parliament was making a significant reform of the Exchequer Chamber in Ireland, providing for the domestic hearing of errors, and then further hearing by Parliament.[71] In a saving clause, the article reserved to the United Kingdom Parliament the power to alter and regulate "from time to time as circumstances" might "appear...to require."

Behind the specific provisions of the Acts of 1800 there was the larger legal question of their fundmental nature. Since it was decided not to use commissioners from England and Ireland along the lines of 1707, thus dispensing with the formality of a treaty, was this action a "fundamental" law? With regard to Anglican Church unification, and some other matters, it seems that was the intent, or at least it could be so interpreted by the Protestant Irish Ascendancy. But in law these were statutes like any others: they could be amended or repealed by a simple majority—and even one without any support from the 100-member Irish delegation.

There was some attempt in article 5 to assert more emphatically the permanent nature of the union: the "united church of England and Ireland" in all respects "shall be deemed and taken to be an essential and fundamental part of the union" and the several provisions "shall remain in full force forever." However, this language could not change the basic legal character; indeed, the disestablishment of the Irish Church in 1869 was the first breach of the union.

Existing legislation was preserved and the long-term association of the Parliaments meant that there were not many cases where major accommodation was required. What was of more consequence was the pattern of legislation under the union. Irish acts were now the business of the United Kingdom lawmakers; the Irish might be subject to general United Kingdom statutes, or to specific measures enacted for Ireland alone. But in both cases, there were five non-Irish MPs for every Irish one and an even poorer ratio in the lords.

For Irish legal questions, there were some important aspects in the new arrangement. The Irish law officers and judges would still be influential, but not in relation to the enlarged legislature. At first this effect was not obvious, and important early legislative measures affecting the Irish legal system did not always come from Parliament.

For example, a large public petition for the change of process in personal actions was published in 1801.[72] This was signed by the Irish law officers and by about 280 solicitors, attorneys, and barristers. It proposed "assimilating the mode of commencing personal actions in Ireland to the practice in England." The ideas were embodied in an act which passed in 1803. This allowed subpoena power in cases of £10 or more. "Special bail" for cases of small value was denied, plus other rule changes.[73]

Most Irish judges were unperturbed by the union, excepting those who sat in the House of Lords; but the Irish peers' attention was absorbed with the elaborate provisions made to provide their elected representation in Westminster, and the careful steps taken to regulate and reduce their number. The sitting judges were not a target, though a few new judges were allegedly promoted as reward for supporting the government in the course of approving the union. Robert Johnson was one of these, and he became a judge in Common Pleas. But Johnson's experience showed how much friction was still present. He wrote scathing attacks on the government in the wake of Emmet's Rebellion (1803) for which he was hauled to London for trial, a move made possible by a radical suspension of *habeas corpus*, though this was only a simple libel case. Johnson was convicted and allowed to resign and retain a reduced pension.[74]

It was noted above that the Irish bench was becoming a predominantly native group, and the union did not reverse that trend. The requirements for barristers' education continued to include time at the English Inns,[75] but the force behind the 1782 act was evidently a rule made by the benchers of King's Inns in Dublin. That body did not provide formal legal education, and a proposal to give the King's Inns a major educational role was beaten back by the Irish bar in 1792–93. But the benchers did adopt a new set of rules in 1793, the import of which has been debated.[76] The Inns were finding new quarters (as the old precincts were the site of the Four Courts buildings under construction, 1786–96). They became a copyright library, acquired a new historian,[77] and enjoyed a revival of sorts in the profession. The foundation stone for the new building was laid on August 1, 1800—the day the union act was passed. Although the King's Inns would never be, or perhaps aspire to be, the same as an English Inn, it had an important role as the central professional body for the Irish bar.

There was indeed a great deal of talk of "assimilation" in legal Ireland around the time of the union; that was predictable. But what stands out more clearly is the continuing independence of the Irish system. Against the apparent merging influence of the Act of Union, there were many other stronger signs of separatism: the growth of Irish Law Reports; the increasing number of treatises on Irish legal topics (leases for lives, custodiams, civil bills), and the appearance of digests of Irish case law.

At the end of the eighteenth century, "revolution" was a decidedly more menacing word in the contemporary vocabulary than a century earlier. It was a term which now evoked change rather than preservation; uprooting of institutions rather than stability. The defense against revolution might be outright resistance, but it was seen by growing numbers that the best defense might be reform. The Commons' Committee on Finance in its 27th Report (13 June 1799) on the Courts of Justice, asked the house for an address to the king requesting a commission "for examining the duties salaries and emoluments of the several officers, clerks and ministers of the courts of justice of this kingdom...reporting what regulations may be fit to be established."[78]

A month later, the reply came that the king "will give directions accordingly." There is no trace in the records of the house that this commission was in fact created or that anyone performed these duties. But the action would be recalled later, when in the next decade such an effort did take shape. What was launched then was a slow and uncertain process of inquiry and reform, one which was a product of, and a blueprint for legal interaction.

Chapter 4

Inquiry and Legal Reform 1799–1850

The first half of the nineteenth century witnessed a dramatic transformation of the United Kingdom. The power which had coordinated the defeat of the Napoleonic Empire by 1815 went on to dominate the world economy by 1850. In the same period, reform of political institutions brought more of the population into political activity, economic relations were forever altered by emerging industry, and these alterations combined to create new visions of social class and social welfare.

All of these changes had vital connections in law and legal interaction. The "true-born Englishman" had a basic sense of the law's protection, despite manifest inequalities, and this shared cultural perspective was a durable foundation for reform. At the same time, the union and "assimilation" with Ireland plus the continuing legal tension with Scotland were naturally linked to changes in law and legal interaction. At its most elementary level, every reform sought some relief or reward in the form of legislation.

For legal thinkers, the new world inspired new formulations. In Scottish law, there were *Commentaries* by David Hume (crime) and George Bell (mercantile law). But there would be no nineteenth-century Blackstone in England, first because tradition was strong enough to sustain the original; but second, because the tide of change was so great that a general project like Blackstone's *Commentaries* was becoming inconceivable. Students and practitioners were engaged in a full-time effort to accommodate the legal inheritance to the currents of innovation, and they found useful instruments for legal reform in the machinery of English politics.

The victory over Napoleon was the product of English ships and money and European troops. The threat of Jacobin subversion was, for practical purposes, dead by 1797. Ironically, radical action was undertaken on behalf of the state. The possibility of a French invasion was a serious threat from about 1796 to 1805. The Ordnance Survey had started mapping the British Isles for defensive purposes; the Defence of the Realm Act of 1798 surveyed the manpower resources of every county and in 1801 Parliament ordered the first census of population. By eighteenth century standards, these were highly irregular government acts. Each was endorsed by Parliament on the ground of national emergency, but each also contributed to an expanding model of state power and authority. None of them, as it turned out, had much to do with victory over Napoleon.

The military success came from fulfillment of the three components of allied strategy. The first was British control of the seas, achieved by Admiral Nelson's famous victory at Trafalgar in 1805. This victory not only ended the threat of French invasion, it established the dominance of the British fleet and enabled a blockade of continental ports. To this, Napoleon's answer was his famous "Continental System," designed to close all European ports to British trade and so to cripple her commercial strength. The embargo did cause serious economic hardship in Britain and elsewhere, but it was no match for the maritime power of the widening imperial enterprise.

The second element of allied strategy was the massing of powerful armies against the Empire. Napoleon was able to subdue Prussia and Austria, but on two fronts he met effective resistance. British forces landed in Portugal and eventually were able to drive the French from Spain (1809–1813). The last stages of this operation were made easier by the massive failure of Napoleon's invasion of Russia. His defeat there was the main turning point of the land campaigns. Retreat and surrender in 1814 were followed by the "Hundred Days" when he returned to power in 1815, only to be beaten by a combined force at Waterloo.

The third reason for the victory was the financial strength of Britain. Unprecedented British economic power had developed during the eighteenth century, but no one knew in 1793 just how resilient and productive it might be. By becoming the most heavily taxed state in Europe, and by assuming a massive burden of debt, Britain was able to raise and equip her own forces while providing generous subsidies for her continental allies. These measures brought military victory, and they also produced domestic turmoil. In a broad view, the massive debt, the income tax, the high rates of customs and excise, and the general acceptance of intensive economic regulation were all significant, though nominally temporary, inconveniences. From another angle, the cost of war meant a multitude of social and economic stresses for large numbers of people, and a significant increase in legal interference in daily life.

Peace brought home soldiers and sailors to a scene of economic distress which lasted for several years. But peace also removed the straitjacket of wartime conformity. Aggravation and agitation led to mass meetings and protests. Those events led to repressive acts, but none had the effects of wartime measures. The postwar crisis was brief, and the 1820s saw the return of economic vitality. The revival, however, did not mean the decline of reform energy. In fact it was the prelude to a period of stunning reform from 1830 onward.

In the first years after Waterloo, there were public meetings and demonstrations many times larger than any in the eighteenth century. While these were disturbing to the magistrates, few of them had serious revolutionary potential. They nevertheless provoked repressive responses, but those, too, were less dangerous than they appeared. It seemed like an echo of the terrible 1790s, but the new context had much less frightening results. At a large meeting at Spa Fields in London in 1816 rioting broke out, leading to the suspension of *habeas corpus* and an act limiting public meetings. An abortive rising of a small group of laborers in Derbyshire in 1817, fomented by a government spy, resulted in the execution of the leader of the rebels.

The most serious of these events was a mass meeting outside Manchester in 1819 at St. Peter's Fields. Tens of thousands of workers, wives and children, marched peaceably to the meeting, in order to hear the address of one of their radical heroes, Henry Hunt. When Hunt tried to mount the platform, local authorities ordered the yeomanry to seize him and disperse the crowd. In the ensuing melee, eleven were killed and hundreds were injured. The event was soon dubbed the massacre of "Peterloo," with mocking and sarcastic reference to the great military event just passed. Peterloo was followed by the notorious "Six Acts," a set of measures to clamp down on meetings and other reform activity, which measures were temporary and not vigorously enforced.

What might have been the most serious threat of all was the Cato Street Conspiracy of 1820, a plan to blow up the Cabinet while the ministers were having dinner. But informers had exposed the plot, and the leaders of this pathetic band were executed. There was no public outcry on their behalf, for the conspirators represented no significant political group or cause, and their revolutionary style was completely out of step with political opinion. After 1821 an improving economy helped to moderate political protests. Of much greater importance in the postwar years, there was a rapid increase in public advocacy of reforms: Jeremy Bentham and his disciples, dubbed the Utilitarians, students of the new science of political economy, and social and political critics of many types filled the pages of newspapers and reviews.

In 1820, when George III died, his errant son and regent George IV assumed the throne. His estranged wife Caroline, who had been living in exile on the continent, tried to reclaim her title as queen. The ensuing legal process, in which she was tried for adultery, was much more distracting and absorbing to London crowds than any political question. The significance of the affair, in which Caroline was found guilty and deprived of her royal title and privileges, was that there was yet another blow to the prestige of the Crown. It is not likely that this meant reform was easier, for the ranks of the establishment were still rigid in resistance. But surely a great amount of potential moral authority was lost, and just as surely the more radical reformers were comforted by the embarrassment of the Crown.

In the 1820s there were numerous reforms which historians labelled as "Liberal Toryism," because Tories continued to control government until the end of the decade. Measures of reform were introduced during the period which were departures from the repressive acts of earlier years. In fact, most of these measures were efforts to reform the operation of government so as to make it more efficient and effective—in other words, measures which were not liberal but were in fact conservative. Nevertheless, reform could come in any garb and still be reform. In 1822, though a Select Committee failed to endorse Robert Peel's ideas for London police, that year saw the formalizing of the Royal Irish Constabulary, the first major paid professional force in the United Kingdom (the "peelers" to Irishmen; just as the London police of 1829 would be called the "bobbies"). The next year Peel steered through a Gaols Act which set out national standards and had provisions for inspection. Also in 1823, the long process of consolidating criminal statutes got underway. A number of statutes requiring the death penalty were repealed; in 1825 some eighty-five old acts relating to juries were removed and replaced by a consolidated act. Similar statutes were enacted for several types of crime between 1826 and 1828. The general purpose was to rid the statute book of obsolete measures and provide new and clearer rules, so as to obtain more effective law enforcement.

A somewhat similar motive might be seen in the repeal of the Test and Corporation Acts in 1828, but the matter was more complicated here. For many years Dissenters had been enabled to avoid penalties thanks to annual indemnity acts. Those acts, however, maintained the principle of religious discrimination while eschewing the penalties. Thus the core grievance remained. The repeal was the beginning of wider official toleration, bitterly opposed by high Tories. The next year saw Catholic emancipation—that is, allowing Catholics to hold public office, including seats in Parliament. This question had been on the reform agenda for a generation. Denied at the time of the union, it was a constant point of dispute, though not one of a party nature. When Daniel O'Connell, the Irish barrister and leader of the Catholic Association, was elected to Parliament in 1828, he could not take his seat in the House of Commons. The leaders of the government (the Duke of Wellington and Robert Peel) chose to defuse the situation. They opted for reform and accepted a restricted measure of Catholic emancipation. That of course led to intra party recrimination which enabled the Whigs to take office.

The new government was committed to some kind of parliamentary reform. The election of members was on an old and arbitrary set of franchise requirements. In 1830 the new government proposed to reform the franchise, to purge some of the more "rotten" boroughs and to reallocate those seats to some of the large, new unrepresented towns. When the House of Lords rejected reform in 1831, an election was called on this issue, the first issue-oriented election in British history. The Whigs won a majority for reform, but still they needed the king's statement that he would create new peers if they were needed to pass the bill, so as to force the Lords to accept the measure. In June of 1832, the reform act, with its companion measures for Scotland and Ireland, became law. Actually the Scottish act created the largest increase in voters, the Irish the smallest. But now there was a more rational system, and, just as important, a major peaceful reformation of one of the most important institutions in the country.[1]

With this barrier cleared, it was easier to tackle further tasks of reform. In the 1830s there were many unconnected areas in which the momentum of reform gained force. In 1833 there was an important factory act, setting standards for construction, safety, and education, all of which were to be monitored and enforced by government inspectors. In 1834 the old Elizabethan Poor Law was reformed. Here the issues were complex, and the tendency of reform was toward efficiency rather than generous welfare. Again there was a central governing agency and rules for the provision of poor relief set down by statute. In 1835 a reform of the old corporate governments of boroughs was enacted, enabling the ratepayers to vote for their governors. In most of these acts, which applied to England and Wales, there were, at some later date, companion or collateral measures for Scotland and Ireland, though they often had different features. In none of these cases were there truly centralized acts which welded all the archipelago into a single structure.

After the work of the 1830s, reformers did not rest. Indeed, some of the most powerful agitations arose in the later 1830s and 1840s. In 1833 the evangelicals and other foes of slavery succeeded in passing a measure to abolish slavery in the British Empire. In 1837 the London Workingmen's Association was formed to pursue wider voting rights for workers. The main instrument of this group was "The People's Charter," a list of democratic reform ideas: universal male suffrage, no property qualification for MPs, pay for members, secret ballot, equal electoral districts, and annual elections. The "Chartists" led numerous protests and petitioned Parliament without success. They were organized in all parts of the United Kingdom, and while the movement did not achieve its goals in its own lifetime, all but the last item eventually became law.

On the other hand, a good many less ambitious reform efforts were successful. Legislation created a variety of public health regulations; the established church was assessed and regulated by government commission; the landed classes saw their protective tariffs ("corn laws") reduced and eliminated by the end of the 1840s. By the middle of the century, then, there had been very substantial reform activity and a respectable amount of accomplishment. When we look more closely at the methods used in these reforms, we will gain a better idea of the role of law and legal interaction.

Inquiry and Legal History

By the beginning of the nineteenth century there was a well-established habit of inquiry in English and archipelago life. It came from two independent sources: a very old tradition of legal inquiry, joined from the seventeenth century on by the new practice of political arithmetic. The latter required the collection of data upon which to base recommendations and decisions on policy, including reform. A number of methods for collection of that information were in use: surveys by private philanthropists, parliamentary committees, and royal commissions of inquiry were among the most common.

There was one other element which historians have not usually noticed when they have tried to explain the advent of legal reform. In the second half of the eighteenth century a vast amount of legal documentation had been published. The work was the product of several factors: looser restrictions on official records, greater facility for publication, and a larger audience were some of the principal causes. Publication had a twofold impact: access to official documents provided valuable sources for reformers and an assumed right of access, whether or not it existed, gave legitimacy to inquiry.

Legal records had always been voluminous; but they were not commonly made public (at least not outside the confines of high politics and the law). Collecting, arranging, and publishing the legal record was a burgeoning enterprise which merits fuller examination than is possible here. It will suffice to note the changes in law reporting, the growth of parliamentary record publishing, and, finally, a new venture in inquiry: the public record commission which began its work in 1800, and extended to all three kingdoms.

The law report was an old feature of English common law, but one which had been through many evolutions. From the Year Books of the Middle Ages to the accounts of volunteer reporters of the early modern period, the English report had been an essential technical document for common law decision-making, but publication had never been a large-scale enterprise. With the reports of James Burrow in Lord Mansfield's King's Bench, English reporting entered an era of more organized and methodical presentation, even though the business of reporting remained essentially private and decentralized for another century. Each of the high courts had recognized reporters. There were also new endeavors like the promptly published *Term Reports* (1785–1800) or the retrospective work of William Cobbett on *State Trials*, begun in 1809 and continued by Thomas Howell.[2]

Scottish decisions were unlike English reports. Until the late eighteenth century, judges treated them as persuasive, not authoritative. The Scottish reports were the first to be systematized, when the Faculty of Advocates directed regular reporting in 1705, but William Forbes only produced a single volume covering 1705–1713. The project was renewed in 1752, issuing in fourteen volumes (1760–1815). Meanwhile, numerous private collections of decisions had been printed. In 1801 William Morison began the huge task of assembling all the earlier decisions into a dictionary, which became a major source for Scottish law. This project was followed by the regular publication of "Session Cases" which superseded the Faculty Collection and became the official record of the Court of Session from 1841. Cases in the High Court of Justiciary were first published in MacLaurin's *Arguments and Decisions, 1670–1773* (1774). Hugh Arnot added *Celebrated Criminal Trials in Scotland (1536–1784)* in 1785. Regular reporting of justiciary cases began only in 1819 and publication dated from 1829. Justiciary cases were included with Session Cases from 1874.

Irish reports were a different story. Sir John Davies had published the first English-style reports in 1615, but he had no successors until the eighteenth century. Then Gorges Howard printed his *Popery Cases* in 1775, and within a decade the first regular printed reports appeared, Vernon and Scriven's *Reports of Cases determined in the King's Courts, Dublin...1786–88*. Thereafter, the number of reporters and private endeavors increased, and by the 1830s the Irish legal system was equipped with a modern apparatus of reporting.

Law reports were most readily usable when their main points were condensed in a classified collection. The earliest English abridgments began to provide this service in the fifteenth century.[3] In our period, Sir John Comyns edited *A Digest of the Laws of England* in five volumes (1762–67) which went through four editions by 1800. John Morgan produced *A Digest of the Common Law* in 1767; Joseph Burchell edited a current form of digest in his *Arrangement and Digest of the Law (1756–1794)* in 1796. More ambitious works also appeared at the end of the century. R. W. Bridgman edited a *Thesaurus Juridicus*, which contained decisions in the equity courts and the House of Lords, from the end of the seventeenth century to 1798 (1799–1800). These early efforts were important additions to the profession, and they provided a foundation on which additions and improvements were made in the nineteenth century.

The publication of the business of Parliament entered a period of growth in the late eighteenth century.[4] Hitherto its work was available to the public only in the printed statutes; its proceedings had been recorded in manuscript journals from the sixteenth century; its debates were privately noted by individual members from time to time. By 1800 published debates and sessional papers joined the formal records to shape the official documentation which still exists today.

The official printing of acts of Parliament in annual volumes began in 1483. There were many collections over the years, and in the eighteenth century these editions became more accurate and reliable. By the turn of the century, English and United Kingdom statutes were appearing in new, currrent editions. Sessional volumes began in 1801, accompanied later by indexes. In Ireland, collected statutes had appeared in the seventeenth century, with Sir Richard Bolton's *The Statutes of Ireland* (1621) and *A Collection of all the Statutes now in Use* in 1678. The latter was reprinted in 1723, and Francis Vesey edited a new *Statutes at Large* (1310–1761) in eight volumes in 1765. This was extended to 1800 by James Goddard Butler in a twenty-volume collection of the acts of the Irish Parliament published between 1786 and 1801. In 1812 Joseph Gabbett began publishing his *Digested Abridgement and Comparative View of the Statute Law of England and Ireland* in order to join the two "and finally lead to the assimilation of the laws in the several parts of the United Kingdom." For Scotland, *The Lawes and Actes of Parliament* had been published by Sir John Skene in 1597. Sir Thomas Murray of Glendook produced an edition of the statutes in 1681; and there were several abridgments of Scottish statutes published in the eighteenth century.

Printed journals formed the next category to appear as public parliamentary information. The Commons journal appeared in print from 1742 and the Lords from 1767. The journals of the Irish House of Lords (1634–1800) were printed between 1779 and 1800; the Commons journals (1613–1800) between 1796 and 1800. Beside the chronicles of actions in the several houses available in the journals, printed sessional papers (reports of committees, accounts, and minutes of evidence) became a regular source within the confines of legislative chambers. And slowly the aversion to publicity in that quarter receded as well. An apt instance for our purposes was that in the Lords, while printed cases had been demanded of appellants and respondents from the beginning of the eighteenth century, these were kept out of public view until the nineteenth century. The ban on publication of the Lords' proceedings was dropped in 1812.

The drive for publication had an important corollary: a campaign to inventory and protect the public records not published. We can get a good picture of this process through the career of Charles Abbot. After a few years as a practising barrister, Abbot retired and took a senior clerical office in the Court of King's Bench. There he worked on organizing the records of the court, which he found in "a ruinous garret" in one of the Inns. After his election to Parliament in 1795, Abbot proposed a committee to investigate expiring laws, and thus he learned more about the condition of parliamentary records. When he chaired a committee on finance, he had to delve into the records of the exchequer. From all of these encounters, he was moved to ask for a committee to inquire into the state of the public records. That committee surveyed over 300 repositories and made a report in 1800, recommending the appointment of a royal commission of inquiry. That was done in 1800. Abbot went to Ireland in the following year as chief secretary, and there he was greeted with a request for a similar inquiry in Ireland.[5] There followed inquiries into Irish and Scottish records as well, and eventually the work of the royal commissions spanned the years 1800–1837.[6]

The great amount of effort put into "published law" at the turn of the century was a sign of a more public political process, and a response to the demand for more legal documentation. These were natural corollaries of increasing interest in reform generally. But as the systems began to open up, there was an escalating concern over the "abuses" and "evils" which came into view. Published law naturally facilitated interaction; the reforming impulse gave interaction a purpose.

That impulse to reform was widely shared in the years 1780–1810. The idea of "economical reform" appeared in periodic bursts of public political debate from 1780 onward. The reformers attacked wasteful and corrupt use of public funds (sinecures, reversions, pensions) as a perversion of public trust. In the course of this period there were in fact significant reductions in these abuses, but periodic scandals took the spotlight, in cases like the mishandling of navy accounts under Lord Melville (1805) or the sale of army commissions by the Duke of York's mistress (1809). In any event, whether conditions had improved or not, the perception remained that "Old Corruption" was still at work, a perception which sustained many different attempts to reform government.[7]

The demand for investigation of the courts of law was a part of this larger reform impulse. The immediate cause came from another source. There had been prolonged discussion of the Scottish Court of Session and its problems, among and between English and Scottish lawyers and judges. Out of this came the first serious investigation of a high court, an investigation by a royal commission. That inquiry was only the first of many into the Scottish court, and the first of a wider series which came to include all of the major courts in England, Scotland, and Ireland. That series was soon followed by inquiries into the laws themselves. In all of this, legal interaction was an ever-present and sometimes vital element.

The Court of Session Inquiry

The Court of Session had been in operation since the sixteenth century, as part of the College of Justice, which included the older bodies of advocates and writers to the signet. The fourteen lords of session and their lord president were the judges of this court, and their traditional proceedings were the cause of much criticism, as to structure, methods and practice. The individual judges took turns sitting singly as lord ordinary (in the outer house). When this judge had ruled on a case, it might be heard again by the whole body of judges (in the inner house). As to method, pleadings were written and cases were argued without requiring the point at issue to be previously agreed upon. Procedure allowed numerous petitions on intermediate rulings (interlocutors) and the judges might review their own decisions. Much of the distinctive character of the Court of Session was owing to the essential fact that it was a court of both law and equity. This was a major reason why it produced a seemingly excessive number of appeals to the House of Lords, some coming even before the final disposition in the case. Critics saw as essential flaws the undue complexity of this procedure, the absence of decisive judgment (e.g., by a jury verdict), and, finally, the inordinate number of appeals from the Court of Session to the House of Lords.[8]

These conditions had been discussed since the 1780s by Scottish reformers. Reform was launched accidentally in 1785 when Henry Dundas proposed to let the number of lords of session decline from 15 to 10 by attrition, thus providing funds for salary increases for the survivors. In 1787 Walter Ross (a writer to the signet) wrote an essay with "Suggestions for Some Reformations in the Forms of Process in the Court of Session." [9] The author suggested that all parties were unhappy with delays, and "that in most cases of importance their judgments are carried by appeal to the House of Lords." He analyzed the "evils" in the current system under three heads: abuse of written pleadings (excessive written documents); wrong method of evidence (disuse of jury trial); and wrong distribution of business (the single ordinary and the inner house).[10] Ross then presented four pages of "regulations for the greater dispatch of business and better administration of justice." The pamphlet embodied a shrewd survey of the court's ills, one which touched the main points of the reform agenda over the next fifty years.

In 1789 John Lord Swinton wrote "Considerations concerning a proposal for dividing the Court of Session into Classes or Chambers and for limiting litigation in Small Causes; and for the Revival of Jury Trial in certain Civil Actions." This was followed by other essays on Scottish reform in the next couple of years.[11] While reformers wrote essays, the judges of the Court of Session took some action before the end of the century to improve the administration of justice. Several Acts of Sederunt (rules of court) introduced procedural changes. Indeed, their introduction caused turmoil in the College of Justice, and provoked some stubborn resistance from the writers, who felt their incomes were in jeopardy. One of these discontented writers, William Jameson, would later be a key figure in the unfolding story of inquiry. Before the new century began, and before there was an effort to reduce Scottish appeals from above, there had been a fair amount of activity, if not much success, in Scotland.

The growth in the number of Scottish appeals reaching the House of Lords continued well into the nineteenth century. As we have seen, appeals in England came in cases from the English Court of Chancery, not from the courts of common law. Therefore, the eligible English cases were limited to the total from Chancery alone. On the other hand, all Scottish civil cases heard in the Court of Session were eligible. Moreover, English cases could only be appealed after a judgment.

Scottish cases might be appealed at intermediate stages, whenever a court order (interlocutor) was given. The third variation was that an appeal in a Scottish case stopped legal proceedings, but in English and Irish process, this had ceased to be the case. In sum, there were very good reasons why there was a relatively large number of Scottish appeals pending in the Lords. Beyond the numbers, Scottish appeals presented more of a challenge. The Lords and the judges were much more familiar with the law in English cases. The most difficult cases from Scotland were apt to be remitted for rehearing, and sometimes not concluded at all. The problem was compounded by the lord chancellor's dual role as the judge of the English Court of Chancery and the presiding officer in the House of Lords. Indeed, this structural difficulty was a key reason why the Scottish appeals caused so much concern.

The reported numbers of appeals at different intervals were usually taken from the records of the House of Lords by the clerks, but in most parliamentary returns, the numbers given do not provide enough information to let us decipher their meaning (parties are not named; the stage of proceedings is omitted, etc.). We can supplement the bald numbers in the returns with evidence from two other sources: the *Calendar of Appeals* prepared for the Lords in the 1820s listed a short description of each case when it was heard; also Paton, Craigie and Stewart's *Reports of Cases* give us somewhat more information.[12] The combined sources show that the Scottish appeal cases covered all areas of the law and presented some inordinately difficult legal problems to the House of Lords. Of course the most pressing problem was to find ways to reduce the numbers, and this was the task to which the peers turned in 1806.

A moderate reform proposal had been drafted by the Scottish judges in 1805 but was never published. When Pitt died in January 1806, the Whig coalition which came to power presented a set of resolutions to the House of Lords.[13] These contained major reforms: division of the lords of session into three equal courts, each with a presiding officer, each to review cases from ordinaries; an end to the ability of ordinaries to review their own orders; and a suitor's choice of either jury trial or traditional hearing. The bill introducing these changes also provided for a Court of Review, which presumably would have cut down the number of appeals going to the House of Lords. The reception by the bench and the profession in Scotland was predictably hostile, in part because there was very little consultation in the preparation of the bill. The Scottish judges wrote to the peers, but their petition was not accepted; instead the judges were summoned to the bar of the house and presented with a set of questions, which they were to answer in writing. The government collapsed in the spring, thus saving the Court of Session in its ancient form for the time being. But Lord Eldon, replacing Thomas Erskine as Chancellor, did not let the matter drop. He proposed the less controversial approach of dividing the court and limiting appeals, while appointing a royal commission to make a further study of the procedure of the Court of Session.[14]

Some thirty-one commissioners, English and Scottish, were appointed, under the nominal leadership of Eldon. The actual working of the commission was a Scottish affair, and the end result was to make minor changes in the court and to shelve the jury question.[15] The case load of the court, and its share of appeals, were virtually unchanged. However, our main concern is with the impact of this breakthrough in government. A commission of advocates and judges had been given statutory powers "to inquire into the administration of justice in Scotland and concerning appeals to the House of Lords." However successful their work was deemed to be, their existence quickly became a precedent for further inquiry. In fact, concurrent events made the process move even faster, thanks to a variety of interacting components, as inquiries were made in increasing numbers after 1810.

Inquiry and Courts

The critique of the economical reformers had revived in the decade before Waterloo, and there were many who wanted to see fuller investigation of government spending. The tradition of committees and commissions of inquiry was well established and about to become even more widely used. In 1809 the House of Commons was debating a "Sale of Offices Prevention Bill" when Lord Folkestone attacked the measure because it omitted court offices ("the most objectionable of any"). During this debate, Folkestone tried to get a committee of inquiry "into the existence of any corrupt practices with regard to the disposal of offices in any department of the state," but his efforts failed.[16]

In May the Committee on Public Expenditure reported on the members who held places under the Crown, as well as those who held positions of profit under other officers, including judges. As noted in the Sale of Offices Act, a statutory ban since the time of Edward VI was supposed to prohibit the sale of judicial offices. In view of the attention attracted by this debate, a "commission on the saleable offices in the [English] courts of law" was appointed in January 1810. It was made up of eight of the high court judges. Its report on May 29 said there were no saleable offices in Chancery or Exchequer. The pertinent offices in Common Pleas and King's Bench were described, and the commissioners recommended a reduction in the number of clerks' positions, with the transfer of the savings to judicial salaries.[17] Elsewhere several groups were at work on the courts of law. The commissioners reported on the Court of Session and recommended a new system of extracting documents, giving compensation to the officials affected. At the same time, another commission was beginning work on the issue of delays in the English Court of Chancery.[18]

These separate efforts were caught up in a new campaign to investigate court fees in 1814. Against the wishes of the law officers, Sir John Newport, an Irish MP, collected a majority in the Commons to demand returns on fees in the courts of law, specifically the *changes* in fees over the past twenty years. Newport had obtained some information from a disgruntled writer to the signet, William Jameson, who was distressed with recent actions by the Scottish lords of session.[19] Jameson was probably not the only writer angered by some reforming Acts of Sederunt, which cut into their profits. Jameson described these laws as "a huge, unseemly, unintelligible volume of as extraordinary acts as ever were made by any court of justice." Jameson sent his tract to MPs and peers to help in "removing national prejudices against rational reform." The returns sought by Newport were slow in coming, as court officers seemed reluctant to cooperate. Ironically, the delays in returns contributed to Newport's decision to seek a royal commission to inquire into "duties, salaries, and emoluments" of the officers of the courts of justice.[20] He drew upon the recent returns—or in some cases, lack of same—to argue that an inquiry was needed. He pointed to the history of inquiries into the courts and the history of unfinished reforms. He added that this inquiry was made even more necessary by the recent union. A tense debate followed, in which judges were defended by ministerial spokesmen and charges of bribery were supported by Romilly and others. The house voted for the inquiry by a margin of 49 to 48 in June 1814.

When by November no commission had been issued, Newport rose to call for an address, reminding the house of the fate of the 1799 proposal. Then an inquiry on the courts had been requested, approved, and then forgotten. Ministers made excuses about the difficulty of finding "persons calculated to fill the situation," but the motion carried. The following February Newport moved for a bill to give the commissioners power to compel the attendance of witnesses. This of course touched off debate on the propriety of compelling officers of the court to testify, thereby impugning their integrity. The measure failed, but there was continuing evidence, by late returns, incomplete information, and assorted foot-dragging, that such powers were probably necessary.

The commissions finally were produced in early February 1815. The original motion of 1814 had called for one commission to examine the courts "within the United Kingdom." But it was determined "for the better execution of the premises, that separate commissions should be issued for the several parts of the United Kingdom." Thus three instruments were produced: the Irish Commission passed under the seal on February 3; on February 8 a warrant was issued for the Scottish commission, and the next day letters patent were issued to the English commissioners.[21] The different instruments were less significant than the varied circumstances of each system in determining the eventual performance of the inquiries. We have to look at the work of the commissions over the next decade or more—their gathering of evidence, their assessments of the courts, and their reports to Parliament.

As the commissioners went their separate ways in 1815, we can follow their activity quite well, not only in their printed reports, but in manuscript minutes (for the Scottish Commissioners)[22] and in published correspondence, returns to Parliament, and occasional publications. In each case, their commissions directed them to "make a diligent examination of the duties, salaries and emoluments" of the judges and officers of the courts of law. The English commission was the only one to mention ecclesiastical courts initially, but in an 1816 edition, the Irish commission included the words "temporal and ecclesiastical courts." Ultimately, all commissioners proceeded to examine at least the highest of church courts in their respective jurisdictions. All commissions listed the courts to be examined, and all included courts at the local level. The Scottish and Irish commissioners examined principal courts at the local level: for Ireland, this meant quarter sessions, the relatively new assistant barristers, and the sheriffs; for Scotland, there were reports on sheriff courts, justice of the peace courts, and burgh courts. The English commission did not pursue its inquiries below the high court level, principally because salaries and emoluments were not to be found in those lower regions.

The basic powers of the three sets of commissioners were the same. They were given power to inquire, to administer oaths, and to send for documents. They were to report their findings, though the instruction was awkward: "certify...all and every your several proceedings" within two years or less! Further, they were to suggest what "regulations" they deemed necessary for the better operation of the courts. The instructions clearly betrayed a lack of experience with this type of work. The actual experience in the field would insure that the commissions stayed on the job and, in some respects went well beyond their mandate. Five members were chosen for each commission. While all were experienced lawyers, some held positions in the law courts or elsewhere in government. But these commissions were not like the elite groups chosen in 1808 and 1810. These were to be working commissioners. They were paid a salary of £800 per annum, and each commission had a secretary and money for expenses.

The English commission included two chancery masters (John Campbell and William Alexander); a retired chief justice from Canada (William Osgoode); a commissioner of bankrupts (James Burrough) who soon was elevated to the Common bench; and a civil lawyer, William Adams. The Scots were headed by the late lord president of the Court of Session, Ilay Campbell, Lord Succoth, and he was joined by four advocates. Of them, James Glassford became well known as a legal writer over the next fifteen years. The Irish commission included John Foster, Bertram Mitford, and three other barristers. The commissioners' terms of service varied considerably. The Scottish commission's reports were all signed by original commissioners. The English Commission had a total of seven different members during its lifetime, and the Irish led the way with 14 different commissioners over 15 years, only one of whom signed all 21 reports.

An early return showed that the commissioners met with varied frequency. The Scots averaged three or four meetings per month, while the English (17) and Irish (18) reported more frequent sessions. The meetings were devoted to collecting and analyzing returns, taking oral testimony and drafting reports. The tasks of the commissioners were harder to accomplish than had been expected. Certainly there was no chance that any of them would be able to certify their findings within two years. Their reports did begin to appear in 1816, and over the next fifteen years a total of 41 reports were presented. As early as 1818, MPs were demanding returns on what the commissioners were spending and what they had accomplished.[23] Over the life of the commissions some £168,605 was spent, approximately £140,000 of that going to the salaries of commissioners. To put these expenses in perspective, we may note that there were reported savings of equivalent amounts *annually* as a result of commission-sponsored reforms.[24]

The form of the reports varied, since there was no central design or control. The English commissioners produced written accounts on each court with a historical sketch and descriptions of the duties of each official. The English commissioners chose not to present the returns of witnesses as appendices, and so it is almost impossible to trace the sources of information in their reports.[25] The Scots, on the other hand, gave a detailed historical sketch in each report, discussing current problems, sketching duties, and listing emoluments. Every report except one had an appendix with documentary evidence, including returns from witnesses, lists of fees, Acts of Sederunt, and other relevant information. The only Scottish report without an appendix was the twelfth and last. That one was unusual in that it examined the charges of law agents in inferior courts. This area was not explicitly covered in the commission, but it was justified in the report as an attempt to address public dissatisfaction over the cost of litigation (and it was aimed at the lower courts because the writers to the signet had blocked such an inquiry in the high courts).[26]

The Irish reports were by far the most voluminous and varied. Here the systematic journey through the courts was diverted on several occasions to address specific problems. Thus the second report looked at the Office of the Clerk of the Pleas in the Irish Exchequer (August 1816). This post was seen as one especially corruptible because of the large discrepancy between the fees taken and the amount paid to deputies who performed the duties. The occasion of the investigation was the death of the Earl of Buckinghamshire, who held the office. The fourth Irish report was also unusual. It looked at twenty-three offices in the disposal of the Crown, offices which were also deputized and seemed to provide large incomes for little or no labor. This line of investigation was suggested to the commissioners by the Irish government. It was meant to buttress a proposal for conversion from fees to salaries for officials' income.

Another diversion in the Irish reports came from a unique source. There seems to have been fairly general cooperation with the commissioners' inquiries. At least there are few signs of resistance in the reports. But the Irish commissioners encountered considerable resistance from the subsheriffs (especially in Dublin). In their thirteenth report the commissioners complained of noncompliance and asked for authority to "transfer sittings from place to place." This apparently led to an act "to facilitate the proceedings before the commissioners of inquiry relating to courts of justice in Ireland." That act gave the commissioners expanded powers, including the power to issue warrants for the arrest of uncooperative witnesses. It did not authorize a travelling commission, but within a year the commissioners had amassed their largest report of all, that on the Irish sheriffs.[27]

Taken together, the reports of these three bodies provide a creditable survey of the state of the courts of law and equity and church jurisdiction in the 1820s. This only met their first goal. There were also many observations and recommendations toward the other goal of regulation stated in the original commissions. Indeed, there were so many comments made by the commissioners, scattered through their reports, and only infrequently collected in summary sections, that it is difficult to give a complete picture of their impact. What is offered here is a sampling arranged around the major questions which prompted the inquiries. These comments will be presented in tandem with the reforms which sometimes followed. There were three main areas of recommendations:

(1) fees and salaries (reduction or conversion);
(2) reorganization and compensation of officers; and
(3) changes in court structure or rules.

In each of these areas, reforms were made by the courts themselves or after intervention by Parliament. As the latter increased during the 1820s, the practice and substance of the law were opened to inquiry as well.

There were two related questions regarding court fees. In the first place, there was a widespread assumption that the cost of legal proceedings was too high. While that opinion must always prevail among litigants, there was surely some ground for it at the beginning of the nineteenth century. Certainly that sentiment was behind the move by Sir John Newport to obtain returns from the courts, and it prompted the subsequent establishment of the commissions. The belated returns to Newport's initial requests were soon drowned by the vast amounts of new information generated by the commissions. Responses to questionnaires (sometimes amplified by oral testimony) came in from all of the officials of the courts. By 1821 the English commissioners alone had collected data on 3,500 fees.[28] In their earliest comments the commissions took varied positions on fees. The Irish in their first report deplored recent increases, some of which were compounded by an increase in the stamp duty in 1806. The Scots were equally committed to reduction. But the English commissioners were much more conservative. They took the position that fees should be judged by "the circumstances of the office, the qualifications which its functions require, the importance of its duties...and the length of time during which such fee has been received." Moreover, the commissioners found an endorsement for that prescriptive approach in an odd quarter. If a fee had been taken for twenty years, there was "a prima facie and possessory title," and that usage was proven by the terms of the 1814 fee returns![29]

There were many examples of scales of fees being recommended by the commissioners and adopted either directly by the courts, or being incorporated in reform statutes. In a number of reports, the commissioners admitted, "It is possible that there may be fees or emoluments actually received by some of the officers or by some of the clerks...of which through inadvertence or otherwise no account has been given." Where that was the case, commissioners said that only the fees they had noted were valid. Any others which persons attempted to assess were deemed illegal, and such a policy was reflected in the reform acts which were passed in the 1820s.

The second issue faced by commissioners was to decide whether fees were an acceptable form of compensation. As the Scots asked, should officers of the courts be "subject to be influenced by those practitioners from whom they obtain employment"?[30] Should they be exposed to temptation and bribery? Or should those officers be paid a salary? It was clear that the Scottish commissioners took the latter position, as did most of the Irish commissioners, and the Irish judges too. The English were again on the other side, and seldom did their reports make any favorable reference to the conversion from fees to salary.

Actually the process of conversion was quite old by the time of the inquiries. The remuneration of judges had been converted to salaries (with certain fees retained) in the seventeenth and eighteenth centuries. Clerks and officers were moving, slowly, in the same direction, before the commissions began their work. So, for instance, the clerks to the accountant general of Chancery were put on salary in 1797; the Irish master of the rolls was paid a salary in 1801; the Scottish commissary's salary was provided in 1806; the English added a vice chancellor, to be paid a salary out of fees owing to the lord chancellor in 1813, and English exchequer salaries were provided in 1817, all by act of Parliament.[31]

According to the Scottish commissioners, "it would be a very beneficial arrangement if all of [the clerks and other officers] were remunerated by fixed salaries in lieu of those fees and perquisites which they at present receive." There was an extreme example in the case of the Irish exchequer's clerk of the pleas. The fees collected amounted to about £11,000 and the deputized work cost about £3,000. The balance was a clear profit for the happy officeholder. Not only that, but in 1803, when some of the court's business was diverted to the Irish courts of King's Bench and Common Pleas, a profitable formula for compensation was adopted.[32] Because of these circumstances, Parliament had already intervened to regulate the finances of the office, before the commission could launch an inquiry. This court was to be the least cooperative of the Irish high courts, earning the criticism of the chief baron, and the appointment of a select committee.[33] The judges of the Irish King's Bench and Common Pleas, on the other hand, supported the fee scales as recommended by commissioners and went further in proposing the abolition of fees entirely.[34]

The work of the commissioners in the area of fees was treated quite differently in the several countries. The Scottish and Irish courts were regulated in detail. The latter were most completely regulated, with statutory fee tables enacted for all the major courts. The Irish chancery led the way with some seventeen tables of fees! Scottish courts were given more leeway for setting fees. The reluctant English judges were empowered to set fees and duties and were "required to take into their consideration as well the reports and recommendations of the several commissions."[35]

The most serious of the "evils" in the courts were those sinecures or ancient and inefficient places whose main function was to collect and disburse fees; whose holders were the profiteers in the administration of justice; who bought and sold their places and used low-paid deputies in case there were any real duties to be performed. But even the most radical reformers recognized a propertied interest in many of these cases. Thus the removal of such offensive posts required either: (a) monetary compensation for outright abolition; (b) compensation (to patrons) for closure by attrition; or (c) compensating regulation for deferred conversion to salary (either to maintain or to merge a post). These were broad, generally recognized types of compensation, and there were different particulars in each system's reforms.

In the English courts, given the modest pressures applied, the process of closure and compensation was slow. An exception was the statutory arrangement in 1825 for "purchase of the office of receiver and comptroller of the seal of King's Bench and Common Pleas and of Custos Brevium of the Common Pleas." This act was probably a further compensation for the acts of the same session which abolished the sale of offices in these two courts and which had provided salaries and annuities in lieu of those lost profits.[36] The English measures also were milder than their counterparts. Scottish commissioners made several surveys of the roster of court officials, and they presented to Parliament a set of summaries of the alterations and the savings which they had produced. The Irish process was more complex and more costly. First, there were more sinecures, hence more closures and claims. Parliament tried to involve the commissioners in the assessment, a long battle ensued, and there were disputes between commissioners.[37]

Besides questions of salaries and emoluments, there were many other questions about duties. Here the commissioners' proposals often went beyond the fuzzy boundaries of their mandates. Numerous regulations were drafted, which would alter the structure and the rules of the courts. These tended to widen the scope of the inquiry, and they helped to open the door to a further phase of examination of the laws which underlay the several systems.

The Scottish commission was the most advanced by virtue of the fact that others had pioneered the study of the Court of Session, and also because it was paralleled by the commissioners for the new Jury Court. These were dubious advantages in that reform legislation was being produced before the results of the inquiries were known, to say nothing of digested. There were many recommendations for streamlining the Scottish courts, only some of which made it to the statute book.

In 1823, after the Scottish reports were complete, it was discovered that the old nemesis of Scottish appeals was as bad as ever. A select committee of the Lords was appointed, and the peers debated the subject once more. Eldon said that the Scots should separate law and equity. There was still something wrong with the Scottish system, and a new inquiry into "the forms and process in Scots law" was set up.[38] Thus the focus was moved closer to the procedural and substantive heart of the system. This inquiry and its report were followed by a controversial review of the jury provision. And both of these were but a prelude to other investigations which lay just ahead. These inquiries demonstrated the way that momentum was created and investigation was extended. As we shall see, the process would inevitably entail further interaction.[39]

The Irish commissioners continued their operations until 1831, but their main reports were completed by 1824. Major legislative enactment followed, and in some cases these acts were explicitly founded on the work of the commission. In the Irish system, there were extensive regulations for the major courts. Statutes were enacted for the Exchequer Chamber, King's Bench and Common Pleas, Chancery, Nisi Prius, Exchequer, and local courts. The courts themselves sometimes anticipated parliamentary action, as in measures by Common Pleas, King's Bench, Nisi Prius, or the Registry of Deeds. Finally, several statutes modified practice regulations: clients should not have to pay for more than 200 copies of a document (!); the issue of exchequer writs was regulated; and the civil bill process before assistant barristers was regulated.[40]

The English commission made nothing like the statutory imprint which was put upon Scottish and Irish courts of law. As already noted, the English judges needed a statute simply to tell them to consider the commissioners' reports. After this unpromising start, it may not be surprising to learn that there were few and only incidental regulations made, and only some of these were linked to the reports of the commission. We have seen already that the single judge acts in 1817 were an effort to adjust the workload in King's Bench and Exchequer; the Admiralty quorum was reduced from 3 to 2; some changes may have had more to do with the need for alternate sites, while new housing for the English courts was under construction in the early 1820s (see chapter 5). Of more moment in the inquiry context were the acts to abolish the sale of offices in King's Bench and Common Pleas.[41]

Inquiry and Laws

Perhaps most interesting of all, a transition was just beginning, barely visible in the Scottish commission of 1824, and emerging clearly in two English commissions at the end of the decade. Inquiry was moving into the examination of the law itself. The famous speech by Henry Brougham on law reform in 1828 played an interesting part in this. Most accounts seem to accept the speech as a landmark event, in that the event is assumed to have inaugurated legal reform.[42]

> The main campaign for the reform of the courts began in 1828 when Lord Brougham delivered a six-hour lecture to the House of Commons on the deficiencies of the existing courts and the measures needed to remedy these defects.

Brougham moved to examine "the state of the law of this country and its administration in the courts of justice with a view to such reforms as time may have rendered necessary and experience may have shown to be expedient." The intent was clearly to continue the trend of inquiry already begun. He referred favorably to the Scottish inquiry, saying "we appointed a commission to investigate the whole administration of justice in Scotland and it ended in altering the constitution of the courts and introducing a new mode of trying causes." Brougham asked for an address to the Crown to take measures to inquire into the courts of common law and "into the state of the law regarding the transfer of real property."[43] The result was a pair of further commissions of inquiry, one into the courts of common law in England and Wales, and the other into real property law. This neatly captures the transition which Brougham's speech represents: he was no originator of reform, but he was important as a catalyst for the extension of inquiry into its next critical stage. By the time of Brougham's speech, there was a rising tide of legal reform, especially visible in alteration of court structures. The work begun in the early 1820s, continued with such measures as the addition of a new Glasgow circuit in 1829, and in the next year the amendment of the Exchequer Chamber in England, the merger of the Admiralty and Jury Court jurisdictions with the Court of Session, and the abolition of the Great Sessions of Wales.

While these court alterations were the main thrust of reform in the 1820s, they occurred against a background of interest in codification, paralleled by intermittent experiments in legal consolidation. The most notable examples are associated with the names of Bentham (Civil Code) and Peel (consolidation of criminal law). But surrounding those luminaries there was a rather large company of activists, beginning with reform-minded neighbors like Joseph Gabbett in Ireland, who produced a three-volume *Digested Abridgement and Comparative View of the Statute Law of England and Ireland between 1812 and 1818*. In Scotland, William Morison had mounted his great project to collect and reprint all *The Decisions of the Court of Session Digested under Proper Heads in the Form of a Dictionary* (38 vols., 1801–1804).

In the first half of the nineteenth century there was a great expansion of reporting and considerable work in digesting reports, plus a beginning of broader (and interactive) approaches to the collection of case law. Expanded current reporting depended upon more efficient means of recording proceedings, and this was made possible by the increasing adoption of shorthand reporting, though there was some delay in the acceptance of this method by the courts.[44] Probably the most important general development in reporting at this time was in criminal cases. Reports of these cases had developed more slowly than the civil side in spite of their sensational nature. Except for state trials and the occasional single report, regular publication of criminal reports began in the early nineteenth century. The one early series, *Old Bailey Session Papers* (which had appeared from 1729 to 1834) was continued by *Central Criminal Court Session Papers* (1834–1913). Cases in the High Court of Justiciary were reported by David Syme (1826–29) in 1829, by Patrick Shaw (1819–31) in 1831, and by a series of successors. These reports were later added to the *Session Cases*, then to the *Scottish Law Reporter*

(1866–1924) and the *Scots Law Times* (1893 to present). The 1840s saw the appearance of a major series containing English and Irish cases, *Cox's Criminal Cases* (from 1846) edited by Edward William Cox.

As case law in print blossomed, there was a natural desire to render the material into useful form in general and special digests. The concept was well established, but after the Union, and in the context of reform and publicity, new digests tried to be more comprehensive and innovative than their predecessors. General digests appeared with more frequency, and the practice was in increasing demand in Ireland and Scotland as well. Somewhat later, the digest developed an interactive dimension. In 1813, Bridgman added Irish cases to his *Analytical Digest*, in a manner used by several editors. Still more ambitious combinations appeared in the 1830s.

Thus the generation of courts inquiry was equipped with more and different tools for the lawyer, but still the questions raised by the early inquiries had not been answered, and new and more probing investigations were soon to follow. In chronological order, the main inquiries of the 1830s were the two English commissions which were inspired by Brougham: a study of the courts of common law and an investigation of real property law. The other major legal inquiries were yet another Scottish Law Commission and a much more original English Commission on Criminal Law. These commissions marked the further advance of the process of inquiry, but more importantly, they required deeper penetration into the workings of the law, to the substance of the law itself.

The first sign of this advanced stage was the Commission of Inquiry into the Law of England Respecting Real Property. This was a fitting target, considering the amount of criticism Brougham had devoted to real actions. It was also the central area of court business, and the one most heavily encrusted with archaisms. The commissioners were directed to investigate the law, the methods of transfer, and to suggest improvements. Their reports (1829–1833) offered a full review of major questions in property, and made proposals for reform. Holdsworth has said[45]

> As a result of these reports, many abuses, anomalies and anachronisms were abolished; and this method of reforming the land law by the piecemeal removal of particular abuses continued all through this period. That this method of reform was adopted was due to the fact that the commissioners were too

> convinced of the essential excellence of the substantive principles of the land law to recommend any very sweeping reforms—except in one branch of it, namely, conveyancing.

The second report argued for a general registry of deeds which Ireland and Scotland had, but England and Wales would wait much longer to get. The commissioners were headed by John Campbell, and in spite of Holdsworth's faint praise, they produced a list of legislative reforms which was quite impressive.

The contemporary Commission to Investigate the Courts of Common Law made six reports between 1829 and 1834. Its mandate was to inquire into "the course of proceeding in actions" in those courts "from the first process...to the termination thereof." As if this were not wide enough, the last two reports branched out to look at courts for small debts and at the Inns of Court. The main body of inquiry, however, looked at the antique process which Brougham had scathingly reviewed. Among the resulting reforms, there was a general reform act of 1830 which added judges, altered terms, and regulated writs of error (with an Irish version a year later). The other piecemeal measures included acts dealing with some major rules for pleading and legal procedure.

In 1834 a commission was appointed to inquire further into Scottish law. George Bell, the professor of law at Edinburgh, was joined by James Reddie (town clerk of Glasgow) and five advocates and two writers to form a body which would look at a cluster of issues: reducing fees in the Court of Session; reorganizing the records of that court; enforcing the court's decrees; examining the procedure of sheriff courts; studying the expense of criminal prosecution; and reviewing the nature of heritable rights and the forms of transfer in Scots law. The latter was the chief deviation from the structural and procedural directions of inquiry up to this point. In the third of its four reports, the commission took a long look at Scottish conveyancing. A set of acts (mostly minor) ensued: allowing bastards to inherit, regulating erasures in documents, abolishing the commissary court, and granting power to sell lands to heirs of entail.

One area which the Scottish commissioners touched briefly, and one which was central to the whole reform movement, was that of criminal law. While Peel had tried to simplify the English laws and reduced the number of capital crimes, there were many other issues and aspects to be dealt with. Among these, not the least were the border disputes with

Scottish and Irish law, some of which we witnessed in the last chapter. It was significant that in 1834 a commission was formed to inquire into the criminal law. The first report addressed the projects of digesting the statute law and digesting the unwritten law, so as to combine the whole into "one body of criminal law." The concept of a digest or code was plainly one cure seen by the reformers.

The reform of criminal law proved to be far more complex than the commissioners had expected; their project went through eight reports by 1845, and then the work was taken up by commissioners "for revising and consolidating the criminal law," who toiled on to 1849. As we shall see in the next chapter, the project was a central feature of midcentury efforts to reconcile the English and Irish systems, and as such it fit into the runup to the great restructuring of the 1870s. But in general, the early efforts to use commissions of inquiry for reform of the law were a disappointment. The task was too great, the tools were too weak, and the time was not ripe. But there was still a significance here which may be too easily overlooked. In 1839 the legal writer John Miller commented on the inquiry process:[46]

> Times have most materially altered. Debates in both houses of parliament, reports of numerous sets of commissioners appointed by the government, books, pamphlets and parliamentary proceedings, all aiming at the improvement of the law and the administration of justice, have followed each other in quick and uninterrupted succession.

This activity was aimed at the improvement of the several legal systems. There was little evidence of an incorporating movement, but there was every sign of extending reforms—for fees, or courts, or laws themselves—to each of the component systems of the United Kingdom. The machinery of inquiry was an important and distinctive tool of modern government. It was significant that its gestation so fully involved the legal systems. But then its promoters and operators were often members of the legal profession. Their active (and interactive) involvement would only grow as the century progressed and the work of legal consolidation continued.

Chapter 5

Building the Supreme Court 1840–1880

Britain assumed the title of "workshop of the world" in the middle of the nineteenth century. Her industrial and imperial power grew apace in a century without major war, a "Pax Britannica." This dominance slipped after 1870, but by then the powerful British economy had forced radical changes in society: the landed aristocracy was infiltrated and surpassed by new wealth; the middle classes became more numerous with rising professional, business, and managerial components; workers began to organize and be heard as never before—first the highly skilled, in craft unions, and by the end of the period, unskilled workers in large industrial unions. At the same time, the shape of government was altered: beside parliamentary reform, a civil service, central inspectorates, and treasury control of expenditure were some of the novel features. In the law, moves toward consolidation were capped by a streamlined English Supreme Court. The interwoven legal and architectural workmanship for that project was set in a context of turbulent politics and crosscurrents of legal change.

The politics of the period had three themes which stood out. In the first place, the political parties were in a state of flux, arriving at some kind of equilibrium by the 1870s. In 1835 Peel had stated, in the famous "Tamworth Manifesto," that the conservative position ought to be to support the new reformed regime. He assumed the leadership of the renovated conservative party. But in 1846, as prime minister, Peel promoted the repeal of the tariffs on grain (the "corn laws") and in so doing he split his party for the next twenty years. It was to be united and revived by Benjamin Disraeli. On the other side of the House of Commons, an assortment of Whigs, Radicals, and "Liberals" was wandering through most of the fifties and sixties, holding office in a variety of coalitions. By 1870 a clearer alliance governed under the leadership of William Gladstone. He and Disraeli, by their notable rivalry in election campaigns and in the House of

Commons, helped to develop the party system in its modern form. But even as they did so, a party of Irish Nationalists was forming in the 1870s, and it would play a very important role in shaping the politics of the next half century.

The second dominant theme in politics was a crescendo of radical thought and activity, which must have seemed to contemporaries to be a sign of danger. The most ominous effort was the campaign of the Chartists, attempting to force the acceptance of the People's Charter by Parliament. With support in all parts of the United Kingdom, for a decade this democratic movement made a loud claim for democracy. It was divided internally, with part of the group committed to "physical force" and part committed to constitutional methods. That division was a major reason why the Chartist movement subsided after 1848. Beside the Chartists, the Anti-Corn Law League brought a new dimension to politics. A group representing businessmen and economists, the league vociferously denounced the Corn Laws as a system of government subsidy for the landowning classes. Their analysis introduced the first well-focused class debate, and their organization (speakers, publications, and organized activities) presaged modern pressure groups. Probably the league was not the reason for Peel's fateful decision on repeal, but the ordinary voter might be forgiven for failing to see that fact, especially since that decision was quickly followed by repeal of the navigation acts and the adoption of a policy of free trade. In any event, a new and powerful device was now in the political system.

Historians often give priority to the third theme, parliamentary reform. However, in 1867 the second reform act was really a story of political maneuvering, in which a conservative ministry under Disraeli passed a bill which was more liberal than one his rival Gladstone had proposed. All the same, the electorate was doubled, and many workers got the vote. In 1872, the secret ballot arrived, again by a circuitous route. Meanwhile women had been enabled to vote in local elections and take positions on school boards. If these assorted reforms had no clear focus, the process itself was significant.

The powerful economic growth of the middle of the century had important legal ramifications in several directions. The 1840s were recorded by some as "the hungry forties." Seeming to belie the economic strength of Britain, there were serious crises. Britain had been in a depression since 1836, and 1842 was "the worst year of distress and disorder that Britain experienced in the nineteenth century."[1] A number of measures, such as renewal of income tax, banking reforms, and some intervention in industry gave the appearance of a successful remedial program. But the inherent strength of the economy was responsible for the recovery. No such good fortune awaited Ireland. When famine arrived there in 1845, in the wake of potato blight, that country suffered a major demographic disaster. Between 1845 and 1850 the population was reduced by 1.5 to 2 million deaths (from starvation and disease) and another million were lost to emigration. The Irish population continued to shrink until the early twentieth century. Britain offered no effective assistance in this crisis. Indeed, the 1846 repeal of the corn laws, which some supported because of the famine, could not help starving Irishmen and women with no money to buy grain at any price. It must be said, however, that there were many relief efforts for Ireland, though perhaps not as many as there were for British cities and towns. There the ugly corollary of industrial and commercial wealth was that the surging population, concentrating in large, smoky towns, working in new and dangerous workplaces, had to struggle to survive in the developing, poorly regulated consumer economy.

It was this mixed picture which lay behind the famous Exhibition of the Industrial Works of All Nations which Britain hosted in 1851. The brainchild of Prince Albert, the exhibition was housed in an appropriately modern, prefabricated, giant iron and glass conservatory in Hyde Park. The show was immensely popular, and more than six million tickets were sold. In the next two decades, the economy of Britain turned in an impressive performance: the growing population produced continuing increases in the staple industries, coal, iron, and textiles; the output of engineering, railways, and shipbuilding also flourished. Profits found their way into the growing area of overseas investment, which quadrupled between 1850 and 1875.

There were many kinds of legal fallout from this commercial cornucopia. The increasing amount of business, with an ever larger community of consumers, naturally meant more cases of small debts. There were some older specialized courts (the courts of requests for example, dating from the sixteenth century) but their provision and their performance were subjects of criticism. In 1846 the Small Debts

Act created a system of 500 county courts (for England and Wales) with a barrister as judge, and an optional jury of five. This large increase in legal jobs might have been rejected as a patronage scheme a generation earlier; now it quickly attracted a growing clientele who wanted swift settlement of small claims. Parties could appear as witnesses, cases could be heard on a simple process, and the appeal of legal points was kept within reasonable limits. This new court structure was only the first major judicial reconstruction of the century.

Another direct outgrowth of the expanding economy was the increased use of arbitration to settle commercial disputes. The common law courts and equity were costly and not always reliable or predictable; merchants and manufacturers found it easier and safer to entrust decisions to private arbitrators who had ample knowledge of the business involved. There were no courts for commercial cases for businesses outside London other than the semi-annual assizes, and in London itself, it was 1895 before a special provision was made for a commercial court, within the Court of Queen's Bench.

The matter of employers' liability was yet another major area of law affected by the economy's growth and, some would argue, the growth of the legal profession. Over our period, by the estimate of one authority, the number of barristers increased by fifty percent, to about 1,000.[2] The number of solicitors rose by a comparable percentage, and the "lower" branch of the profession probably was more directly involved in commercial business and its expansion.[3] In a direct way, legislation such as Factory Acts and Mines Acts were setting limits on employers and thereby defining their liability. The courts meanwhile were beginning to try cases of injury to workers, and developing (in English law) doctrines which limited tort liability (the doctrine of common employment, for example, which is explained in chapter 6). On a higher level, corporate liability was reformed by the enactment of limited liability in 1856, meaning that in suits against a corporation, shareholders were only liable to the limit of the value of their shares.

While the economy grew and forced or induced legal change, the contours of society were seriously affected as well. In 1851 the total British population was 21 million, about triple the number of a century earlier. But now in addition to a census, and as important, civil registration of births, marriages, and deaths was gradually being applied to all parts of the archipelago. The impact of population went further, for it was the movement of large numbers into the manufacturing towns which had forced the advances in public health legislation of the second quarter of the century.

The working class, recently a much more articulate entity, found advocates who campaigned for remedial legislation such as the laws prohibiting women and children from working in the mines, limiting hours of work, and prescribing safer conditions in workplaces. Workers themselves sought to protect their rights in organizing. The law saw this activity as unlawful "combination" in restraint of trade. That maxim had been made into a statute in 1799, but by the 1820s it was challenged. Further investigation and legislation gave grudging recognition to lawful organization later in the century, and meanwhile the workers continued to bolster their cause, by forming the Trades Union Congress, a lobbying agency, in 1869.

Another problem in social and political terms was the legacy of Irish disaster. To the nationalists, the problem was Britain. In the 1830s and 1840s, an aging Daniel O'Connell had led a movement to repeal the act of union. Among other things, O'Connell had held "monster meetings" to promote the cause. One such meeting at Clontarf in 1843 was banned, and O'Connell and a group of his lieutenants were tried for seditious conspiracy. The case went all the way to the House of Lords, where several lay Lords tried to sit as judges and were denied that right—the first formal recognition that only the "law lords," that is, senior judges, active or retired, were really expected to vote on "House of Lords" appeals. More directly related to the economy, there was a progression of legislation (and litigation) stemming from the devastating damage to property and property values in Ireland. This is taken up in chapter 6 under the subject of landlord and tenant acts.

A third major area of legal "fallout" was what we may call reconstruction of government. This was not a contemporary phrase: there was no movement to achieve this goal, except in limited areas. Rather, a retrospective view shows that a collection of developments amounted to a substantial reconstruction. The main components of that were: legislative expansion, administrative "revolution," and casual centralization. On the first head, the process we have already seen of the growing number of statutes continued and escalated in the nineteenth century. At first there was not much thought given to it, but by the 1860s there was a concern for unlimited growth and uncontrolled verbiage on the statute book. Statute revision and improved drafting requirements were to be adopted in the third quarter of the century. Even more important, by the 1880s political leaders were quite concerned about the crowded legislative calendar, and soon the ability of individual MPs to move bills forward was going to fall before the imperatives of party government and control.

The administration of government business increasingly was the province of boards and bureaucrats. The salaried and trained career civil servant was replacing the relative or friend of the family in government jobs. Just as important, the job was more likely to have statutory goals and requirements, and even penalties for failure to abide by those terms. Thus a new breed of administrator came to occupy a position much like a public prosecutor for specific areas of conduct (factories, housing, poor law administration, and so on).

The final effect to notice was a trend toward centralization. This was a complex subject, for most opponents of nineteenth century regulatory acts were anxious to prevent this trend and happy to denounce the prospect in debate. For example, police reforms were delayed and diverted for years because of the fear of a centralized police force. The result in that case was a masked form of centralization: control by the Home Office of chief constables in charge of large regional districts; divided funding responsibilities and diffuse regulatory patterns. In other cases, central boards were used in experimental ways, either freestanding, under Parliament, or under department heads. One feature which emerged during this period, connected to the vigilant critics of government, was the central control of expenditure, situated in the Treasury and designed to audit and restrict spending.

Legal Architecture

The expanding economy necessarily impressed itself on the old legal systems, forcing growth in some areas, alteration or restriction in others. The altered social and economic landscape dramatized the awkward and antiquated structures which survived from earlier days.

However venerable these institutions might be, they were bound to be under pressure to reform, remodel, and rebuild.

While royal commissions worked on the law and the courts, they had noted an ever-expanding list of defects during the first half of the nineteenth century. In that period the physical setting of the courts was occasionally remodelled. These two themes grew and merged in the shaping of the supreme court in the 1870s. This was an English court, but not an English reform. All the systems were engaged in some way in the process of reconstruction.

The Judicature Act of 1873 is a well-known milestone in the nineteenth century. But general historians give it a wide berth, and legal historians have not been overly anxious to fill the void.[4] The story is interesting, instructive, and interactive. The building project which would eventually house the new supreme court dated from the 1840s. By that time groundwork was being done on consolidating the sources of law and reforming criminal and civil practice. In short, a complicated foundation, legal and architectural, was being laid long before the appointment of the Royal Commission on Judicature in September 1867.[5] That commission, with its Irish chairman Lord Cairns, was soon followed by another Scottish Law Commission in 1868, led by Duncan MacNeill, Lord Colonsay, the first Scottish law lord. The Cairns Commission reviewed the English structure and proposed consolidating the high courts and replacing the Lords' appellate jurisdiction with a new Court of Appeal. The Colonsay Commission made an extensive survey of Scottish judicature and also looked at the subject of appeals. When the Judicature Act was passed in 1873, the appellate role of the Lords was terminated. It was soon clear that the ramifications of this change had not been fully considered, and between 1874 and 1876 the appeal process was thoroughly examined. English, Scottish, and Irish appeals to the House of Lords were restored, and Scottish and Irish law lords were created.

This point also marks the beginning of the actual construction of the supreme court buildings. The life of the new statutory regime took shape after the first enactment and its later adjustment. The new high court judges did not occupy their quarters in the Strand until 1882, but they wrote new rules of court after 1873; they began to sit in their new capacity from 1876; their example encouraged the collateral changes of Irish judicature in 1877; and a series of further consolidating measures followed in the 1880s. In the end, the new court was, like its predecessors, an English venue. After decades of consolidation, there was not much assimilation. Each legal system was modernized; the essential connections between them were not.

The outward structures of the English, Scottish, and Irish court systems were all undergoing reconstruction between 1795 and 1825; the interior patterns of the systems were likewise being refurbished; and the professions which staffed them were reforming and retooling. Westminster Hall had been the home of the English royal courts since the thirteenth century, but it was physically outgrown by the beginning of the nineteenth century. There were several efforts made to remodel or rebuild within the precincts of Westminster. A variety of expedients was used to shift the courts' locations: the chief justice of King's Bench was allowed to try Middlesex issues at *nisi prius* "elsewhere than in Westminster Hall." The next year the justices were allowed to sit in Serjeants' Inn. In 1822 the Court of Exchequer was allowed to move during rebuilding to "any convenient place in the county of Middlesex."[6]

Work on a new setting for the royal courts was begun in 1820. The space beside Westminster Hall was selected, and Sir John Soane was chosen to design a new court complex; funds had been appropriated to the amount of £30,000 for this work. The project was reviewed and criticized by a Select Committee on Public Buildings in Westminster, and its plans and cost figures were revised. The estimate published in 1827 was £18,612. The reduced project was being outgrown almost at once. When the famous fire of 1834 destroyed St. Stephen's Chapel, it left the hall intact, along with the remodelled housing for the courts. The English building project was not alone in being inadequate, or subject to criticism. The old Parliament House in Edinburgh was in need of improvements, and work was begun early in the century. The reconstruction of Parliament Close was interrupted, and additional work was required, after a serious fire in 1824. New construction in Dublin had preceded all of these projects, beginning with the Green Street court building in 1792. Later the Irish Four Courts were rebuilt, after the design of James Gandon, between 1786 and 1796, and the new King's Inns were built between 1800 and 1817.[7]

The contours of the legal profession were also changing in the several systems during the first decades of the new century. The practitioners were adjusting to new social and economic conditions, while traversing the shifting terrain of the reformed legal systems. Legal education, legal associations, and legal publication marked new departures which were early signs of the development of the profession before its transformation in the 1870s. The matter of legal education, always a tempting target for reformers, was again in their sights. In this instance, there was an interesting episode of interaction. Members of the Irish bar, motivated in part by their required attendance at the English Inns, developed their own educational programs (e.g. the Dublin Law Institute). This effort was coupled with the work of Thomas Wyse, MP, leading to a new inquiry into legal education. In the wake of a Select Committee on that subject (1846), the Inns formed a Council of Legal Education which led to the beginning of examinations there. In the next generation law teaching expanded in the universities.[8]

Foundations, 1840–1865

From the 1840s a variegated process of consolidation gained momentum, a process which was as essential to the foundation of the new Supreme Court as its physical design. And in this process of consolidation there were many instances where legal interaction played an important role. The effort to rehouse the English high courts moved into a more aggressive phase in the early 1840s. This effort was to last for thirty years because of site problems and money problems. But at least the idea of consolidating the courts was so familiar by the 1860s that it encountered no significant opposition. Since early reconstruction in Westminster had not been successful, a select committee was appointed in 1842 to consider the construction of a building for the courts in the vicinity of the Inns. This committee was followed by still another, which reprinted the original report in 1845. The testimony of witnesses, representing most sectors of the legal profession, concurred in the view that the old courts were poorly situated and preferred only by those lawyers whose practice required them to be near the Houses of Parliament. The majority of practitioners (and their clients) would be better served by courts located nearer the precincts of lawyers' chambers. The 1842 report contained plans for a new structure in Lincoln's Inn Fields. The design proposed for this site was by James Barry. There were rival interests in the Lincoln's Inn site and a site in Carey Street, and both proposals had problems of finance and design.

Other matters were involved in consolidation. When significant progress was made with them, the building project gained momentum. There were very extensive changes in both criminal and civil practice, changes which cut across the different systems and showed that serious reform was underway. By 1840 there was a general notion that something had to be done to consolidate laws, especially criminal statutes. Indeed, some things had been done already, but early action underscored different definitions of "consolidation." Did the word mean combining, or did it also mean codifying and thus revising the laws? Did it include statutes only, or did it include common law rules as well?[9] In the 1820s, Peel led the way in consolidating (i.e., reducing) English criminal statutes, while others proposed codification; in the 1830s, we saw the establishment of a royal commission to compose a digest of criminal law. That body was reconstituted in 1845, "for revising and consolidating the criminal law." Both commissions produced reports in the form of general criminal statutes which were not enacted. The task was then given briefly to a statute law board, and then another commission was created but that effort failed as well. The reason for failure was that the concept of consolidation was fatally flawed: to the English lawyer "a code of common law is a contradiction in terms."[10] But that is what was at issue: should the law grow and evolve in its old way, or was it more desirable to review and refine it? There were instances in the midcentury which showed that many lawyers and legislators took the latter view. The statute law commissions themselves were one example, and in the latter stages they were given strong support by Lord Chancellor Cranworth, though to no avail. But there were some other instances in the field of criminal law which showed that legal interaction might be promoting some advances in consolidation.

In theory the criminal law of England and Ireland were the same. In practice, in those very different social settings, the administration of justice meant very different things. The structure of law enforcement was markedly different. The operation of Irish criminal trials was also unlike the English. Even the basic criminal statutes were not the same. This last was perhaps the easiest to amend, though the consequence of amendment might not be significant. In any event, it was interesting that in the period of early statute consolidation, one of the areas of achievement was between English and Irish criminal laws. The first act was the result of applying the Peel principle to Irish law: the number of capital crimes was seen to be excessive. In 1842 a bill was introduced "to assimilate the law in Ireland, as to the punishment of death, to the law in England." This measure rescinded the death penalty for popish priests and reduced their sentence to transportation, as it did for for ship-burning by owners, for embezzling banknotes, and for serving the king of France. These and other provisions were outdated, were not enforced, and were not found on the new and shortened list of English capital crimes. Of course the act, like the earlier English ones, only deleted laws, it did not rewrite them.[11]

A more significant development came in 1848, when England and Ireland simultaneously were reformed by the "Crown Cases Act." It had long been possible for judges to reserve cases for the consideration of points of law by the full bench; at this point, some effort was being made to introduce a criminal appeal. Most of the legal profession were against the idea of appeal (as distinct from "error" in law), because an appeal as to the facts was thought to cast a cloud over the jury verdict. In their creation, the Courts of Crown Cases Reserved were identical. But in operation, the Irish court tended to become an appeal court; indeed, in the Irish law reports it was called the "Court of Criminal Appeal." The English court was strictly held to points of law, and was not allowed to develop as its cousin did.[12]

In 1861 a set of acts passed "to consolidate and amend the statute law of England and Ireland" for larceny, forgery, offences against the person, malicious injury to property, and offences relating to the coin of the realm. As a prelude, Parliament repealed a large number of existing statutes.[13] The consolidating acts made some changes in the respective laws of both countries, but it is hard to estimate what broad general impact they may have had, except to say that they reflected a general desire for uniformity and consistency.

There was something of the same consolidating effort behind a push to reform the method of prosecution in England and Wales. Both Ireland and Scotland had forms of public prosecution; in England and Wales the prosecution of criminals nominally depended on the action of the injured private individual. In practice, the new police forces were slowly assuming a role in this area from the 1840s. But for some time, the matter of public prosecution was a focus of debate, the general concept only receiving a limited endorsement with the creation of a director of public prosecutions in 1879. In Scotland, the lord advocate had supervised prosecutions by the local procurators fiscal since the sixteenth century. In Ireland, crown solicitors had been assigned to judicial circuits since 1800, and sessional solicitors sat with quarter sessions since 1830. In England, the practice of private prosecution came in for criticism, but very slow alteration. The criminal law commissioners observed in 1845 that[14]

> intrusting the conduct of the prosecution to a private individual opens a wide door to bribery, collusion, and illegal compromises. Independently of these obvious objections..., it frequently happens that there is no person who can legally be called upon to prosecute; as in cases of homicide.

The effort continued with bills for the creation of public prosecutors. In 1855 a select committee was appointed, including the English attorney general, the Irish solicitor general and the Scottish lord advocate. Having looked at an experiment in Leeds, and considering U.S., Irish, and Scottish parallels, the report favored district agents.[15] The districts would be the same as those of the county courts, each of which would have a qualified barrister to act as the public prosecutor. There were too many problems and disagreements at this stage and the report was shelved. In civil litigation there were important forms of interaction as well. These coincided with early stages of internal English consolidation—especially between law and equity and between secular and ecclesiastical jurisdiction. In addition there were important procedural reforms which were further evidence of legal interaction.[16]

The movement to fuse law and equity was a necessary prelude to the reconstruction of the English courts. Here there was potential for interaction of two kinds: the Scottish Court of Session offered an example of fusion. It had an equity jurisdiction, which made its decisions less intelligible to English judges, but which gave its own members a sense of superiority to their English brothers. The second kind of interaction came from Ireland. There the Court of Chancery suffered from some of the same problems as its English model, but the application of remedies was easier for an English legislature. In the 1850s a new Court of Chancery Appeal was instituted in England and a similar one in Ireland. The discussion and implementation of these measures attracted more attention, and in 1859 a commission reported on duties in the Irish chancery. Two years later another commission was created to look at courts of common law and equity in both England and Ireland.[17] During the 1850s tentative steps were taken to move chancery and common law procedure closer together. In the Common Law Procedure Act of 1854, the limited use of injunctions was introduced in courts of law. In the Chancery Amendment Act of 1858, the awarding of damages in combination with injunctions was permitted. Such steps showed that the gap between the courts was being closed, however cautiously.

As of 1857, the old ecclesiastical jurisdictions in probate and in marriage and divorce were ended. New secular courts for those matters were established by statute. These laws "put an end to civilians as a separate branch of the legal profession." There was some continuity of personnel, of procedure, and of substance, but these separate bodies had been merged with common law courts, as a first step toward a larger combination.[18]

While there was some convergence, or at least cooperation in these structural areas, there were also procedural changes designed to improve the joint operation of the legal systems. In 1859 there were two acts of this kind. In April one act authorized taking evidence by commission from witnesses outside the jurisdiction of the court. The courts specifically empowered were "Her Majesty's superior Courts of Common Law at Westminster and in Dublin respectively, the Court of Session in Scotland, and any supreme court in any of Her Majesty's colonies or possessions abroad." The judges of the several jurisdictions were authorized "to frame such rules and orders as shall be necessary or proper for giving effect to the provisions of this act, and regulating the procedure under the same."[19] Later the same year another area of cooperation was opened. Courts in one dominion were allowed to remit a case for a legal opinion "on any point on which the law of such other part of Her Majesty's dominions is different from that in which the court is situate." These opinions were subject to review on appeal to the House of Lords. This was amended by the Foreign Law Ascertainment Act of 1861.[20]

A further step toward integration was taken in 1868 when Parliament passed "an act to render judgments or decreets obtained in certain courts in England, Scotland and Ireland respectively effectual in any other part of the United Kingdom." "Certain courts" meant the courts of common law in England and Ireland, but since fusion was anticipated, there was no intent to exclude equity from the comprehensive system.[21] All of these steps were useful, if small. One large area still was a source of difficulty, namely the old matter of appeals to the House of Lords. In 1856 a select committee was appointed to look into this matter yet again. The peers had virtually admitted that lay Lords should not vote in appeals, but in the 1850s there was a shortage of legally trained peers. When an attempt was made to create life peerages for lawyers, the house resisted. This forced the issue of appellate jurisdiction to be studied once more. The Select Committee proposed a more professional judiciary in the House of Lords, but those recommendations were not enacted.

By the 1860s there were several converging trends which seemed to shape a movement for more consolidated administration of justice. The differences between jurisdictions were still great, but there was a new openness and even eagerness to address these problems. James Paterson, a barrister of the Middle Temple, produced a topical work in 1860, which he called *A Compendium of English and Scotch Law stating their differences. With a dictionary of parallel terms and phrases*. In his preface, Paterson observed (pp. vii–viii):

> Each code speaking a barbarous language to the other—ignoring and being ignored—has groped its way alone... A common legislature, and in many respects a common supreme court have latterly, no doubt, confined them very much within the same channel. Yet notwithstanding many approximations, assimilations, and rounding of angularities, the law of the one country is still a sealed book to the other. England rather glories in her ignorance; and Scotland confidently rebukes this insular pride by counting over the adaptations from her own code, which have now and then been paraded by her neighbour under new names as original reforms.

Paterson offered a "key of intercommunication"—that is, a translation. In one sense this was an admission of defeat for assimilation. But in another sense, it was evidence of a step beyond some dreamy combination, in the direction of a practical method of harmonizing, which by definition meant preserving separation.

Still assimilation had some powerful advocates. John MacQueen was asked by Lord Westbury to study the subject of a digest of law, covering the several systems, in 1863. According to MacQueen, "much reflection and many conferences ensued." When MacQueen spoke to the Social Science Association in 1866, he advocated comprehensive digests, both English and Scottish.[22]

> To digest the law of England alone, without any reference to Scotland, would be a pretty sure way to widen the existing segregation; but to digest two systems harmoniously together, would be to realise quickly that amalgamation which was desiderated by Bacon at the union of the crowns and desiderated by Somers at the union of the kingdoms.
>
> I have not mentioned Ireland; but if my argument be correct, it must apply to the sister country, which cannot well be overlooked in a work essentially imperial.

MacQueen clearly was envisioning a code which comprehended both major systems; and he also saw no urgency to fit Ireland in. The imagination of some ran to such projects of assimilation, though the numbers of lawyers who supported them was small. Still, the vogue of consolidation rolled on.

It appears that the move for greater currency merged with the urge for digested law to help advance a consolidated structure of law publishing. Weekly reporting had been tried as early as 1844 (*Legal Chronicle*), and there were periodical issues in *The Law Digest Index to Reports and Statutes* in 1845 (n.s. 1846). E.B. Lovell edited the *Monthly Digest*, 1850–54; and the *Weekly Reporter Digest* appeared in the later years of the decade, 1853–59. Current digested reporting in Scotland and Ireland was somewhat slower to appear: the *Scottish Law Reporter Digest* began in 1863; Thomas Brunker's *Digest of Cases in the Superior and other Courts of Common Law and Admiralty* was printed in 1865; and Shaw's *Digest* was extended in 1869. William Green produced the *Digest of Irish Reports* in 1879. In 1870 R. A. Fisher had edited *A Digest of the Reported Cases in the House of Lords*, and the supplement for 1870–1880 added a selection of Irish Reports. This was taken over in 1880 by Chitty and Mews, whose pioneering effort was the *Digest of Decisions,* with all English and Irish courts. By this point, annual digests had become common and numerous. The modern era of reporting had arrived, and with it a new departure in consolidation.

It was in 1859 that structural consolidation got another push. A royal commission under Lord Coleridge was established "for providing sites for bringing together the superior courts of law and equity." Its report cited general support for "concentration" of the courts, laying stress particularly on physical location and increasing efficiency, as well as the by then evident trend toward fusion of law and equity. The Commission's report reviewed the project and discussed the concept of concentration, the possible sites for building, and the manner of funding. Proposals were made for the use of suitors' funds, the paradoxically named accounts which held vast sums from past litigation, which suitors had in fact lost, thanks to the malfunctions of the courts. A Treasury minute of 1864 estimated that £1 million of the cost of land and buildings, or about two-thirds of the total cost, could be provided from these funds. This time, after twenty years of committees and proposals, there was some concrete action: bills were introduced, and in 1865 there was legislation on the site and the building.[23]

Blueprints, 1865–1876

The foundation on which the Supreme Court was erected had many elements; consolidation of law in several forms; the fusion of English law with equity; the displacement of English ecclesiastical courts; and the linkage of English and Irish Chancery appeals. A number of reforms had made it easier for the courts to work together. How soon would the builders be able to construct a new central court? And what judicial blueprint would be provided by Parliament?

Although it had been discussed for twenty years, the Supreme Court still lacked a detailed plan. Some preliminary drawings were made during the discussion of site acquisition, 1861–65. But the final site selection, the choice of an architect, and the method of funding for the new law courts were outstanding public questions in the late

1860s. In order to choose a design, a royal commission was issued to the judges, law officers, members of government, and leaders of the architectural profession. This group conducted the competition that led eventually to the selection of G. E. Street as the architect. But his work was delayed while another select committee looked into disputes over the site. Then there was a flurry of pamphlet debate before construction began. The work dragged on through the decade, and Street died before the project was complete.[24]

There has been nothing but criticism for the competition which led to the selection of Street's design in 1866–68. The method of handling the competition was controversial. The jury had five members: two politicians, two lawyers, and the commissioner of works, to whom were added two architectural clerks later in the evaluation. After the public exhibition of rival designs, the jury could not reach a decision, so it proposed joint winners, Barry and Street, an impractical and highly unpopular decision.[25] While Parliament was reviewing the decision in May 1868, the treasury took charge and appointed Street. This touched off a Commons debate. At the same time, a select committee was examining the proposal of yet another site (the Thames Embankment), but it eventually endorsed the work in progress. After all this commotion, Street went to work and produced three new plans within a year of his selection. But his work was far from finished: final revisions were still being made in 1871. A public debate swirled around Street and his designs even as the site was cleared and excavation began in the spring of 1871. Meanwhile, in the area of judicial administration, the blueprint for the English Supreme Court was not much further along.

Walter Bagehot published his famous study of *The English Constitution* in 1867. He is often quoted on the subject of the judicature, although his qualifications in that area were not those of a specialist or a practitioner (p. 168):

> The supreme court of the English people ought to be a great conspicuous tribunal, ought to rule all other courts, ought to have no competitor, ought to bring our law into unity, ought not to be hidden under the robes of a legislative assembly.

In other words, the House of Lords should not be the highest court and there should be some august replacement. Bagehot's formula had literary quality but lacked legal clarity. Still he was in harmony with the legal reformers. The Queen's Speech in 1867 promised consolidation of probate, divorce, and admiralty, and examination of "the means of disposing" of the business of the common law courts. The plan became public with the issue of yet another royal commission in September 1867.

The commission was under the direction of Hugh Cairns, Belfast MP, recent attorney general, and future lord chancellor (1868, 1874–80). He was the first Irishman to head the English bar, and he was simultaneously head of the English judiciary. The commission's first report was published in March 1869 and recommended the consolidation of the high courts and the creation of a court of appeal. The Cairns Commission was paralleled by a new inquiry into the Scottish courts, this one under Duncan McNeill, just made the first Scottish law lord, with a life peerage as Baron Colonsay and Oronsay. The Colonsay Commission began fourteen months after Cairns, but its first report was issued at about the same time and consisted of minutes of evidence; in fact, its collected observations were not presented until July 1870.[26] According to its mandate, the Scottish inquiry was to examine the constitution and jurisdiction of all courts, the forms of writs and pleadings, rules of procedure, privileges of agents, "and also to inquire into the system of review of, and appeal from the decrees, interlocutors, and orders issued by these courts respectively." The Scottish commission issued five reports, between 1869 and 1871. The second report of the English commission only appeared in 1872, after a supplemental commission extended its authority to local courts. The third, fourth, and fifth reports were presented in 1874, after a second supplemental commission to study "tribunals of commerce."

With courts being designed and debates continuing over the new buildings, ministers did not wait for the end of the inquiries to begin the legislative process. In 1870 the government introduced bills to implement the major recommendations of the Cairns Commission: first an appellate jurisdiction bill to consolidate appeals by dropping the old exchequer chamber, abolishing the newer courts for chancery appeal and crown cases reserved and replacing them with a Court of Appeal with four special judges augmented by three high court judges. This measure kept the House of Lords as "the ultimate court of appeal." Next came a High Court of Justice Bill for "consolidation of all the superior courts of law and equity" to be called "Her Majesty's Supreme Court."

The thorniest question for legislators was the issue of the House of Lords' role as the final court of appeal. Any consolidation or reconstruction of the English high courts had to deal with what Bagehot called "the robes of a legislative assembly." And those robes were draped over English, Scottish, and Irish legal systems. By 1870 there had been considerable discussion of the peers' appellate role, and there was a consensus that a full-time professional group of judges was preferable to the traditional body. The senior judges who were peers were not always sufficiently numerous to do the job, and the house had resisted proposals to create life peers. Moreover, the work of the Judicial Committee of the Privy Council presented analogous problems of jurisdiction and staffing. Would a new, ultimate, professional court of appeal solve these problems?

Whatever sensible solution reformers might design, the political conditions of the early 1870s made it impossible to implement a new appellate system. Gladstone's Liberal government was losing its momentum by 1873, but the major obstacle to rational judicature reform was a matter of legal interaction. Ironically, debates over Scottish and Irish appeals created enough of a problem to delay and then to derail the creation of a novel court of appeal. A majority of MPs and peers, for varied reasons, wanted to retain the appellate role of the House of Lords. One part of the resistance was obviously from the conservative elements who revered the traditional constitution. The other main support was from those who were concerned about the future of Scottish and Irish appeals: either that they might have no higher jurisdiction, or that it might be a new English Court of Appeal quite distinct from the broadly constituted upper house.

The Judicature Act of 1873 was a close rendering of the report of the Cairns Commission of 1869, except in the matter of appeals. The commission envisioned appeals to the Lords only when leave was given, and it was assumed that that route would dry up over time; under the act a new Court of Appeal displaced the peers. Composed of nine appeal judges (plus *ex officio* judges) it would hear all English appeals; Scottish and Irish appeals were expected to be handled in those jurisdictions. As it happened, the ending of the Lords' jurisdiction went through easily. When Gladstone did propose sending all appeals to the new court, he aroused some Scottish and Irish opposition.[27] Therefore the Judicature Act as passed in 1873 did away with the House of Lords' jurisdiction in English appeals. It also made no provision for Scottish or Irish appeals. The appellate jurisdiction had not been carefully handled by the reformers. It exposed the new court to rearguard action, and some delays in implementing the judicature act allowed time for conservative forces to muster support for the Lords.[28]

In early 1874, Cairns was again lord chancellor in a new Tory government. He introduced a bill for the court of appeal which was to end Scottish and Irish appeals to the Lords, sending them to the new imperial Court of Appeal. That court would be made up of judges from the bench and bar of any of the three jurisdictions. The First Division of the Court of Appeal would hear Scottish and Irish appeals as well as rehearings of English cases in which the other divisions had not attained unanimity. In the next few months, Cairns seemed to be on the verge of success; but in July the Cabinet balked, and the bill was dropped. The effective date of the Judicature Act was put off for a year (until November 1875) pending resolution of the appeal issue.

At this point, agitation for retaining the Lords' jurisdiction was gaining momentum. Thus when the session of 1875 saw Cairns reintroduce the bill of 1874, it encountered much tougher opposition. A new bill was introduced in April, letting Scottish and Irish appeals remain unchanged and modifying the English provisions; this delayed the opening date until November 1876. Meanwhile the cabinet decided to retain the appeal to the Lords, but changes would be made: there would be more permanent sitting and there would be a committee of judges including members of the Scottish and Irish bar. With the appellate jurisdiction finally ironed out, the Supreme Court's blueprint was at last complete, in time for its "opening" date in November 1876. The buildings were still six years from completion, and there was still more legal construction to be done.

Construction, 1876–1882

The structure of the new Supreme Court was not complete in 1876, either physically or juristically. The building work continued until 1882. Meanwhile, the court itself wrote its rules and put final touches on the shape of its staff and structure.

The impact of the new Supreme Court at the center of the empire produced shock waves which in turn induced reaction elsewhere—in the abortive Canadian Supreme Court of 1876 and the more successful Irish Judicature Act of 1877. Finally, as the Supreme Court swung into action, there were other forms of consolidation made in the 1880s. The job of converting the high courts was a massive one. The work began as soon as the 1873 act passed, but its completion and implementation took several years. We can glance at some of the work done on personnel, rules of court, and appeals. A Legal Departments Commission was set up in 1873 to study the effects of the Judicature Act on court personnel, particularly to look at the issue of compensation, at the provisions for annuities, and at the possible employment of excess court personnel. The commission under Lord Lisgar made two reports, December 8, 1873, and July 30, 1874.[29]

In March of 1875, another committee was organized, under the master of the rolls, George Jessel, who was to be the presiding judge in the new Chancery Division. The "Departmental committee on the system upon which the legal business of the government is conducted" made three reports in 1875. The committee's task was to review the "solicitors' departments attached to public offices." It shied away from endorsing a treasury solicitor but proposed a virtual equivalent. In any event, it was definitely engaged in consolidating the legal staff of the government. The office of treasury solicitor was created by act.[30] This was one of many examples of how the business of judicial reform opened up new avenues of change; others happened in the extended probes of the Cairns Commission: the assize and local court examination and the extension into commercial courts pointed toward future reforms.

The judges were not immune from examination. In 1877 returns were ordered of "the number of days on which each of the judges of the supreme court of judicature sat, in court or in chambers, for the transaction of business." While the Home Office complained about the great difficulty of compiling figures where none had been kept, the resulting tabulation was fairly impressive in terms of sitting days. Study went ahead with a Judicature Acts (Legal Offices) Committee, which studied the treasury lords' queries about the arrangement and functioning of the Supreme Court, looking to some consolidation of offices, continuing the work begun by the Lisgar Commission. This effort was soon followed by the Central Office of the Supreme Court Act.[31]

The Rules of Court were rewritten and printed in 1873. Collected in some fifty-seven orders, these rules explained the new form of writs, rules for pleading, the use of district registries, and a wide range of procedural points. The rules were widely available in a very large number of private publications, copies of the acts with rules and/or relevant cases.[32] It is ironic that the most significant change affected English appeals. As many commentators noted, the act of 1876 gave a statutory right of appeal to the House of Lords in English cases for the first time. With Irish cases, the act of the next year recognized an existing appeal, and with Scotland, the right of appeal remained as it had been. The latter confirmations were of course what most participants desired; the real innovation was in the English sector. Now an English appeal stood on the same footing as its cousins; a look at the numbers of cases shows that a shift occurred in the late 1870s. As Stevens says, "Only after the passage of the Appellate Jurisdiction Act of 1876 did the House of Lords finally become primarily an English court," meaning that appeals from English jurisdictions, now being recognized on the same footing, began to outnumber both Scottish and Irish appeals combined. This paradoxical result was achieved in the same process that for the first time assured representation for Scotland and Ireland in the appellate court.[33]

The major overhaul of the English courts quite naturally suggested related changes in other dominions, especially those where a rough imitation of the English court structure was in place. In 1875 the government of Canada, with its newly contrived dominion status, proposed to establish a supreme court from which appeal could not be made to the Judicial Committee of the Privy Council. The famous clause 47 caused considerable opposition in London and the act was repealed. In 1877 the Irish courts were remodelled in the Judicature Act. This was not a simple imitation of the English reform. The successive reforms of the previous generation caused simplified business and declining incomes.[34]

> The combined effect of the Judicature (Ireland) Act 1877 and the County Courts (Ireland) Act 1877 was to sweep away 'a large amount of purely artificial business' and to direct work to the less expensive and more accessible county courts.

The Supreme Court in operation continued to invite further ideas for its reform and for its consolidation. So the old divisional structure, plainly adopted to ease the transition, became a target for simplification, and in 1880 the old common law divisions were merged into a new Queen's Bench division. The main judge in the Chancery division was the master of the rolls; he was removed as a divisional judge and placed as the senior judge in the Court of Appeal in 1881. Jessel continued to sit as the presiding judge in the Chancery division, but he was not replaced in that capacity after his death in 1883.

A general change affecting the lords justices of appeal was the adoption of life peerages in 1887. At the outset, they were "official" peers, which meant that their title terminated with their service. This rather niggardly provision was eventually removed, and the lords justices were elevated to life membership in the House of Lords. The 1876 act had also provided for four lords of appeal in ordinary; they were given life peerages from the outset, which was entirely appropriate as they were now the embodiment of the judicial function of the house.[35]

The establishment of the Lord Chancellor's Office in 1885 was another step toward consolidation. The chancellor's job had long been the subject of criticism: could it be split into political and judicial halves? could the administrative detail (justice of the peace appointments, church duties, ceremony) be separated from the elevated judicial place? Recognizing the enormous burden of his combined positions, a full-scale office staff was created, and the ungainly post of lord chancellor was left unchanged. There were a great many other consolidating measures which could be inserted here. The erection of the Supreme Court seems to have given the idea an official blessing. Consolidation came to mean something closer to code by the end of the nineteenth century. But one thing it did not mean was the merging of the structures of the legal systems. There were signs of consolidation of the laws, and there was surely closer cooperation than in the eighteenth century. But the work of Victorian consolidation was ultimately the rationalization of a large amount of English heritage.

Queen Victoria dedicated the Royal Courts of Justice on December 4, 1882. It was only months after the murders of English officials in Dublin's Phoenix Park, and in the midst of the "dynamiters'" campaign of terrorist bombings. Brownlee has a story about a Fenian enlisting in the honor guard which attended Her Majesty. But the ceremony went off without any disturbance. The Supreme Court judges marched from Westminster to their new quarters that morning, and the courts were declared open. The reformation of the English high courts was a highlight of the Gladstonian Liberal renovation of British government. Together with collateral political and institutional reforms, it should have braced the government for the rigors of a dawning democratic era. However, the legal changes and interactions prompted by democratic reform would severely test the capacity of any new Supreme Court.

Chapter 6

Law and Democracy 1880–1930

Judges and lawyers were content to have the new Supreme Court settlement be final. Legal changes in the next fifty or sixty years were typically the product of piecemeal adaptation or surrender. Some even called it an "age of stagnation."[1] However, ongoing changes in society at large would not permit true stagnation, and when the high court successfully resisted change, there was always a statutory escape route to extrajudicial safety in new tribunals. The age of democracy had begun, and no amount of hidebound judicial resistance would be able to stop it. The power of this change will be better understood when we look at the breadth of alterations. For democracy involved much more than political reform. Political democracy was not created in isolation. A vital context was provided by complex social and cultural change. Strong intellectual currents steered the thought patterns of a growing segment of society. Finally, the political process itself had many essential alterations beside expanding the right to vote.

The society we call "Victorian" vanished in this period. The forces that supported the Anglican church, the idea of individual responsibility, and the concept of a separate sphere for women all declined in influence, and each of these declines had important legal causes and consequences. The role of religion (and the Anglican establishment) had been paramount before 1880, but it had already come under pressure from several directions. Various surveys raised doubts about the extent of religious worship; internal stresses (heresy and other trials) showed a stern face of repression; a number of rival groups (especially the Salvation Army, founded in 1878) took a message of charity outside the walls of the traditional church; several campaigns undermined the edifice of Anglican authority (the parliamentary oath; admission to university; various charitable reform movements). As a final (legal) blow, a campaign for disestablishment was gaining strength at the end of the century. The Church of England and Ireland (Anglican) was disestablished in 1869; the Church of England in Wales in 1914.[2] Actually earlier steps had already taken away some of the established church's powers: monopoly on the certification of birth, death, and marriage; probate of wills; provision of education; and power of taxation (tithing) had all been reduced or removed by 1880. What was left was a more symbolic, though still privileged, position in government. The Church of England did not lose this status, and its bishops still sit in the House of Lords.

A second radical feature of the late nineteenth century was the confrontation between liberal individualism and collectivism, ideal and practical. At midcentury, the ideal held up for emulation was typified by Samuel Smiles's *Self-Help* (1859), a manual on the virtue and value of rugged individual enterprise. The message was echoed in sermons and government policies, but of course the early nineteenth century had seen numerous examples of collective action as well. The earliest (and most durable) was the Friendly Society, organized locally, chartered under statute, providing death benefits and mutual support for members. The more ambitious idea of a cooperative society for workers, for commerce and other benefits, was tested early, and by the later nineteenth century had grown into a large movement. Perhaps the best known form of cooperation was in the trade union. As noted already, this form was declared illegal in 1799 (Combination Act), but unions continued to form, and their legal status continued to be challenged and altered throughout the century. In the later decades employers found ways to challenge strike action in suits for damages, and with friendly judges they were in a position to bankrupt unions.[3]

The espousal of individualism was under further assault from a new generation of students of society, able to amass a large body of evidence to support its findings. Charles Booth collected seventeen volumes of information on *Life and Labour of the People of London* (1889–1903). Seebohm Rowntree produced *Poverty: A Study of Town Life* (1901) which examined the city of York. Both studies estimated that 30 per cent of the population lived in poverty. These and other works were not composed as political tracts, but they provided ammunition for activists like Sidney and Beatrice Webb, leaders of the Fabian Society, a group of intellectuals determined to influence leaders of government to institute social reforms. In the early years of the twentieth century a significant number of these reforms were enacted: free school meals, old age pensions, and a limited program of government-assisted health insurance were the first steps toward the welfare state. The social credo of Victorian liberals had been dealt a mortal blow.

The woman's place in Victorian society had been to occupy a "separate sphere" wherein she was responsible for hearth and home and bearing and raising children. The outside world was a place too rugged for her delicate condition, be it employment or public affairs. This mythic condition never existed for working-class women, and it barely applied to sisters in the classes above. As the century wore on, it was increasingly clear that the "ideal" so stated was a convenient tool to deny women greater ability to compete with men. The taboo was dismantled in the generations after 1880, by early legal battles, by the campaign for the vote, and by the massive impact of the Great War.

One of the early legal clashes in 1877 saw Charles Bradlaugh and Annie Besant on trial for publishing a pamphlet on contraception, and the sales of the pamphlet skyrocketed. A group called the Malthusian League followed up on this victory with mass distribution of other informational leaflets. An egregious example of the renowned double standard was in the Contagious Diseases Acts (1865–69), which allowed arrest, inspection, and detention of prostitutes in an effort to stamp out venereal disease. There was no punishment for the male customer. That fact probably contributed to a successful repeal campaign and to the passage of acts outlawing brothels (1885–86).

The campaign for women's suffrage lasted for two generations and was a remarkable turning point for women in public life. National organizations were formed in the later nineteenth century to promote the extension of the parliamentary franchise. Respectable advocacy gave way in the early years of the twentieth century to aggressive tactics, but neither was successful by 1914. At the war's end in 1918, the first breakthrough came with the granting of the vote to women over thirty years of age. This was, in fact, the start of gradual enfranchisement, completed finally in 1928. Here as elsewhere, the war, with its massive use of female labor and military auxiliary service, created a clear obligation on society to end the arbitrary exclusion of women. So also, in 1919 the Sex Disqualifications (Removal) Act abolished restrictions on women entering professions. The professions of barrister and solicitor were opened to women, the first of whom were admitted in 1922.

The advent of the democratic electorate is typically and properly measured by the number of voters. But it is well to observe that there were many other features of the political process which were changing even before the new voters were added to the rolls. These features also have a claim to consideration. Political campaigns, political organizations, the regulation and reporting of political activity, and the selection of political candidates were all changing in the period, and each had a part in the overall process. In 1879 Gladstone's notorious Midlothian campaign was a radical invention. Going to the people, making a speaking tour to arouse the electorate, was unseemly to many, particularly Tories. It was, however, forging an essential link in an emerging process. So, too, after the second reform act, was the work of Joseph Chamberlain and others in forming local constituency organizations. His famous Birmingham Caucus was a device to coordinate the votes of liberal supporters in the new, three-seat district created by the recent reform. Through this caucus it was possible to direct voters (who were so inclined) to support the party's several candidates in a more efficient manner. This was but one of many local organizing efforts. A more general change came in 1883 with the passage of a Corrupt Practices (Removal) Act. This law imposed restrictions on candidates' spending, which in turn made the candidate more amenable to direction by party organizations. Comparing the elections before and after the act, spending dropped about 60 per cent, and the frequent petitions claiming bribery at elections all but disappeared.

A close adjunct to political campaigning was the press. This was no novelty, but until the 1880s and 1890s, the press catered to a well-educated clientele, with relatively small circulations. In 1896 Alfred Harmsworth began publishing the *Daily Mail*, and in three years he reached a circulation of 540,000. That number was roughly equal to the circulation of all newspapers twenty-five years earlier. This paper was the first cheap daily directed at a working-class audience. Using a style suited to its readers, its stories were simpler and more vigorous. In 1903 Harmsworth inaugurated the *Daily Mirror*, the first morning daily, planned as a paper for women. The *Daily Express* was founded by Arthur Pearson in 1900 and the *Daily Herald*, a Labour party paper, in 1912. The latter two reached circulations of two million in the early 1930s. These outlets surely brought more political information and opinion to their readers; their net value to the political process is harder to determine, but certainly was important.

Candidates were, until the turn of the century, still mainly from the affluent upper ranks of society. The first worker MPs were miners elected in 1874; the first effective national figure was another miner,

Keir Hardie, elected for West Ham (London) in 1892, and later for Merthyr Tydfil (Wales) from 1900 to 1915. Members of Parliament were first paid a salary in 1911 (£400), but the key to unlocking nominations was in the formation of a workers' party. Labor candidates had been working under the aegis of the Liberal Party, for lack of another home. The Independent Labour Party, led by Hardie in 1893, was the first break from the old party structure. There followed a period of experimental collaboration with socialist groups (the Labour Representation Committee) which produced a real party presence by 1906, and a formal organization in 1918. Meanwhile the political party scene was being altered by growing division among Liberals (especially from the 1890s); the combination of some departing Liberals and old Tories to make up the Conservative and Unionist Party; and the continued strong showing of Irish nationalists (through 1918). The collected effect of all of these changes was reform of the electoral system which was independent of the size of the electorate.

Voters' Rights and Registration

The creation of electoral democracy occurred in the period 1880–1930. In simple terms, the portion of the adult population which could vote increased in that period from about 17 per cent to over 90 per cent. But equally important in terms of law, this change aided or reinforced a fundamental shift in legal perceptions. English lawyers did not (and do not) think in terms of abstract rights. But the campaign to assert a right to vote (actually an expanding cluster of rights) supported that new way of thinking. In turn, the germ of this new thinking spread to other areas, and the legal consequences, amid much legal interaction, were extensive and profound. The intrusion of rights (natural and positive) into English legal practice helped to undermine insularity and prepare for twentieth century openings. Our aim here is to learn what part legal interaction played in the achievement of electoral reform, and then to find out how interaction was involved in the expansion of other legal rights.

In the nineteenth century, voter franchises were seen by most politicians as a privilege, a concession from higher authority. Debates centered on whether certain people were "fit" to vote. A franchise was a kind of property and often had its roots in property. There was no single "right to vote," but rather a curious assortment of rights. This was why the uniform £10 franchise of 1832 was so important. It began the process of establishing a uniform right. The new franchise brought with it the voting register, and registration was the key to using the franchise. Registration was by no means uniform or simple. Indeed, the century of franchise reform after 1832 was also the century of unification for electoral law. At the outset, the scene was one of great variety.[4]

> For most of the nineteenth century the United Kingdom was neither administratively united nor politically integrated. Its actual, as distinct from supposed, condition was one of informal devolution. The legacy of different histories and a tenderness toward tradition combined to preserve that chaotic half-understood collection of national anomalies known as the Victorian electoral system.

With voter registration, the "national anomalies" were a source of comparison, dispute, and assimilation, until the 1914–18 war brought a simple uniformity with universal (male) suffrage. In one view, the older register kept voters out. It was [5]

> so replete with technicalities, complications and anomalies, that every obstacle is put in the way of getting on, and every facility exists for getting struck off, the register.

In another view, the register was used to give party agents ways to drag voters in. In any view, the years before 1918 were a busy time for revising barristers and all those attending the business of voter registration. And all parties were acting to verify the *right* of individuals to the franchise.

Electoral registers were revised differently in England, Scotland, and Ireland. In England (and Wales) the overseers of the poor prepared lists of ratepayers, and those lists were expected to indicate the persons who met the £10 qualification. The overseers were to present the list by a certain date; claims were to be made for additions, and objections presented to names already on the register for determination at a revising court.[6]

In Ireland in 1832, an assessment system replaced the voting certificates which had been issued since 1727. But in the circumstances it was impossible to achieve reliable assessments. In 1841 an inquiry was made, and in 1850 an Irish Franchise Act overhauled registration. An occupier franchise was introduced, using valuations from the newly instituted poor law administration. The voting lists were made up by clerks of the peace, and the chairman of the Court of Quarter Sessions was responsible for revision.[7] In Scotland, a much older system of assessment was in use; valuations were made and used for various local purposes. Revision courts were held by the sheriff (or sheriff-substitute). The period from 1860 to 1890 was an especially busy one for debate and action on the provisions for registration. This discusssion paralleled the active debate on the franchise and electoral practices in the period. There were separate measures for county registration: Scotland in 1862, Ireland in 1864, and England in 1865. These were followed by borough registration measures.[8]

With the extension of the electorate in 1867, there was more attention paid to registration. One effort proposed the combination of the register for municipal with that for parliamentary elections. This report called attention to the apparent superiority of the Scottish model of registration, noting that "objections and claims are of rare occurrence." The Committee proposed to "assimilate the English system to that which has acted so satisfactorily in Scotland." Alas, such a change would have required a major overhaul of English local government, so it was not attempted.[9]

In the 1870s, more major change was made, especially with the Ballot Act. This was accompanied by several registration measures (Registration [Ireland], 1873; Revising Barristers, 1873). Instead of settling questions and concerns about registration, there were growing inquiries into the varied aspects of voting, even as the momentum was building for the next great expansion of the franchise. The conjunction is not surprising: the piecemeal additions of ever-larger numbers of qualified voters was bound to produce growing anxiety about the way new voters would be certified as to their qualification.[10]

In the 1884–85 round of electoral reform, registration in counties and boroughs was "assimilated." The entire process was reviewed and reformed in a set of acts for England, Scotland, and Ireland. The results were not satisfactory, at least in the eyes of a reformer like Sir Charles Dilke:[11]

> In the case of registration reform the...potent obstructing force has been the conflict between London liberalism and the opinion of expert radicals in rural

> parishes under the usual English County Council. In London, all were willing to trust the county nominees to prepare the register. In Wales, the Liberals are willing to trust the counties, as in Scotland, but the Tories have their doubts. In the rural counties of England the more a Liberal knows about registration the more he fears to find the local Tory agent put in to supervise it officially for the county.

Divisions such as these were stumbling blocks to wider and more uniform improvement. Actually the statutes on electoral reform were becoming more uniform by the 1880s. Where there had been separate reform acts for England, Scotland, and Ireland in 1832 and 1867, the Ballot Act of 1872 addressed the United Kingdom as a whole and the reform acts of 1884 and 1885 were of the more general variety. The next major step came at the end of the war. In 1918 the revising barrister and his colleagues disappeared. Town and county clerks assumed the duties of registering the new and much more uniform electorate, under a general U.K. statute.

While separate English, Scottish, and Irish provisions were being replaced by general U.K. legislation, there was an increase in consolidated case law. The publication of registration cases and election manuals for lawyers was a busy field down to the war. But after 1918, and especially after 1929, the demand withered as the statute book recorded the last major stages of electoral reform.[12] Lawyers may have seen their election work decline between 1880 and 1930 but democracy brought more than enough added work in the newer democratized areas of legal action. The legal position of tenants, the right of injured workmen to compensation, and the status of women seeking divorce were just a few of the cases which were debated and acted upon in this new era of democracy. And in each of them there were significant forms of legal interaction.

Tenants' Rights and Land Purchase

The law of landlord and tenant was revolutionized between 1870 and 1914. The amazing series of legislative interventions, for Irish tenants (1870–1903), Scottish crofters (1886–1907), and English smallholders (1892) drew historians' attention particularly as a reflection of the expanded electorate:[13]

> As Britain moved inexorably in the direction of democracy, it invariably followed that the political parties would be obliged to woo the mass electorate and that administrations would be increasingly compelled to take the side of the tenant rather than the landlord, the crofter rather than the laird, the poor rather than the rich.

And observers expected communication within the British Isles: "Once the legitimacy of landed property was successfully challenged in one part of the kingdom, it was bound to be threatened elsewhere." But this type of argument glosses over the central legal issues which animated the struggles of the later nineteenth century. The rights of tenants in the land were at issue; economic pressures on landlords made concessions acceptable; and to a degree, there were signs of legal interaction throughout the land wars.[14]

The land reforms were an impressive collection of legislative interventions: they all asserted parliamentary power to remake the law, to revise the relation (customary or statutory) of landlord and tenant, and to establish courts or other means to enforce the changes. In sum, these acts were a major assault on the existing system of land law. In one view, the end result was what F. M. L. Thompson called "the liquidation of the landed interest."[15] Our main question is, to what extent was the renovation of the land law a product of legal interaction?

The foremost case comes from Ireland, where the debate over land reform goes on. Since the 1970s, the older views of landlordism have been modified, albeit slowly, and the scholarship in legal history has been part of the story.[16] From this point it was possible to move beyond the overly dramatized accounts of the "land war" and the depiction of all events in a context of violence and bloodshed.[17] One interactive illustration of the improvement was in the clearer understanding of "tenant right" in the careful analysis in Steele's *Irish Land and British Politics*. Steele removed the confusion caused by equation of the English concept (compensation for improvement) with the Irish version, a heritable interest in a tenancy and a marketable "goodwill" which the tenant could sell. That considerable asset was only very slowly accounted for in English legislation, though its real definition was understood as early as the Devon Commission, which inquired into Irish landholdings in 1845. The critical moment in this legal interaction was the conversion of Gladstone, upon reading a pamphlet by George

Campbell which argued that the clash "between two sets of laws" (Irish custom and English common law) was at the root of the issue. The prime minister recognized the "historical and traditional rights" of the Irish tenant, and with the Land Act of 1870, he began a process of accommodation.[18]

Unlike the Irish tenant, the Scottish crofter's status was a creation of the nineteenth century. To cope with the human residue of clearances, families were resettled on small properties. This resettlement infringed on a traditional right of occupancy, while it confined the crofter to a nonviable unit of land.[19] The crofter as a rule was not an aspiring owner, though he clearly desired a larger tenancy. According to one historian, "The Highlanders had no interest whatsoever in owning their holdings."[20] They sought lower rents and more secure tenancy on larger plots. In the economic distress of the early 1880s, they began to resist evictions and rent collections with physical force. Probably the Irish experience helped to gain the crofters an early government inquiry.

The action at the national level began with the Napier Commission in 1883, which investigated recent public protests of crofters. The crofters and their parliamentary allies (especially the Highland Land Law Reform Association) were interested in a reform like that of the Irish Land Act of 1881, which they did get in 1886. But as some pointed out at the time, this was not what they needed: the demand for larger landholdings had not been part of the Irish agenda. So the crofters' act was opposed by some of their most ardent champions. Just the same, it produced a commission which heard complaints and adjudicated rent disputes. Only later, at the turn of the century, did the government intervene to purchase land and lease it to the crofters.

The many varieties of land reform agitation in England after 1870 seem to have neutralized one another. From "free trade in land," to schemes of nationalization, to taxing unearned increments, there was an excess of remedies. Also after 1880 there was a serious decline in the earnings and hence land values in English agriculture. These conditions laid the groundwork for a sustained effort to promote smallholdings: its major milestones were acts giving authority for county council acquisition (1892) and more power to compel transfers (1907). A radical plan of Jesse Collings and Joseph Chamberlain in the 1880s promised that "three acres and a cow" would provide the means to resettle workers and repopulate rural areas. The idea now seems too naive for serious consideration. But it was part of the mosaic of cures prescribed for an unusual situation. After English agriculture had prospered from 1850 to 1875, much more difficult times ensued in some areas. The new circumstances were not the best in which to sort out the complex relations between landlord, tenant, and agricultural worker.

Landowning and tenancy in England were on very different terms from those of Ireland and Scotland. In the early 1870s the "new domesday" survey of landowners provided some useful data for contemporaries.[21] The basic numbers showed 166,000 landowners in England and Wales, 21,000 in Ireland, and 8,000 in Scotland. These represented one owner for every 130 persons, for every 257, and for every 400 respectively. Of course, ownership differed in kind and in quantity. The English owner, examined against European and other countries, was uniquely separated from farmers and laborers, principally because of the custom of primogeniture and the use of the strict settlement to perpetuate estates. These provisions were addressed in 1882 in the Settled Land Act. Heirs obtained the power to sell or mortgage their estates, powers which many would exercise in the turbulent economic times of the 1880s and 1890s.

The English tenant farmer, who typically did not own his land, was represented by the Farmers' Alliance, a group formed in 1879, primarily for electoral purposes. It drafted a Landlord and Tenant Bill in 1881 and helped to promote the interests of tenants, but it never attained the position of the equivalent interest groups in Ireland and Scotland. A form of English tenant right was provided on a voluntary basis in the Agricultural Holdings Act in 1875 and made mandatory in 1883.[22]

While the English scene did not have a major tenant reform, it did have a set of related reforms for occupiers of small properties. These consisted of laws which pertained to leaseholds, allotments, and smallholdings. In 1884 the Leaseholds Enfranchisement Association was founded: for holders of leases (mainly urban) they advocated easier methods to convert leasehold to freehold. This movement was only temporary.[23]

> It may be mere coincidence, but the enfranchisers largely fell silent when property values began to rise again in the 1890s. Although it raised a considerable stir in the 1880s, leasehold enfranchisement, like the analogous movements for allotments and smallholdings, could only tap a limited reservoir of discontent.

In 1892 an act for smallholdings made public acquisitions possible, but the powers of councils in this regime were limited, and the act was little used. In 1894 new powers were given to local governments to make allotments of pieces of land smaller than smallholdings, sometimes defined as nonsubsistence or supplemental plots. The smallholdings powers were broadened in 1907, but the total amounts of land involved were never very large.

The measures of public acquisition were paralleled by powerful economic forces which induced landlords to sell estates in the first quarter of the twentieth century. One author noted that the reforms prepared the country for "a hectic bout of postwar selling, a shift without parallel since the dissolution of the monasteries and the confiscations of the civil war."[24] It is clear that sale of land which was declining in value was a much more powerful engine of reform than all the legislative acts put together.

To what extent were English reforms inspired by Irish and Scottish acts? Politicians and popular organizations easily communicated and capitalized on the generality of tenant anger and landlord depression. Still the specific formulae had little to share across legal boundaries.[25] Irish tenant right was unlike the customs in England or Scotland, and though the variety was ignored in some legislation like the Crofters Act of 1886, it remained an obstacle. These differences are part of the reason Irish precedent failed to influence British land law reform. The massive state-aided land transfer in Ireland simply had no counterpart elsewhere. There were large private sales and modest state-aided voluntary transfers in Britain.

Workers' Rights and Compensation

The tort of negligence did not exist in English law at the beginning of the nineteenth century. At that point there was only a remedy for injury which was the result of a criminal act. In Scots law, there was an old concept of compensation ("assythment"). In the course of the nineteenth century, a concept of noncriminal responsibility developed in English law. That evolution was accelerated by industrial activity, and it was bound up with a fair amount of legal interaction.

Our story begins with a period of erratic reconciliation of English and Scottish concepts (1800–1880). This was followed by the introduction of workmen's compensation, a major manifestation of the influence of democracy on policy, by the Act of 1897. The awards under that law were made subject to appellate review, and the practice which thus blossomed (1898–1946) was a truly "U.K." legal phenomenon: appeals from English, Scottish, and Irish jurisdictions were freely cited by the courts and collectively reported in several series. This unique example of "assimilation" thus has a special interest for our study, even if its long-term significance was diminished by the termination of workmen's compensation when the welfare state introduced a statutory program of insurance for industrial injuries in 1946.

Given the common law's insistence that negligence must be criminal, coupled with the difficulty of choosing the correct form of action, it is not too surprising that the first record of a worker suing his employer is found as late as 1837 in the case of *Priestley v. Fowler.* On the other hand, in general liability, there was a long line of precedents in road accident cases, a series about to be mightily augmented by the railroad. As a matter of fact, Priestley was riding in the overloaded van of his employer, which overturned and caused his injury. Priestley had won an award of £100 at the Lincolnshire assizes, but in a hearing on arrest of judgment in the Court of Exchequer, Lord Abinger said, "If the master be liable to the servant in this action, the principle of that liability will be found to carry us to an alarming extent."[26]

While Lord Abinger conjured up a vision of unlimited liability and acts of negligence by servants, the next few years saw the English courts allow employers to defend themselves on the grounds of "common employment"—that one servant might be injured by the negligent act of the other without liability on the employer; or "contributory negligence," where the worker bore some part of the blame for his injury; or use of a prior waiver, called *volenti not fit injuria*, that is, that the worker assumed the risk in taking the job. It was interesting that in Scottish law in the same period, these principles were not observed, because they conflicted with the older concept of compensation and with some contemporary developments.[27] There were several times when the contrasting systems interacted. We may look closely at a pair of instances, to see the highlights of this complex process.

At the beginning of the nineteenth century, English law had no way to compensate victims of fatal accidents or even felonies. A felon's goods were forfeited to the Crown; and in wrongful death, the action died with the victim. In the famous case of *Baker v. Bolton* in 1808, Mrs. Baker died a month after injuries suffered in a coach accident, and the judge told the jury that they could only consider [28]

> the loss of his wife's society, and the distress of mind he had suffered on her account, from the time of the accident to the moment of her dissolution. In a civil court, the death of a human being could not be complained of as an injury.

There were and are questions about this decision, but it did embody the basic principle in force in the early nineteenth century. The reporter in the Baker case was John Campbell, the Scottish emigré, a graduate of St. Andrews who entered Lincoln's Inn and became a well-known barrister and judge. Campbell had not practiced in the courts of Scotland, but he was doubtless aware of the wide gap between English and Scottish laws for accident victims. In Scotland the old action for "assythment" gave victims or their relatives compensation; this was supplanted in the eighteenth century by the *actio injuriarum.* Campbell sponsored a bill to remedy the defect in English law, which said that "whereas no action at law is now maintainable against a person who by his wrongful act, neglect or default, may have caused the death of another person," that if the deceased would have been entitled to an action if alive, then his survivors might bring that action.[29] Ironically, Campbell's Act gave England a somewhat wider form of protection than that existing in Scotland, though courts in the North viewed the position of survivors more generously. The effect of the Fatal Accidents Act was limited. It was costly, uncertain, and for some occupations quite out of reach; but the change in principle was still important.

While this import seemed to have a Scottish label, the trade moved in both directions across the Tweed. We saw that Priestley failed to get a verdict in suing his employer in 1837; in a Scottish case in 1839, a quarry worker was injured in a blast and sued. The sheriff ruled for the owner, but the lords of session reversed because "the pursuer sustained the serious injury in question, through the culpable negligence or rashness of those for whom the defenders are responsible."[30] In an even more dramatic case in 1853, a worker named Reid was thrown from a pit cage when his co-worker failed to stop the engine. Reid was killed instantly after a 60-foot fall. His widow and children sought reparation, but the company's defense was that it was not liable because of the doctrine of common employment. The Court of Session unanimously agreed with Lord Deas:[31]

> I think the cases are conclusive. And whether the law of England would or would not except such a case as this from liability on the part of the master, the law of Scotland certainly does not.

The case was appealed to the House of Lords and decided in 1858 after some sharp disagreement between the respective law officers. Two years elapsed while Lord Chancellor Cranworth "took time to consider." When he stated his decision, it was a flat rejection of Scots law on the ground that there could be no difference between the law of England and Scotland! It seemed that the English bench was determined to impose its reading on the Scots.[32]

By 1880, there were signs of change in English law. In that year, Parliament passed the Employers' Liability Act. This was not a major turnaround, but there were limits placed on the defense of common employment in some very specific cases (negligence of supervisor or co-worker, or where the injury was direct result of rules or orders—or even of railroad signals). In court there was a similarly modest reversal of direction in 1883. A worker fell off scaffolding and sued the dock owner. He was cleared by Queen's Bench, but the Court of Appeal held the owner liable, even though he was not the employer of the injured worker.[33]

In the 1880s, with the widening franchise, more and more political attention was paid to workers' grievances, perhaps as part of what Joseph Chamberlain called the "ransom" being paid by property to keep its privileges. There were many measures considered in the 1880s and 1890s to meet the demands of workmen. They were, of course, in the process of organizing themselves in large industrial unions and political associations, and Parliament saw a number of bills on the subject. In a related area, there was the Fatal Accidents Inquiry (Scotland) Act in 1895, which created something like a coroner's inquest, to be conducted by the Sheriff Court, with a jury.[34]

As early as the debates on the 1880 act, a new idea had been mentioned: using insurance to cover injury awards and dispensing with litigation. This was added to a bill in 1893, and in 1897, under a

Conservative government, it became the centerpiece of a new departure, the Workmen's Compensation Act.[35] This law was applicable to the whole of the United Kingdom. No actual clause said this, but the conventional regional exclusions were omitted, and multiple definition was given—for example, to the term "dependent." The major innovation was "no fault" procedure. The only legal questions were related to deciding whether the worker was covered by the act, and as we shall see, these left large enough areas of debate.

In its original form, the Workmen's Compensation Act sent cases to county court judges, to be settled by arbitration. Few cases were expected to go further, since a fund for compensation was available, and insurance protected (and insulated) employers. Of course, insurers' legal points would need some forum. And an amendment to the act allowed appeals from these awards to courts of appeal. This set the stage for continued debate over the exact meaning of terms (what was an "accident"? when was one duly "employed"?). While comments have been made frequently about the massive number of cases, it seems that only a small percentage of the eligible claims went to arbitration, and perhaps "less than one per cent of cases in which compensation was payable resulted in litigation."[36] Of those few cases, a fraction (2 to 6 per cent) were appealed to the high court. It is impossible to say how significant these numbers were. What is clear is that these cases provided a new field, a new set of reports, a new line of work (or one radically altered)—and one which was strikingly new in its broad, intersystem coverage. A few sample cases can suggest the implications of this novel format.

One of the exercises in definition was deciding the meaning of "accident." There were ample opportunities to define the term. Lord Macnaghten called it "an unlooked-for mishap or untoward event which is not expected or designed."[37] Would this apply to the case of an undernourished worker who suffered heatstroke as a trimmer on a steamship? The Belfast County Court and the Court of Appeal in Ireland said yes. But in the Lords, the ruling was upheld, with Lord Macnaghten dissenting: "It was...just what anybody would have expected who saw the man and knew what a trimmer has to do," namely to work in the heat of a stokehole.[38] At another point, this case was interesting in that Lord Ashbourne cited the reasoning of a Scottish case (Lord Maclaren):[39]

> If a workman in the reasonable performance of his duties sustains a physiological injury as the result of the work he is engaged in, this is an accidental injury in the sense of the statute.

Many other questions arose which engaged varied legal principles. Widow Potts made a claim for child support under the act. Her husband had left her with four children, and she had won an action for aliment (legal award for maintenance) in 1909. He died as a result of an accident in 1911, and her claim was upheld in the Sheriff Court, but overturned by the Court of Session. Was the court competent to deny the award of an arbitrator? The House of Lords said no.[40]

Probably one of the most unusual cases under workmen's compensation was that of John Kelly. An assistant master at the Trim Industrial School, Kelly was attacked by a group of the schoolboys, struck on the head with a block of wood, and killed. The Irish County Court awarded his mother £100 compensation, and the award was upheld by the Court of Appeal. But the school district took the case to the House of Lords, where a lengthy debate ensued as to the possibility of an accident resulting from a deliberate assault.[41] "One view has been taken in England and Ireland and another in Scotland," but the latter was rejected.[42] Lord Shaw said that Macnaghten's famous definition had been "asserted over and over again in the courts of each of the three kingdoms." But he felt that definition was distorted; employment was the key, and that was a finding of fact by the lower court which bound all others. Lord Reading concluded the debate by arguing that injury from an unforeseen cause could readily (and "legally") come as the result of a deliberate act. A bare majority upheld the award.

The next year a case arose over the mysterious drowning of a ship's steward.[43] An arbitrator's findings were held incomplete by the Court of Session. On appeal to the House of Lords, an interesting debate followed on the process of treating arbitration. Lord Dunedin had stated a rule that the conclusion of an arbitrator should be "such as a reasonable man would reach."[44] But here, on the same ground, Lord Dunedin dissented. The Court of Session was reversed.

In one respect at least, the advent of workmen's compensation was not a success. The procedure had been expected to remove these cases from the courts and to establish an administrative procedure without long and complex and costly argument. Even though the raw number of cases was small, the potential for debating exact statutory definiton was great.

Whether that was due to loose drafting, or clever lawyering, the act opened the door to argument. But beyond that, it created a unique opportunity for interaction. Here was a piece of U.K. legislation, designed to assist the worker (and the employer) regardless of which legal system they lived in. A novel legal relation was created, without regard to separate legal traditions. Indeed, we can see how, in some of the arguments, a unified case law, with *dicta* and *ratio* from all corners, was being created. This experiment in United Kingdom case law would come to an early end, as in 1946 the welfare state superseded workmen's compensation with national insurance. And that, in turn, was a further step in the direction which was taken at the end of the nineteenth century—toward meeting the demands of an enfranchised but legally unprotected segment of society.

Women's Rights and the Law of Divorce

The law of divorce was vastly different across the United Kingdom, and those differences were instrumental in the reforms between 1857 and 1937. In that same period, women's suffrage was grudgingly granted, a parallel which may explain some of the delays in finally conceding legal equality to women. The first breakthrough in divorce reform came with the Divorce Act of 1857; the next major stage was reached in the Married Women's Property Act of 1882; and the final stage came between the Gorrell Commission (1912) and Herbert's Act (1937). At each stage there was important legal interaction which helped to determine the direction of reform.[45]

After the Reformation, divorce was not recognized in English law, as it was elsewhere in Europe. A marriage could be put aside on grounds of nullity (incest, lunacy, bigamy, abduction) or it could be suspended by separation (from bed and board, *a mensa et thoro*) with a bond not to remarry. The latter was confined to cases of adultery and it was administered in the courts of the Anglican Church. Near the end of the seventeenth century, Acts of Parliament came into use as instruments of divorce *a vinculo* (i.e. final decrees) and the same practice applied to Ireland, though it was rarely used. In all of these instances, the woman was technically able to sue, but in the latter two the cases were rare. On the other hand, a Scotsman could obtain a divorce *a vinculo matrimonii* from a church court, on grounds of adultery. A Scotswoman could apply for a divorce on the same ground. And the Scottish Commissary Court could grant a divorce on the ground of desertion after four years (Act of 1573). By the nineteenth century, the English divorce involved a decree of separation from the church court, a common law case against the adulterer (for "criminal conversation"), and then a private act of Parliament. This was the route taken by about 200 Englishmen, between 1680 and 1800. Needless to say, the majority of failed marriages were treated in extralegal if still effective ways. For women, the obstacle course was even less inviting than for men. The first female applicant for a parliamentary divorce was recorded in 1801, and there were only four in all in the first half of the nineteenth century.

At the beginning of the century, a series of cases drew the attention of lawyers and legislators to the contrasts between Scottish and English laws of marriage and divorce. A key question was whether a Scottish dissolution could apply to an English marriage. In the course of resolving this, the lawyers got a chance to debate and determine which marriages were in fact English, and which of those were (or were not) within the jurisdiction of Scots law. This theme was persistent and pervasive. Modern authors have noticed it and given some attention to Anglo-Scottish variation.[46] But none of them allows the contrasts a key role. Yet the prominence of Scots lawyers and civilians,[47] plus the ubiquitous and well-known distinctions, make this a vital backdrop (if not blueprint) for the discussion of reform.

In the first quarter of the nineteenth century, there were quite a few circumstances which might have contributed to cases that mixed English and Scottish divorce law, aside from the essential presence of spouses from each jurisdiction. There was accelerating migration between the countries of England and Scotland and within the empire generally; one of the legal consequences had been a growing debate on several fronts over the law of domicile; finally, wartime circumstances (until 1815) certainly help to explain the trend, if only in their role of promoting impulsive marriages. The case of Elizabeth (Utterton) Teush illustrated some of the legal differences. She was married to Frederick Teush in 1790. He lived in open adultery from 1796, and she sought a decree of separation while she repeatedly sued for support. She then sought a parliamentary divorce and it was denied in 1805. At this point, the husband went to Scotland and was sued in a (collusive?) bill to the

Commissary Court of Edinburgh. The judges there found that he had not established a domicile and refused to revoke the English marriage. But on appeal, the Court of Session remitted the case and a new hearing led to a divorce *a vinculo*.[48]

This case was followed by a number of others. Indeed, James Fergusson, one of the Commissaries, was moved to produce a set of reports because he saw[49]

> an alarming collision between the respective judicatories of the two countries...which equally affects the sister kingdom of Ireland and all the other British dominions.

The court had previously made no distinction between Scots and "foreigners," but the "alarming increase" of the latter "led the commissaries in the year 1811, upon the first case now reported [Teush]...to attempt a more deliberate mode of investigation."

The concern south of the border was much the same. In two cases, English courts rejected Scottish dissolutions of English marriages. In 1812, Lolly was charged with bigamy. He had married in England, moved to Edinburgh, and there was divorced on a charge of adultery. He returned to England, remarried, and was tried and convicted for bigamy because his Scottish divorce was invalid. He spent some time in the hulks before he received a pardon.[50]

In 1813 a Scotsman (Lindsay) who married an Englishwoman (Tovey) in Gibraltar, was sued twice for divorce—for adultery in England and in Scotland. There were many points of dispute in the case, but Mrs. Lindsay died and the case was dropped.[51] But before long, there were enough cases for Fergusson to print a second edition in 1823. In this version, he featured five cases from the years 1814 to 1816, and he added thirty-five more from earlier periods in an appendix, cases he found in manuscript. Four of the principal cases involved parties married in England, of whom three were granted Scottish divorces on appeal to the Court of Session. The commissaries were not pleased, and Commissary Gordon said in 1815 that he disagreed with decisions to follow Scots law "in these English cases," but he was happy in the knowledge that he was supported by "the infinitely higher authority" of the twelve English judges and the lord chancellor.[52]

We may assume that the "infinitely higher" English authorities felt the same. But they made no headway. In 1823 the jurisdiction of the inferior commissary courts was transferred (except Edinburgh) to sheriff courts. But in 1827 the notorious case of Ellen Turner (the unhappy bride of the English colonial reformer Edward Wakefield) brought more attention to Scottish marriage, as it was terminated by a parliamentary divorce. In 1829 a motion was made in the House of Commons for a return of Scottish divorces for adultery in the Commissary Court of Edinburgh for the years 1822–1829. According to the return, the average was less than twenty-one per year, but in the English climate (about eight parliamentary divorces per year) that number may have seemed large.[53] This information was evidently part of the case made to merge the last of the commissary courts into the Court of Session in 1830, along with the Jury Court and Admiralty Court. But reforming the court structure in Scotland did not deal with the questions raised in legal interaction. The first important step came with English judicial acceptance of the validity of Scottish divorce.

The breakthrough occurred in the case of *Warrender v. Warrender* in 1834. Warrender was a Scot who married Anne Boscawen, an Englishwoman, in 1810. They executed a deed of separation in 1819. She went to France, he returned to Scotland. In 1834, he sued for divorce on grounds of her adultery. Henry Brougham (now lord chancellor) made an ambitious judgment. It hinged on the domicile of the wife following that of the husband. In that case, the two must have had a Scottish marriage, and thus a Scottish divorce was valid. The case of Lolly was distinguished (those parties had not intended their marriage to be valid in Scotland), and finally in a bizarre twist, Brougham argued that since English courts allowed the validity of Scottish ("Gretna Green") irregular marriages, they could hardly reject Scottish divorce.[54]

> But we have it now firmly established as the law of the land, and daily acted upon by persons of every condition, that, though the law of England incapacitates parties from contracting marriage here, they may go for a few minutes to the Scotch border, and be married as effectually as if they had no incapacity whatever in their own country.

Not only that, these same parties on return could have the aid of English law

> in securing the enjoyment of all the rights incident to the married state. Surely there is neither sense nor consistency in complaining of the risk, infraction or evasion arising to the English law from supporting Scotch divorces, after

> having thus given to the Scotch marriages the power of eluding, and breaking and defying that law for so many years.

In the 1840s the subject attracted widespread professional interest, as Brougham seemed to have lifted a sort of taboo. In legal literature, Leonard Shelford wrote his *Practical Treatise on the Law of Marriage and Divorce* in 1841. In this he included sections on Scotland and Ireland. He recognized that "the canon law is the basis of the laws of marriage throughout Europe" and was still effective in Scotland. On the other hand, Ireland was still under the law "which prevailed in England before...1753." Shelford disguised any reformist impulses he may have had, but he made clear the thinking since Warrender, discussing marriage as a branch of contract. "A man who contracts in a country, engages for a competent knowledge of the law of contracts in that country" and thus was obliged to observe local laws (pp. 85–88).

In 1842 John Fraser MacQueen, former writer to the signet and now Chancery practitioner, produced a major treatise on the Lords' appellate jurisdiction, to which he appended the first major study of parliamentary divorce.[55] MacQueen gave a detailed description of the acts for divorce, and he showed a detailed knowledge of Scots law, which he discussed intermittently and by way of comparison. He noted the equal standing of women in Scottish cases, and he lamely added that it was "merely a matter of accident" that no wife had applied for an English parliamentary divorce before 1801.

In 1846 Patrick Fraser published his first work on Scottish domestic relations, including a section on husband and wife. He became the leading authority on this field, his work later being expanded and subdivided into three treatises; he also was a keen observer of the *Conflict of Laws in Cases of Divorce* (1860). The 1840s also saw stirrings of political and legislative action. After the judicial alteration, further collection of data and further committee work examined the state of marriage laws. In 1842 there was a flurry of interest in Irish divorce. In a pair of cases which were widely reported, the discrepancies of Irish practice were highlighted. The discussion led to overhaul of Irish marriage in 1844.[56]

A Royal Commission was formed in 1847 to examine the prohibited degrees of affinity, especially in "marriages solemnized abroad or in the British Colonies." At the same time a Select Committee was set up to review "the state of the law of Scotland as regards the constitution of marriage." The fifteen MPs were predominantly Scots and included the lord advocate and solicitor general. They made no recommendations, merely directing the chair to print evidence. The "evidence" consisted of statements by Brougham, Campbell, and Lushington. There had been some debate about other evidence, but on a split vote they only considered "legal authorities upon the present law." Brougham wanted tougher requirements because Scottish marriages were too easy to perform and too hard to prove in a court of law. Out of the committee came a bill to amend the Scots law of marriage which provided a 14-day waiting period.[57]

The rising interest, both academic and legal, merged around 1850 with a church-state showdown and a surge of interest in women's rights. The result was a Royal Commission on Divorce chaired by Lord Campbell. The commission did not recommend any major change in English law, but it did propose removal of matrimonial causes from the ecclesiastical courts. The commission heard ample testimony from Scottish witnesses, including the lord advocate.[58] Scotland's transfer of jurisdiction was now twenty years old, but indeed was much older than that, given the Court of Session's old appellate power. Several bills were introduced, first to shift divorce to Chancery, then to the Privy Council.

Finally, a new English Divorce Court was created by the Divorce Act of 1857. The charade of parliamentary divorce and the legal process of "crim. con." were ended, and divorce was to be adjudicated in a single process. Women were given access, and the promise of security of property for separated wives. The terms for a wife to sue were still unequal (adultery aggravated by cruelty or incest or bestiality). Nevertheless, the new access proved immediately successful, for in the first year there were 340 petitions, of which 97 were from women.[59]

The Divorce Court brought several Scottish equivalents into English law.[60] By eliminating parliamentary divorce and shifting to a secular court, the new jurisdiction came close to that of the Court of Session. The admission of women petitioners was not yet as equitable as in Scotland, but there was a start. And as Stone said, the debates on the act did help to set an agenda[61]

> for the changing attitudes towards divorce for the next century right up to 1960. In the course of the debate, suggestions were made which were not to become law for another eighty years—for example, about extending the cause of

> divorce to include desertion [as in Scotland], and about setting up cheap, local divorce courts.

However, the act probably seemed to some contemporaries, as it does to modern feminists, a cramped, male-oriented effort, making as few concessions as possible and keeping women in a subordinate place. The property sections, in particular, reflected an ambivalence still deeply rooted in social and legal attitudes, however strongly some men spoke for the equality of women. This awkward stance was soon challenged.

The next phase of development saw the focus shift to married women's property rights. The common law idea of "coverture"—that a woman on marriage was subsumed in the legal personality of the husband—had to be breached before there could be any idea of equality for women. A married woman in England could not own property or make contracts or otherwise have an independent economic existence. In 1856–57, the property issue was raised when divorce was under discussion, and a bill to reform this aspect was introduced but failed. The idea of the married woman possessing and controlling property within a marriage was too radical for the 1850s.

In Scotland, the basic principle of male control was the same, but the Scottish wife had more leverage. She might have a separate estate or heritable estate and/or paraphernalia (personal belongings) over which her husband had a limited *jus administrationis*.[62] The other property of the couple was subject to his *jus mariti*, a legal power like that of the English husband. Finally, the wife enjoyed *jus relictae*, rights after death or dissolution as the surviving spouse. These distinct and durable legal rights became more important in the 1860s, both as subjects of a series of legislative changes for Scotswomen, and as a model for their sisters, whose organizing and agitating was on the rise after 1860.

When after considerable debate a Conjugal Rights (Scotland) Act passed in 1861, it marked an important advance in several areas, and it could have been a road map for English women.[63] The act said that if a wife succeeded to property, the husband could not claim it unless he made a reasonable provision for her maintenance. If she were deserted or separated, the property became hers.[64] The act simplified the process for proving desertion (the action could be raised at the end of four years' absence without the preliminaries previously required). There were also provisions allowing various third parties to appear and testify.[65]

While this progress was being made, elsewhere the variation of marriage laws was still being seen and treated as an "evil," and in 1866 a new Royal Commission was created to inquire into "the state and operation of the various laws in force in the United Kingdom with respect to the constitution and proof of contract of marriages."[66] Lord Chancellor Chelmsford (Frederick Thesiger) sent circulars to bishops and others, and this way a large amount of "evidence" was collected on the cheap. One section of the report was devoted to the discussion of the "desirableness of uniformity in the marriage laws of the United Kingdom," but no one volunteered to revise the laws of a particular system. This example underscored a sense of the discrepancies, and a general notion that "uniformity" (an unfortunate choice of words) would somehow be better than variety. But if there was to be convergence, it would not come through this commission. It was more likely to come piecemeal, from acts pressed on the legislature by reformers.

Advances in the condition of the English married woman vis à vis property began in the 1870s. A series of acts began to realize the goals first put forward by Caroline Norton and Barbara Leigh-Smith. They both helped to bring about the legislation (1870–1882) which started to give married women justice in their property relations. Meanwhile, concurrent changes in the structure of the courts might have had some influence: the reform of judicature which was a de facto merger of common law and equity (with priority given to equity rules wherever there were differences) might have been a factor in tilting the balance toward recognizing women's property rights.[67] In 1870 a diluted measure passed, giving slight improvement regarding "separate property."[68] An amendment came in 1874 (the "creditors' bill") which tried to sort out legal status with regard to indebtedness. But these measures were not wholly sympathetic, and as Shanley points out, they coincided (negatively) with the first efforts to gain the franchise in parliamentary elections.

It was perhaps the contemporary land agitation which helped property legislation over the hump in 1882. Separate Scottish and English bills were introduced in 1881. The English bill extended the equity concept of "separate property" to married women generally. The Scottish measure, on the other hand, followed a series of earlier acts.[69] In other words, the legislature had been busily trying to settle Scottish law in this area, and would have to continue to update it in the future. What the statute book shows, among other things, is that there seemed to be access (for Scots) to legislative alteration, and attention paid to the increasing influence of this issue.

The cause of women in divorce made significant strides in the twenty-five years between the Divorce Act of 1857 and the position in the Married Women's Property Act in 1882. But the law was still tilted against women, and there was one more major difference between English and Scottish law which would be at the center of the next phase of reform. Since the sixteenth century, Scots law had recognized that a husband who deserted the matrimonial home effectively destroyed the marriage.[70] It was clear that desertion was ground for a decree *a vinculo,* and even an offer to restore, after four years' time, was held unacceptable in the early nineteenth century.[71] Ireland presented still another prospect. There, where full divorce was anathema, either in the Roman Catholic or the Anglican church, there was no comparable reform in the nineteenth century. Even the Act of 1857 failed to reach Ireland. But a custom of informal separation was evidently widespread.[72]

The issue of divorce, in the context of laws in the British Isles, was a matter of great interest. In 1888, Harry Quilter, a barrister, edited a selection from 2,000 letters sent to the *Daily Telegraph* on the questions of marriage law.[73] The writers from all parts of the country gave their views, generally unflattering, of English laws of marriage. The low opinion was not confined to the general public. In fact the English divorce *a mensa et thoro*, or legal separation, was attacked in 1912 by the majority report of a royal commission as[74]

> one of the most corrupting devices ever imposed by serious natures on blindness and credulity. It was tolerated only because men believed, as a part of their religion, that dissolution would be an offence against God.... As the fruits of compromise we have this ill-begotten monster of divorce *a mensa et thoro*, made up of pious doctrine and worldly stupidity...an unnatural and unsatisfactory remedy.

This law of separation was blocking the rational treatment of deserted wives in England. And from the 1880s, there were signs that various forms of mistreatment were being addressed by the lawmakers: in 1878 the Matrimonial Causes Act extended provision for separation as a result of abuse; in 1886 there was maintenance for deserted wives; in 1895 there was some addition to summary jurisdiction on cases involving married women.[75]

In 1892 an explicit attempt was made to use Scottish law as precedent for change. W. A. Hunter, MP for Aberdeen, moved for a bill to assimilate Scottish and English law on divorce (as to desertion and as to similar process for adultery of husband or wife). The opposition of the attorney general helped to defeat this measure.[76] This attempt was not followed up for a decade, but the idea was not lost. In the Divorce Court, John Gorrell Barnes (appointed in 1892, president, 1905–09) was aware of these discrepancies. The partially reformed English law was now its own worst enemy, for it invited further change, and offered little or no ground for defense. The Scottish example was brought forward often as a critical comparison, and cases and acts of the new century seemed to push toward resolution.

Barnes was elevated to the peerage as Lord Gorrell in 1909; the same year he was made the chair of a Royal Commission on Divorce and Matrimonial Causes. In its report, the commission gave full consideration to the regional variety in the British Isles and elsewhere.[77] The recommendations included granting wives the same [Scottish] grounds as husbands (adultery without compound offence), plus the new [Scottish] ground of desertion for a period of three years. The commission also proposed expanding access via regional divorce courts. These proposals were sufficiently provocative to cause a minority of the commission to report against them, and the divided result was enough to stall any immediate action. The war deferred it further, but that same event soon stimulated attention with the cascade of marital difficulties it produced. The rate of divorce jumped by a factor of six between 1913 and 1921.[78] Lord Buckmaster's private bill (his second attempt) in 1920 proposed the allowance of desertion as a ground, but the bill failed.

In 1921, another bill (by the son of Lord Gorrell, who had died in 1913) was attempted and failed; but in 1923 an "equal adultery" bill passed. The interwar years saw further weakening of resistance (decline of church authority, rise of women and suffrage, new social attitudes). After the 1923 act, there were many "hotel bill cases" in which a husband's adultery was proven by simply presenting incriminating receipts. These brought the same derision as the old collusive actions, and helped to clear the way for reform. Also by 1925, progress was being made in reform of access, with the new Poor Person's Rules extended to include divorce cases.

In 1937, a private bill brought in by A.P. Herbert finally gained the adoption of the 1912 recommendations. Herbert was a barrister and author of the novel *Holy Deadlock* (1937). His bill added the ground of desertion (and cruelty, habitual drunkenness, and incurable insanity), which became available only after five years of marriage.[79] The debates were lengthy and the opposition was in disarray, though notably the measure still had to be a private bill. The Scottish example was cited, but it was not a major theme of the debates; indeed, it was hardly necessary to belabor this contrast after so much exposure.[80]

Thus on the eve of the Second World War the law of divorce finally stood on an even footing in England and Scotland. Meanwhile, in Ireland, the years 1920 to 1939 saw a stiffening of the position against divorce. The last imperial measure was a marriage act in 1918. After the Anglo-Irish Treaty, the issue of divorce was not even allowed free discussion. Bills for parliamentary divorce were ruled out of order in 1925.[81] In 1937, just as the English law was being "liberated," the Irish ban on divorce was written into the new republican constitution (Article 41.3). Indissoluble marriage, long a reality in Irish society, was now a fundamental law in the Republic, but not in the North.

Marital breakdown and inevitable separation had been treated with very different legal and social solutions. Scotland adhered to canon law after the sixteenth century. Ireland evolved a marital pattern which discouraged legal separation in favor of an "informal" variety. The English form of legal separation was devised as a way of deflecting divorce. It receded, slowly at first, and then rapidly after the First World War. The Scottish model was an irresistible comparison, strengthened by the coincidence of enfranchised women and secularized society.

The lawyers in an emerging democracy had to work with new clients in changing contexts. The tenants, workers, and women they met were by and large new to the formal work of the law, and their counsel were likewise testing a new environment. Rules were being rewritten, courts were being created and modified. At the same time, the politics of the period saw national revivals and imperial crises. The sequel to universal suffrage was a radically altered society and legal system, or systems. They cohabited in a constitutional framework which their Victorian forebears would barely recognize. The late Victorian image of the constitution was indeed one which soon lost its link to reality. The uprooting of that image was the next important step in the history of legal interaction.

Chapter 7

Law and the Constitution 1900–1950

Queen Victoria's Diamond Jubilee in 1897 was a massive display of imperial power. The naval review, in the channel off the Isle of Wight, mustered ships in a column formation thirty miles long; troops from all continents paraded in London, in what the *Daily Mail* called "a living gazeteer of the British Empire." Fifty years after the Diamond Jubilee, the British government was hastily withdrawing from India. The British military was rapidly demobilizing after the second world war in twenty years had drained the treasury. And in domestic affairs a socialist government was implementing a revolutionary agenda of social legislation rather than maintaining the vestiges of empire. In order to understand these dramatic changes, we need to review the outline of events between 1900 and 1950, prior to our detailed study of the developing constitution. For it was the rapid pace of events which made constitutional formulation a hazardous exercise.

British intervention in the Boer Republics in South Africa followed hard on the heels of the Jubilee, and it showed a very different aspect of the empire. The Boer War (1899–1902) saw British and colonial forces conquer two small colonial states (Transvaal and Orange Free State). They only did so after embarrassing losses and blunders (including the use of concentration camps for settlers' families). This situation exposed Britain to general European hostility. The boast of the government had been its policy of "splendid isolation"—that is, that British power was too great to require an alliance, and that power would be used to tilt the European balance as and when it was necessary. Soon after the war, and out of fear of German naval rivalry, Britain began to increase its diplomatic engagement, first with an alliance with Japan (1902) and later with an entente with France (1904) and with Russia (1907). In this loose fashion, the British Empire entered the alliance "system" as an opponent of the Triple Alliance of Germany, Austria-Hungary and Italy. The empire was not as powerful as the show in 1897 seemed to indicate; or else its managers had lost their nerve.

The atmosphere of domestic affairs would account for some loss of confidence. In the period before 1914 there were numerous conflicts, and the disputes they generated found only fitful aid from the ordinary courts of law. Party political battles were increasingly bitter, and acts or threats of violence became a common tool of strikers, suffragettes, and Ulster unionists. In 1906 the Liberal Party won a landslide victory after two decades of Conservative domination. Part of the success came from collaboration with candidates of the emerging Labour Party. The two had agreed to avoid direct contests in many constituencies, and that helped a number on each side to defeat Tory opponents. Most workers' candidates formerly had run under the Liberal banner, and so the electoral bargain was also a sign of the growing independence of the new party.

A Labour Representation Committee had been formed in 1900 to act as liaison between the trade unions and socialist political organizations. One of the main concerns was to defend union strike activity against the hostile rulings of the courts, which had accepted the argument that unions could be sued for damages incurred during strikes—a clear threat to any hope of solvency on their part. The Liberal government passed a Trades Disputes Act which gave unions immunity from such damage suits. But in another field, the law was used to threaten the continued growth of the Labour Party. The House of Lords (in its appellate capacity) ruled in 1909 that the compulsory dues of trade unions could not be used for political purposes. If implemented, this spelled the doom of a workers' political party.

Having already obstructed a large number of the government's measures, the House of Lords used its legislative power to veto the 1909 budget, which included increased death duties and progressive rates of income tax. The Lords had rarely tried to veto a financial measure since the seventeenth century, and this crisis was a serious threat to the conventional relation between the two houses. Prime Minister Herbert Asquith brought in a bill to reform the Lords and deprive it of an effective veto. After two elections and months of debate, the Parliament Act of 1911 passed. It denied the Lords any power to vote down a money bill; if other bills passed three consecutive sessions in the Commons, they became law; and the time between elections was reduced from seven years to five.

To pass the Parliament Act, Asquith needed the support of the Irish Nationalists in Parliament. Their price for this support was the introduction of another Home Rule bill for Ireland in 1912. Knowing that this would become law in 1914, Ulster unionists recruited units of volunteers and collected arms. Large meetings were held where supporters swore oaths to support an "Ulster Covenant." The former English solicitor general, Sir Edward Carson, was one of the leaders of this movement. There was also strong support from Tory leaders and army officers. This activity, with its tinge of sedition, brought no legal action, even after a number of army officers resigned rather than lead their regiments into Ulster to enforce Home Rule.

The prewar years saw some important legal changes, alas few of them instigated by the officers of the law. The use of tribunals and boards of arbitration increased steadily. Where the system set up for workmen's compensation had faltered, new arrangements were made in 1908 for old age pensions (local authority committees, appeal to the Local Government Board). For claims under national insurance (1911) the Friendly Societies were employed, appeals going to national Insurance Commissioners. For unemployment claims under the same law there were three levels: an insurance officer, a court of referees, and (at the national level) an umpire. Tribunals continued to multiply, indicating both a degree of failure in the traditional courts and a sign of the flexibility of the politico-judicial system in the United Kingdom.

Britain did not have a clear objective for fighting the Great War which began in 1914. With a halfhearted commitment to France, and a traditional desire to keep the coastline opposite Britain in friendly hands, the German invasion of neutral Belgium was the principal excuse for declaring war on the Triple Alliance. The expected short war turned into a nightmare of trenches, barbed wire, artillery, and machine guns. In the end, British (and Irish) losses numbered 700,000 lives and 1,700,000 wounded. The dominions had participated willingly, and India, Australia, New Zealand, Canada, and South Africa sent nearly 3 million to join the 5.7 million troops from the United Kingdom. At first these troops were all volunteers, but after years of terrible losses, the British government decided to impose conscription in 1916. Most of the dominion governments balked at this requirement. Their losses in the end totalled over 200,000 dead and 420,000 wounded.

The legal impact of war was very significant, but it needs to be seen in context. There were very important changes in public order law in the last quarter of the nineteenth century, changes which prepared the ground for the rapid alteration of the war years. The Fenian outrages of the 1860s saw last use of a traditional tool: the suspension of *habeas corpus* (last used in England in 1818) was enacted for Ireland in 1867–69. The purpose, as always, was to allow arrest and detention (internment) of suspected traitors, without the troublesome safeguards of the Habeas Corpus Act. In 1871 a turning point was reached with an act known as the Westmeath Act, which prohibited the use of the writ, but created the power to intern suspects temporarily (34 & 35 Vict c. 25). In the next decade, an explosive substances act was prompted by the "Dynamite War"—a campaign of terrorist bombing. Other threats of foreign and internal subversion prompted developments in the areas of secret service, regulation of aliens, official secrets, and martial law in the decades before 1914. Thus it was easier, when war was declared, to accept the Defence of the Realm Act. This law gave the authorities sweeping powers over the civilian population and over the physical resources of the nation. The act was to be implemented under regulations made by the ministers of the Crown, enforceable at first by courts-martial. Jury trial was restored in 1915, but ordinary courts were augmented at different stages of the war by new tribunals, for munitions workers, for veterans, and for relatives of deceased soldiers. Probably the most profound legal impact of the war came through the Representation of the People Act of 1918. Universal male suffrage and the vote for women over 30 pushed the electorate from about 7.5 million to nearly 20 million, the largest single reform of its kind. This was a harbinger of the powerful momentum which the war and its brutal cost brought to domestic political and legal issues.

The complex questions of postwar settlement were dealt with by the Paris Peace Conference of 1919. The reward for dominion support in the war was to be included as participants in the conference and as members of the League of Nations. The idea of collective security, that the international body would adjudicate disputes and members would enforce its judgments, appealed to most member states, at least in the abstract. But the League never had the consistent participation, the widespread support, and the effective sanctions it would have needed. But most important of all, the corollary to collective security had been a call for general disarmament. The conference to achieve this was only organized in 1926 and convened in 1932. Meanwhile some naval disarmament had been accomplished, but by the 1930s there were several powers intent on rearming.

The domestic issues of the postwar period had very significant legal impact. There was a sense of entitlement like that behind the electoral reform of 1918. But this positive trend was paralleled by some disturbing signs of unrest. Demobilization was a primary concern, and in 1919 and 1920 the economy showed positive signs. A number of programs for reconstruction had been planned, for housing and education and unemployment. But when the economy showed signs of weakness in 1921, many promised programs fell by the wayside. More serious matters had to do with two hostile opponents of the government: labor militants and Irish republicans. The former were headed by an extreme group in Glasgow: many thought that the Clydeside labor group was affiliated with the Communist Party, and the official action, including the calling of troops, was excessive if understandable. In the case of Ireland, there was clear revolutionary potential. The Easter Rebellion of 1916, a small movement easily put down, was followed by stiff punishments which made the victims martyrs. When conscription was adopted in 1918, there was further resentment. The general election at the end of the year produced a majority for Sinn Fein, the nationalist republican party. Those who won refused to go to Westminster, stayed in Dublin, and formed the Dail Eireann, the provisional government of an Irish republic. Two years of civil war followed, and a treaty in 1921 led to the creation of the Irish Free State. This was a new government for the twenty-six counties of southern, Roman Catholic Ireland. Meanwhile, the North (Ulster) had accepted a Parliament provided by the Government of Ireland Act of 1920, thus effectively dividing Ireland.

The 1920s brought a new age of legal regulation in peacetime. In 1920 the Emergency Powers Act provided for special authority, like that of the war period, to deal with political emergencies like a general strike. Such an event occurred in 1926, after a prolonged period in which the government had tried to extricate itself from wartime subsidies and other regulations, particularly for the operation of the coal industry. At the same time, the legal powers of the government were extending into new areas such as electricity supply and radio broadcasting.

During the Great Depression (1931–1935) there were profoundly important events with legal significance. First, on the national level, when the Labour cabinet would not accept budget cuts, its leader Ramsay

MacDonald resigned and then resumed office at the head of a coalition. His unprecedented act alienated his entire party and reshaped the politics of the 1930s. Those same budget proposals included cuts in judges' salaries. The judges, however, insisted on maintaining what many others thought were very generous incomes, seeming to be uninterested in joining the efforts to bring national recovery. The recovery efforts had other connections with legal problems. Perhaps the most signfiicant was judicial obstruction of some welfare legislation, in spite of the traditional stance taken by judges against "lawmaking." On another front, the continued growth of arbitration procedures was the subject of a study by the Peel Commission in 1934.

But the most important activity of the 1930s was well outside the realm of the judges. The process of collective security under the League of Nations had faltered, as had the process of international disarmament. With the rise of dictators in Germany, Italy, and Japan, Britain and others were faced with a novel threat to peace. The response was one of piecemeal rearmament and diplomatic appeasement. Unfortunately, that formula was no deterrent to further aggression. The hostilities which became World War II began in the Far East with Japan's invasion of China in 1937. Hitler's invasion of Poland in 1939 opened the fighting in Europe. In this case, both Ireland (the South now a self-declared republic) and India (its independence promised but grudgingly stalled) decided to remain neutral. The old dominions joined the contest, albeit reluctantly. Equally serious was the anticolonial mood which had spread through the empire from the 1920s. India, Egypt, and African and Asian colonies all experienced a rising sense of their own capacity to govern, a feeling which British soldiers and administrators seemed unable to understand. In one dimension, the British export of law had invariably become a tool of liberation.

In the Second World War there was another episode of emergency powers, this time more extensive and better prepared. When war was declared in 1939 there was a "War Book," a set of bills immediately enacted which had provisions like those of the last war. There was another plan for internment of suspicious persons; there were laws for censorship; there were numerous manpower provisions, and of course all of the rationing and other controls perfected in the earlier war. The war itself was slow to reach the British Isles, but by May 1940, Germany invaded and quickly defeated France. Within weeks the Battle of Britain began with heavy German aerial bombardment. Combined with intensive submarine warfare, the prospects were bleak. British resistance held up for a year, and in 1941 first the Soviet Union and then the United States were attacked and forced into alliance with the United Kingdom. It took four years of campaigning to defeat German and Japanese forces.

The aftermath of the Second World War brought some profound legal developments. In international affairs the establishment of the United Nations and a number of specialized international bodies was predicated on the acceptance of general principles of international law, some of them laid down in instruments like the Atlantic Charter, drawn up by Winston Churchill and Franklin Roosevelt in 1941. Domestically, the decisive Labour victory in the election of 1945 set the stage for the establishment of the welfare state and the nationalization of industry. All of the programs and measures involved had significant legal dimensions. Although there was no question of resisting or challenging the power of Parliament to enact such programs, the national health service, national insurance, and nationally owned mines, railroads, and utilities necessarily required a long list of legal adjustments.

One task was not necessary in 1945. There was no need to rewrite any provisions of the constitution. There was no written constitution. That was unchanged from earlier times. In fact, lawyers, judges, and scholars regarded earlier written formulae on the constitution as being still sound and accurate. But the events we have retraced here had in reality rendered the older definitions obsolete.

The Victorian Canon

The nineteenth century constitution had been delineated in an outpouring of historical and interpretive literature between 1870 and 1900. The resulting canon prevailed well into the twentieth century. But serious reappraisal is necessary if we want to understand twentieth century legal interaction. Even as the old interpretation was being composed, the seeds of three major constitutional revolutions were being sown. Those revolutions, separately and collectively, put legal interaction on an entirely new footing by 1950. In brief, they forced English law and the English legal system on the defensive for the first time.

The first revolution was a fundamental internal shift of power to the executive or ministerial part of government. The supreme power of statute, in the control of ministers, was used to delegate the authority to make rules, to hear petitions, and to judge complaints. This innovation seemed to infringe upon the place and power of the courts of law, but its real significance was the creation of a whole new system of interactive administrative tribunals.

The second revolution was the radical change in the constitution of the United Kingdom. Irish Home Rule was stalled long enough to force rebellion. The republican resistance to British rule and Ulster's defiant unionism produced two new Irish legal systems after 1920. Thus a reformed United Kingdom was forced into some very new directions in legal interaction with Ireland.

The third alteration saw power in the imperial legal system dissolve or disperse. While these experiences were unlike Irish separation, the severely truncated imperial legal authority and the new judicial autonomy within the commonwealth helped to form a new English (British) position in international law by 1950. The three revolutions altered the place and power of the English judiciary: it lost a chance to play a major role in the modern state, it accepted written constitutions for a partitioned Ireland, and it surrendered the last of its dwindling direct legal powers over the empire. The change in the constitutional position of the English legal system disposed it toward practical accommodation, in spite of canonical insularity.

In the last half of the reign of Queen Victoria, there was a burst of writing about the unwritten English constitution.[1] These works are hard to classify, for each had elements of history, politics, and law in different combinations. Our primary concern is with their treatment of the law. As all the writers acknowledged (or boasted), there was no written "law" of the constitution. Convention and custom were preeminent. But the English high courts had just been redesigned by statute in the 1870s and the next generation would bring still more definition. Thus we have a central paradox: at the very time that a canon of constitutional interpretation was being asserted, the courts of law were being molded by novel influences. This may help to explain why the position of the courts in the constitution was not addressed fully or effectively by the constitutional writers in this period. Holdsworth's history was unique in reaching 1875 (but his detailed volumes on the nineteenth century appeared after 1950); modern authors were absorbed with politics (parties, elections, and ministers); jurists like Dicey were overtaken by current affairs even before 1914 (e.g., Irish Home Rule). These writers had another difficulty. They were only interested in the "English" constitution, a reasonable aim for the medievalist, but less so for the modern author.[2]

The canon is commonly described (or denounced) by recent authors in terms of the work of Albert Venn Dicey.[3] While he was certainly one of the foremost figures, it is misleading to personify and simplify in this way. The canon fused long-standing ideas shared by many interpreters. The major tenets were:

> 1. an act of Parliament is the supreme law of the land and may not be superseded by any court;
>
> 2. the ministers of the Crown are responsible to Parliament and may be held accountable by the people's representatives;
>
> 3. no subject may be punished by a court without a hearing; all subjects have equal standing at law; and
>
> 4. the independent judiciary guards and pronounces the law.

Even as a statement of the English constitution, these terms were no longer adequate by 1885, and they were hopelessly outdated by 1914. But as H. J. Hanham observed,[4]

> the events of the 1880s undermined the foundations of classical Whig theory. Liberal intellectuals continued to talk the language of the Whig constitution down to 1914, but there were no new Whig theorists after 1885.

Their theory was overtaken by changes in government, which we may recount under the tenets enumerated above. As to the power of statutes, there was a reformation which followed the midcentury commissions: consolidation or revision (repeal of useless statutes); publication of new collections; and the beginning of an authorized annual series (1887). Even more important from a judicial point of view, there was a collateral effort to standardize the language of statute law. A parliamentary draftsman was appointed in 1869, and within the next decade two major works were published on statutory interpretation.[5] At the same time, the courts were expounding the basic principle of parliamentary sovereignty, so they were sure to welcome assistance in this critical area.[6] The most authoritative guidance came in 1889, with the passage of the Interpretation Act. This listed a large number of standard terms and their definitions, laying down exact meanings for statutory language for the first time in general form.[7]

Beyond formal legislation, this period saw the rapid growth of delegated legislation: the supreme Parliament endowing ministers with quasi-legislative power.[8] This touched the first two tenets cited above, and it particularly affected the work of the legal system. Much nineteenth century legislation involved rule-making, and it was at this point that that process began to be standardized, much as the writing of statutes had been. In 1893 the Rules Publication Act was passed. This act provided guidelines for public notification of rules. In 1896 a collection of statutory rules and orders was published for the first time, beginning a rapidly expanding sector of legal documentation, one which is now designated "statutory instruments."[9] This was a major extension of the power of ministers as agents of the supreme Parliament, far beyond what was envisioned in the Whig constitution.

But the change did not end there. In some areas, especially commerce, the courts had not been efficient. Litigants therefore sought other solutions like arbitration. A recent historian has shown the significant extent of this activity before 1870.[10] But the courts of law showed a marked aversion to engaging in the new work, as manifest in the episode of early railroad regulation. Judges abdicated in this area of legal work, and Parliament was left to find other solutions. In 1873 a Railways Commission was established to settle disputes in that area. In 1888 this was converted into the Railways and Canals Commission, with a high court judge, recognized as a court of record.[11] Meanwhile in 1883 the Patents and Designs Act replaced the legal authority of the law officers of the Crown with the Comptroller General of Patents and an appeal tribunal.[12] In the next decade, the Merchant Shipping Act of 1894 provided for Board of Trade Inquiries.[13] With these new legislative ventures, there were numerous questions raised as to the courts' powers to review the acts of tribunals. Under the Patent Act, a Court of Session ruling in 1894 held that the Board of Trade had acted *ultra vires*, but this was reversed by the House of Lords, ruling that some delegated legislation was exempt from judicial review. That issue was to remain a continuing subject of litigation.

The English courts were also engaged in a different kind of delegation. In 1895 the High Court established a "Commercial List," a special sitting of a single judge in London to expedite commercial cases. This became known as the Commercial Court, but it was a unique accommodation of new legal business.[14] The significance of these actions was in the *ad hoc* variation of the relations between the ordinary courts and the ministers of the Crown. The strategy was not yet general. The Commercial Court was the best example of adjustment, but it did not establish a new pattern. When Parliament enacted workmen's compensation in 1897, it tried to involve the ordinary courts in a limited way. But the courts displayed their penchant for technicality and vitiated the simplified process for injured workers. Thereafter, as we noted already, Parliament was inclined to bypass the courts in projects like pensions and health and unemployment insurance.[15]

When we consider the second tenet of the Victorian canon, we must pay special attention to the prinicipal "legal" minister, the lord chancellor.[16] His position was unusual. One of the oldest servants of the Crown, the most senior judge (although his court was the youngest), he was a political servant who took office when cabinets changed. Yet he had no department like other ministers, at least not until the 1880s. Then the offices of Principal Secretary and Clerk of the Crown in Chancery were combined. Kenneth Muir Mackenzie assumed the new post in 1885 at the head of what came to be called the "Lord Chancellor's Office," later the Lord Chancellor's Department.[17] There was more to this process than merely consolidating the massive patronage work, though that in itself would conceivably have significant indirect impact on the judicial workload.

Beside the Chancellor's Office, other departmental changes occurred, but reform met with great resistance, especially because there was a strong English bias against a minister of justice along continental lines. Thus when the director of public prosecution was established in 1879 in response to lengthy agitation against England's tradition of private prosecutors, the office was starved of funds and only gained importance slowly. Criminal administration was historically under the home secretary, and this tradition stalled any major move toward public prosecution until 1985.

The third tenet, that the law was the guardian of liberty, was also challenged. Liberty was always hostage to security. When Parliament perceived danger, it assumed what came to be called "emergency powers." The dangers of the 1880s included Fenians, dynamiters, land leaguers, and crofters. Responses included the formation of the Special (Irish) Branch by 1883, which was transformed into the Special Branch by 1886. For foreign dangers, the first Official Secrets Act was passed in 1889. These fears (plus threats from organized labor and organized women) were shared by the judicial establishment. The only significant positive change in this area was the creation of the (English) Court of Criminal Appeal in 1907.[18]

The final tenet of the canon, that of judicial independence, requires a careful assessment. While there were no direct attacks on the judiciary, there were very important changes in their situation and operation which might have had subtle effects on their sense of independence. The foundation of judicial independence was laid at the end of the seventeenth century, when it was enacted that judges were to enjoy their office during good behavior, rather than at royal pleasure. They could only be removed from office by an address of both houses of Parliament (a step taken but once, in the case of the Irish judge Jonah Barrington, in 1833). Beside this, in the Act of Settlement (1701), judicial salaries were made a part of the consolidated fund, and as such, they were not subject to annual review by the House of Commons. It was interesting that the lord chancellor's salary (or the £6,000 which was paid him as head of the Court of Chancery) was only given this protection in 1869. His salary as the speaker of the House of Lords (£4,000) was not protected. But by the 1870s, even after years of intense criticism of the legal structure, there was no danger of political tampering with judges. This was not to say that their political views had no bearing on their appointments.

There were other, more subtle influences on judicial work, whose total impact has never been assessed. In 1870 the Incorporated Council of Law Reporting created the (unofficially) coordinated system of law reporting. This step (duplicated in Ireland) was a very important one in updating and standardizing case law, possibly a conscious parallel to what was happening with statutes. Qualified reporters, working with the same general guidelines, were employed in preparing a reliable and consistent record of case law.[19]

After the judicature act and the appellate jurisdiction act, peerages were given to those sitting as law lords in both the Privy Council and House of Lords. The peerages must have given added security to their holders, though at first they were only in effect while the holder was in office; later they became life peerages.[20] The rules of the Supreme Court gave some added form to the position and the place of the judges, and indeed, this put them in the special category of government officers who made their own rules. The Supreme Court's Rules Committee consisted of judges and practitioners. By 1925, when the committee laid rules before Parliament, they became statutory instruments.[21]

Altogether, our review of the last years of the nineteenth century suggests that no canon could accurately describe the English (or British) constitution at the beginning of the twentieth century. As Geoffrey Elton said of Maitland's posthumous *Constitutional History*:"Splendid lectures though they must have been to hear [in 1887], they embodied a state of learning already out of date at the time of publication [1908],"[22] for of course no one, not even the "sainted Maitland" was able to write the history of an evolving constitution. And evolution was going to turn into revolution in several quarters in the early twentieth century.

"New Despotism"

The title of Chief Justice Hewart's book in 1929 was inaccurate.[23] Nevertheless, he was not mistaken, at least not from the standpoint of the place of the courts in the old Whig constitution. But as we have seen, that structure had begun to decay before 1914. The Parliament Act of 1911 was the most important constitutional change in the twentieth century, for it gave the House of Commons by statute a precedence which it had exercised by custom since the seventeenth century. What effect if any did this have on the judiciary? Two points may be made: in the immediate political context, the act magnified the sole remaining power, that of the highest appellate court (even though it was now exercised by a committee of professional judges); but in the longer term, that legal authority would be hard to translate into effective constitutional authority. And that truth would be made even clearer in the short term by world events.

In the Great War, the judicial transformation was carried further. The emergency powers taken by government were a drastic affirmation of the long-term trend. Many, but not all, of these powers were surrendered after the armistice, but still the growth of ministerial authority continued. "By 1920...the judges had been removed, had removed themselves or had been restrained from entering large areas of competence of the modern state."[24]

The effect on the judicial system which Hewart saw in the interwar years may be described under several functional headings: power to make rules and orders; power to make judgments; and power to appeal or review judgments. The sum total of the changes in these areas added up to a revolution in terms of the constitution. It was no despotism, but it was a significant transfer of traditional judicial power to ministers of the Crown. Whatever the safeguards, they too were mainly beyond the control of courts of law.[25]

Making rules and orders was already a well-established function of ministers.[26] The ministerial acts of the Great War, acts which drew upon the reservoir of power created by the Defence of the Realm Acts (DORA), were a further source of alteration. In quantity, the change seemed dramatic but short-lived: Allen listed an average of 1,349 orders annually (1901–1913), rising to 1,459 in the war and to 2,275 for the years 1919–1921, before returning to about 1,500 for the interwar years.[27] But quantity was less important than content. DORA provided special powers to assure "public safety and the defence of the realm." But what might come under this umbrella? First, there were effective powers under some laws already on the books. For instance, railroad controls were implemented under Acts of 1871 and 1896. Further, the government was able to enact new laws like the Munitions of War Act (1915), which banned strikes, took control of some factories, and set up tribunals. But in large areas outside specific wartime needs, there was a wide space for ministerial ingenuity. Cecil Carr wondered in 1921:[28]

> Who could have foreseen at the beginning that the Defence of the Realm Regulations would have embraced the acquisition of factories, the appropriation of materials, such as hay, wool or flax, the control of food supply and food production, the disposal of securities, the felling of timber, and the taking over of mines, railways, shipping and the liquor industry? Who would have guessed that those regulations would be extended to prohibit the holding of dog-shows, the sale of opium or the whistling for cabs in London,—all in the

name of the defence of the realm?....The greater the emergency, the wider the delegation of legislative power, and the more incomplete the statute book.

Rules would be a much less significant ministerial power if they had to be enforced by the ordinary courts. But the administrative tribunal solved that problem.[29] There is a consensus that the extrajudicial requirement was appreciated by 1908–1911, and varied methods were tried. Unemployment courts of referees were most innovative. Local pension committees and appeal tribunals were multiplied in the war. Industrial courts (1919) probably followed the experience of munitions tribunals in the war.[30] Postwar problems invited further experiments, with Scottish pioneering in rent tribunals, and other efforts in agriculture. Studies of tribunals seldom examine the U.K. aspect. There were some significant differences in Irish and Scottish cases, but the field has barely been explored.[31] In Scotland there was a long history of the Court of Session's involvement in supervising various administrative bodies. Many tribunals were merged with or overseen by the ordinary courts. New tribunals probably entered this system on a very different footing.[32] Irish tribunals, on the other hand, grew up in the climate of emergency laws and colonial rule, which had to color their evolution.

The final function we must look at is the right or power of the ordinary courts to review or hear appeals from administrative tribunals. There was and is a power to review and adjudicate an issue in which a tribunal has acted illegally. But the ordinary courts did not often become involved in the work of tribunals.[33] By and large, the tribunals continued their work without infringing on court jurisdiction for two reasons: (1) their own areas of jurisdiction were created by the authority of statute; and (2) those fields were specialized, and thus there was no appropriate ordinary court to deal with the issues.

The tribunals were a part of the larger issue of the organization of government which was taken up before the end of the war. In 1917, Lloyd George appointed Lord Haldane to head a committee on reconstruction, looking at "the machinery of government," and Heuston was moved to say that "for the first time, the extraordinary artifact of the English Constitution was subjected to logical analysis."[34] However, Haldane's report called for a ministry of justice, and it was shelved. It is doubtful that the changes proposed would have radically altered the history of administrative law, for in the matter of tribunals, the report was silent, spending more time on proposed shifts of power between the lord chancellor and the home secretary. Still a new tradition of studies of government was begun, which one must say appeared to be designed to alleviate the pressure periodically built up by angry judges. Certainly that was the cause of the next committee, which followed Hewart's outburst. The Donoughmore "Committee on Ministers' Powers" was also ignored. Allen says the report "passed quietly into the oblivion which is the fate of so many reports." The system of tribunals continued to grow. By the 1950s, there were about fifty permanent tribunals, and they were subjected in 1955–57 to another study and the predictable inaction.[35]

The first half of the twentieth century experienced an administrative and a judicial revolution: special courts were added to ordinary courts. The resolution of the boundary disputes was unlikely as long as tribunals continued to increase and diversify. The Donoughmore and Franks inquiries may have misunderstood the main question (what was the place of these novel units of government?) because of lingering Hewart-like assumptions. But the major point is now clear. The administrative tribunals constitute an entirely new judicial system to complement the modern structures of social service. The advent of this administrative revolution was especially difficult in the context of English law (at least for English judges). Modern administration came to Scotland and Ireland by different routes. And while the impacts were different, the general application of the new system meant a new dimension of assimilation, beside the older legal systems. For many of the tribunals were joined to the modern provisions for all subjects in the United Kingdom. Thus tribunals had to be instituted in England, Scotland, and Ireland, much as the arrangements for workmen's compensation had been. Even if the new tribunals brought no new accumulation of U.K. case law, there was widely shared innovation in judicial systems. But for Ireland, new courts were an old subject.

Irish Separation

The legal constitution of the United Kingdom was severely tested in Ireland. The creation of new court systems for the Free State and the North (plus an abortive all-Ireland structure) were the products of the period of upheaval from 1919–1922. The impact of these changes may have been tempered by the history of legal innovation in Ireland. For a century the Irish had been given frequent emergency laws, constant experimentation with police agencies, and regular overhaul of criminal statutes.[36] The creation of two "home rule" legal systems was probably a welcome respite.

The critical background to this episode of legal interaction was in the last decade of British rule in Ireland. In that period, a crisis occurred which effectively tied the government's hands in all later dealings with Ireland. For the explosion of Unionist resistance (1911–14) fatally divided British and Irish leaders, raised the specter of civil war, and simultaneously posed the dilemma of military justice. Who would coerce Ulster into accepting home rule? Who would impose any longer delay on the South? At bottom, the questions were constitutional and legal in the most fundamental way.

The Parliament Act of 1911 was passed with the support of Irish Nationalists. The Liberal government was obliged to press on with another home rule bill. But under the new law, Tory opponents knew that the Lords could only delay the measure for two years. There began an extraordinary story of Unionist organization, led by the onetime English solicitor-general, the Irish-born Sir Edward Carson. Oath-taking, recruiting, drilling, and gunrunning were all on the agenda, and all were tolerated by the London government.[37] Of course equivalent actions were taken in the southern counties. By the spring of 1914 there were two armed camps in Ireland, and it was at this point that army officers stationed near Dublin declined to enforce the expected act. The standoff was overtaken by the outbreak of war in Europe in August, at which time the parties agreed to suspend the home rule measure for the duration of the war. But much more important for the legal future was the implementation of the Defence of the Realm Acts in all of the United Kingdom. As Charles Townshend pointed out:[38]

> The transformation of the minimal state through organizational problems like conscription and munitions production has commanded much attention. Less spectacularly, but perhaps more permanently, its legal structure was modified by the final appearance of a new type of emergency law. The Defence of the Realm Acts brought the United Kingdom under a statutory form of martial law, a form that was—even after Lord Parmoor's amendment in 1915—a marked redirection of English legal tradition.

The acceptance of this change was surely prompted by the war in Europe, and made tolerable by the short war most people expected in

August 1914. But just as surely, the tension and the confusion of the Irish crisis had prepared the ground by exposing the unsettled state of the law and the lack of adequate power (not to mention political will) to enforce the law.

While being a part of the inspiration for DORA, Ireland would also be the scene of the only major application of martial law during the war. The lord lieutenant's proclamation of April 25, 1916, put all of Ireland under martial law for one month, and General Maxwell was dispatched from London to take command in Dublin.[39] It remains unclear what added value the proclamation had when DORA was already in place. In fact many officials were unable to separate the two. The well-known immediate impact of martial law was the execution of fifteen leading rebels after secret military trials. Far worse were the deaths of Francis Sheehy-Skeffington and other civilians at the hands of British soldiers. These irresponsible actions discredited British rule and martial law, and they were instrumental in mobilizing political separatism.[40]

By 1918 further events completely undermined British control, after which the issue of martial law was almost irrelevant. The London government imposed a conscription law which, while never enforced, served as a final goad to the Irish electorate; the proclaiming of "special military areas" gave the authorities a little more power at the expense of general alienation. The result was clear by December, when the general election gave Sinn Fein candidates a commanding seventy-three seats in Parliament. Their decision to remain in Dublin and establish a revolutionary government in 1919 began a new stage of the drama. The Sinn Fein MPs met in Dublin in January to establish the *Dail Eireann*. They created a *de facto* republic alongside the Dublin Castle regime. This meant two things: a new separatist legal regime was developing in the South, while a new unionist legal regime was developing in the North. But for the moment, the law was martial in a different, revolutionary sense. Until the truce of July 1921, the Irish secessionists were in a state of war with Britain and Ulster. Such circumstances were corrosive to settled legal systems. Courts could not sit because of assault, arson, theft, and obstruction. Decrees of judges were flouted or ignored. But the turmoil of revolution was plainly a part of the eventual settlement, and recent writers have begun to unravel an extremely complicated story.[41] It is a tale of three governments, London, Dublin, and Belfast, each trying to fashion legal systems attuned to their communities. There were several phases in the process: the first was the period of revolution 1919–21; the second was a period of renovation, 1922–24; and then there was a long period of rehabilitation, 1925–1945. Our sketch will outline the new structures and their relations with one another. During this entire story, the major legal change was the creation of two new court systems based upon *written* constitutions: the Government of Ireland Act of 1920 and the constitutions of the Irish Free State (1922) and the Republic of Ireland (1937).

The provisional republican government decreed the establishment of its own set of courts in August 1919. The first court session was not until May 1920. The "Dail courts" were meant to replace the British courts with popular, accessible, and inexpensive venues. At first these courts were arbitration tribunals "which, since their jurisdiction depended on consent, were not technically unlawful."[42] But soon the provisional government granted more powers to the courts, and it employed personnel to enforce their decisions. At this point they encountered resistance from the colonial regime.[43] The aims of the revolutionary government went well beyond forming alternative courts. In a 1920 pamphlet a set of court rules encouraged the use of ancient Irish laws, Roman law and continental codes, adding that "no legal textbook published in Great Britain shall be cited to any court."[44] But the effort to uproot English law was not going to succeed.

Indeed, the passage of the Government of Ireland Act in late 1920 was a key event in the revolutionary period. It was the London government's solution to the breakdown: a pair of home rule measures for North and South, plus a fig leaf of union in the form of a few all-Ireland provisions which both parts of the island could choose to endorse or not. This act provided the basis for the new court system in Northern Ireland, which came into being after King George V opened the first session of the Stormont Parliament in June of 1921. The Ulster courts maintained their prewar outline, with one departure in the creation of a Supreme Court with an appeal to the House of Lords. The Supreme Court of Northern Ireland had its first sitting in October 1921.

The Dail courts seemed to be quite active in the period between the truce and the treaty in the later months of 1921.[45] But in spite of their apparent popularity, under the terms of the Anglo-Irish Treaty, the new Free State government announced (January 1922) that it would retain the bulk of the instruments and the personnel of the old anglicized court system:[46]

> When the Constitution has been finally settled by the Irish Parliament there must necessarily be a reorganisation of the judicial system according to the requirements of the Irish people. In the meantime the Government proposes to do away with unnecessary duplication and to let the people have the full advantage of the Judiciary and staffs for which the people are paying, and which have complete machinery for dealing with all kinds of cases.

This was a renunciation of the innovative courts of the revolution, and a concession to the pro-Treaty forces. There may have been some truth to the last point as a pragmatic excuse. Nevertheless the decree marked a "retreat from revolution." The laws to be enforced were similarly derivative. The Free State Constitution said [47]

> subject to this constitution and to the extent to which they are not inconsistent therewith, the laws in force in Saorstat Eireann immediately prior to the date of the coming into operation of this constitution shall continue to be of full force and effect until the same or any of them shall have been repealed or amended by enactment of the Oireachtas.

The new government also decreed that personnel should remain at their posts:[48]

> And we do hereby direct that all Law Courts, Corporations, Councils, Departments of State, Boards, Judges, Civil Servants, Officers of the Peace, and all Public Servants and functionaries hitherto acting under the authority of the British Government shall continue to carry out their functions unless and until otherwise ordered by us.

Whether or not all the personnel remained, the new legal systems were destined to have difficult early years. In the Free State, renewed civil war followed the ratification of the 1921 Treaty. On June 30, 1922 the Four Courts Building in Dublin was blown up by the anti-Treaty republicans. This was a symbolic gesture in the political world; in the world of lawyers, it was a major blow to the reconstruction of the system. The judges had to meet in the King's Inns until the colonial government vacated Dublin Castle; they were then able to take up places in the old seat of government during the rebuilding period.

But there was even more renovation going on. When the Dail Courts were closed by the Dail Courts (Winding Up) Act in 1923, there was a collapse of local justice, and the government had to appoint a number of district justices to replace the former justices of the peace, resident magistrates and Dail Court judges.[49] In 1924 two important laws were enacted affecting the judicial system. Under the Courts of Justice Act (April 1924) many features of the English system were removed (petty sessions, resident magistrates, grand juries), and a paid professional magistracy was provided in a three-tiered system of district, circuit, and central courts. A Supreme Court was created. The chief justice and his two fellow judges also constituted a Court of Criminal Appeal. A minister of justice was made responsible for the operation of the system under the Ministers and Secretaries Act (1924). In 1924 all the high court judges in the South retired. The government asked two (O'Conor and Wylie) to return, and it appointed two others from the old lower courts. Thus there was some continuity of personnel. There were a few new wrinkles as well: barristers of twelve years standing were eligible for the bench, and the new law set a retirement age for justices.

In the North, the 1920 Act had more or less recognized the status quo. The existing replica of the English system had a new supreme court added, from which there was an appeal to the House of Lords. Nevertheless there was a considerable amount of work involved in establishing separate operations. Current litigation which crossed the new border had to be resolved. The solicitors in the North organized the Incorporated Law Society for Northern Ireland in 1922. The barristers of the North set up a Committee of Fifteen to represent their interests. But as of 1921 they were not allowed to award the degree barrister-at-law, and they had to admit Dublin barristers before the courts of Northern Ireland. These distinctions would prove intolerable, and the profession would finally split in 1926.[50]

In a more public sphere, the transfer of police power allowed the introduction of emergency laws in the North under the provision in the Government of Ireland Act, which delegated power to legislate "for the peace, order and good government" of the province. The wartime powers were replaced by the Special Powers Act (Northern Ireland) of 1922. This remained the basis of police authority for arrest and detention of suspected enemies of the state (see chapter 8).

One area of renovation with great potential was a complete failure. The treaty had provided the means for the two Irelands to work together and move toward reunion. The High Court of Appeal for Ireland which was provided in the 1920 act was meant to be one of the bridges for this process, if both court systems used it as a course of appeal. But the new court only sat from 1921 to 1922 and it was abolished by the Irish Free State (Consequential Provisions) Act of 1922, which also repealed the 1920 act insofar as it applied to "Southern" Ireland.[51]

In the two decades after 1925, the main theme was recovery and rebuilding after the tumult of the previous five years. Both Irelands were still preoccupied with militants in their midst, and both governments were beholden to emergency powers, but they were beginning to fashion some new elements as they worked to rebuild civil society. For the South, continuity and English influence were paramount until 1937, and for some years after, as the potential of the new constitution waited to be realized. For the North, continuity was not just convenient; it became an article of faith. Even so, the desire to emulate the English still produced a singular legal system in Ulster. Actually, British legislation and English case law were powerful influences for both Irelands, far more than each was for the other.[52]

In the Free State, one important feature of the new system was the development of the office of minister of justice. This officer combined the functions of the chief secretary and the lord chancellor in the old regime. And as Mansergh noted, the post marked "the achievement of reforms so frequently urged upon the Home Office in England."[53] Further legislation spelled out the contours of the new system—for example the Court Officers and Orders Act, 1926. The minister was also responsible for the police and the prison system.

In the new republican Constitution of 1937, the courts were founded (art. 34) in very general terms, and no major changes were made in the existing structure. Provision was made (art. 58) for further revision by the *Oireachtas*, but no substantial alterations were made until the 1960s. Also by that date the judges in the high courts took more activist positions and began to develop the system in ways which were permitted by the 1937 document, but which had not been previously exploited.[54]

In Northern Ireland there was understandably greater interest in legal continuity. The lord chief justice (assuming the lord chancellor's authority over the province in 1921) presided over the several divisions of the supreme court. One striking departure for the courts was the creation of a power to declare laws unconstitutional (i.e., judicial review). Since there was a Constitution and a specified sphere of legislative authority for the Stormont Parliament, the courts of the North could be called upon to rule on the validity of legislation. However the impact of judicial review was far greater in the courts of the Republic, if only because of the difference in legislative powers. The *Oireachtas* was the sole legislative voice for the South; the Stormont Parliament (until 1972) was but one of two legislatures for Northern Ireland. This contrast produced many significant statutory variations, and it might have operated against the growth of a power of judicial review in the North. However, the very features of the 1920 act which set limits on Stormont's legislative power had to be monitored by the courts of Northern Ireland. In other words, the principle of parliamentary supremacy was divided and interdicted in Northern Ireland.

In both new jurisdictions there was considerable continuity. Regular series of law reports were maintained in the North and the Republic. Courts in both jurisdictions admitted citations of cases from English, American, and other courts. Statute law was applied from the time before 1920, though on a more restricted basis in the south. In other words, the fundamental features of the two systems were rather close to their mutual parent. But their later development was free to proceed in quite different directions. The two parts of Ireland were in some respects moving in the same direction as many other parts of the empire. But Ireland had a very long and troubled history behind its relations with Britain. The states of the Commonwealth had only begun to alter their legal relations with the United Kingdom in the second half of the nineteenth century.

Imperial Dissolution

There was no fixed imperial legal system. There was a shared allegiance to the Crown which acknowledged sovereign authority in a wide variety of mixed legal systems.[55] This allegiance fostered the growth of anglicized laws, courts, and legal professions throughout the empire. But from the late nineteenth century the central controls began to dissolve. The common allegiance, the legislative primacy, and the judicial centrality were gone by 1950.[56] Thus there was a prolonged period of redefining the shape of legal empire. In our sketch, there will be several focal points: changes in the law of nationality, the locus of legislative power, and the course of judicial appeal.

The law of nationality was at the root of any legal empire: being a subject determined whether one was under the judicial authority of the sovereign. This definition had been laboriously developed over the centuries. The two basic categories were natural subjects (born of subject-parents) and naturalized subjects (those granted status by an official act). A general act for the latter was passed in 1844, but some doubts were not settled: how long did Americans retain British nationality? what of the large numbers of emigrants from the United Kingdom in the nineteenth century?[57] The Naturalization Act of 1870 served to "overthrow the old doctrine of the indelibility of allegiance" and removed the disabilities of aliens in private law. But the act did not "introduce a new or revived system of Imperial naturalisation."[58] In other words, the new definition implicitly acknowledged the power of colonies to provide their own procedures. Imperial nationality was left to be reformed in the Act of 1914, by which time it was arguably too late.[59] The powers of local authorities were preserved, and imperial naturalization was explicitly a joint enterprise. "The scheme neither created a real unity of nationality throughout the Commonwealth nor met the needs of national self-awareness in its several parts."[60] Each member country pursued its own interests in terms of nationality. Such was the trend eventually acknowledged in the British Nationality Act of 1948: the separate member states of the Commonwealth bestowed citizenship which was a precondition of British nationality.[61] As one of the expert commentators said, citizenship in the Commonwealth "is in itself of no effect, for its value depends essentially on the local law."[62]

The lawmaking power of the colonies was another example of the corrosive power of definition. The Colonial Laws Validity Act, 1865, had attempted to state the relation of colonial and imperial legislation. A colonial law was to be held invalid when and to the degree that it was "repugnant" to imperial legislation. This anomalous "judicial review" was to be monitored by the responsible minister (and at law by the Privy Council).[63] There was considerable irony in the use of judicial review by colonial legislatures (under their constitutions) and by the imperial Parliament, which otherwise tolerated no such judicial power in the British constitution. But the Colonial Laws Validity Act, according to one of its modern students, "was intended to reduce restrictions on the legislative powers of colonies by removing conflict with the English common law as a ground for invalidating colonial laws."[64] In other words, the statutory supremacy proclaimed here masked an important concession in the operation of legal empire. The need for the law arose from a complex dispute in Australia, wherein a colonial judge had aggressively challenged the Torrens system of land title registration, declaring certain provisions unconstitutional. Parliament was cautiously interposing a limited check on colonial legislation, knowing that it risked meddling with essential constitutional provisions.[65]

The effort to reconstruct imperial legislation was bound up with the movement for what was called "imperial federation."[66] The central idea was that closer coordination would make the laws of the United Kingdom and the colonies more compatible. This idea appealed especially to British officials and MPs who were afraid that Parliament was becoming swamped with imperial business. But for colonial leaders, the prospect of closer association meant reducing their power. Thus the only visible result of the idea of federation was periodic meeting in colonial, then imperial conferences (1887, 1897, 1905) and the formation of an imperial general staff and an imperial war cabinet. The latter were reasonable efforts to link the action of wartime allies, but they had less utility in peacetime. Indeed, the end of fighting brought the senior dominions a new international presence via participation at the Paris Peace Conference and membership in the League of Nations. The imperial conferences of the 1920s were devoted largely to working out an acceptable formula to state the new relation. By 1926 the imperial conference agreed[67]

> They are autonomous communities within the British Empire, equal in status, in no way subordinate to one another in any aspect of their domestic or external affairs, though united by a common allegiance to the Crown, and freely associated as members of the British Commonwealth of Nations.

Thus was the question of British legislative power resolved. It only remained to state it in the highest form, which was done in similar language in the Statute of Westminster in 1931.[68]

The imperial judicial power consisted of several components. The long-standing power to establish colonial courts was fully enunciated in the British Settlements Act of 1887.[69]

> It shall be lawful for Her Majesty the Queen in Council from time to time to establish all such laws and institutions, and constitute such courts and officers and make such provisions and regulations for the proceedings in the said courts and for the administration of justice, as may appear to Her Majesty in Council to be necessary for the peace, order and good government of Her Majesty's subjects and others within any British settlement.

In addition, there was the power to monitor the acts of these courts, manifest in measures like the Colonial Laws Validity Act. A more flexible and adaptable form of supervision was present in the appellate role of the Privy Council (or, since 1833, its Judicial Committee). In colonial cases there were two courses of appeal, either by right or by special leave. The right of appeal was created by specific legal act, and might be similarly denied—for example, by colonial court, legislative act, or order in council. In the event of denial, special leave to appeal might be sought from the Judicial Committee. Special leave might be sought either where no right of appeal existed or where such right was refused by the court below.

The Privy Council had a jurisdiction which was "the most vigorous in its daily operation and at the same time the most archaic in form."[70] It was attended in early days by any councillors, but after reform in 1833 nonlawyers were excluded and assessors who had been colonial or Indian judges were added. The Judicial Committee was modified in 1871. Four paid judges were provided for the committee, mainly to address the problem of a rising caseload. For the next half century, the caseload grew and complaints from the colonies grew along with it. In 1895 further legislation allowed added membership, making judges from the dominions eligible to serve, although the numbers sitting were never large.[71]

The number of cases heard annually by the Privy Council had grown in the course of the nineteenth century. The number of cases in 1800 was about 23; by 1820 it had grown to 40; by 1870 there were about 80; and in the early years of the twentieth century, from 90 to 100 cases were the norm.[72] But complaints about the appellate jurisdiction were about other matters: the process was slow, expensive, unreliable, and far removed from the setting of the cases. And of course the appeal represented a clear statement of constitutional inferiority. Over the last half of the nineteenth and first half of the twentieth century, the Privy Council appeal was challenged and in many cases eliminated by dominion governments.

The earliest challenge to the appellate power came from Canada. The first dominion proposed a new supreme court for Canada in 1875, from which appeal to the Privy Council would not be allowed. Extensive discussions went on in London, and the act was left on the books on the understanding that the restriction only applied to appeal as of right. The Judicial Committee was provoked in this situation to declare in unusually blunt terms that the effect of the act would[73]

> obviously be to destroy one of the most important ties connecting all parts of the empire in common obedience to the courts of law, and to renounce the last and most essential mode of exercising the authority of the Crown over its possessions abroad.

The Canadian effort was relaxed when a new government took office. Although there were some important decisions in the 1880s and 1890s on federal-provincial issues, in the rest of the century there was only one other act taken in Canada to oppose the jurisdiction. The Criminal Code of 1888 stated that

> no appeal shall be brought in any criminal case from any judgment or order of any court in Canada to any court of appeal or authority by which in the United Kingdom appeals or petitions to Her Majesty in Council may be heard (s. 1025).

This provision was not challenged until 1926, when in the case of *Nadan v. the King* it was overruled by the Judicial Committee. And that decision was the prelude to final termination of the appellate power.

At the turn of the century there were some unusual developments. When the Commonwealth of Australia Constitution Act was adopted in 1900, there were supreme courts in each of the six states, plus a high court of the federal government. One of the key provisions regarding that court stated that no constitutional issue (between the Commonwealth and the states)

> shall be capable of final decision except by the High Court, and no appeal shall be permitted to the Queen in Council from any decision of the High Court on any such question unless by consent of the executive government or governments concerned.

At the same time, there was interest in forming a new imperial court of appeal. This was a revival of an idea debated at the time of Brougham's act in 1833. Other proposals in the 1840s and 1870s had reached the discussion stage. When the proposal surfaced again in 1900, it was supported by Australian opponents to appeals in the debate over the dominion constitution.[74] The idea was considered at a Conference on Imperial Appeals in 1901 and it resurfaced several times over the next half century. But its promise of genuine central control always doomed the idea for some observers both in London and in the dominions.

In yet another area, the creation of the Union of South Africa added one more dominion constitution, one in which there was a variation on the dominion theme. The South Africa Act of 1909 gave extensive amending powers to the South African Parliament, which was the legislature of a highly centralized state. Thus there was considerable power to form and regulate the courts of the new state. As provided in the 1909 act, the appeal as of right from the superior courts of the South African colonies was abolished, and only an appeal by special leave was allowed.

Still another form of adjustment appeared with the creation of the Irish Free State. According to its constitution, it was a dominion patterned on the Canadian model. This explicit reference was made in order to give a stronger assurance of maintaining Privy Council appeal in Irish cases. In the 1920s the frequent negotiations between British and Irish representatives were often snagged on the issue of imperial appeal, and indeed, the Irish eventually resorted to enacting statutes to override unwanted appeal decisions.

Thus, in the several dominions between 1875 and 1925, a variety of limits and inroads on the appellate power had accumulated. It was therefore not surprising when more generalized opposition appeared. In the Imperial Conference of 1926 an important decision was reached, though as a conference resolution it had no legal force. The conference stated that [75]

> it was no part of the policy of His Majesty's government in Great Britain that questions affecting judicial appeals should be determined otherwise than in accordance with the wishes of the part of the Empire primarily affected.

This statement embodied a growing consensus on the place of appellate jurisdiction. But there was no general application of the principle. For appellate courts there was nothing comparable to the Statute of Westminster. But in the 1930s a number of decisions of the Judicial Committee referred to that act in allowing further limitation of appeals.

In *Nadan v. the King* the Canadian ban on criminal appeals was overturned, the Judicial Committee saying that it was possible only by an imperial act, in fact citing measures to that effect in Australia and South Africa.[76] The Canadian Parliament passed a new bill to end criminal appeals, and it was tested in the case of *British Coal Corp. v. the King*, where the denial of special leave was upheld.[77] The Canadian Parliament went on to debate bills to end appeals in civil cases in 1938 and 1939. The issue was not pursued during the war, but a bill was introduced again in 1947. After more delay, the measure finally passed in 1949.[78]

The Irish Free State, led by the old republican Eamon de Valera, passed legislation in 1933 to amend the constitution and end appeals. In a test case in 1935, the Judicial Committee said that "the Statute of Westminster gave the Irish Free State a power under which they could abrogate the Treaty [of 1921], and that, as a matter of law, they have availed themselves of that power."[79]

In the Dominion of South Africa there were very few appeals to the Judicial Committee. Only the most serious cases were expected to be appealed, in accord with the constitution. It was a case which failed to meet such criteria which forced the issue of appeals into South African politics.[80] The issue was debated in the late 1930s, but again the war intervened. When the nationalists came to power after the war, a Privy Council Appeals Act was passed in 1950.

The ending of Privy Council appeals was untidy. The new republics of India and Pakistan joined Ireland in abolishing the link in 1949 and 1950. Australia very slowly disengaged: appeals regarding federal jurisdiction were terminated in 1968; all appeals from the high court were ended in 1975; and a final end to all appeals was enacted in 1986. New Zealand and a number of East Asian governments retained the appeal even longer.

The judicial ties in the empire and Commonwealth were an important means of linking the sovereign identity of the different parts of the British global enterprise. But the interaction between them after 1870, and especially after 1900, was in the direction of dismantling an outdated piece of machinery.[81]

1870, and especially after 1900, was in the direction of dismantling an outdated piece of machinery.[81]

> While the Empire strode forward politically, its law stood still. The rules which it needed...it formulated in...the language and sanctions of constitutional convention. When, therefore, the Empire became the Commonwealth of Nations, its fundamental law was still in all substantial respects the law of George III, the same law which lost Britain the American colonies.

Latham endowed the law of 1776 with unlikely powers, but he suggested a problem of historical myopia which we have followed throughout this chapter. The constitutional ideal of the Victorian canon had ceased to correspond with reality before the midtwentieth century, but in spite of the three revolutions we have traced, it clung to a vestige of support. In the 1950s there would be formal recognition of an Irish Republic (with affirmation of the Union for the North); there would be a Council of Tribunals and other signs of formal endorsement of administrative law; there would also be an end to the Privy Council's role for most new Commonwealth members, ending "the last and most essential mode of exercising the authority of the Crown over its possessions abroad."

One dramatic case in the 1950s resurrected several of these constitutional elements. They converged in a way that could not restore faith in English law, but even worse, would exacerbate some already inflamed Scottish opinion. During the invasion of Rangoon in 1942, the Crown had ordered the colonial authorities to destroy the oil refineries belonging to the Burmah Oil Company so as to deny them to the Japanese. After the war, the company received a sum of £5 million in compensation. Regarding this as insufficient, the company sought the balance of its claim, but this was denied by the Burmese courts in 1960. As that country had left the Commonwealth, there was no question of appeal to the Privy Council. However, the company was registered in Scotland, and it sought redress there. The lord ordinary ruled for the company, the Inner House ruled for the government; the case was appealed to the Lords, where a 3-2 ruling went in favor of the company. Then a most extraordinary thing happened. The government introduced a War Damage Bill to reverse the decision of the Lords:[82]

> Her Majesty's Government believe that the law as it now stands, after the Burmah Oil judgment, is utterly wrong: it is opposed to the public interest; it is

This action was to be retroactive, and even the lord chief justice described it as blatant confiscatory legislation. It was entirely within the power of Parliament to overrule an incorrect judicial decision, if somewhat bruising to do so in this fashion. Lord Kilbrandon said the original decision stood upon firm Scottish precedent. But the case seemed to show an old English tradition of interference, an old exercise of imperial power: the main difference here was an unusual double reversal, judicial plus legislative. Imperial legal interaction had changed a great deal in the early twentieth century; and the aspect of Anglo-Scottish confrontation was another area which was about to produce some surprising results.

Chapter 8

Modern Legal Interaction 1950–1990

The world after 1945 looked different from almost every angle: in global politics, in the affairs of the archipelago, and in domestic matters. It was not surprising that the place and performance of legal systems were subject to unprecedented review and reform.

Britain's victory in 1945 was bittersweet. The expenditure of over £7 billion represented a fourth of the national wealth, a cost which permanently altered Britain's capacity. Her two major allies emerged as superpowers, and the United States and the Soviet Union soon began to engage in a Cold War of global maneuver and confrontation. Britain had been one of the "Big Three" and became a permanent member of the U.N. Security Council. But realities of political and economic power forced Britain to make concessions. She had to retire from principal colonial outposts (India, 1947; Palestine, 1948) because of earlier promises and current weaknesses. The "special relationship" with the United States assigned Britain to a subordinate role in an Anglo-American alliance. One key product of the relationship was the continuing American role in Europe. Paradoxically, Britain failed to define its own relation to Europe while clinging to the remains of empire.

In July of 1945 at Potsdam the British were still involved in drawing postwar boundaries for central Europe. But Stalin's armies were in a position to override diplomatic decisions. Germany was divided into zones of occupation, but Soviet troops and their political allies created a much wider zone in central and eastern Europe. When Winston Churchill coined the phrase "iron curtain" in 1946, there was clearly an emerging Soviet empire, which Britain and the United States were trying to decide how to contain. When Britain withdrew its military forces from Greece and Turkey in 1947, President Truman made a public commitment to resist a Communist takeover there. The blockade of supplies to Berlin (in the Russian zone) was countered by the Berlin Airlift in 1948. But more serious than these symbolic moves, Russian scientists (helped by western spies) produced an atomic bomb, and then its more powerful cousin, a hydrogen bomb. Here the British government, denied a joint role with the United States, had launched its own atomic weapons program in 1946. In the end, it was more important that there was a strategic agreement as to missiles (land and submarine), whereupon the United Kingdom became a launching pad for U.S. weaponry and from time to time pretended to be an independent nuclear power.

Throughout the postwar period the United States was a lender of last resort. This relation dated back to the lend-lease program of 1940. President Roosevelt and Congress had established a program to provide military equipment and supplies when Britain was in its greatest peril under German attacks by air and (more dangerously) by the U-boat. The program was abruptly ended in 1945, but British penury was not so easy to terminate. Postwar loans and monetary crises were recurrent features of the later 1940s.

In the 1950s relations with the empire continued to weaken, as it became clearer that Britain could no longer maintain the role of an imperial power. One alternative at this point was to join other European nations in the formation of common institutions. Britain had, after all, helped to form the North Atlantic Treaty Organization. When given the opportunity, Britain opted not to join the early forms of European economic integration. Unable to surrender the idea of empire, Britain held back, only trying to join the Common Market in 1963, and after being rejected, applying again and finally entering in 1972.

The legal fallout from these global events was extensive. In general, the shift in Britain's world position was reflected in developments in international law. In particular, by joining the United Nations, the several cold war treaty organizations and (eventually) the European Community, the United Kingdom accepted numerous treaty commitments. These actions involved subscribing to codes and charters—that is, quasi-constitutional documents. In dealing with Europe, for example, Britain signed the European Convention for the Protection of Human Rights and Fundamental Freedoms and opened the door to possible recognition of "constitutional rights."[1]

On a different plane, the cold war brought attention to other critical areas of public law. In one direction, the whole question of "official secrets" and the collateral government control of information, ostensibly for security and the defeat of espionage, led to tougher acts and restrictions. On the same plane, but in another direction, organized protests such as the Campaign for Nuclear Disarmament brought into view a range of questions about control of public assembly, rights of expression, and power to regulate those areas. Finally, the connection with Europe introduced a new set of questions of jurisdiction which we will explore at some length below.

It would be quite surprising if the shift in global and in imperial relations was not reflected in changes in the "internal" relations in the British Isles. The relations between England and her immediate neighbors had shifted during the war, and the postwar period saw continued movement, some of it in the legal realm. Irish neutrality seems to have underscored the independence of the newly proclaimed republic. In 1949 the Westminster Parliament acknowledged that status with the Republic of Ireland Act. Eire had of course been functioning under its own constitution, adopted in 1937. The new constitution was drafted by the Dail and adopted by plebiscite. The document omitted references to the British Crown, asserted that its provisions were superior in law to any statute or common law, and claimed to govern the whole island of Ireland. The document also acknowledged the special position of the Roman Catholic Church.[2]

The Ulster government was not happy with the act of 1949. The North had fully supported Britain in the war, its industry being an important contribution to the total effort. The war economy and the postwar welfare state gave the North a boost, relative to the republic. Per capita incomes rose, very much on the strength of British legislation, from a prewar ratio of 57 per cent of the U.K. level to 84 per cent by the 1960s. Ulster had the benefit of health services and unemployment insurance plus improved educational and other social programs, subsidized by the British taxpayer. That is, Protestants in Ulster received these benefits; Catholics were discriminated against by municipal regulation. And the general level of unemployment, higher than other parts of the United Kingdom, was higher still in Catholic communities. It was the attempt by Terence O'Neill, prime minister of Northern Ireland (1963–69) to begin to reduce these differences which triggered protests, civil rights marches, and the clashes which brought down the unionist government in 1972. The legal impact of these developments and their effect on English and U.K. legal practice are discussed below.

The interwar years had seen some resurgence of nationalist activity in Wales and Scotland, although as before, there was nothing comparable to Irish intercommunal violence. The interest in devolution or "home rule" for these parts of the United Kingdom was an issue of long standing, if not of an explosive character. Actually, in 1936 three Welsh nationalists set fire to an RAF installation, and they used their trial as a platform to proclaim Welsh nationalist objectives, though these were mainly cultural in nature.[3] There was very slight political support for the Welsh nationalist party (*Plaid Cymru*). After the war, there was some attention given to the complaints of the Welsh: a secretary of state for Wales (1964) and a Welsh language act (1967) marked the beginning of serious recognition. In the 1970s there were some small parliamentary victories for the Welsh nationalists.

In Scotland the level of political interest was somewhat higher, but the organization of a Scottish Nationalist Party was plagued by factional disputes. In the early postwar years, there was a dramatic episode when extreme nationalists rescued the Stone of Scone from its "captivity" in Westminster Abbey, but this, too, was an isolated and pathetic protest. More significantly, the movement to decentralize authority did show some sign of achievement. Many years earlier Scotland had a cabinet member, a secretary for Scotland. In the eighteenth century this post was an office for managing patronage and keeping track of Scottish votes in the House of Commons. It was abolished in reaction to the Jacobite rebellion of 1745. The secretary of state for Scotland was restored in 1885, in response to rising nationalist feeling. That office was made quite powerful during the war, and the secretary, Tom Johnston, amassed considerable authority. One enduring legacy of that period was the establishment of the North of Scotland Hydroelectric Board (1943). The powers of the secretary were reduced after the war, but in subsequent years they increased again. The Scottish Office came to supervise most departments of domestic government in Scotland.

The creation of cabinet posts has been called "administrative devolution," to distinguish it from legislative delegation of power. The latter was, of course, the goal of most nationalists, the more extreme seeking complete independence. By the 1960s there was enough concern about the growth of nationalist sentiment that the Westminster government set up a Royal Commission on the Constitution. The reports of the Kilbrandon Commission (1973) were inconclusive. The majority held that there should be elected assemblies in Scotland and Wales. A minority report recommended assemblies for English regions as well.

The government was inclined to shelve the matter, but with nationalist gains in the elections of 1974, the issue revived. The Labour government enacted legislation which provided for assemblies, but it required the approval of the voters in a referendum. Moreover, the referendum needed the approval of 40 per cent of all registered voters. Thus when these votes were taken in 1979, the Welsh proposal was defeated outright, while the Scottish measure was approved, but only by 33 per cent of registered voters. Similar measures were introduced again after twenty years, and the Welsh Assembly and Scottish Parliament were approved and established in 1999. The political and legal consequences of both new bodies can only be judged in the future. They do indicate, however, a willingness to decentralize authority not seen until the late twentieth century.

In domestic politics—English and general—there were numerous new directions after 1945, many of which had significant meaning for the making and the enforcement of law. It is a commonplace that the Second World War was a "total" war. All classes, all communities in society were involved, either as targets or as combatants or as war suppliers. This common experience engendered a powerful sense of unity in the years of struggle. And since the early postwar years saw continued rationing and tight controls on some economic activity, there was a postwar extension of the phenomenon. But there was also a strong sense of entitlement which was cultivated during the war: for national programs for unemployment insurance, for health insurance, or for educational reform. All of this was swept up in the landslide election victory of the Labour Party in 1945. The new government was "socialist" in name; its program was radical enough to seem to merit the title, but on closer examination, the government of Clement Attlee was not one of social radicals. Many of its members were from affluent backgrounds; most of them supported established institutions; none of them espoused serious expropriation of property or massive transfers of wealth. What was achieved in the 1940s was a strong injection of social democracy through government-directed welfare programs and government supervision of selected sectors of the economy.

Beside the renovation of social services, legal systems were under extensive review from 1945 on. It is tempting to say that they were receiving a continuing assessment, because of the number and regularity of committees, commissions, and reports on varied aspects of the systems. More accurately, the frequency of reports and reforms was a reflection of the number and range of remedies being sought.

Law Reform and Interaction

In the first postwar decade there were many government efforts to examine and improve the legal system. In 1946 a royal commission was established to study Justices of the Peace; in 1947 a committee examined the county courts; in the same year another committee looked at supreme court practice; a major study of legal aid led to the Legal Aid and Advice Act of 1949. These were but a few of the escalating number of studies and proposals which came forward. The generation after the war would encounter very extensive and significant reform, much of it classified as administrative. There was also a large category we might label cultural—or "moral." The Obscene Publications Act, 1959; abolition of capital punishment, 1965; legalized abortion, 1966; legalized homosexual activity, 1967; and the Sexual Discrimination Act, 1975 were all in that category. There was another field we could call "technical" or professional, including tort reform acts in 1945 and 1948; a restrictive practices court in 1956; and the beginning of Crown courts in Liverpool and Manchester in 1956, which would eventually replace the assize courts (Courts Act 1971). In short, there was very broad and general interest in and action for legal reform, and this activity generated and was generated by interaction around the archipelago.

Since 1950 dramatic changes in the the legal systems of the British Isles have made legal interaction seem almost routine. The climate for this development was set by the postwar wave of legal reform, culminating in new mechanisms for that purpose. The entrenchment of the new mode of interaction was assisted by some fundamental encounters between legal systems. We will examine several major episodes of legal interaction which contributed to the general reformation. Perhaps the most surprising of these legal changes has been the convergence of English and Scots law. Despite Scottish protests about English domination, which reached a peak at the time of the coronation of Elizabeth II in 1953, English procedure and substantive law have been significantly modified in recent years, sometimes under more or less acknowledged Scottish influence.

The second major interactive change followed the shock of renewed unrest in Ireland. In the 1970s Ulster was visited by a regime which used the British army, draconian police powers, and resumption of direct rule, the sort of powers which would have provoked an Irish rebellion in the nineteenth century. These powers did produce serious distortions of the criminal justice system in Ulster and Britain, and they fuelled collateral movements for a bill of rights and criminal law reform which still are being debated.

The third change came with the entry of the United Kingdom and Ireland into the European Communities in 1972. This act involved an unprecedented English legal concession: the regular subordination to "foreign" law (a problem with which Irish and Scottish lawyers had some experience). The change was made by statute in the United Kingdom and by a constitutional amendment in Ireland. New rules were made for U.K. and Irish courts in cases involving the law of the communities. This obviously was an interaction of some magnitude, and the extent of its effect is still being determined.

These alterations were not just coincidental reactions. There had been a gathering movement of legal reform since the prewar years. A consensus emerged in favor of reconstructing the machinery of justice, featuring new machinery for reform which helped to regularize legal interaction. Law reform was once the enemy of the establishment. Attempts to reform aimed at specific "evils" of a particular system. There were gradual changes in these contests between authorities and their critics; by the nineteenth century the official inquiry aided more systematic study and change; by the twentieth century, reform seemed less threatening, and its formulation became less insular in origin. Now reform is more likely to produce, or be produced by interaction.[4]

It became increasingly clear as the twentieth century unfolded that a more systematic approach to law reform was desirable. Ireland resembled some European countries where reform might be undertaken by a minister of justice.[5] England and Scotland did not have an official with such responsibility, and they relied on the reform efforts of judges and parliaments. The drawbacks of both were well known. Judges may once have been the custodians of community values, but they had difficulty with that role after 1900. Moreover, the reactive and unpredictable case law method of reform could not keep pace in the new century. The answer then had to lie with statutory reform. But this method also had perils; indeed, its long history suggested to David Walker that "the main responsibility for the defective state of the law rests on Parliament."[6] The legislature responded willy nilly to complaints, always with an eye on the political aspects, and its alterations of law often created new problems.[7] A new approach emerged when Lord Sankey appointed a Law Revision Committee in 1934 [8]

> to consider how far, having regard to the statute law and to judicial decisions, such legal maxims and doctrines, as the Lord Chancellor may from time to time refer to the Committee require revision in modern conditions.

This revision by referral, with emphasis on judicial decisions, was resumed by Lord Simonds in 1952.[9] In 1954 a Scottish Law Reform Committee was formed, which reported to the secretary of state and the lord advocate on such matters as they directed it to investigate. For the criminal law in England and Wales, the home secretary established the Criminal Law Revision Committee in 1959, to report on "aspects of the criminal law" which he might refer to it.

These measures had their counterparts in Ireland. In 1962 the minister of justice established a Committee on Court Practice and Procedure.[10] A White Paper on reforms was also published and the early aftermath saw the enactment of several measures. At the same time, there was a change in the atmosphere in the Irish legal profession, which one author described as the "discovery of the constitution."[11]

In 1963 Gerald Gardiner and Andrew Martin, co-editors of *Law Reform NOW!* advocated a new departure for England and Wales. They said "much of our English law is out of date, and some of it shockingly so." They proposed a permanent body "kept in continuous operation and minded by full-time personnel." The following year Gardiner became lord chancellor in the new Labour government, and he proposed the legislation which created the Law Commission. Its mandate was[12]

> to take and keep under review all the law...with a view to its systematic development and reform, including in particular the codification of such law, the elimination of anomalies...and generally the simplification and modernisation of the law.

The act also created a Scottish Law Commission, which some said was an afterthought, while others thought it a ploy "to develop a common system of law" for England and Scotland.[13] But the two commissions were quite separate; the (English) Law Commission had five full-time members, the Scottish Law Commission one full- and four part-time.[14] The goal of both commissions was to study areas of the law suggested or approved by the lord chancellor or the lord advocate. The commissioners consulted many sources, gathered evidence, and produced working papers for discussion.[15] After the period of study, the commissions put forward legislative proposals. In their first twenty years, the English commissioners made seventy-five reports on a wide range of reforms.[16] Of course there were limits on the action of the commissions. In each case, their proposals had originally been authorized by the lord chancellor, and customarily the commissions deferred to the jurisdiction of government departments. Finally, the rate at which English proposals were actually implemented was quite low. The Scottish Law Commission made thirty-eight reports on reforms in the first two decades, and a relatively large number of these found their way to the statute book.

The original law anticipated joint work by the English and Scottish commissioners. The relevant section of the act said, "In the exercise of their functions under this Act the Commissions shall act in consultation with each other."[17] On a number of occasions they made joint studies and reports, some twenty-six between 1965 and 1982.[18] The joint work tended to bring out the Scottish commissioners' concern for the preservation of Scots law. In making numerous and sweeping changes, they sought harmony but shunned assimilation. This is one reason why the joint efforts had mixed results. For instance, a great deal of work went into the joint project to reform the law of contract (1966–1972), but one English commissioner conceded that "we speak different legal languages," when discussing the failure of the project.[19] Other joint efforts have included statutory interpretation (1974), the mental element in crime (1978), and the law of domicile (1987). As well as specific projects, perhaps the most important product of the relationship was the establishment of routine communication on the programs and projects of the two commissions.

Nothing like the same level of communication exists with the other law commission in the British Isles. The Irish Law Commission was announced in 1974 and enacted in 1975. It was patterned after the English and Scottish commissions and also the Australian and Canadian versions which were established by that time.[20] The Act of 1975 gave a very detailed outline of the mandate, probably based upon the experience of sister commissions. Section 4 (3) said the commission might

> (a) receive and consider for inclusion in a programme being prepared by it, proposals for law reform; (b) examine and conduct research into the legal systems of other countries; (c) prepare or cause to be prepared draft Bills for inclusion in its proposals for reform; (d) consult with persons qualified to give opinions on any relevant matter; (e) establish working parties or advisory committees; (f) publish preliminary working papers prior to formulating any proposal for reform; (g) indicate the desirability, priority, scope and extent of any proposals for law reform.

This section suggests the amount and manner in which the commission idea had evolved in only ten years.

One subject which law commissions encountered early and often was the effect of precedent. The concept of *stare decisis*, that the previous case (decided by a higher court) must be followed, was apt to stand in the way of reform, certainly by judges, and perhaps also by commissioners. However, this potential obstacle to reform fell rather easily, and it happened in an interesting interactive manner. It had been established in 1898 that the House of Lords considered itself bound by its past decisions. The same principle was adopted by the Irish Supreme Court after 1922. But in 1965 that court reversed itself and overruled an earlier case.[21] Also in 1965, the Scottish Law Commission was examining the role of precedent in the Scottish legal system, and it had decided (after consulting the English commissioners) to recommend a simple statute declaring that decisions in the House of Lords in Scottish appeals would not be considered binding on courts in Scotland. While this did not represent a major change in Scottish legal thinking, it did prompt the English lord chancellor to reconsider the basic doctrine. Within a few months, he issued a Practice Statement, or rule, which said that the House of Lords would regard its decisions as "normally binding," but it might depart from them if it was right to do so.[22] Thus the several systems had interacted to produce one of the major legal alterations of the century.

That the Scottish Law Commission had assumed such a role in the process of making this change might have surprised a casual observer. But it was no surprise to Lord Kilbrandon, the head of the commission. The act was "one in which we may claim a modest but important success....The fruit of consultations among their Lordships was not the legislation we had suggested, but something which will be equally effective."[23] This influence from Scotland was a vital part of the new trend in interaction.

The Invasion of Scots Law

One of the basic issues in legal interaction in modern times has been the preservation of the independence of Scots law. Since the Union of 1707, the potential for English interference has been present in appeal cases and in statute law. At the same time, vigorous defenders have urged Scottish solutions for English legal problems. In the 1950s there seemed to be an escalation of both tendencies: open and hostile resistance to the English threat, and a growing number of incidents in which Scots law helped to change English law or practice. A brief survey can only sketch the outline of English invasion and show the strengths of Scottish resistance.

In the first two-and-a-half centuries of Anglo-Scottish union, many commentators foretold the demise of the separate Scottish legal system. They cited abuses of the treaty of union, an array of discriminatory legislation, and the futility of appeals to the anglocentric House of Lords. In addition there was a group of Scots who seemed to favor closer alignment. But English influence was more of an attitude than a campaign. To illustrate this mind-set, we may examine a little-noted phenomenon which we will call "mistaken identity." English judges, who sometimes should have known better, insisted that English and Scottish law were "the same" when that was manifestly untrue. Whether to make their work easier by applying English rules to Scottish cases, or whether because of genuine misunderstandings, cases such as these could produce a vexing precedent against Scottish history and practice.[24]

This assumed similarity was a convenient but irregular judicial step. It was established procedure to treat cases or principles from other systems as matters of fact, to be introduced in evidence and proven before the court. The judicial equation was a shortcut around that practice (which *was* the same in Scotland and England). Judges could state equivalence without proving it. Proving (or disproving) identity should not have been a problem. There were, after all, some well-qualified Scots who came to the English bar, though not all with experience as advocates.[25] One who did fit that description was Henry Brougham, the first lord chancellor to have had training in Scots law. He and others (John Campbell for one) were employed in Scottish appeals at the bar of the House of Lords. Indeed, that experience may have given Brougham an inflated sense of his acquaintance with Scots law. In a case dealing with a partnership, Brougham delivered a lengthy judgment concluding that Scottish and English partnership law were the same "in principle," and therefore the Court of Session should be reversed. Actually, in this case the Scottish judges had claimed to be following English practice, and in the Lords an English judge (Baron Wynford) quoted Lord Stair against the Court of Session! [26]

In *Bartonshill Coal v. Reid* in 1858, Lord Chancellor Cranworth displayed the stereotypical English attitude: "in England the doctrine [of common employment] must be regarded as well settled; but if such be the law of England, on what ground can it be argued not to be the law of Scotland? The law, as established in England, is founded on principles of universal application, not on any peculiarities of English jurisprudence." Therefore a unanimous Court of Session, certain that this was not the rule of Scots law, was overturned.[27]

In the law of charity, a mistaken identity was noted more than once in the nineteenth century. In 1868 Lord Westbury said in a Scottish appeal:[28]

> The doctrine of trusts has the same origin and rests on the same principles both in Scots and English law, and it is desirable that it should be developed to the same extent in both systems of jurisprudence.

This idea has been rejected in more recent times. Lord Normand said that "the history of the origin and development of the law of trusts in Scotland is not at all the same as the history of the origin and development of the law of trusts in England."[29]

Alongside these cases of mistaken identity, and perhaps because of them, there was a growing awareness in the last century that the Lords' jurisdiction required more professional judges, and more non-English judges. Lay peers were no longer a factor in Lords' decisions, but there was no way to insure the presence of enough senior judges to do the work of the House. One option was to use life peerages to add legal talent to the House. James Parke was created a life peer (as Lord

Wensleydale) in 1856. The first Scottish law lord was Lord Colonsay and Oronsay in 1867. With the reform of appellate jurisdiction in 1876, further provision was made for the addition of Scottish and Irish law lords. This was done to address the anomaly of English judges sitting on "foreign" law cases. By the twentieth century, the apparitions of mistaken identity began to disappear.

The threat of English influence must be balanced against the very substantial weight of Scottish tradition. The latter proved to be more than equal to occasional English interference in statutes and appeals. Scottish tradition was well documented and had a stable structure. Its history was tended unevenly, but since the 1920s, that too was converted into a major asset. It is commonly said (at least by Englishmen) that Scots law belongs to the family of continental systems of law. It is in fact in between the common law systems and the continental, taking important elements from each, and hence Scots law is *sui generis*.[30] This is its primary strength. That solid durability rests upon both its institutional writers and its substantial body of case law. These are collated and reviewed in a literature which contains encyclopedic works and digests as well as a stream of treatises and a steady flow of periodical commentary. This more positive picture has only clarified in the last century, though some elements have been present over the entire modern period.[31]

The organization of Scots law has also been a source of strength. Here the main feature is the centralized court structure: the College of Justice comprises the high court judges, both civil and criminal. Under them the sheriffs form an organized hierarchy. The most distinguishing feature is the totally independent system of criminal law in Scotland. Under the central direction of the lord advocate are the procurators fiscal, the public prosecutors in the several localities (49 districts, 6 sheriffdoms). The sheriff courts also have civil authority; indeed, they have jurisdiction unless it is given to others by statute, which is the opposite of the English county court.

Another asset of the Scottish legal tradition is in the historiography of Scots law. Here a durable (if sometimes devalued) old foundation has been strengthened by new academic energy in the past half century. The foundation of modern historiography was in the work of Lord Kames and his peers in the eighteenth century, who collected and catalogued decisions and added their insights in numerous essays. The next major stage came in the work of Thomas Thomson and Cosmo Innes in assembling records in the early nineteenth century. Their generation also boasted the accomplished historical work of John Burnett on the criminal law, and that of Archibald Alison, who wrote in the same field, but who was better known as a writer of European history. For the next few generations there were occasional bright spots: Henry Cockburn in the nineteenth century; John Dove Wilson and William Dickson, ca. 1900. In the 1920s some important developments marked the beginning of a revival in Scottish legal history. The National Library was established on the foundation of the Library of the Faculty of Advocates (1925). In 1934 the Stair Society was founded for the scholarly study of Scots law. There was no instant flow of modern history, but a definite rise in interest.

There has also been a long tradition of comparative study of English and Scottish law, one which offers powerful antidotes to mistaken identity. These Scottish authors explained differences and sometimes championed the Scottish solutions over the English. The earlier practitioners in the field were Innes, Forbes, and MacDowall. The early twentieth century saw a renewal of the same interest. J.W. Brodie-Innes wrote *Comparative Principles of the Laws of England and Scotland* in 1903. In 1924 Hector Burn Murdoch published his *Notes on English Law as Differing from Scots Law*, and Andrew Graham Murray (Viscount Dunedin, lord president from 1905 to 1913 and lord of appeal from 1913 to 1930) gave a David Murray lecture which he called *The Divergencies and Convergencies of English and Scottish Law* in 1935.

After World War II there was an angry upsurge in the study of Anglo-Scottish legal relations. In April 1949 in his inaugural lecture as professor of law in the University of Aberdeen, Thomas Broun Smith addressed the "Severalty of the Administration of Justice in the United Kingdom."[32] The same year Lord Cooper (Lord President of the Court of Session) published *The Scottish Legal Tradition*. These would turn out to be the opening salvos of a counterattack on the English intrusion. The next year, the most bruising of these shots was fired by Andrew Dewar Gibb (Regius Professor of Law in the University of Glasgow) in his *Law from over the Border*, which criticized the House of Lords appellate jurisdiction, aiming chiefly at the years 1707–1876. He concluded that "in respect of competence for its task it would appear to be in theory completely indefensible." But Gibb conceded that[33]

> The Scottish jurisdiction of the House has given an impetus to certain legal reforms in Scotland. For some of these such as the civil jury Scotland has small cause to be thankful. Others were beneficial; they were right even if for a wrong reason. Finally, through the House of Lords, the example of the law of Scotland has from time to time affected the law of England. A little reciprocity may be thought to have enhanced the value of a very strange experiment.

The 1950s saw a set of disturbing cases and a number of critical essays which suggested that a showdown was brewing. Beside the rise in Scottish nationalist sentiment, would this be the basis for some kind of legal secession? The most notable of these conjunctions was in 1952. John MacCormick, the rector of the University of Glasgow, brought a suit against the application of the royal titles act in Scotland, on the ground that Queen Elizabeth could not use the numeral "II" in her northern realm. The case was dismissed, but not without a sympathetic statement from Lord Cooper, who underscored the Scottish hostility to the doctrine of parliamentary sovereignty.[34]

> The principle of the unlimited sovereignty of Parliament is a distinctively English principle which has no counterpart in Scottish constitutional law. It derives its origin from Coke and Blackstone, and was widely popularised during the nineteenth century by Bagehot and Dicey.... Considering that the union legislation extinguished the Parliaments of England and Scotland and replaced them by a new Parliament, I have difficulty in seeing why it should have been supposed that the new Parliament of Great Britain must inherit all the peculiar characteristics of the English Parliament, but none of the Scottish Parliament.

Lord Cooper died in 1955, but T. B. Smith carried the torch for a long period, producing numerous essays on the theme.[35]

Even while the alarm was being sounded, Scottish tradition continued. We will never know how serious a threat was posed or whether Scotland's defenders were over-reacting. The interesting fact is that the "tide" of influence had never moved in only one direction, and by 1960 it had begun to move significantly southward. There were no dramatic shifts, only assorted interactions. For instance, in one important case in 1956, the House of Lords decided that it was not bound in a Scottish appeal to follow a previous ruling it made in an English appeal.[36] This would be followed in a decade by the Scottish-influenced decision to limit *stare decisis*, already noted.

Outside of case law, there were signs of energy in other areas. Important Scottish legal writing was on the increase. Leading the way was David M. Walker's *Law of Damages in Scotland* (1955); in 1957 the Stair Society's cooperative *Introduction to Scottish Legal History* was published; in 1959 David Walker's single-volume account of *The Scottish Legal System* broke new ground. Scots law was alive and well; there had been a political crisis; but in law, a tide was already moving in the opposite direction: the point had been noted even by Gibb ("the example of the law of Scotland"). That view was amplified by Lord Denning in his David Murray Memorial Lecture in 1961 (published as *Borrowing From Scotland* in 1963).[37]

There was never any systematic "borrowing," but the record of the twentieth century suggested that interaction went deeper than Lord Denning thought. His superficial blend of "principles and men" belonged to an older historiographical tradition, whereas it is possible, in the twentieth century, to show quite extensive borrowing in the process of the law. These episodes came to constitute a completely new level of sustained interaction, quite unknown to earlier periods. Looking closely at a few key examples of this kind of interaction will simultaneously deflate the conventional idea of English invasion and demonstrate the salient Scottish extensions in the opposite direction.

Scottish law, as we have seen, had long had the capacity, in opportune situations, to influence English law, whether or not the English lawyer chose to acknowledge it. The different approaches of the northern system could from time to time fit the circumstances of a case more precisely than the English, and they might be accepted in a decision. Of course, acceptance had varied forms and levels of acknowledgment. The significance of the landmark case of *Donoghue v. Stevenson* in 1932, which saw English adoption of the principle of "culpa" (what English lawyers called "duty of care") was that it also contained a public recognition of Scots influence.[38] This signalled a new era in Anglo-Scottish legal interaction, and over the next few decades, the influence of Scottish law would increase, in tandem with Scottish nationalist feeling. There were several key areas, and though no discernible general pattern was present, there was a very significant set of alterations.

The story of Donoghue is well known. A shop assistant became ill after drinking a ginger beer which contained a decomposed snail. She sued the maker, and against all the odds, her claim was upheld in the House of Lords. This departed from the English ideas of liability and negligence, and introduced a "duty of care" which was very much like the Scottish *culpa.* Denning later said "it seems to me that unconsciously they introduced the Scottish law about delict or *culpa* into our English law" and that the English law "is now of the same breadth."[39] This sounds like an echo of the old "mistaken identity," though now in reverse.

In the area of "common employment" where there had been so many collisions in the nineteenth century, and where workmen's compensation had been invented to soothe matters, the English courts persisted into the 1940s with the traditional view. But that became harder and harder to maintain. In a series of cases involving coach and tram accidents, where drivers employed by the same company were injured, the doctrine took on an especially ugly appearance.[40] The judges seemed to be incapable of extricating themselves, and a statute was drafted "to repeal the defence of common employment," the Law Reform (Personal Injuries) Act of 1948. However it was explained, this was a case in which a doctrine had been forcibly extended to Scotland in the 1850s (Bartonshill) but within a century, it was rejected by the political leadership.

Probably the most interesting, and surely the most explicit, borrowing from Scotland occurred in the realm of criminal sentencing. In the 1950s, an English campaign against capital punishment had reached a crescendo with the formation of a Royal Commission. The English debate became entangled with a long-running controversy over the insanity defense and the so-called "McNaghten Rules." McNaghten was a Scot, and he had shot and killed the secretary of Sir Robert Peel, mistaking him for his employer. The English court set the standard rule that one who was incapable of understanding the crime was legally insane. In Scotland there was a sentencing option for "diminished responsibility." In a case where a deranged person was found guilty, the mental state was introduced *after* the conviction, and only to mitigate the sentence.

This method had been evolving in Scottish criminal process since 1867. In the leading case, Alexander Dingwall had stabbed his wife with a carving knife in the early hours of January 1. Dingwall suffered from chronic alcoholism, but according to Lord Deas[41]

> not such as to warrant an acquittal on the ground of insanity, and he could not therefore exclude it from the consideration of the jury here...in making up their minds whether, if responsible to the law at all, the prisoner was to be held guilty of murder or of culpable homicide.

The doctrine developed slowly. The English borrowing came late in the process. The concept evidently appealed to the Royal Commission, the support of which was responsible for inserting it in the Homicide Act of 1957. Indeed, the attorney general said "what we have done is to adopt and adapt the Scottish law of diminished responsibility in cases which do not amount to insanity."[42] In practice, as Nigel Walker has shown, the adaptation may have actually produced a more liberal result in English law.[43] But the basic point was quite clear. Scottish principles were not only received, their reception was more plain and less problematic than in the past.

Scottish legal procedure also offered some models for English reform. In both countries a key area of legal reform was in legal aid. There had been sporadic efforts to improve this side of the legal system since the early twentieth century in England. There the pauper litigant had to have less than £25 of property even after reform. In Scotland, since the fifteeenth century there had been a looser method of providing assistance. Both systems engaged in reviews and restructuring in the late 1940s.

In a variety of other ways, proceedings were haphazardly rendered more uniform. For instance, Crown proceedings were treated differently in England and Scotland until 1897.[44] In 1947 a statute set aside the older immunity. Another special area was the review of official action, known as "judicial review." This was a difficult concept, except in Ireland where a written constitution made the idea sensible even if the implementation was slow.[45] Allied to review was the question of statutory interpretation. This seemed to take new life from some cases involving the boards of the nationalized industries.[46]

Another area of concern was in jurisdiction. Where there was a choice of court, how was it made? A number of cases arose in which English and Scottish and Irish venues were in the balance, and some of these helped move the courts toward adopting a Scottish rule called *forum non conveniens*, namely that the case ought to be moved because the court was not the most convenient (for the parties). This had been anathema to English judges.[47]

There were other procedural areas, such as arbitration, where English-Scottish differences came to the surface. Here, in the well-known case of *Miller v. Whitworth Estates* some of these differences were epitomized.[48] An English architect had contracted for work in Scotland. In a dispute, arbitration was conducted according to Scottish procedure and the architect objected. The Court of Appeal supported the Scots company, but the House of Lords said that since the parties had used the R.I.B.A. form for the contract, the English law of arbitration applied and the Court of Appeal was reversed.

Contemporary Scottish invasion seems benign, and there is more open and genuine sharing of legal tools and ideas with somewhat less chauvinism. There now is occasional, nonthreatening but ongoing interaction and both countries have facilitated that with new reform agencies.[49] Regrettably there have been less benign areas of interaction, where mutual action has had a darker side. The Anglo-Irish conflict continued to foster special legal provisions, particularly in the years after 1969, and this interaction had wide and enduring impact.

Emergency Powers and Interaction

Since 1914 emergency powers have been in force in the United Kingdom and Ireland for considerable periods of time, indeed longer than the periods of mere, unaided ordinary criminal laws. But rather than a substitution, emergency laws have always operated alongside criminal law, sometimes with special structures (police, courts, statutes) but always with overlapping personnel (lawyers, judges, legislators). Thus there has been no way to insulate, and some opportunity to infect, the ordinary systems. Similarly, between Ireland North or South and the rest of the United Kingdom, there has been continuing interaction. Variety in the details of emergency powers and their incidence has not negated strong parallels in development. To illustrate and explain this phenomenon we may begin with a sketch of the recurrent issue of these laws in the half century before the latest crisis. Then looking more closely at the period since 1969, some deeper analysis will display the varied nature of interaction: in the definition of crimes, in the constitution of courts, and in the rights of accused parties.

Only weeks after the Home Rule Act passed (with its companion suspension), the Defence of the Realm Act became law in August 1914. This law gave powers to ministers to make and enforce regulations, with military courts (including the death penalty, until the amendment act of 1915). DORA did not suspend normal courts or criminal laws, but it spawned a huge volume of Defence of the Realm Regulations. These measures were due to expire at the end of the fighting, but they were extended in a variety of ways. At first, there were delays in general and there were specific extensions (Courts Emergency Powers Acts, etc). In addition, a peacetime Emergency Powers Act (1920) was modelled on DORA and aimed at dealing with the threat of civil disorders in Britain, specifically major industrial disturbances.[50] Most critical, however, was the enactment of the Restoration of Order (Ireland) Act in 1920 (ROIA), which virtually reenacted DORA for the troubled community of postwar Ireland.[51]

As we saw in the last chapter, the Irish situation had remained explosive after the Easter Rebellion of 1916. The Sinn Fein victory in the 1918 election allowed the formation of a provisional government. Those who won (and were not in captivity) proclaimed the Dail Eireann in Dublin, and thereafter the colonial government was in disarray. British attempts to retain control met with violent resistance, which was countered with emergency powers.

In 1920 the British Parliament passed the Government of Ireland Act, providing the legal basis for partition; that was endorsed by the Treaty of 1921 and ratified by the Dail in 1922. The antitreaty republicans then took up arms against the Free State, while the government in Belfast squared off against its domestic minority and republican invaders. Both governments assumed emergency powers: in Ulster the Civil Authorities (Special Powers) Act was passed in April 1922. This act was a slimmed-down version of the ROIA, without courts martial. The minister of home affairs was to make regulations "for the preservation of the peace and maintenance of order." The act also contained the remarkable section 2 (4):

> If any person does any act of such a nature as to be calculated to be prejudicial to the preservation of peace or maintenance of order in Northern Ireland and not specifically provided for in the regulations, he shall be deemed to be guilty of an offence against the regulations.

At first the Special Powers Act was renewed annually, then for a five-year period in 1928. In 1933 the act was made permanent. Up until its replacement in 1973, the act was subject to alteration via the changes in regulations, but it was a permanent fixture in the law enforcement structure of Northern Ireland.

In the Free State during 1922, there was some use of martial law and of the Restoration of Order regulations, but these provisions were of doubtful legality, especially in light of the new constitution's stance on fundamental rights (arts. 65, 66). Matters came to a head in August 1923 when the Court of Appeal decided that a state of war did not exist, and thus martial law powers were no longer valid.[52] The Oireachtas quickly passed the Public Safety (Emergency Powers No. 2) Act which made provision for power to intern suspects. Before this expired a year later, further laws were enacted: the Public Safety (Powers of Arrest and Detention) Act, 1924; the Public Safety (Punishment of Offenders) Temporary Act, 1924; and the Firearms (Temporary Provisions) Act, 1924. These Acts expired in 1925, but they were replaced by permanent measures: a Firearms Act, 1925, and Treasonable Offences Act, 1925, plus a new Public Safety (Emergency Powers) Act in 1926 (for internment) which was activated by declaration of a state of emergency. In the wake of the assassination of the minister for justice, Kevin O'Higgins, a new, five-year emergency law was passed in 1927, but repealed a year later. In 1931 a permanent mechanism was designed to activate special powers. In an amendment to the Constitution (art. 2A), provisions were made for a special tribunal, special police powers, and the by now standard features of emergency legislation.

In the 1930s, while open civil war had subsided, there were other conditions which provoked anxiety and the knee-jerk response of emergency powers. In demonstrations by the unemployed and marches by political extremists, British authorities perceived a growing threat to internal security. There was a particular concern over "private armies" such as the black-shirted followers of Oswald Moseley's British Union of Fascists. It was precisely the uniformed procession which was the object of the Public Order Act of 1936. This law gave police special powers to "give directions" to organizers of processions "necessary for the preservation of public order" (s. 3). Specific conduct in these circumstances was made an offense (possession of a weapon, threatening words, refusing to give identity, ss. 4, 5, 6). The Public Order Act remained on the statute book until replaced by the Public Order Act of 1986.

In 1937 the Free State adopted a new constitution, rejecting the dominion status granted in 1922 and unilaterally creating the republic. In the new constitution, which contained a bill of rights and the provision for judicial review, there were sections to facilitate exercise of emergency powers. Article 28.3.3 recognized laws "for the preservation of public safety and the preservation of the state in time of war or armed rebellion." Article 38.3 allowed the establishment of special nonjury courts so long as those courts were established by proper legislative acts. In 1939 it was deemed necessary to proceed with such emergency laws. The Offences Against the State Act, 1939, provided for a Special Criminal Court (part V) and for internment (part VI). An Emergency Powers Act also passed in 1939 which conferred broad powers on the government. The Special Criminal Court ceased to meet in 1946 but it was not terminated until 1962. The declaration which was issued under the act of 1939 was only rescinded in 1976. Once again, emergency laws showed unexpected longevity.

Due to a rash of IRA bombings, the British government in 1939 adopted the Prevention of Violence (Temporary Provisions) Act. The measure was quickly passed in the last week of July, during the height of the crisis. It was supposed to expire in two years, but it was extended annually until 1954. The Prevention of Violence Act permitted the police to expel suspects against whom there was insufficient evidence to convict. It gave the power to arrest on suspicion and detain for up to seven days and gave authority to issue search warrants to senior police officers rather than to justices of the peace. The draconian emergency powers of the war were soon to follow. On August 24, 1939, the Emergency Powers (Defence) Act became law. The Crown was empowered to make "Defence Regulations" for "securing the public safety, the defence of the realm, the maintenance of public order, and the efficient prosecution of any war in which His Majesty may be engaged, and for maintaining supplies and services essential to the life of the community" (s. 1). The act further specified powers to apprehend and try violators and to detain persons whose detention "appears to be expedient." The operation of the law provoked some strenuous debate, especially as to internment practices. These powers remained in force until the end of the war.

The two decades after 1945 represent the longest period in the twentieth century free of emergency legislation, though it must be noted that colonial sites were providing opportunity for the exercise of this special talent. However the postwar lull in emergency powers may have distracted contemporaries, it cannot alter the fact that the preceding half century had seen those features become a regular part of the legal landscape. That degree of permanence had to smooth the way for the reintroduction and reestablishment of emergency powers in the 1970s.

With widespread disorder in Ulster in 1969, British troops were sent in and emergency powers implemented once again. At first the authorities used the long-standing special powers from the interwar period. But because these had attained such a bad reputation, and because they were not geared to a British army occupation, and because of embarrassment caused by the implementation of internment under the old powers, when London assumed direct rule of the province in 1972, it began to search for alternative legislative solutions. The result was the Northern Ireland (Emergency Provisions) Act of 1973 (EPA). This Act provided special police powers, a set of scheduled offenses, and a method of nonjury trials.

In the following year, after several spectacular IRA bomb attacks in Britain, the mainland also saw renewed emergency powers. The Prevention of Terrorism Act of 1974 (PTA) combined some features from the 1939 Prevention of Violence Act with some of the elements of other special powers acts to combat the newly christened "terrorist" foe. Both EPA and PTA were enacted for limited terms, in the tradition of emergency powers. And in that same tradition, both were renewed readily and regularly, remaining in force into the 1990s. The paradox of emergency permanence appeared once again. To better understand the significance of emergency or special powers and their special variety of legal interaction, it is necessary to look closely at different aspects of the process. By examining special offenses, special courts, and special procedures, we may get a clearer view of how these techniques caused or were caused by legal interaction.

One of the cardinal features of special powers was the definition of particular offenses. At the most elementary level, this was a justification for the creation of the powers: namely that there were prospective acts which the criminal law might not recognize or punish. Further, the particular offense prescription enabled separate treatment as to definition, conviction, and punishment. Some of the precursors of special offenses dated from the nineteenth century. For example, in the Dynamite War of the early 1880s, when radicals bombed a number of targets, the Explosive Substances Act provided elaborate definition of the lawful means of producing and handling explosives, creating a number of offenses for those uses which fell outside the statute.

An even older power concerned proscription of hostile organizations. The history of this usage dates from at least as early as the proscription of Daniel O'Connell's Catholic Association in the 1820s. The proscription power was revived by ROIA and by both Public Safety (IFS) and Special Powers (NI) acts. Proscribed organizations were central to the EPA 1973 and the PTA 1974. In the former, fines and imprisonment awaited those convicted of belonging to or supporting the listed organizations (s. 19). In schedule 2 the specified groups were the Irish Republican Army, Cumann na m'Ban, Fianna na h'Eireann, Saor Eire, Sinn Fein, and the Ulster Volunteer Force. A year later, the PTA included membership, support, addressing a meeting, or wearing any "item of dress" or displaying "any article" which would "arouse reasonable apprehension that he is a member or supporter of a proscribed organisation." Schedule 1 listed only one body, the Irish Republican Army. In both acts, there were provisions for the secretary of state to add to or delete from the list of organizations. The purpose of both was plainly to suppress the public appearance of members and to provide the authorities with a relatively simple charge for use in any related prosecutions. Any sense that these measures would actually suppress the organizations was not apparent. In fact, the public order laws on the books would achieve the same result as the proscription clauses: the latter were primarily a gesture of political disapproval by the communities and their leaders.

Another particular offense in EPA 1973 was unlawful collection of information with respect to the police or her Majesty's forces "likely to be useful to terrorists" (s. 20). In addition, escaping from custody or aiding in an escape was added to the scheduled offenses (schedule 4). The full list of scheduled offenses (those triable under the act and the courts created therein) included common law offenses (murder, manslaughter, arson, and riot) and a long list of statutory offenses dating from 1861.

The approach of the PTA was decidedly different. In addition to proscribing the IRA, that act gave the secretary of state the power "in such way as appears to him expedient to prevent acts of terrorism (whether in Great Britain or elsewhere)" (s. 3). This was the basis for the power to issue exclusion orders against those "concerned in the commission, instigation or preparation of acts of terrorism." Exempting long-term residents of Britain, this measure allowed the authorities to monitor travel between Ireland and Britain.

The subsequent amendments and extensions of both EPA and PTA have added more special offenses: unlawful training in munitions (EPA 1975); joining a public demonstration being disbanded (EPA 1978); unlawful collection of information (EPA 1978); withholding information about "an act of terrorism" (PTA 1984); and financial assistance to a proscribed organization (PTA 1989). The general point on special offenses is simply that they reflected powerful political impulses in both communities, and they contributed to varied forms of legal interaction, including duplication, inspiration, and exhortation. Commentators like Walker, Hogan, and Townshend share a sceptical view of their value as supplements to criminal law.

There was not the same need to create special courts as there was to create special offenses. By and large, the authorities preferred to rely on the existing courts, fortified by statutory offenses and procedural changes. Over time there were exceptions to this rule. There were situations where some issues seemed to require special expertise, as for example in the industrial courts and the munitions tribunals (1919). There was occasional use of an extraordinary jurisdiction, the best example being the Special Criminal Court in Dublin (1923, 1935, 1972).

Seeing this context explains the singular importance and unusual status of the so-called "Diplock courts" in Northern Ireland. Lord Diplock's inquiry into the legal disarray in Ulster was one of several attempts to understand the situation. According to the home secretary, William Whitelaw, the object of the Diplock Commission was to "consider whether changes should be made in the administration of justice in order to deal more effectively with terrorism without using internment under the Special Powers Acts."[53] In other words, the British government was attempting to fashion a new approach to the problem which would avoid the old instrument of arrest without charge and replace it with effective judicial action.

Working under pressure, in the midst of the heaviest violence of the unrest, the Diplock Commission recommended a list of procedural changes, the most serious of which was trial of scheduled offenses by a judge "sitting alone with no jury." In addition, denial of bail, shifted burden of proof in firearms cases, easier admission of confessions and written evidence were the major procedural recommendations aimed at more effective court operation.

The Diplock report proposals went into the Emergency Provisions legislation of 1973. These nonjury courts have been subjected to extensive analysis and criticism.[54] It is not our purpose here to add to that critique. We are concerned with what the Diplock courts tell us about legal interaction, and in that context, how they were significant. The interaction in this instance is decidedly triangular. As Hogan and Walker note:[55]

> In the light of history and corresponding experience in the Republic, the existence of a special trial system in Northern Ireland is unremarkable. However, the nature of special trials and the facility with which they can be developed rightly cause concern.

Some of that concern might arise from the fact that, while both parts of Ireland experienced special courts, the same has not been the case with England. And Lord Diplock had his legal roots in that jurisdiction, as did all of the commissioners. Why did it occur to English commissioners to dispense with juries in Northern Ireland? Would they have had the same inclination dealing with disorder in England?[56]

The context of the Diplock courts helps to explain the radical step. In trying to end internment, the British authorities wanted to institute a legal process insulated from the extreme emotions in the community. The courts represented a step away from the non-judicial internment of suspects without trial. In the short term, the Diplock courts were thus a positive step. That the courts failed to evolve toward the norm of trial by jury, and that they continued in operation more than twenty years later was yet another reminder of the staying power of "emergency" provisions.

The creation of special powers and procedures has always, by definition, been a repudiation of the traditional system of criminal justice. One saving feature has been temporal limitation (the strength of which we may doubt). Another saving feature has been the invisible (imaginary?) wall between emergency powers and procedures and those of the ordinary criminal justice system. This also has shown serious weakening recently, particularly in the area of the right to silence.

The right to silence, or the protection against self-incrimination, has a long history in English law. Its most notable early record was established by the Court of Star Chamber, which in the seventeenth century frequently used a simplified procedure of *ore tenus*—that is, the silence of an accused person was held to imply a confession.[57] In modern times, the provision applied to police questioning and to trial. The suspect was to be warned that should he choose to answer questions, those answers could be used against him. This had the dual effect of protecting the suspect, and validating such answers as were given.

In recent years there have been varied pressures to reduce or eliminate the right to silence. Some criminal law statutes have explicitly curtailed the right. The first formal proposal to limit the right generally came from the Criminal Law Review Committee in 1972. The Committee did not compile empirical evidence, but it recommended that if an accused chose not to answer questions, in pretrial proceedings or at trial, a judge or jury should be able to draw such inference from that silence as they deemed appropriate.

The Royal Commission on Criminal Procedure in 1981 reasoned that abridging the right to silence was inconsistent with the basic rule that the prosecution had the burden of proof in criminal proceedings. Much of the commission's findings went into the formation of the next important measure on procedure, the Police and Criminal Evidence Act of 1984 (PACE). This law was meant to enhance the protections offered to a suspect, and some argued that this gave enough new protection to render the right to silence unnecessary. The Codes of Practice issued under the act gave added protection to suspects under interrogation, including the practice of tape-recording of interviews with the police. Yet the defenders of the right argued that PACE was based on assumed retention of the right, and thus it would be incorrect to use its improved protections as arguments to reduce or eliminate the right to silence.

In the next phase of the debate, several actions related the situation in Northern Ireland directly to the ongoing discussion. On the one hand, in the PTA renewal of 1984 a section was introduced which made withholding of information an offense (s.11). That provision was retained in PTA 1989 (s.18). In the Irish Republic, the Criminal Justice

Act of 1984 restricted the right to silence. Inferences could be drawn when the accused failed to account for certain physical evidence (s. 18) and when the accused failed to account for his presence at the scene of an offense (s. 19).

In 1987, the government reviewed the PTA's most recent version and recommended the abolition of the right to silence. This was based upon the difficulty faced by the Royal Ulster Constabulary (RUC) in mounting successful prosecutions in the face of determined silence by suspected terrorists. The Criminal Justice Act lately passed in the Republic was used as an example to be followed. The government formed a Home Office Working Group in May 1988 to study the right to silence, but its work was preempted by the issue (in November 1988) of the Criminal Evidence (Northern Ireland) Order. In that order, it was made permissible to draw inferences from the silence of the accused in specific situations, in terms which appear to follow some provisions of the Criminal Law Revision Committee (1972) and of the Irish Criminal Justice Act (1984).

In general, the pressure to restrict the right has arisen from police and judicial complaints of abuse by "professional criminals" in the police station and of "ambush" defenses in court. These complaints gain added emphasis when they arise from the terrorist milieu. The Irish dimension added what may have been the decisive weight in this instance. The Royal Commission on Criminal Justice (1991) was established in the wake of the series of miscarriages of justice involving the Birmingham Six, the Guildford Four, and others. Those accused terrorists had been sentenced to long prison terms, based on tainted evidence and forced or altered confessions. The tone of the commission's terms of reference was not at all apologetic. In fact, in the area of our subject, the commission was to look at

> the extent to which the courts might draw proper inferences from primary facts, the conduct of the accused, and any failure on his part to take advantage of an opportunity to state his position.

With this tone, it was no surprise that the next legislative proposal from the government continued in the restrictive direction of the 1988 Criminal Evidence Order. The Criminal Justice and Public Order Act of 1994 (c. 33) spelled out the consequences of the accused's failure to give evidence before trial (s. 34), or at his trial (s. 35), or his failure to account for physical evidence (s. 36), or his failure to account for his presence at a particular place (s. 37), namely that a court or jury "may draw such inferences from the failure or refusal as appear proper."

The compound effects of emergency laws enacted in the multiple jurisdictions of the British Isles have been enhanced by the temporal extension of emergency and by the physical interaction of the several jurisdictions. The general consequence has been a toughening of the criminal law, especially but not exclusively with respect to the terrorist. In that process, some of the traditional marks of the English and allied systems of criminal justice have been injured or lost: jury trial, right to silence, and several other assumed (but unwritten) rights—freedom of assembly, protest, and speech. No one has been able to prove that the traditional criminal law might have handled this branch of crime without special powers; everyone would admit that the pressure of political emergency made it impossible to test that thesis.

In 1971 the Irish government made use of the European connection to challenge the use of internment and alleged torture by British army personnel; this was an early and important example of yet another novel form of legal interaction in the late twentieth century. Although the case of *Ireland v. UK* was not concluded until 1978, and although its legal effect may have been limited, it was an example of another major form of interaction, the entry of European law.

Community Laws in the United Kingdom and Ireland

Throughout the modern period English law has taken a formal position against allowing "foreign" law to be cited, putting Scottish and sometimes Irish law in that classification. Any rule of foreign law had to be proven as fact before the court, to receive it in evidence, while relegating it to an inferior position as just one more fact for the jury and the court to consider. But this public stance was always false to some degree. There could never be a total exclusion of foreign law, but the pretence that there was gave lawyers and judges a convenient excuse to exclude or ignore foreign elements. However, much of what we have studied in this book was a continuing challenge to the insular myth. The actual shift, toward acceptance of foreign law, was a long, involved story, deserving its own full scholarly exploration. We may offer a simple sketch here to suggest the dimensions of the problem.

Insular treatment was modified from the midnineteenth century onward by a series of statutory changes aimed at improving international legal interaction. The law of extradition led the way here, with agreements and statutes being shaped between 1840 and 1870. There were also acts to permit "foreign law ascertainment," that is, to improve the method of putting foreign law before English courts. And there were, from 1890, foreign judgments acts: laws to provide a way to recognize and enforce the judgments of foreign courts. These clearly were responses to the growth of international law and its organization after 1850.

But a century later a truly remarkable change occurred in Europe. In the wake of the Second World War, the search for economic recovery plus the threat of Soviet political and military expansion produced the early steps toward a European Community. First there were the postwar rescue efforts of the International Monetary Fund (IMF) in 1946 plus the General Agreement on Tariffs and Trade (GATT) and the Marshall Plan in 1947. European states moved toward organized structures through the Organization of European Economic Cooperation (OEEC) and the multinational union of Belgium, the Netherlands, and Luxembourg (BENELUX) beginning in 1948. More general groupings came with the North Atlantic Treaty Organization (NATO) in 1949, the Council of Europe in 1950, and the European Coal and Steel Community (ECSC) in 1951.

The Treaty of Rome of 1957 established the Common Market (European Economic Community, EEC) and the European Atomic Energy Community (Euratom). These were merged with the ECSC, and by 1958 there was a new degree of economic unification, a process expected to lead to more legal, political, and military concentration. The United Kingdom had been a party to most of the postwar groupings, but it chose not to sign the Treaty of Rome. The country honored its continuing ties to the Commonwealth and Empire, and the resulting illusion of power made it appear that Britain did not need the kind of desperate measures which war-ravaged continental states did.

By 1961 the British government was applying for membership in the EEC. This attempt and a second one in 1967 were vetoed by France. In 1972, negotiation finally succeeded. There was a very heated and involved domestic political debate on the issue of membership, but we need to focus on the questions raised by lawyers. What did entry mean, and was it acceptable on legal grounds? There was a White Paper on the "Legal and Constitutional Implications of United Kingdom Membership of the European Communities" published in 1967.[58] This document admitted the radical change involved: "The Community law having direct internal effect is designed to take precedence over the domestic law of the Member states." Also Parliament "would have to refrain" from passing acts in conflict with community law. The authors tried to soothe anxiety: "This would not however involve any constitutional innovation. Many of our treaty obligations already impose such restraints," namely, the UN Charter, ECHR (the European Convention on Human Rights), and GATT. To a traditional English lawyer, this was no comfort. Similar assurances were given in another White Paper on the negotiations in 1971.[59]

> The English and Scottish legal systems will remain intact. Certain provisions of the treaties and instruments made under them, concerned with economic, commercial and closely related matters, will be included in our law. The common law will remain the basis of our legal system and our courts will continue to operate as they do at present.

These reassurances were quite necessary, for the United Kingdom was undertaking a totally unprecedented departure. The treaty itself, by constitutional law, was a prerogative matter. Neither Parliament nor the courts had anything to do with the executive power to negotiate and sign the Treaty of Brussels in January 1972.[60] But it was necessary, under English law, to have a statute passed to effect the terms of any treaty. The European Communities Act of 1972 was drafted for that purpose.[61]

The EC Act said that rights and obligations as well as remedies and procedures created by the several treaties of the communities were "recognised and available in law" and were to be "enforced, allowed and followed accordingly" (s. 2-1). Moreover, the test of any right was the community law, and the interpreter of that law was the European Court. In addition, the act provided for the implementation of the wide range of "secondary legislation" which the community produced. There were several forms, which were of varied impact: directives, regulations, and decisions of the European courts all were involved, and each would require a distinct level of adherence. But for the initial effect, it was now necessary to adhere to a whole new body of administrative law, another "new despotism" to some.

This sweeping change was both less and more than it seemed. Less because it only came into play when there was a breach of community law. More because it required the creation of an entirely new field of law for the profession in the U.K. and Ireland. Though the process now has nearly thirty years of experience, it is still early for an effective evaluation. But we can sketch the changing effects on United Kingdom law from two perspectives: how did European law come into U.K. courts and what has happened to U.K. litigants going into European courts? [62]

The first impression of what community law's entry would mean was unsettling. Lord Denning made a famous (over)statement in *Bulmer v. Bollinger* in 1974:[63]

> The treaty is like an incoming tide. It flows into the estuaries and up the rivers. It cannot be held back. Parliament has decreed that the treaty is henceforward to be part of our law.

The case concerned the right of two English manufacturers to use the word "champagne" for their cider and perry beverages. The French makers of champagne insisted that this violated community rules, but the first English judge declined to refer the case to the community court. His refusal was challenged in the Court of Appeal and this gave the court the chance to rule on the method of seeking a preliminary ruling from the Court of Justice. This provision of the treaty (article 177) was unsettling to English judges as a loss of jurisdiction (via an unfamiliar procedure). Denning put forth guidelines in his opinion and said that only the highest court should make a reference. These rules conveyed the nervous early reaction of the English judiciary. But references to Luxembourg and usage of community law in the courts both grew in the next two decades.

Scottish and Irish courts have not had very many occasions to apply community laws in comparison with the English courts.[64] The cases have been predominantly commercial and agricultural, in which instances there are many community regulations which come into play.[65] There have been others in which community rules are held to have been compromised, or in which national laws are found inconsistent with the treaties. The fundamental point is that the member states have the basic job of enforcing community law, with the occasional assistance of the Court of Justice in interpreting that law, thereby maintaining uniformity.

The road to some sort of consistent application of community law has been very bumpy. In one early case, a German plaintiff demanded repayment of a debt in marks, the county court refused to grant the plea or to make a reference; the Court of Appeal upheld the plea without a reference, assuming the authority to rule on a point of community law.[66] It was natural for the English court to assume the ability to interpret regulations, but it could not possibly put them into the European context. The need for such references was only slowly appreciated.

Along the way, related questions were raised. Would legal aid apply to references? This was declared valid in a case in 1977.[67] Would equal pay provisions be subject to community law on equality? [68] Here the case was over inconsistent U.K. law, and the European view prevailed. Even the criminal law was involved: *DPP v. Henn and Darby* found the defendants guilty of importing pornographic material from Denmark. They tried to argue a defense under the rights of import (art. 30), and the English ruling used the issue of public morality (art. 36) for its judgment. A reference was made in order to assure the finding.[69]

Community influence was not confined to cases bearing directly on some EEC regulation. Under the aegis of the community there is a new procedure for enforcing foreign judgments. Article 220 of the EEC treaty called for a new process, and the Brussels Convention of 1968 laid the groundwork. After accession, the United Kingdom agreed to the new framework in 1978, and Parliament passed the Civil Jurisdiction and Judgments Act in 1982. Under this law, courts in the United Kingdom now have rules laid down for recognizing and enforcing judgments in the courts of other contracting states.[70] This new procedure produced a number of anomalies for English (and Scottish and Irish) law. We may simply note the effect on the matter of foreign jurisdiction.

English law had a doctrine called *lis alibi pendens*; this allowed the court to either discontinue, to stay, or to ignore a proceeding. This is no longer allowed under the convention. While the requirements of the convention are not completely clear, this innovation may have been one factor encouraging the acceptance of the related Scottish doctrine, *forum non conveniens*, the stay of proceedings which allowed a case to proceed in a more convenient court. Another recent English legal development is related to the convention and the European courts. The "Mareva injunction" has evolved since the 1970s, a device used in other courts, by which the assets of a party may be frozen pending the outcome of a case.[71]

The cases where community law is applied in the courts of the United Kingdom are just one part of the story. The contact with community law also takes place in the court in Luxembourg, either in cases involving a member state or involving individuals or companies. Decisions in such cases obviously become part of community law, and even if precedents are not recognized, they are still of some influence in future cases, perhaps even guidance for future action in member states, their courts and/or legislatures. The United Kingdom has been brought before community courts on several occasions, sometimes, as we saw earlier, under the Human Rights Convention. More recently, some terms of the EEC treaty were at issue. In 1979 the commission brought a case on agricultural policy, relating to the United Kingdom's attempt to ban the import of potatoes.[72] The import ban was held illegal.

Elsewhere, the community claimed authority over fisheries, and unilateral acts of members were not allowed. In 1977, the United Kingdom disallowed certain nets, and the French government decided to sue. The court found against the United Kingdom for not having sought permission to institute the regulation. Community authority was clearly asserted in Ireland for the first time in *Pigs and Bacon Commission v. McCarren Ltd.* [73] Here a complaint was made against an existing Irish agency and its fees; the system was held in violation of EC regulation, and the Irish agency had to be reformed.

There are limited rights of individuals and companies under the treaties, and there have been cases where these parties have succeeded in the European Court. Miss Van Duyn was refused entry to the United Kingdom because she was connected with the Church of Scientology; this was challenged as a violation of community rules on free movement.[74] The case revolved around the rights conferred by European directives and their enforceability in United Kingdom courts.

In 1977 the commission found the Distillers Co. Ltd. in violation of art. 85 (distorting competition) on the complaint of Scottish whisky dealers.[75] Distillers were charging higher prices for exported spirits than for domestic sales. The company appealed the commission ruling to the Court of Justice but the verdict was upheld. The direct power of community law came up in another company case.[76] The plaintiff exporting butter in bulk claimed it was wrongfully denied permission by the Milk Marketing Board. An injunction was sought under art. 86 but not granted. Damages were awarded by the first judge, overturned, and then restored. Were they based on EC or English law?

It seems quite clear that the European connection brought a new dimension to law in the British Isles. There is no room now for an insular view of foreign law. Indeed, the legal profession has been forced to move toward more open contact between jurisdictions. In 1977 a European Community directive said that lawyers from one member state might appear in the courts of another member state. This did not have immediate effect, but now in Scotland there are provisions "for the admission of legal practitioners qualified in England and Wales or Northern Ireland to appear and conduct litigation in Scottish Courts."[77] In the same vein, there has been statutory recognition of the right to form multinational practices. The Courts and Legal Services Act of 1990 reversed previous restrictions on this type of work, clearly as a response to the growing demand for work in the EC and between English and other jurisdictions.

That same legislation was the product of yet another interactive experience. In the 1980s there was a major debate on the nature and regulation of the legal profession. In part it was about the cost and efficiency of lawyers and in part about their division into two groups, the solicitors and the barristers (or advocates). The governments of the United Kingdom and Ireland raised questions about the monopoly of audience and of practice, leading to reports and papers proposing major reforms. The Fair Trade Commission in Ireland commissioned a "Report into Restrictive Practices" in 1984. In Scotland the question of solicitors joining with accountants, surveyors, or others in "multidisciplinary" practices was studied in formal reports (1987–1990). Meanwhile in England and Wales discussion documents were produced by the lord chancellor which promised major overhaul of the profession in the later 1980s. The result of these studies has been a series of reform acts.[78] The laws have not radically changed the structure of the courts or the professions, but they have introduced new elements, the effects of which will only be clear in the future.

The effect of the European Community may be that the mixing of law is only more obvious than before. It is certainly not a complete innovation. As we have seen, the last few decades have experienced several levels or branches of interaction, not entirely new, but much more open and much more readily and continuously engaged with the national systems. The Scottish "invasion" and the Ulster emergency legislation, taken together with the impact of the European Community are evidence of the latest and most advanced stage of relations between the legal systems, that of very advanced and much less hostile legal interaction.

Conclusion

Law and the British Isles

> There is nothing that sets a man thinking and writing to such good effect about a system of law and its history as an acquaintance however slight with other systems and their history.
>
> Frederic W. Maitland
> "Why the History of English Law Is Not Written"
> (1888)

Maitland's inaugural lecture as Downing Professor of Law at Cambridge was a gloomy commentary on the failings of English legal historiography and the poor prospects for teaching legal history in the university.[1] This great scholar found gaps in comprehension between the study of English and continental systems and greater gaps between the thinking and working of lawyers and historians. While he thought the former might be curable, on the latter problem he was quite pessimistic. Must we reach a similar conclusion? Could it be that the history of the laws of the British Isles has not been written because of the gulf between systems and professions?

Law and History

It is a commonplace that law permeates modern society. What then prevents law from infiltrating general histories? Three answers come to mind, which relate to the law itself, the legal profession, and the profession of the historian. The law is paradoxically pervasive and private. While statutes, decisions, and legal traditions are public, criminal cases, private suits, and arbitrations are screened (in part or whole) from the media and the general public. The methods vary, but the judge in his private chambers may rule on motions without explanation, he may use the threat of contempt proceedings to control pretrial information or the comments of jurors. When cases are concluded, there may be other impediments. Only selected cases are recorded in regular series of law reports. Others are not "reported," but they may be recovered on computer files. There is some question as to whether these cases can be cited in court. Whatever the answer, the "unreported" cases, even more than their published cousins, remain well out of the view of the public.

The realm of lawmaking appears to be open, at least the statute book is open in nature. But details are worked out in cabinet or in committee or in private. Much "secondary" legislation is drafted and settled inside government departments. Cabinet meetings maintain a façade of unity, and we only learn later of disputes and differences from minutes and memoirs. Yet these point to another critical void. We have many probing and revealing reflections of politicians, sometimes long after the fact. In the law, however, there is a traditional aversion toward revelatory accounts of official business. Chancellors, law officers, judges, and barristers and solicitors have only produced a small amount of autobiographical work dealing with the workings of their craft.

The preservation of legal traditions might seem to give useful insights into legal systems. Yet these apparently "historical" features of the law are frequently discovered to be mythical survivals of past glories, and, however historically true they were in earlier centuries, their validity in modern times may be in question. A tradition can even shield quite contrary present conditions. For example, the image of the English jury as the bedrock of liberty obscures the fact that in the current legal system the English jury is a seldom-used instrument. Likewise, the notion of individual liberties (e.g., freedom of the press, speech, and public meeting) can be easily shown to rest on bad history and no current evidence.[2] A particularly egregious example can be found in the paeans to *habeas corpus*, a nearly moribund device in English criminal law (though it is still healthy in Ireland as is its parallel in Scotland).

However the law might be shielded from the public eye, we could expect the trained and vigilant historian to penetrate those barriers in order to lay out the contours of this vital activity. But here we encounter the other serious obstacles. The legal profession is by nature closed and unhistorical. The complex mysteries of the law are essential to practitioners. The vocabulary and the substance, the ritual and the rules establish the need for a profession.

The basic insularity is sometimes manifested in legal study. Maitland commented on "the traditional isolation of the study of English law from every other study." As a professor of law, he felt he could not connect the study of English law with that of other countries or even with its own legal history. The English common lawyer looked for precedents, but they were oddly unhistorical. The lawyer was thought to know about the past, but he gained little knowledge of the past from precedent because "the more modern the decision, the more valuable for his purpose." Moreover, the historian found the working of precedent was "almost of necessity a process of perversion and misunderstanding."

The ultimate blame for the absence of law from general histories must lie with the historian. Why would he or she eschew this rich mine of evidence? Maitland's answer was that "there are large and fertile tracts of history which the historian as a rule has to avoid because they are too legal." But even a century ago that view was overstated. Many monographs successfully mined the legal treasure-trove, among them Maitland's own brilliant interpretations.[3]

The historian typically does not need and does not acquire the expertise for decoding the law; for studying or composing a survey of the law; or for making a concordance of legal and general history. And these formidable tasks would only be the prelude to the much more difficult work of integration: how did the legal culture interact with all other aspects of domestic life, and beyond that, with other countries? This agenda is enough to deter any hardy historian who might have given a thought to legal integration. While that group has never been very large, there are positive signs for the future.

Law and History in the British Isles

Several fields in British history have had, for varying lengths of time, a strong component of legal or constitutional history. While that component has often been subordinated to political or social analysis, it nevertheless can form the basis for more integrated histories. Indeed, as noted at the outset, there have been some pioneering efforts, and the prospect for greater inclusion of law in English and archipelago history seems encouraging.

In the study of the empire, for example the field of "Atlantic history," the constitutional questions raised by the American Revolution have been treated in the stimulating works of Jack P. Greene and John Philip Reid. Willard Hurst, Morton Horwitz, and Peter Charles Hoffer have examined the early American legal systems in ways that have expanded our understanding of social history. While these works have given the legal communities and their relationships a key role in the general history of American colonial development, one may ask whether this could be done in a way that included Scottish and Irish laws and lawyers as well as English ones? [4]

The tremendous amount of work on crime and police since the eighteenth century opens up another vista for integration. Combining the study of popular demonstrations, ordinary crime, and innovative policing and punishment seems to offer an excellent avenue toward integrated social and legal history. There will be much more work required to explore the equally valuable history of civil litigation.[5]

The modern period displays manifold shapes of reform, social and political, which have powerful but little remarked legal dimensions. In social reform, the self-conscious society of the nineteenth century addressed the dangers and destitution of modern life with a battery of legal powers. In all parts of the British Isles there were significant changes in the law, which were part of the larger theme of social reform. In many reform efforts, genuine change was often frustrated. One example was in the story of imprisonment for debt. Parliament tried to end imprisonment for debts below £20 in 1844 but failed. The Small Debt courts (alias County Courts) set up in 1846 in England and Wales were another attempt, which met with limited success. In 1869 an act to abolish imprisonment for debt merely changed the crime to refusal to pay, and the numbers of imprisoned debtors increased.[6] Failures such as these were repeated in all parts of the British Isles. The lurching steps, changes of direction, and frequent defeats were important components of the "march of progress." But even with their inherent limitations, lawmaking and legal decisions deserve a more developed treatment in general social histories.

Researchers in many topical areas have deployed legal study: in the changing place of the established churches in the British Isles; in explaining the powerful force of industry and its corollary of organized labor; on the erratic and sometimes violent constitutional changes under the innocuous rubric of "home rule." These subjects and others are tied to essential legal conditions and alterations, matters which have to be explored more fully to enlighten general narratives. Fortunately, as we noted earlier, there are some pioneering works which show movement in this direction, albeit from different directions. W.R. Cornish and G de N. Clark have broken ground with *Law and Society in England*, a survey of general and legal history, mainly aimed at the student of law, providing a broad general context for legal developments. Norman Cantor, on the other hand, took a long view of Anglo-American legal history. In *Imagining the Law* he collected extensive contextual material, from the Middle Ages to the present, and on both sides of the Atlantic, to weave a description of the shared legal tradition. Paul Langford provided a vivid description of *Public Life and the Propertied Englishman, 1689–1798*. In his Ford Lectures, Langford detailed the response of property owners to the challenges of the eighteenth century, especially through the administration of the land law and the public activities of the propertied classes. In an important essay, Christopher Brooks has charted a course through "Litigation and Society in England, 1200–1996," showing that neglected but numerically dominant civil cases provide valuable insights for social historians.[7]

The potential for "legalized" historical narratives has existed for some time. Now it would seem that the inhibiting factors which bothered Maitland may be losing some of their power. The time seems right for more ambitious integration of law and general history and more comprehensive study of the law and legal systems in the British Isles.

Legal Interaction

In the course of this book, we have followed the story of legal interaction in the British Isles, particularly from 1660. This is only one approach to the plurality of legal systems at work in the modern world. For over a century lawyers have studied and compared legal systems. They have made a field of study of the conflicts which occur between them and the international law which would seem to embrace them all. More recently there have been studies of plural systems, that is, how native and colonial and metropolitan laws overlap and operate within a common area.[8] Obviously these broader forms of "interaction" have larger dimensions than those we have tried to comprehend here. But for our limited area of study, there are some valuable conclusions which can be made.

Legal interaction in the British Isles has been an *ad hoc* affair. There has been no plan to unite or federate the legal systems. Aside from the addition of Scottish and Irish law lords in the nineteenth century, there is hardly any act which even hints at unification. There is no uniform case law, though some proposals for consolidation or codification had that as a distant goal. Even statutory reconciliation had clear limits. Interaction has been and remains a collection of separate events, planned or otherwise, which juxtapose two or more systems. Over the last three hundred years the nature of legal interaction changed from conquest to convergence. For a century or more after the Restoration, there was an imperial era. It was supplanted, after decades of revolution, by an urge for reform which loosened many of the traditional foundations. The last century has consequently seen major constitutional changes: shifting laws and doctrines along with new courts and procedures have encouraged further interaction. At present, interaction does not carry a threat of foreign invasion but is instead part of a widening and almost routine engagement. Interaction has been a significant factor in most major alterations and innovations in modern law. Major changes in one system usually had an impact elsewhere. Solutions to problems have come from foreign systems with increasing regularity. In short, legal interaction has become an important, if neglected, part of modern legal history.

The story of modern interaction as we have traced it suggests three main stages of development. In the first stage, from the Restoration to the later eighteenth century, there were pronounced assertions of imperial legal power. These encouraged a variety of adaptations, but they did not produce amalgamation. From 1660 his Majesty's dominions had one royal master and three councils and parliaments and legal systems. To these were added the many separate colonial jurisdictions. The king's judges around the empire were his agents in his courts. Those courts had no central structure, nor did the events of the seventeenth century (the reign of James II in particular) encourage the creation of such a structure. The Privy Council was in the best position to assume such a role, but it was kept to the simpler task of hearing judicial appeals. These were numerous enough, as the right to petition was exercised around the royal dominions. All courts had unhappy suitors who might attempt to find justice from a higher authority. For civil cases, Scotland had the best ordinary provision for hearing an appeal (suspension and advocation). England and Ireland only allowed the writ of error for common law courts, but the petitions for equity appeals were allowed to grow and to gain new means of hearing. The House of Lords was well placed to play a key role, and it was soon hearing appeals from all three kingdoms. But its contribution was substantially different for England, Scotland, and Ireland. Those differences underscored the separation which still prevailed in 1720. The absence of any central judicial structure under the Crown was evidenced by the separate bodies of case law, collections upon which the appeals to the House of Lords were added as separate supplements.

The English Lords and Commons did jointly wield legislative power with the Crown. That power should have been supreme in the dominions of the Crown, but in various ways the authority of statute was less than complete. It was the fortune of the eighteenth century to see that power asserted, defended, and defied. Declaratory Acts, penal laws, and specific laws such as the Scottish Treason Act were powerful assertions of imperial authority; but they all proved to be incapable of forcing legal (legislative) uniformity. Lawmaking remained a divided enterprise even when legislatures were amalgamated.

Revolutions caused and were caused by constitutional debates. These debates engaged legal professionals from all parts of the empire. Whether it was the Stamp Act, the repeal of Poynings' Laws, or the defense of seditious Scots, there were qualified participants on both sides. Interaction was caught up with the fundamental political disputes of the age of revolution. But as there was no upheaval in Britain, legal systems remained intact, and interactive energies were channelled into reforms.

The second general stage of interaction began with the appearance and growth of the reforms of the nineteenth century. This activity was facilitated by a number of legal changes at the turn of the century and by responses to the revolutionary era (police and political reform) which brought about what Townshend called a "new image of public order."[9] The processes of inquiry, publicity, and legislative action were bound to stimulate and reflect comparison and interaction between legal systems. Legal inquiry was an early element in this process, and it was destined to go on for some time: it spurred several types of interaction and served as a main component of the reform trend.

The inquiries which probed the Court of Session, the courts generally, and the branches of the law itself, may have weakened some of the barriers between the systems, but separation was never threatened and was never put on the agenda as a target. Royal Commissions studied most of the courts, and they contributed to the demise of some and the reconstruction of others. The single most visible reform was the Judicature Act of 1873. The new English Supreme Court was ready to drop Scottish and Irish appeals. But in a scramble to amend the act, appeals were restored and new Scottish and Irish law lords were added. This essentially restored the status quo; there was no new British and Irish supreme court, but only the previous *ad hoc* review of some Scottish and Irish decisions. Interaction continued much as before.

The third stage of interaction began with the advent of democracy. The widening franchise shifted the place, the pattern, and the powers of courts of law in all systems. The most basic alteration was the democratizing of the clientele, first the voters themselves, and soon particular classes of clients such as tenants, workers, and women. By opening the courts to increasing numbers of the less affluent, democracy not only forced the expansion of legal aid and the dispersal of legal advice; it accelerated transformation of the court structures and the legal professions, as well as affecting their procedures. These changes made interaction much more natural, for example, with the general introduction of workmen's compensation and its attendant U.K. case law. Revision of the constitution was surely propelled by democracy. The Victorian constitution was quickly overtaken by change. New tribunals were created for new functions, and in many cases they served all communities in the British Isles without regard to old legal boundaries. The growth of tribunals created a parallel legal system of specialized judges beside the common law courts. The constitution also changed, inside the United Kingdom and outside it. The major internal change was the fracture of the Irish system into two parts, one remaining in the United Kingdom and the other becoming structurally independent. These alterations were responsible for more and different interaction since the 1920s. At the same time, the empire was forced to review its legal connections. In the process, there were reformulations of nationality law and the legislative and appellate links between the Crown and the colonies. These events coincided with a new English outlook on international law from the middle of the twentieth century. There was much more room for interaction and less chance for English imperial assertiveness; in all, interaction was becoming more healthy, which may have contributed to the most recent major development.

In the second half of the twentieth century, after extensive alterations in legal machinery in the generation after the Second World War, an established state of interaction was achieved in several different forms. The essential innovation in all cases was the creation of a relationship in which interaction was accepted as a continuing and healthy feature. There were several major examples: Scots law was extensively borrowed by the English, reversing what for some time looked like an English invasion. Helped somewhat by parallel law commissions, the dissimilar systems no longer were at odds as much as they were in tandem. In a much more hostile variation, Ulster was given emergency provisions for administration of justice (1973); those followed a long tradition of emergency laws, and were behind the prevention of terrorism laws which were adopted in the rest of the United Kingdom (1974). While both were intended as temporary measures, they were amended and renewed regularly into the 1990s, and in several instances they influenced amendments to English criminal procedure. There was a still different, and in its way more radical, change with the entry into the European Community. The recognition of community law broke down a long-standing English resistance to foreign law and caused the creation of methods to allow European law to be cited in U.K. courts, and for U.K. litigants to be heard in European courts.

These provisions show a greatly increased propensity to cross the boundaries between legal systems. We have seen that those boundaries were never as rigid as some may have wished, and that there had always been opportunity for interaction. The novelty here was that as barriers appeared to come down or become porous, there was a shift toward routine, established interaction. The story continues at the end of the century with the restoration of a Scottish parliament and the establishment of a Welsh Assembly, even as the government of the United Kingdom contemplates a future without a House of Lords. Each of these steps holds very important historical, political, and legal significance. The historian of the future, perhaps even the writers of general surveys, will surely be expected to explain them all, in all their relevant contexts.

Notes

Introduction **Insularity and Interaction**

1 W. R. Cornish and G. deN. Clark, *Law and Society in England, 1750–1950* (1989) is a particularly good example, written as a history text for law students. Norman F. Cantor has written for students of both history and law in a transatlantic framework: *Imagining the Law: Common Law and the Foundations of the American Legal System* (1997).

2 This movement began with a seminal article by John Pocock, "British History: A Plea for a New Subject," 47 *Journal of Modern History* (1975) 601–628. Early efforts to answer the plea included Christopher Haigh, *Cambridge Historical Encyclopedia of Great Britain and Ireland* (1986); Richard S. Tompson, *The Atlantic Archipelago: A Political History of the British Isles* (1986); and Hugh Kearney, *The British Isles: A History of Four Nations* (1989).

3 The only broad treatment of the several legal systems so far has been W. R. Cornish, "Legal Systems and Legal Literature," in Elizabeth Moys, ed., *Manual of Law Librarianship*, 2nd ed. (1987). A unique contribution which examined the separate systems in a collected series was George W. Keeton, ed., *The British Commonwealth: The Development of Its Laws and Constitutions*, 14 vols. (1955–1967).

4 There have been mobile lawyers. It was a requirement for the Irish bar that one spend a number of terms in an English Inn of Court. In the other direction, a number of English barristers became judges in Ireland, mainly from the sixteenth to eighteenth centuries. A good many Scots enjoyed legal careers in England, some of them reaching the pinnacle of the profession, the office of Lord Chancellor. For the most part, the latter were trained in and practiced English law; the recent case of Lord Mackay (1989–97) was a notable exception.

5 In England the citation of a case or rule from another system traditionally required that the matter be presented in court as a piece of evidence for the consideration of the jury. Over the last century there have been varied efforts to facilitate interaction, including some statutory measures, such as the Foreign Law Ascertainment Act (1861), the Foreign Judgments Act (1870) and the Fugitive Offender Act (1880). These changes are discussed further in chapters 7 and 8 below.

6 Liam Breatnach, "Lawyers in Early Ireland," in *Brehons, Serjeants and Attorneys: Studies in the History of the Irish Legal Profession*, Daire Hogan and W. N. Osborough eds. (1990), p. 5.

7 H. G. Richardson and G. O. Sayles, *Law and Legislation from Aethelberht to Magna Carta* (1966), pp. 22–23.

8 For another view, see M. T. Clanchy, *England and Its Rulers, 1066–1272* (1983).

9 *Tractatus de legibus et consuetudinibus Angliae,* ed. G. D. G. Hall, 1965. The work was ascribed to Henry's chief justiciar Ranulph de Glanvill, but it was actually written by Hubert Walter, Glanvill's nephew.

10 W. D. H. Sellar, "The Common Law of Scotland and the Common Law of England," in R. R. Davies, ed., *The British Isles, 1100–1500* (1988), p. 87. See Geoffrey Barrow: "The Scottish Justiciar in the Twelfth and Thirteenth Centuries," *Juridical Review* (1971) 97–148; *The Kingdom of the Scots* (1973); and his Ford Lectures, *The Anglo-Norman Era in Scottish History* (1980).

11 The charter of 1210 has not survived; on its context, see Paul Brand, "Ireland and the Literature of the Early Common Law," 16 *Irish Jurist* (1981) 95–113.

12 A. Gwynn, "Edward I and the Proposed Purchase of English Law for the Irish, c. 1276–1280," 10 Royal Historical Society *Transactions* (1960) 111–127. This may have been a plan to uproot the brehon law: see A. J. Otway-Ruthven, *Medieval Ireland* (1980), pp. 188–190.

13 Samuel E. Thorne, ed., published by the Selden Society, 4 vols. (1968–1977). Also see *Bracton's Notebook*, F. W. Maitland, ed. 3 vols. (1881), containing a collection of about 2,000 cases from the thirteenth century.

14 The Scottish king obtained the lordship of Man in 1266, but over the next half century that title was caught up in the disputed Scottish succession and came under English control by the 1330s.

15 Lord Cooper (Thomas Mackay), *The Scottish Legal Tradition* (new enl. ed., M. C. Meston and W. D. H. Sellar, eds., 1991). For medieval Scots law generally see Hector MacQueen, *Common Law & Feudal Society in Medieval Scotland* (1993).

16 Robin Frame, *English Lordship in Ireland, 1318–1361* (1982) offers an overview, while Katharine Simms provides a closeup of "The Brehons of Later Medieval Ireland," in Hogan and Osborough, *Brehons, Serjeants and Attorneys*, pp. 51–76.

17 Steven Ellis, *Tudor Ireland, 1470–1603* (1985), p. 46.

18 R. R. Davies, *Conquest, Coexistence and Change: Wales 1063–1415* (1991), pp. 419-422..

19 Glanville Williams, *Recovery, Reorientation and Reformation* (1987), pp. 10–14.

20 G. R. Elton, *The Tudor Constitution,* 2nd ed. (1982), p. 148.

21 For the various editions of Balfour's works, and information on other jurists, see David M. Walker, *The Scottish Jurists* (1985). For a general overview of the government, see Maurice Lee, *Government by Pen* (1980). Lee points out that resignations *in favorem* (consigning one's seat to a relative) continued into the seventeenth century (p. 43).

22 Ellis, *Tudor Ireland,* pp. 156, 158, 166.

23 S. G. Ellis, *The Pale and the Far North: Government and Society in Two Early Tudor Borderlands* (1988) and *Tudor Frontiers and Noble Power: The Making of the British State* (1995).

24 Ellis, *Tudor Ireland,* p. 166.

25 Hans S. Pawlisch, *Sir John Davies and the Conquest of Ireland: A Study in Legal Imperialism* (1985), pp. 9–10.

26 Ibid. The purported cases of tanistry and gavelkind were collective resolutions against traditional Irish landholding customs; Pawlisch suggests an involuted effect on doctrines of precedent (chapter 3).

27 Bruce Galloway, *The Union of England and Scotland, 1603–1608* (1986) and Brian Levack, *The Formation of the British State: England, Scotland and the Union, 1603–1707* (1987).

28 Speech to the House of Commons, March 21, 1610 (*Political Works*, ed. C. H. McIlwain [1946] p. 310).

29 Galloway, *Union of England and Scotland,* p. 148; Louis A. Knafla, *Law and Politics in Jacobean England* (1977), p. 202. A reprint of Edward Coke's report of the case is in 77 E.R. 377.

30 Sir Thomas Craig, *De Unione Regnorum Britanniae Tractatus,* 1605 (Scottish History Society, v. 60, 1909), pp. 303–304.

31 See the strong dissent in Pawlisch, *Sir John Davies.* Perhaps he is right to see civilian and other influence in the law's *operation,* while John Pocock is right to see Coke as the insular symbol of the *explanation* of the common law. *The Ancient Constitution and the Feudal Law* (new ed., 1987), p. 263.

32 J. P. Kenyon, *The Stuart Constitution* (1969), pp. 91, 177. In his speech of March 21, 1610, James criticized "every court striving to bring in most moulture to their own mill." *Works*, p. 313.

33 G. J. Hand and V. W. Treadwell, "His Majesty's Directions for Ordering and Settling the Courts within his Kingdom of Ireland, 1622," 26 *Analecta Hibernica* (1970); Hugh Kearney, *Strafford in Ireland*, 2nd ed. (1989); Aidan Clarke, *The Old English in Ireland, 1625–42* (1966), p. 48.

34 Gordon Donaldson, *Scotland: James V–James VII* (1968), pp. 310, 313.

35 Kearney, *Strafford*, p. xxi.

36 *A Justice of the Peace for Ireland* (1638), p. 1.

37 J. Rushworth, *Historical Collections of Private Passages of State*, v. 4, 1131–1136, cited in Kenyon, *Stuart Constitution*, pp.197–203.

38 Stuart Prall, *The Agitation for Law Reform during the Puritan Revolution, 1640–1660* (1966); Donald Veall, *The Popular Movement for Law Reform, 1640–1660* (1970).

39 William Cole, *A Rod for the Lawyers* (1659), cited in Veall, *Popular Movement*, p. 230.

40 Bodl. Rawlinson Ms A. 189, ff. 390, 397, cited in T. C. Barnard, *Cromwellian Ireland* (1975), p. 268. A *supersedeas* was a writ ordering a stay of proceedings.

41 F. D. Dow, *Cromwellian Scotland* (1979), pp. 33, 166, 221.

Chapter 1 **Making Appeals, 1660–1720**

1 In England the lord chancellor, lord chief justice of King's Bench, and three junior justices; a similar cast in the Court of Common Pleas, a lord chief baron and three barons of the Court of Exchequer, a master of the rolls assisting in Chancery, plus an attorney general and solicitor general; Ireland's cast was the same, minus a junior judge in each court. Scotland's College of Justice was a unique combination of judges, lawyers, and clerks. There were fifteen lords of session (including a lord president and a lord justice-clerk) plus the lord advocate, the law officer of the Crown.

2 There are two excellent recent studies on the House of Lords: Andrew Swatland, *The House of Lords in the Reign of Charles II* (1996) is a political and institutional

study; James S. Hart, *Justice Upon Petition: The House of Lords and the Reformation of Justice, 1621–1675* (1991) examines the Lords' judicial capacity.

3 The subject of religious uniformity is explored in numerous works. See John Miller, *Popery and Politics in England, 1660–1688* (1973) and Ronald Hutton, *Charles the Second: King of England, Scotland, and Ireland* (1991).

4 Hart, *Justice Upon Petition* gives the first detailed treatment of this aspect, using the voluminous archival material of the House of Lords.

5 The Irish Lords only sat for short periods: 1613–15, 1634–35 and 1640–41; only in the latter two periods were journals kept. There is some evidence of copying English practice, but that becomes much clearer at the end of the century.

6 Henry Elsynge, *The Ancient Method and Manner of Holding Parliaments in England* (1620). Elizabeth Foster, ed. *Judicature in Parliament* (1991) contains one chapter of Elsynge. See also [John Selden] *A Brief Discourse Concerning the Power of the Peeres and Commons in Parliament in Point of Judicature* (1640) and Henry Scobell, *Remembrances of Some Methods, Orders and Proceedings Heretofore Used and Observed in the House of Lords, extracted out of the Journals of that House* (1656).

7 9 H.L.J. 9, 69; also see Book of Orders and Judgments, H.L.R.O., B.19, p. 35; and Hart, *Justice Upon Petition*, p. 223. On the large quantity of petitions, see Swatland, *House of Lords*, p. 71 f.

8 The record of the appeals is in the Manuscripts of the House of Lords (in H.M.C.). Cases are also found in H.L.J., and in the *Calendar of the Journal* and the manuscript Book of Orders and Judgments (1660–1693) in H.L.R.O. From 1702, the House required all cases to be printed, and the printed cases are in the H.L.R.O.

9 May 18, 1661, Book of Orders and Judgments, H.L.R.O., B.20, p. 7.

10 *The Jurisdiction of the Lords' House* (1796), p. 154, as cited in Thomas Bevan, "The Appellate Jurisdiction of the House of Lords," 17 *Law Quarterly Review* (1901) 365.

11 *History of His Own Time* (1714), v. 1, p. 271.

12 *Forasmuch as upon writs of error returnable...* an order printed on December 13, 1661.

13 Bevan, "Appellate Jurisdiction," pp. 155–170. His work was used by William S. Holdsworth, *A History of English Law* (1922), v. 1, p. 365, and it was accepted by most later writers. See Maurice Bond, *Guide to the Records of Parliament* (1971), p. 107; Louis Blom-Cooper and Gavin Drewry, *Final Appeal : A Study of the House of*

Lords in Its Judicial Capacity (1972), p. 21; and Robert Stevens, *Law and Politics, The House of Lords as a Judicial Body, 1800–1976* (1978), pp. 6–14.

14 An interesting list of 198 claims of breach of privilege was compiled for the years 1660–1697, and it was cited in *Stockdale v. Hansard* (1839) 112 E.R. 1117.

15 *Skinner v. East India Company* (1668) 6 S.T. 719.

16 Thus the journals of both houses are silent on the Skinner case. But enough manuscript material remained in the Lords' archives for the Historical Manuscripts Commission to collect a supplement to its 8th Report, which described the case in considerable detail (8 H.M.C. 107).

17 12 H.L.J. 348.

18 9 H.M.C. 56. Both Bevan and Holdsworth evidently thought that it was literal, and they invented a reason for the Commons relaxing their position: that they realized the Lords' power was better than "jurisdiction by a special commission appointed by the Crown" (Bevan, "Appellate Jurisdiction," p. 170; Holdsworth, *History of English Law*, v. 1, p. 375). Hart sees a plan to oppose the king's "legislative programmes." *Justice Upon Petition*, p. 251. See 6 S.T. 1122.

19 Hart, *Justice Upon Petition*, p. 257.

20 Each had served as Lord Chief Justice and they were among the most respected of the judges of the period. Holdsworth discussed this opposition, and he acknowledged that it lasted into the next century. *History of English Law*, v. 1, p. 374.

21 *Calendar*, p. 638; see John F. MacQueen, *A Treatise on the Appellate Jurisdiction of the House of Lords and Privy Council* (1842), p. 32, and Bond, *Guide to the Records of Parliament*, p. 115.

22 Roll of Standing Orders, 1664–1715 ("Roll B") printed in *Manuscripts of the House of Lords*, n.s., v. 10 (1965), p. 15.

23 11 H.M.C. (pt. 1) 200.

24 Roll "B" in *Manuscripts of the House of Lords*, n.s., v. 10.

25 *Regina v. Paty* et al. (1705) 92 E.R. 232.

26 7 A.P.S. 500.

27 8 H.M.C. 115. This may be the first recorded Scottish appeal to the House of Lords. The tie vote meant of course that the committee nearly accepted a Scottish appeal; such a decision could have been reversed by a vote of the whole house.

28 P. Hume Brown, ed., *The Register of the Privy Council of Scotland*, third series, v. 4 (1910) p. 395.

29 2nd ed. 1693, Book IV, tit. 1.

30 9 A.P.S. 154, 159, 170, 175, 186.

31 9 A.P.S. 355, 463–490.

32 On the legal aspects of union during the course of the seventeenth century, see Levack, *Formation of the British State*.

33 A. J. MacLean, "The 1707 Union: Scots Law and the House of Lords," 4 *Journal of Legal History* (1983) 50.

34 *Manuscripts of the House of Lords*, v. 17, pt. 7, p. 20; 18 H.L.J. 253.

35 8 Anne c. 16; the Treason Act of 1709 is discussed in chapters 2 and 3 below.

36 Actually the Parliament of the United Kingdom of Great Britain was proclaimed on April 29, 1707 whereby the sitting English Parliament was converted to the new model. The cases referred to may be found in Lord Fountainhall, *Decisions of the Lords of Council and Session* (1759–61): 2 *Fountainhall* 368, 381.

37 *Brand v. Mackenzie* (1709), *Manuscripts of the House of Lords*, v. 8, p. 273.

38 2 *Fountainhall* 643.

39 David M. Walker, *Oxford Companion to Law* (1980), p. 540. See Richard S. Tompson, "James Greenshields and the House of Lords: A Reappraisal," in W. M. Gordon and T. D. Fergus eds., *Legal History in the Making* (1991), pp. 109–124.

40 2 *Fountainhall* 523.

41 19 H.L.J. 127. Henry Sacheverell was an ardent Tory and High Churchman, charged with preaching a seditious sermon in St. Paul's Cathedral in which he denounced Dissenters and Low Church Anglicans. Geoffrey Holmes, *The Trial of Doctor Sacheverell* (1973).

42 Clyve Jones and Geoffrey Holmes eds., *The London Diaries of William Nicolson* (1985) and letters of Nicolson in British Museum, Additional Manuscripts (Add. MS 6116).

43 1 E.R. 357.

44 David Robertson, *Reports of Cases on Appeal from Scotland* (1807), pp. xvi–xvii.

45 *A Seasonable Caution to the General Assembly* (1711), p. 8.

46 Sessions were held in 1661–1666, 1692–1693, 1695–1699 and 1703–1714. The *Journal* of the House of Lords shows procedures like the English house, and some similar conflicts between the Lords and the Commons. 1 I.H.L.J. 236, 243, 364, 367, 378, 391, 393, 430.

47 Paul O'Higgins, *A Bibliography of Irish Trials and other Legal Proceedings* (1986) does not list these cases separately, but some of his entries are included in this tally.

48 See the case of Viscount Loftus in 1660 (7 H.M.C. 112) and the petition from "divers of Irish nobility" on double taxation (7 H.M.C. 120) and the Earl of Cork's request for a private act "to proceed at law or equity against such persons as took away their goods" (9 H.L.J. 123, 151).

49 In the two decades 1664–1684 there were twenty-eight Irish cases which were included in the English nominate reports.

50 23 E.R. 133; 22 E.R. 1039.

51 84 E.R. 926; 89 E.R. 179.

52 23 E.R. 369, 340, 405; 87 E.R. 223.

53 1 I.HL.J. 454.

54 Ibid., 543, 509, 524, 526, 535, 547, 548.

55 *Manuscripts of the House of Lords,* new series, pt. 3, pp. 16, 24–56; 1 E.R. 54.

56 February 11, 1704; 1 I.H.L.J. 52; also see an undated document in Marsh's Library, Dublin which appears to be a draft of the resolutions in the form of a bill (Z 2.1.7 [100]) "An Act declaring that ye Parliament of England cannot bynde Ireland against writts of error and appeals to be brought..."

57 The case is in 15 S.T. 1302. There is further discussion of the act in chapter 2.

58 2 I.H.L.J. 655–660.

59 6 George I c. 65. See Isolde Victory, "The Making of the 1720 Declaratory Act," in Gerard O'Brien, ed., *Parliament, Politics and People: Essays in Eighteenth Century Irish History* (1989) pp. 9–29; and M.S. Flaherty, "The Empire Strikes Back: *Annesley v. Sherlock* and the Triumph of Imperial Parliamentary Supremacy," 87 *Columbia Law Review* (1987) 593–622.

60 MacQueen, *Appellate Jurisdiction*, pp. 232–240, 290–295.

Chapter 2 **Imperial Legislation, 1689–1766**

1 The numbers here are taken from the *Chronological Table of the Statutes*. P. D. G. Thomas, *The House of Commons in the Eighteenth Century* (1971) tabulated all private and public acts from 1689 to 1820, with similar results, although his tabulation does not include the shift from 1660 on (p. 61).

2 For an introduction to the subject, see H. T. Dickinson, "The Eighteenth Century Debate on the Sovereignty of Parliament," 26 Royal Historical Society *Transactions*, 5th series (1976) 189–210. The beastly quote is from Bruce Lenman, *The Jacobite Risings in Britain, 1689–1746* (1980), p. 33.

3 The constitutional question attracts American colonial historians interested in the onset of rebellion. Some legal historians have made significant recent contributions: Barbara A. Black, "The Constitution of Empire: The Case for the Colonists," 124 *University of Pennsylvania Law Review* (1976) 1157–1211; Jack P. Greene, "From the Perspective of Law," 85 *South Atlantic Quarterly* (1986) 56–77; and the extensive work of John Phillip Reid, especially his *Constitutional History of the American Revolution* (v. 3, *The Authority to Legislate*, 1991).

4 Sheila Lambert, *Bills and Acts: Legislative Procedure in Eighteenth-Century England* (1971); P. D. G. Thomas, *The House of Commons in the Eighteenth Century* (1971); and David Lieberman, *The Province of Legislation Determined: Legal Theory in Eighteenth Century Britain* (1989).

5 T. W. Moody and W. E. Vaughan, *A New History of Ireland*, v. 4 (1986), p. 64.

6 1 I.H.L.J. 454.

7 J. G. Simms, *William Molyneux of Dublin, 1656–1698* (1982).

8 Maureen Wall, *The Penal Laws* (1961). The eighteenth-century Irish laws were distinct in the imposition of specific burdens and in providing payment to informers to enforce the laws

9 Louis Cullen, "Catholics under the Penal Laws," 1 *Eighteenth Century Ireland* (1986) 23–36; Colum Kenny, "The Exclusion of Catholics from the Legal Profession in Ireland, 1534–1829," 25 *Irish Historical Studies* (1987) 337–357; T. P. Power and Kevin Whelan eds., *Endurance and Emergence: Catholics in Ireland in the Eighteenth Century* (1990); and Thomas Bartlett, *The Fall and Rise of the Irish Nation* (1992).

10 An Act for the Abrogating the Oath of Supremacy in Ireland and Appointing other Oaths, 3 William & Mary c. 2. This law revoked the oaths of the Patriot Parliament. Disarming and banishment were contained in 7 William III cc. 4, 5 and 9 William III c. 1 (Irish).

11 1 William and Mary cc. 15, 9 and 26; 11 William III c. 4; for forfeited estates see 1 Anne St. 2, c. 26; and c. 18; 2 & 3 Anne c. 19; 4 & 5 Anne c. 11; and 7 Anne c. 29. For background, see J. G. Simms, *The Williamite Confiscation in Ireland, 1690–1703* (1956). The Scottish act of 1703 is in 11 A.P.S. 104.

12 12 *Irish Historical Studies* (1960) 105–118; 2 Anne c. 6.

13 6 Anne c. 2 (Irish) was for "public registering of all deeds, conveyance and wills" and cited several English acts (2 & 3 Anne c. 4, 5 Anne c. 18, and 6 Anne c. 35). See Peter Roebuck, "The Irish Registry of Deeds: A Comparative Study," 18 *Irish Historical Studies* (1972) 61–73.

14 As this discussion is one mainly involving twentieth century authors, the individuals and the issues are discussed more fully below in chapter 8. For a partisan overview, see Michael Upton, "The Marriage Vows of the Elephant," 105 *Law Quarterly Review* (1989) 79–103; for a better historical account of the lawyers in the union process, see A. J. MacLean, "The 1707 Union: Scots Law and the House of Lords," 4 *Journal of Legal History* (1983) 47–65

15 9 A.P.S. 27; and see journals in 9 A.P.S. appendix, pp. 145–161.

16 9 A.P.S. 107 and 136.

17 4 & 5 Anne c. 15.

18 6 Anne c. 41; amended by 8 Anne c. 15.

19 6 Anne c. 53.

20 Leading Scottish commentators on the subject were John Lord Swinton, *Abridgement of Public Statutes in Force and Use Relative to Scotland*, 2 vols. (1755), and Henry Home, Lord Kames, *Statute Law of Scotland Abridged, with Historical Notes* (1757).

21 Most of the acts listed were repealed in the twentieth century, especially by the Statute Law Revision Act of 1906. The list does not designate acts repealed as a result of the union.

22 6 Anne c. 40.

23 10 Anne cc. 10, 21.

24 7 Anne c. 15; 10 Anne cc. 6, 39, 40.

25 7 Anne c. 21.

26 David Murray, *The York Buildings Company* (1883; new ed. 1973).

27 20 George II c. 43.

28 21 George II c. 19.

29 Cited in Basil Williams, *The Whig Supremacy* (1962), p. 274.

30 1 *Institute* ix and 2 *Institute* 527.

31 Greene, "From the Perspective of Law"; Reid, *Authority to Legislate;* and Philip Lawson ed., *Parliament and the Atlantic Empire* (1994).

32 Louis B. Wright ed., *An Essay upon the Government of the English Plantations* (1701; reprinted 1945), p. 23.

33 J. R. Pole, *Political Representation in England and the Origins of the American Republic* (1966), pp. 57, 71, 94; Jack P. Greene, *Peripheries and Center: Constitutional Development in the Extended Polities of the British Empire and the United States* (1986), p. 125.

34 *The Administration of the Colonies,* 4th ed. (1764), pp. 70–71.

35 E. S. and H. M. Morgan, *The Stamp Act Crisis* (1953); P. D. G. Thomas, *British Politics and the Stamp Act Crisis* (1975). The Stamp Act was 5 George III c. 12; the Declaratory Act was 6 George III c.12.

36 Reid, *Authority to Legislate*, p. 5.

Chapter 3 **Revolution and Law, 1760–1801**

1 Stanley Katz ed., *Commentaries on the Laws of England* (1979), introduction, p. iii.; J. C. D. Clark, *English Society, 1688–1832* (1985), p. 200; I. R. Christie, *Stress and Stability in Late Eighteenth Century Britain* (1984), p. 13.

2 Blackstone is the starting point for any modern discussion of English law in the eighteenth century. See David Lieberman, *The Province of Legislation Determined: Legal Theory in Eighteenth-century Britain* (1989) and Michael Lobban, *The Common Law and English Jurisprudence, 1760–1850* (1991).

3 1 *Commentaries* 204–209.

4 Ibid., 147, 151, 245, 257.

5 Judges did enjoy another form of independence. They might choose what Michael Lobban called internal or external bases for decisions, common law precedent or other sources. However, this was not an item likely to appear on Blackstone's list. 1 *Commentaries* 258–259.

6 For a recent survey of the "mischiefs" and the multitude of acts, see David Lieberman, "Blackstone's Science of Legislation," 27 *Journal of British Studies* (1988) 117–149.

7 1 *Commentaries* 93–106.

8 S. F. C. Milsom, "The Nature of Blackstone's Achievement," 1 *Oxford Journal of Legal Studies* (1981) 1–12. Other critics are noted in Julius S. Waterman, "Thomas Jefferson and Blackstone's Commentaries" in David H. Flaherty ed., *Essays in the History of Early American Law* (1969), pp. 451ff.

9 On the influence of Wilson, see Waterman, "Thomas Jefferson," pp. 475–479.

10 Adrienne Koch and William Peden, *The Life and Selected Writings of Thomas Jefferson* (1944), pp. 293–311.

11 Peter Charles Hoffer has characterized it differently in "The Declaration of Independence as a Bill in Equity," in William Pencak and Wythe W. Holt Jr., eds., *The Law in America, 1607–1861* (1989), pp. 186–209.

12 Elizabeth Gaspar Brown, *British Statutes in American Law. 1776–1836* (1964), p. 21.

13 For background, see Bradley Chapin, *The American Law of Treason: Revolutionary and Early National Origins* (1964) and Frederick B. Wiener, *Civilians Under Military Justice* (1967).

14 The best short survey is Peter Charles Hoffer, *Law and People in Colonial America* (1992).

15 A. G. Roeber, *Faithful Magistrates and Republican Lawyers: Creators of Virginia Legal Culture, 1680–1810* (1981), chapter 4.

16 Lois Schwoerer, *"No Standing Armies!"* (1974); Reid, *Defiance* relates the issue to the colonial legal situation; the Quartering Act (1765) was officially titled the Mutiny Act (North America), 5 George III c. 33; see Wiener, *Civilians under Military Justice*, p. 68.

17 Chapin, *American Law of Treason*, p. 28.

18 Ibid., p. 37.

19 Ethan Allen, *A Narrative of Colonal Ethan Allen's Captivity* (1799).

20 George Chalmers, *Opinions on Interesting Subjects of Public Law and Commercial Policy Arising from American Independence* (1784), pp. 154, 156.

21 Donald S. Lutz, *The Origins of American Constitutionalism* (1988), p. 50.

22 Anthony Stokes, *A View of the Constitution of the British Colonies in North America* [1783] contains extracts and contemporary evidence.

23 Ibid., p. 8.

24 Grace Cockcroft, *The Public Life of George Chalmers* (1939).

25 *Royal Commission on American Loyalists*, ed. H. E. Egerton (1915), based on the notes of Daniel Parker Coke, lawyer and commissioner; also see John Eardley-Wilmot, *Historical View of the Commission for enquiring into the Losses, Services and Claims of the American Loyalists* (1815).

26 Brown, *British Statutes*, p. 24.

27 See p. 503; also see Lieberman, *Province of Legislation*, p. 189, n. 39.

28 Andrew S. Skinner, "Adam Smith: The Demise of the Colonial Relationship with America," in Prosser Gifford ed., *The Treaty of Paris (1783) in a Changing States System* (1985).

29 19 George III c. 54; and see Report of the Committee on Transportation, 1784. Sheila Lambert, ed., *Sessional Papers of the House of Commons in the Eighteenth Century*. 145 v. (1975–1976), v. 49, pp. 1–13.

30 James Walvin, "The Public Campaign in England Against Slavery, 1787–1834," in David Eltis and James Walvin, eds., *The Abolition of the Atlantic Slave Trade* (1981), pp. 63-79.

31 The accounts are in *State Trials*, vols. 22–25. A good modern summary is given in Alan Wharam, *The Treason Trials, 1794* (1992). For political aspects see Henry Meikle, *Scotland and the French Revolution* (1969); Albert Goodwin, *The Friends of Liberty* (1979) studied "interlocking dimensions" of radicalism; Roger Wells, *Insurrection: The British Experience, 1795–1803* (1982) is also multinational.

32 May 21, 1792; 47 H.C.J . 813.

33 22 S.T. 357; Wharam, *The Treason Trials, 1794* (1992), p. 35.

34 H. T. Dickinson, "Popular Loyalism in Britain in the 1790s," in Eckhart Hellmuth ed., *The Transformation of Political Culture* (1990), pp. 503–533.

35 *Institutions*, Bk. III, tit. 3, par. 29.

36 Henry Lord Cockburn, *Examination of the Trials of Sedition...in Scotland*, 2 v. (1888), v. 1, p. 1, citing David Hume, *Commentaries on the Law of Scotland Respecting Crimes* (1797–1800).

37 A.J. MacLean, "The House of Lords and Appeals from the High Court of Justiciary, 1707–1887," 1985 *Juridical Review*, 192–216.

38 Cockburn, *Examination*, p. 133; see his statement that "there was no need of such a statute in Scotland, because in this, as in a thousand other cases, our law was in advance of that of England, and had never fallen into the error which in England required the interference of Parliament."

39 Ibid., p. 138; in the English trials for sedition the results were mixed: about half were acquitted; those convicted were fined and imprisoned for an average of two years. 22 and 23 S.T.

40 Hume, *Commentaries*, v.1, pp. 354–365.

41 Cited in Cockburn, *Examination*, v.1, p. 183.

42 23 S.T. 237.

43 William Cobbett, ed., *Parliamentary History*, v. 30, p. 1346.

44 Watt was hung and then beheaded, and the remainder of the grisly English ritual was foregone.

45 23 and 24 S.T.

46 36 George III c. 7.

47 36 George III c. 8, s. 1.

48 V. 1, p. 556.

49 Cockburn said that Hume's publication was "in a great measure for the purpose of vindicating the proceedings of the Criminal Court in the recent cases of sedition, and was therefore hailed with the loudest acclamations by the friends of those whose proceedings stood so much in need of defence." He added that "there is no book that has worse stood the test of time"—a judgment which modern Scots lawyers might find amusing. *Memorials of His Time* (1856), ed. W. Forbes Gray (1945), p. 101. The 1795 act was temporary, made permanent in 1817, and replaced by the Treason Felony Act of 1848.

50 On the general body of legislation see Clive Emsley, "Repression, 'Terror' and the Rule of Law in England during the Decade of the French Revolution," 100 *English Historical Review* (1985) 801–825. The measures included the Seduction from Duty Act and the Unlawful Oaths Act of 1797, and the Treasonable and Seditious Societies Act and Illegal Combinations Act of 1799.

51 For the older view, Matthew Hale, *Pleas of the Crown* (1682) p. 77; Edward East, *Pleas of the Crown* (1803), v. 1, p. 48.

52 Michael Lobban, "From Seditious Libel to Unlawful Assembly," 10 *Oxford Journal of Legal Studies* (1990) 307–352 shows the essential change but treats the years 1790–1815 rather lightly.

53 R. B. McDowell, *Ireland in the Age of Imperialism and Revolution* (1979), p. 64. The ratio for the period 1714–1760 was 17 English to 21 Irish.

54 Ibid., p. 261; and see J. L. Clifford, ed., *Dr. Campbell's Diary* (1947), pp. 94–95.

55 William T. Ayres, *Comparative View of the English and Irish Statute and Common Law*, 2vols. (1780) published in Dublin and reprinted in London. Ayres provided a set of notes on the *Commentaries* of Blackstone, pointing out variations in Irish law for the guidance of barristers with anglocentric training.

56 D. S. Greer, "The Development of Civil Bill Procedure in Ireland," in John McEldowney and Paul O'Higgins, eds., *The Common Law Tradition* (1990), pp. 27–59.

57 J. F. McEldowney, "Crown Prosecutions in Nineteenth–Century Ireland," in Douglas Hay and Francis Snyder, eds., *Policing and Prosecution in Britain, 1750–1850* (1989), pp. 427–457.

58 On the origin of this requirement see Colum Kenny, *King's Inns and the Kingdom of Ireland* (1992), pp. 40–48.

59 The Irish act dropped about half of the text of the English act (1679), especially parts pertaining to jurisdiction overseas; the essential right to challenge custody was retained, but it was subject to intervention by the lord lieutenant as well as the parliaments of Ireland and Great Britain. Kevin Costello, "A Constitutional Antiquity?" 23 *Irish Jurist* (1988) 240–254.

60 Stanley Palmer, *Police and Protest in England and Ireland, 1780–1850* (1988) provides a very detailed multinational account. Also see Daire Hogan, *The Legal Profession in Ireland, 1789–1922* (1986).

61 Marianne Elliott, *Partners in Revolution: The United Irishmen and France* (1982).

62 R. B. McDowell, "The Personnel of the Dublin Society of United Irishmen, 1791–4," 2 *Irish Historical Studies* (1940-41) 12–53. There were records of 30 barristers and 26 attorneys.

63 Jacqueline Hall, "The Legal Profession and the Defence of the *ancien régime* in Ireland, 1790–1840," in Daire Hogan and W. N. Osborough, eds., *Brehons, Serjeants and Attorneys* (1990), pp. 181–209.

64 *Tandy v. Westmorland* ; see reports listed in O'Higgins, *Bibliography of Irish Trials,* 4.169 and 4.170.

65 J. F. Larkin ed., *The Trial of William Drennan* (1991).

66 26 S.T. 1191.

67 G. C. Bolton, *The Passing of the Irish Act of Union* (1966); Oliver Macdonagh, *Ireland: The Union and Its Aftermath* (rev. ed. 1977); Edward Brynn, *Crown and Castle: British Rule in Ireland, 1800–1830* (1978).

68 *A Report of the Debate of the Irish Bar* [December 9, 1798] (1799).

69 The Irish act was 40 George III c. 38; the British counterpart was 40 George III c. 67.

70 A proposal to create appeal committees for Irish and Scottish cases was made at this time. Marquis of Buckingham to Lord Grenville, November 17, 1799: H.M.C. 6 Fortescue 26.

71 40 George III c. 39, one of the last Irish acts, said that all Irish judges would sit together and hear writs of error; a clerk was provided, with an annual salary of £300. Royal assent was given immediately after the Act of Union.

72 *Case of the Suitors in the Courts of Law in Ireland* (1801).

73 43 George III c. 53.

74 44 George III c. 92 was the repeal, removed by 45 George III c. 92; Irish and English trials are reviewed in 29 ST 81; the trial in England is found in 103 E.R. 26.

75 21 and 22 George III c. 32 [Irish] required a student to be registered in King's Inns for five years, or for graduates, three years. This was in addition to keeping terms at a London Inn. Hogan, *Legal Profession*, p. 17.

76 Kenny, *King's Inns and the Kingdom of Ireland*, pp. 247–265.

77 Bartholomew Duhigg, *King's Inns Remembrances* (1805).

78 54 H.C.J. 620, 640, 728.

Chapter 4 **Inquiry and Legal Reform, 1799–1850**

1 The main legal effect of the reform acts was the creation of a system of voter registration, and the need for a new legal process to certify voter qualifications. For more on this subject, see chapter 6.

2 The first such collection had been that of Thomas Salmon (1719), with four later eighteenth century editions before Howell's *Complete Collection of State Trials and Proceedings for High Treason*, 34 v. (1809–1828) covering the years 1163 to 1820.

3 John Cowley, *A Bibliography of Abridgments, Digests, Indexes and Dictionaries of English Law to the year 1800* (Selden Society, 1932; reprinted 1979).

4 Bond, *Guide to the Records* sketches the evolution of published debates (pp. 36–39). Sheila Lambert in volume 1 of *Sessional Papers of the House of Commons in the Eighteenth Century* explains the printing of bills, reports, and accounts.

5 Bartholomew Duhigg, *A Letter to the Rt. Hon. Charles Abbot on the Arrangement of the Irish Records, and the Assimilation of Irish to English Statute Law* (1801).

6 Peter Walne, "The Record Commissions, 1800–1837," 2 *Journal of the Society of Archivists* (1960) 8–16.

7 Philip Harling, *The Waning of 'Old Corruption': The Politics of Economical Reform in Britain, 1779–1846* (1996) gives a very good survey of the economical reformers and their political impact, but he does not include an examination of the reforms of the courts of law.

8 Nicholas Phillipson, *The Scottish Whigs and the Reform of the Court of Session, 1785–1830* (1990); Stevens, *Law and Politics,* pp. 7–23; and A. J. MacLean, "Jeremy Bentham and the Scottish Legal System," 24 *Juridical Review* (1979) 21–44.

9 This essay is bound with *An Historical Account of the Privileges of the College of Justice* [1785] in the Law Library of the University of Edinburgh (FOL KK ROS).

10 Phillipson, *Scottish Whigs* gives a detailed account of the court's procedure (chapter 2) and he notes the comment from Lord Swinton that in a year's work a judge might have to read 25,000 pages of papers relating to cases in the inner house alone (p. 54).

11 P. R. D., *A Letter Addressed to...the Lord President of the Court of Session* (1790); [John Russell], *New Form of Process before the Court of Session*(1791). Earlier editions were printed in 1768 and 1786; Walter Ross, *Lecture on the Practice of Law in Scotland* , 2 v. (1792).

12 *Reports of Cases Decided in the House of Lords upon Appeal from Scotland, from 1753 to 1813* , 6 v. (1849–1856).

13 Phillipson describes the judges' proposal of 1805 as a thoughtful and promising contribution. (Melville Mss, 57–9. National Library of Scotland). The Whig scheme of 1807 is in 45 H.L.J. 715.

14 The terms were embodied in the Judicature (Scotland) Act 48 George III c. 151. The Commission is printed in the first report, S.P. 1809.IV.381.

15 The introduction of the civil jury was only delayed. A Jury Court was established in 1815, working as an adjunct to the Court of Session, into which it was absorbed in 1830.

16 14 P.D. 68, 114.

17 49 George III c. 126; the committee report is in 13 P.D. cclxix; the commission report is in S.P. 1810. X. 131.

18 S.P. 1810. X 53.93.115; 1811. III and 1812. II. 343.

19 William Jameson, *Letter to Lord Melville* (1814); Jameson also petitioned the House of Commons in 1821.

20 See his speeches in June and November (28 P.D. 375 and 29 P.D. 475); also see S.P. 1813–1814. XIII 1. 11. 33 and 1814–1815 XI. 159. 191.

21 S.P. 1814–1815. VII. 136, XI. 5, and 153.

22 Scottish Record Office, Law Courts Commissions (COM).

23 Account of days of attendance, S.P. 1818. XV. 103; Irish expenditure was reported annually from 1819, but similar accounts were not required from English and Scottish commissions.

24 For more detail, see S.P. 1821. XX and XXI and 1822. XXI.

25 An explanation was given in S.P. 1821. XXI. 374.

26 See S.P. 1822. VII. 293.

27 6 George IV c. 10; S.P. 1825. XV. 175 and 1826. XVII. 20.

28 This figure was used in a letter from Henry Dealtry, secretary to the commission, responding to an order of the House of Commons regarding fees and the commissioners' recommendations thereon. S.P. 1821. XXI. 374.

29 S.P. 1817. X. 2 (Irish); 1816. XVIII (Scottish); 1816. VII. 97 (English).

30 S.P. 1816. VIII. 368.

31 37 George III c. 64, 41 George III c. 25, 46 George III c. 49, 53 George III c. 24 and 57 George III c. 60.

32 See the sums reported in S.P. 1813–1814. VII.

33 S.P. 1821. VIII. 465.

34 S.P. 1820. VIII. 197.

35 The Irish statutes were 1 George IV c. 68 (Exchequer Chamber); 4 George IV c. 61 (Chancery); 4 George IV c. 70 (Exchequer); 1 & 2 George IV c. 53 (King's Bench and Common Pleas). The English order to the judges was in 3 George IV c. 69; the justices of King's Bench and Common Pleas were waiting to be told to read the commissioners' reports. Their letters were printed in S.P. 1821. XXI.

36 6 George IV cc. 82 and 83 (abolition) and 6 George IV c. 89 (compensation).

37 1 & 2 George IV c. 53 and 4 George IV c. 38 dealt with Irish offices.

38 For debate, 9 P.D. 1348; 4 George IV c. 85; and report in S.P. 1824. X. 1.

39 Phillipson, *Scottish Whigs*, chapter 6.

40 1 George IV c. 68; 1 & 2 George IV c. 53; 4 George IV c. 61; 1 & 2 George IV c. 54; 4 George IV c. 70; 7 George IV c. 61. For court-initiated actions, see S.P. 1820. VIII. On practice regulations: 4 George IV c. 89; 5 George IV c.4; 6 George IV c. 55; and 7 George IV c. 36.

41 57 George III cc. 11, 18; 3 George IV c. 19; 3 George IV cc. 87, 102; 6 George IV cc. 82, 83.

42 Brian Abel-Smith and Robert Stevens, *Lawyers and the Courts* (1967), p. 29.

43 Brougham's speech was reported in 18 P.D. 166.

44 The question of suppressing a report was raised in Lord Melville's trial in 1806 (*Gurney v. Longman* 33 E.R. 379); in the trial of Andrew Hardie in 1820 the publication of proceedings in progress was restrained (1 New State Trials 609); in the Thistlewood trial in 1821 a fine was levied for publishing a report while the trial was in progress (106 E.R. 918). For cases from 1824 to 1880, see Matthias Levy, *Shorthand Notes and the Practice Relating to Them* (1888).

45 Holdsworth, *History of English Law*, v. 13 , p. 270.

46 *On the Present Unsettled Condition of the Law and Its Administration* (1839), p. 2.

Chapter 5 **Building the Supreme Court, 1840–1880**

1 Norman Gash, as cited in William Rubinstein, *Britain's Century: A Political and Social History, 1815–1905* (1998), p. 75.

2 Daniel Duman, *English and Colonial Bars in the Nineteenth Century* (1983) pp. 6–9. Since all those who were called to the bar did not practice, there can be no definitive number. Thus Duman gives a range for 1835: 450 to 1000; and for 1885 from 660 to 1450.

3 There were about 10,000 solicitors in 1841, rising to 17,000 by 1911, a figure not exceeded until after 1945. Cornish, *Law and Society in England*, p. 51, citing Harry Kirk, *Portrait of a Profession: A History of the Solicitors' Profession, 1100 to the Present Day* (1976), p. 108.

4 Robert Stevens, "The Final Appeal: The Reform of the House of Lords and the Privy Council, 1867–1876," 80 *Law Quarterly Review* (1964) 343–369.

5 David B. Brownlee, *The Law Courts: The Architecture of George Edmund Street* (1984) gives a thorough examination of the combined history with the heaviest weight on architecture.

6 1 George IV c. 21; 1 & 2 George IV c. 16 and 3 George IV c. 87.

7 W. N. Osborough, *Law and the Emergence of Modern Dublin* (1996).

8 Colum Kenny, *Tristram Kennedy and the Revival of Irish Legal Training, 1835–1885* (1996). Christopher W. Brooks, *Lawyers, Litigation and English Society since 1450* (1998), chapter 6.

9 A. H. Manchester, "Simplifying the Sources of the Law," 2 *Anglo-American Law Review* (1973) 395.

10 *The Jurist*, 1853, ibid., p. 407.

11 5 & 6 Victoria c. 28.

12 10 & 11 Victoria c. 78; see A. H. Manchester, *A Modern Legal History of England and Wales, 1750–1950* (1980), p. 183. Rosemary Pattenden, *English Criminal Appeals, 1844–1994* (1996).

13 24 & 25 Victoria cc. 95–100.

14 Eighth Report, S.P. 1845. XIV. 184.

15 S.P. 1856. VII. 347.

16 In civil law the equivalent of Peel's consolidation acts would be found in the laws of 1845: Companies Clauses Consolidation (8 & 9 Victoria c. 16; Scotland c. 17); Land Clauses Consolidation (8 & 9 Victoria c. 18; Scotland c. 19); and Railroad Clauses Consolidation (8 & 9 Victoria c. 20; Scotland c. 29).

17 S.P. 1859. XII. 361.; 1863. XV. 463; 1866. XVII. 83.

18 Court of Probate 20 & 21 Victoria c. 77 (Ireland c.79) and 21 & 22 Victoria c. 95; also Vital Registration c. 25 and Legitimacy c. 93. Holdsworth, *History of English Law*, v. 15, p. 27.

19 22 Victoria c. 20.

20 22 & 23 Victoria c. 63; 24 & 25 Victoria c. 11; J. H. Baker, "Ascertainment of Foreign Law: Certification to and by English Courts prior to 1861," 28 *International and Comparative Law Quarterly* (1979) says that the act was never used.

21 31 & 32 Victoria c. 54.

22 National Association for Promotion of Social Sciences, *Transactions*, 1866, p. 178.

23 For the Coleridge Report see S.P. 1860. XXXI. 89; the Treasury Minute is in S.P. 1864. XLVII. 431; the site and building acts were 28 & 29 Victoria cc. 48, 49.

24 Royal Commission, June 25, 1865 , S.P. 1871. XX; Select Committee on Site, S.P. 1868–1869. X. 625

25 Brownlee, *The Law Courts*, chapter 3; John Summerson, "A Victorian Competition: The Royal Courts of Justice," in *Victorian Architecture: Four Studies in Evaluation* (1970); and M. H. Port, "The New Law Courts Competition, 1866–67," 11 *Architectural History* (1968) 75–93.

26 Fourth Report, S.P. 1870. XVII. 461.

27 Stevens, "Final Appeal," pp. 352–355; for debate see 216 P.D. 1561.

28 Judicature: 36 & 37 Victoria c. 66; Appeal: 39 & 40 Victoria c. 59.

29 S.P. 1874. XXIV. 557. 583, and minutes of testimony S.P. 1875. XXX. 163. The second report was useful for its detailed history of the question of fees in the courts of law. It also contained lengthy sketches of the major legal offices as they were on the eve of consolidation.

30 39 & 40 Victoria c. 18.

31 42 & 43 Victoria c. 78.

32 S.P. 1874. LIV. 411–453.

33 Stevens, *Law and Politics*, p. 69.

34 40 & 41 Victoria c. 57, amended by 41 & 42 Victoria c. 27 and later acts. The comment is from Daire Hogan, *Legal Profession*, p. 83. On the numbers and salaries of judges and clerks, see S.P. 1877. LXIX. 495.

35 The salary scale provided £6,000 for law lords and appeal court judges and £5,000 for high court judges. For details see J. C. Sainty, *The Judges of England*. Selden Society (1993).

Chapter 6 **Law and Democracy, 1880–1930**

1 Abel-Smith and Stevens, *Lawyers and the Courts*, p. 93.

2 There was a distinct variation on this theme across the archipelago. In both Wales and Ireland, Anglican establishments were alien institutions to Welsh Dissenters and Irish Catholics. In England (Anglican) and Scotland (Presbyterian), the establishments were native and ingrained. For a comparative analysis see Rubinstein, *Britain's Century: A Political and Social History, 1815–1905*, pp. 298–303.

3 The leading case of this kind was *Taff Vale Railway v. Amalgamated Society of Railway Servants* [1901] A.C. 426.

4 K. Theodore Hoppen, *Elections, Politics and Society in Ireland, 1832–1885* (1984), p.1.

5 S. Buxton, *A Handbook to Political Questions of the Day* (1892), pp. 114–115, cited in Neal Blewitt, "The Franchise in the United Kingdom, 1885–1918," *Past and Present* (no. 32, 1965), p. 28, n. 6. Blewitt estimates that 1 million were kept off the register (p. 36) out of a total that rose from 3 million (1880) to 8 million (1911).

6 The 1832 acts were amended by the registration act (for England and Wales) of 1843, 6 & 7 Victoria c. 18. For later reforms, see 42 & 43 Victoria c. 71.

7 13 & 14 Victoria c. 69; on valuations, see Hoppen, *Elections*, pp. 18 ff.

8 24 & 25 Victoria c. 83; 27 & 28 Victoria c. 22 and 28 & 29 Victoria c. 36.

9 Select Committee Report, S.P. 1868–1869. VII. 301, 307.

10 See reports on registration: S.P. 1874. XI. 167; 1878. XIII. 573 and 1884–1885. XI. 1.

11 Speech to the National Liberal Club in 1901, British Museum, Dilke Papers, Add. Mss. 43943, ff. 175–186, cited in Blewett, "Franchise in the United Kingdom," p. 53.

12 Between 1860 and 1914 there were at least twenty-five different manuals and fifteen independent casebooks. Since 1918 there have been but a few manuals and no separate publication of election cases. Here also the structure shifted from specific English, Scottish, and Irish works to a general United Kingdom coverage.

13 David Cannadine, *The Decline and Fall of the British Aristocracy* (1990), p. 66. For general studies see J. P. D. Dunbabin, *Rural Discontent in Nineteenth Century Britain* (1974) and Roy Douglas, *Land, People and Politics: A History of the Land Question in the United Kingdom, 1878–1952* (1976).

14 E. D. Steele, "Ireland and the Empire in the 1860s: Imperial Precedents for Gladstone's First Irish Land Act," 11 *Historical Journal* (1968) 64–83; J. C. Brady, "English Law and Irish Land in the Nineteenth Century," 23 *Northern Ireland Legal Quarterly* (1972) 24–47; Clive Dewey, "Celtic Agrarian Legislation and the Celtic Revival," *Past and Present* no. 64 (1974) 30–70.

15 F. M. L. Thompson, *English Landed Society in the Nineteenth Century* (1963), p. 332. See also Harold Perkin, who said that no fundamental land reform was in fact ever accomplished ("Land Reform and Class Conflict in Victorian Britain," in J. Butt and I. F. Clarke eds., *The Victorians and Social Protest* (1973), p. 178.

16 E. D. Steele, *Irish Land and British Politics: Tenant-Right and Nationality, 1865–1870* (1974) gave an important new view of the subject. J. C. Brady, "English Law and Irish Land in the Nineteenth Century," 23 *Northern Ireland Legal Quarterly* (1972) 24–47 and C. F. Kolbert and T. O'Brien, *Land Reform in Ireland: A Legal History of the Irish Land Problem* (1975) represent the older interpretation.

17 An early correction came with the essay by W. E. Vaughan, *Landlords and Tenants in Ireland, 1848–1904* (1984). The same author has since produced a landmark revisionist work: *Landlords and Tenants in Mid-Victorian Ireland* (1994).

18 The episode is recounted in Steele, *Irish Land*, p. 104.

19 "Clearance" refers to the conversion of highland estates and removal of tenants, in the 1790s, 1820s and after. A corollary of the traditional occupancy was an aversion

to written leases; see James Hunter, *The Making of the Crofting Community* (1976), p. 157.

20 Leah Leneman, *Fit for Heroes? Land Settlement in Scotland after World War I* (1989), p. 2 n. 5.

21 Return of Owners of Land, S.P. 1874. LXXII. pts. I & II.

22 Dunbabin, *Rural Discontent*, pp. 174–177.

23 Avner Offer, *Property and Politics, 1870–1914* (1981), pp. 151–158.

24 Cornish, *Law and Society in England*, p. 171.

25 This section has not tried to integrate Welsh and other jurisdictions, on which there has been some very good work—for example, David W. Howell, *Land and People in Nineteenth-Century Wales* (1978). Sir George Shaw-Lefevre, *English and Irish Land Questions* (1881) has an excellent essay on "The Land System of the Channel Islands," pp.165–186.

26 150 E.R. 1030; discussed in A. W. B. Simpson, *Leading Cases in the Common Law* (1995), chapter 5.

27 Robert Black,"A Historical Survey of Delictual Liability in Scotland for Personal Injuries and Death," 8 and 9 *Comparative and International Law Journal of South Africa* (1975 and 1976) 46, 189, 318, and 9.

28 170 E.R. 1033.

29 "Campbell's Act," 9 & 10 Victoria c. 93; see Black, "Historical Survey," 9:59.

30 *Sword v. Cameron* 1 D. 499.

31 17 D. 1017.

32 3 Macq. 266; ironically a Scottish case 90 years later precipitated the ending of common employment by statute: *Neilson v. Pantrini* 1946 S.C. 446; the Law Reform (Personal Injuries) Act of 1948.

33 43 & 44 Victoria c. 42; *Heaven v. Pender* 11 QBD 503.

34 58 & 59 Victoria c. 36. See Fatal Accidents (Scotland) Act 1906, 6 Edward VII c. 35.

35 60 & 61 Victoria c. 37.

36 P. W. J. Bartrip, *Workmen's Compensation in Twentieth Century Britain* (1987), p. 24.

37 *Fenton v. Thorley* 1903 A.C. 443.

38 *Ismay, Imrie and Co. v. Williamson* 1908 A.C. 437 at 442.

39 *Stewart v. Wilson's and Clyde Coal Co.* 5 F. 120.

40 *Potts v. Nidrie and Benhar Coal Co.* 1913 A.C. 531.

41 1914 A.C. 667.

42 *Murray v. Denholm* 1911 S.C. 1087.

43 *Kerr [or Lendrum] v. Ayr Steam Shipping Co.* 1915 A.C. 217.

44 Mackinnon v. Miller 1909 S.C. 373; 2 B.W.C.C. 64.

45 The "model of legal change" suggested here goes beyond that which Lawrence Stone used in *Road to Divorce: England, 1530–1987* (1990), pp. 18–21. He saw three stages: lay disobedience, lawyers' manipulation, and legislators' alteration. This concentration on groups of actors tends to obscure the dimension of legal interaction.

46 Allen Horstman, *Victorian Divorce* (1985), pp. 163–164; Stone, *Road to Divorce*, pp. 357–359.

47 A veritable "who's who" of the profession, including Henry Brougham, John Campbell, Patrick Fraser, and among civilians Stephen Lushington, Sir Robert Phillimore, and William Scott, Lord Stowell.

48 MacQueen, *Appellate Jurisdiction*, p. 602.

49 James Fergusson, *Reports of Some Recent Decisions by the Consistorial Court of Scotland in Actions of Divorce, Concluding for Dissolutions of Marriages Celebrated under the English Law* (1817), p. 1.

50 Ibid., p. 9; also see 6 E.R. 1268 and 168 E.R. 779.

51 *Tovey v. Lindsay* (1813) 3 E.R. 643, 648.

52 *Gordon v. Pye* (1815) Fergusson (1823), p. 276.

53 S.P. 1830. XXIX. 399.

54 Gretna Green was the well-known Scottish town close to the English border, where eloping English couples found it possible to marry quickly and easily. The Warrender case is reported in 5 ER 1235. Brougham's Marriage Act of 1855 set a 21-day waiting period before Scottish marriages. 19 & 20 Victoria c. 96.

55 *Treatise on Appellate Jurisdiction;* the divorce section is in pp. 465–548; cases are at pp. 550–668.

56 *Regina v. Millis* and *Regina v. Carroll* 8 E.R. 844; return S.P. 1844. XXXVIII. 155; 7 & 8 Victoria c. 81.

57 S.P. 1847–1848. XXVIII. 233; 1849. IV. 147. 155.

58 S.P. 1852–1853. XL. 249.

59 20 & 21 Victoria c. 85; Number of Causes, S.P. 1859. XIX. 331; Divorce Court Rules, S.P. 1859. XXII. 71.

60 The act did not include Ireland. A comparable measure was expected but did not appear. David Fitzpatrick, "Divorce and Separation in Modern Irish History," 114 *Past and Present* (1987) 174, 185.

61 *Road to Divorce*, p. 389.

62 This right of the husband was restricted by acts of 1861, 1877, and 1881. It was abolished in 1920.

63 24 & 25 Victoria c. 86.

64 See notes in Stair Society, *Introduction to the Study of Scots Law,* p. 102.

65 But see the remarks of the lord chancellor in the debate. He made it sound as if English features were being imported into Scots law! 164 P.D. 1783.

66 Report in S.P. 1867–1868. XXXII. 1.

67 Mary Lyndon Shanley, *Feminism, Marriage, and the Law in Victorian England, 1850–1895* (1989), pp. 68–69.

68 33 & 34 Victoria c. 93; see also the Irish act, 33 & 34 Victoria c. 110.

69 The acts concerned intestate widows (1875); married women's property (1877); marriage notice (1878); married women's policies of assurance (1880); and married women's property (1881).

70 Act of 1573 (c. 1), 3 A.P.S. 81.

71 *Murray v. M'Lauchlin* (1838) 1 D. 294.

72 Fitzpatrick, "Divorce and Separation," pp. 172–196.

73 Harry Quilter ed., *Is Marriage a Failure?* (1888; reprint 1984).

74 Royal Commission on Divorce, S.P. 1912. I. 91 and II. 51, 62, 79; Stone, *Road to Divorce*, p. 391.

75 41 & 42 Victoria c. 19; 49 & 50 Victoria c. 52; 58 & 59 Victoria c. 39.

76 4 P.D. 1437.

77 S.P. 1912–1913. XVIII. 17. See section on the "law of other countries" including Scotland, Ireland, Isle of Man, Channel Islands, and the dominions.

78 Stone, *Road to Divorce,* p. 394 and fig. 13.1.

79 317 P.D. 2083.

80 105 P.D. 831; Stone, *Road to Divorce*, p. 400.

81 Fitzpatrick, "Divorce and Separation," p. 190.

Chapter 7 **Law and the Constitution, 1900–1950**

1 There is as yet no full-scale historiography for this remarkable phenomenon. See the Selden Society lecture by C.H.S. Fifoot, "Law and History in the Nineteenth Century," 1956. The void is the more surprising since the key figures are so well known: in history William Stubbs, Frederic Maitland, Frederick Pollard, Sir William Anson, James Bryce, and William S. Holdsworth; in the study of the modern constitution, John Stuart Mill, Walter Bagehot, and Albert Venn Dicey; and for the working of government Thomas Erskine May, Peter Maxwell, and Henry Thring.

2 Here Maitland was once again exceptional (proving the rule?); see his *Constitutional History of England* (1908) "Sketch of the Public Law at the Present Day, 1887–8," p. 330. Brougham wrote *The British Constitution* as early as 1844. Leonard Baron Courtenay published *The Working Constitution of the United Kingdom* in 1901 and J. H. B. Masterman wrote a *History of the British Constitution* in 1912. But the British usage only seems to have become common ca. 1930. English precedence was in part the product of the flood of printed sources (Record Commissions, 1802–; Rolls Series, 1858–; Historical Manuscripts Commission, 1870–).

3 Dicey's *Law of the Constitution* remained in print far longer than other works (10th edition in 1959). See the exegesis of F. H. Lawson, "Dicey Revisited," 7 *Political Studies* (1959) 120–126 and 207–221. For Dicey's career, Richard A. Cosgrove, *The Rule of Law: Albert Venn Dicey, Victorian Jurist* (1980).

4 *The Nineteenth Century Constitution* (1969), p. 4.

5 Henry Thring (1818–1907) was appointed First Parliamentary Counsel to the Treasury in 1869. He had produced some important legislative work in the 1850s and 1860s, and he published *Practical Legislation*, a handbook for drafting, in 1877. Shortly before, Sir Peter Maxwell, a colonial judge, published a work on *Interpretation of Statutes* (1875) which saw its eleventh edition in 1962.

6 *River Wear Commissioners v. Adamson* (1877) endorsed strict interpretation. 2 App. Cas. 743.

7 52 & 53 Victoria c. 63. See D. Neil MacCormick and Robert S. Summers, *Interpreting Statutes: A Comparative Study* (1991), especially chapter 10, by Zenon Bankowski and D. N. MacCormick,"Statutory Interpretation in the United Kingdom."

8 One of the earliest students of the subject was Sir Courtenay Ilbert, *Legislative Methods and Forms* (1901); see chapter 3.

9 56 & 57 Victoria c. 66; Alexander Pulling, *Statutory Rules and Orders...issued prior to 1890 and now in force* (8 v., 1896); revised edition, to 1903 (13 v., 1904); continued by annual supplements.

10 Harry Arthurs, *"Without the Law": Administrative Justice and Legal Pluralism in Nineteenth Century England* (1985).

11 51 & 52 Victoria c. 25; J. R. Spencer, *Jackson's Machinery of Justice* (1989), pp. 108–109.

12 46 & 47 Victoria c. 57. C. K. Allen, *Law and Orders*, 2nd ed. (1956), p. 296.

13 57 & 58 Victoria c. 60.

14 *Institute of Patent Agents v. Lockwood* [1894] A.C. 347; for the Commercial Court see Abel-Smith and Stevens, *Lawyers and the Courts*, pp. 87–88; also see the Arbitration (Scotland) Act 1894, 57 & 58 Victoria c. 13.

15 Ibid., p. 116; Cornish, *Law and Society*, p. 95.

16 R. F. V. Heuston, *Lives of the Lord Chancellors*, 2 vols. (1964–1987); introduction, v.1, pp. xv–xxiii.

17 D. N. Chester, *The Organization of British Central Government* (1957) classifies the Lord Chancellor as a "departmental" minister, but calls it a "borderline" case (p. 19).

18 7 Edward VII c. 23.

19 W. S. Breem, "Primary Sources: Law Reports," in Elizabeth Moys ed., *Manual of Law Librarianship* (1987), chapter 4; C. G. Moran, *The Heralds of the Law* (1948); W. T. S. Daniel, *History and Origin of the Law Reports* (1884).

20 39 & 40 Victoria c. 59; 50 & 51 Victoria c. 70.

21 Allen, *Law and Orders*, p. 101.

22 G. R. Elton, *F. W. Maitland* (1985), p. 8.

23 *The New Despotism* (1929) was an outspoken attack on administrative tribunals, or the perceived tendency to endow them with unchecked powers. Hewart's work was a compilation of cases and acts, with long extracts from a debate (1928) on a rating bill, pp. 119ff. Without naming his target, he made scathing comments on the able account of W. A. Robson, *Justice and Administrative Law* (1928; 3d ed., 1951).

24 Abel-Smith and Stevens, *Lawyers and the Courts*, p. 117.

25 For our purposes the best work in this field is R. E. Wraith and P. G. Hutchesson, *Administrative Tribunals* (for the Royal Institute of Public Administration, 1973), which has a section on Scottish background and chapters (9 and 10) dealing thoughtfully with the judicial ramifications of tribunals.

26 Delegated legislation had been explained by C.P. Ilbert, *Legislative Methods and Forms* (1901); after the war, Cecil Carr wrote *Delegated Legislation* (1921) and later Sir John Marriott, *The Mechanism of the Modern State* (1927) and Frederic J. Port, *Administrative Law* (1929) joined the works of Robson and Hewart.

27 Allen, *Law and Orders*, p. 31.

28 Carr, *Delegated Legislation*, p.18.

29 Wraith and Hutchesson say tribunals "found their way back" after exclusion in the wake of 1688, *Administrative Tribunals*, p. 24. This sense of continuity is also found in Robson; but one may question the equation of old justices of the peace and modern tribunals, especially at the time when the justice of the past had already been replaced by county councils (1888).

30 Gerry R. Rubin, *War, Law and Labour: The Munitions Acts, State Regulation, and the Unions, 1915–1921* (1987). Also see Tribunals of Inquiry (Evidence) Act, 1921, 11 & 12 George V c. 7.

31 M. R. McLarty, *Source Book and History of Administrative Law in Scotland* (1956) and Ronald M. Stout, *Administrative Law in Ireland* (1985) are good surveys of their respective fields.

32 A. W. Bradley, "Administrative Law," in *The Laws of Scotland. Stair Memorial Encyclopedia*, v. 1, p. 59. In Scotland there was a more substantial history and more theoretical discussion; the principle of judicial control was the same in England and Scotland, but the judicial remedies were different (p. 61).

33 For early case law, see Allen, *Law and Orders*. Wraith and Hutcheson, *Administrative Tribunals* examines links to ordinary courts (appendix I). For comparison of courts and tribunals, J.A. Farmer, *Tribunals and Government* (1974). For more recent law see Supreme Court Act 1981 on judicial review, that is, the power to oversee (and reverse) the decisions of tribunals.

34 *Lives*, v. 1, p. 227; Haldane said the committee was his idea: see his *Autobiography* (1928). Also see C. H. Wilson, *Haldane and the Machinery of Government* (1956).

35 Allen, *Law and Orders*, p. 49; see Franks Committee Report, 1957.

36 See the discussion of emergency laws in chapters 3 and 8; the nineteenth century experience is carefully traced in Virginia Crossman, *Politics, Law and Order in Nineteenth Century Ireland* (1996); for the police, see Palmer, *Police and Protest*.

37 There was a veneer of legality over some of the actions. For instance, justices of the peace could permit loyal drilling, and there was no active ban on gun imports (beyond an old customs law). There is useful contemporary background in J. H. Morgan, ed., *The New Irish Constitution* (1912).

38 "Military Force and Civil Authority in the United Kingdom, 1914–1921," 28 *Journal of British Studies* (1989) 279.

39 Civilian courts had been suspended. Townshend, "Military Force," p. 281.

40 Max Caulfield, *The Easter Rebellion* (1995).

41 The most extensive studies are Mary Kotsonouris, *Retreat from Revolution: The Dáil Courts, 1920–1924* (1994) and Colm Campbell, *Emergency Law in Ireland, 1918–1925* (1994).

42 W. N. Osborough, "Law in Ireland, 1916–1926," 23 *Northern Ireland Legal Quarterly* (1972) 49.

43 H. Hanna, *Statute Law of the Irish Free State, 1922–1928* (1929), said that there were 900 parish courts and 77 district courts in operation (p. 30).

44 Minister for Home Affairs, "The Judiciary Rules and Forms of Parish and District Courts" (1920), as cited in New Ireland Forum, *The Legal Systems, North and South* (1983), p. 14.

45 See the entry from Cahir Davitt's memoir quoted in Kotsonouris, *Retreat*, pp. 59–60.

46 Decree of January 17,1922; quoted in Osborough, "Law in Ireland," p. 51.

47 Free State Constitution Act, 13 George V (sess. 2) c. 1 (article 73); see comment in New Ireland Forum, *Legal Systems*, p. 15.

48 Proclamation of January 16, 1922, quoted in Osborough, "Law in Ireland," p. 58.

49 Decree, October 26, 1922; District Justices (Temporary Provisions) Act, 1923.

50 Osborough, "Law in Ireland," pp. 52–54.

51 13 George V (sess. 2) c. 2; V. T. H. Delaney, *The Administration of Justice in Ireland,* 3rd ed. (1970), p. 35.

52 The New Ireland Forum made an interesting survey of cases cited between 1922 and 1975, which showed that courts in Northern Ireland cited English cases 61 per cent of the time, and cases from the Republic 1 per cent. In the Republic, English cases were cited 50 per cent of the time, and cases from the North 3 per cent. *Legal Systems,* p. 7.

53 *The Irish Free State: Its Government and Politics* (1934), p. 304.

54 See list of rights found to have constitutional protection in New Ireland Forum, *Legal Systems,* p. 22.

55 Only anglicized systems are treated here; for native systems interacting with Europeans, see M. B. Hooker, *Legal Pluralism: An Introduction to Colonial and Neo-colonial Laws* (1975).

56 The active pursuit by England/Britain of a new role in international law was confirmation of this development. New organizations were founded: British Institute of International and Comparative Law (1952); U.K. National Committee on

Comparative Law (1951); and the Institute of Advanced Legal Studies, in the University of London (1947). Also see publications and periodicals: *The British Commonwealth, the Development of Its Laws and Constitutions*, 14 v. (1955–1967); *British Practice in International Law* (1962–); *British Digest of International Law* (1965–); and *British International Law Cases* (1964–1973) the latter offering "a collection of decisions of courts in the British Isles on points of international law."

57 Of particular concern here were the emigrant Irish; if naturalized in the United States, were they no longer subjects under British law? Or Irish law? Lord Chief Justice Cockburn treated some of these themes in his *Nationality: Or the Law Relating to Subjects and Aliens* (1869).

58 33 & 34 Victoria c. 14; Clive Parry, *Nationality and Citizenship Laws of the Commonwealth and of the Republic of Ireland* , 2 v. (1957), v. 1, pp. 79–80.

59 4 & 5 George V c. 17; Parry, *Nationality*, v. 1, p. xiv.

60 Ibid., p. 85.

61 11 & 12 George VI c. 56; the Irish case was a major exception here: a year later the Republic of Ireland Act recognized the independence of Ireland, but it was not a foreign country.

62 Sir Ivor Jennings, *Constitutional Laws of the Commonwealth*, 2nd ed. (1952), p. 19.

63 28 & 29 Victoria c. 63.

64 D. B. Swinfen, *Imperial Appeal: The Debate on the Appeal to the Privy Council, 1833–1986* (1987), p. 4.

65 D. B. Swinfen, "The Genesis of the Colonial Laws Validity Act," 1967 *Juridical Review* 29–59.

66 Michael Burgess, *The British Tradition of Federalism* (1995).

67 The conference report was printed in *Annual Register*, 1926, part ii, pp. 93–107.

68 22 & 23 George V c. 4.

69 50 & 51 Victoria c. 54, s. 2.

70 R. T. E. Latham, "The Law and the Commonwealth," in W. K. Hancock, *Survey of British Commonwealth Affairs*, v. 1 (1937), pp. 540–541.

71 By the 1930s the Committee contained, in addition to senior English judges, the judges of the Supreme Court of Northern Ireland, the Court of Session of Scotland, the supreme courts of Canada, South Africa, Newfoundland, and the high courts of Australia and India, plus superior court judges from New Zealand, the Australian states, and Canadian provinces, plus others specially appointed. Latham, *Law and Commonwealth*, pp. 546–547.

72 Swinfen, *Imperial Appeal*, p. 4; Stevens, *Law and Politics*, pp. 72–73.

73 Committee Memorandum, in Swinfen, *Imperial Appeal*, p. 16; quoting from J. S. Ewart, "Judicial Appeals."

74 Chamberlain drafted a bill to create the court; Haldane proposed such a solution in an address to the Scottish Law Society in 1900; see "The Appellate Courts of the Empire," in 1900 *Juridical Review*, p. 1.

75 Quoted in Latham, *Law and the Commonwealth*, p. 549.

76 Commonwealth of Australia Act, 1900, s. 74; Union of South Africa Act, 1909, s. 106; see Jennings, *Constitutional Laws*, pp. 415, 444.

77 [1935] A. C. 500; ibid., 159–169.

78 George F. G. Stanley, *A Short History of the Canadian Constitution* (1969), pp. 187–189.

79 The amendment was in The Constitution (Amendment No. 22) Act; the test case was *Moore v. Attorney-General* [1935] A. C. 484. The case was extracted and discussed in Jennings, *Constitutional Laws*, p. 158.

80 *Pearl Assurance Co. Ltd. v. Government of the Union* [1936] A. C. 570; see Swinfen, *Imperial Appeal*, pp. 157–161.

81 Latham, *Law and the Commonwealth*, pp. 512–513.

82 Lord Sheppard speaking in the House of Lords, quoted in Blom-Cooper and Drewry, *Final Appeal*, p. 371.

Chapter 8 **Modern Legal Interaction, 1950–1990**

1 The convention was the work of the Council of Europe in 1950, ratified by the United Kingdom in 1951 and in force in 1953. Implementation was the work of a European Commission on Human Rights and a European Court of Human Rights.

See S. H. Bailey and M. J. Gunn, *Smith and Bailey on the Modern English Legal System* (1996), pp. 109–112.

2 Raymond Byrne and J. Paul McCutcheon, *The Irish Legal System* (1996), chapter 15.

3 The British government transferred the case from the Welsh court to the Old Bailey in London, whereupon the defendants would only give evidence in Welsh. They were imprisoned for nine months. Kenneth O. Morgan, *Rebirth of a Nation: Wales, 1880–1980* (1981), pp. 254–257.

4 Good recent overviews of the legal systems are Bailey and Gunn, *Smith and Bailey on the Modern English Legal System*; Robin M. White and Ian Willock, *The Scottish Legal System* (1993); Byrne and McCutcheon, *Irish Legal System*; and Brice Dickson, *The Legal System of Northern Ireland* (1988). Also useful are J. R. Spencer's exemplary edition of *Jackson's Machinery of Justice*, 8th ed. (1989); Enid Marshall, *General Principles of Scots Law*, 5th ed. (1991); and V. T. Delaney, *Administration of Justice in Ireland* (1970). It is noteworthy that the more recent surveys contain descriptions of the process and apparatus of reform.

5 Norman Marsh, "Law Reform in the United Kingdom: A New Institutional Approach," 13 *William and Mary Law Quarterly* (1971), 270 and n. 19.

6 D. M. Walker, "Reform, Restatement and the Law Commissions," 1965 *Juridical Review* 245.

7 Efforts had been made to improve drafting. Sir Noel Hutton, "Mechanics of Law Reform," 24 *Modern Law Review* (1961) 18–31.

8 Quoted in John H. Farrar, *Law Reform and the Law Commission* (1974), appendix, p. 133.

9 A good account of the work of this committee is given in E. C. S. Wade, "The Machinery of Law Reform," 24 *Modern Law Review* (1965) 3–17.

10 Programme of Law Reform, as cited in John O'Connor, "The Law Reform Commission and the Codification of Irish Law," 9 *Irish Jurist* (1974) 14.

11 Bryan MacMahon, "Developments in the Irish Legal System since 1945," in J. J. Lee, ed., *Ireland, 1945–1970* (1979), p. 87.

12 1965 c. 22, s. 3 (1).

13 Walker noted rumors to this effect in "Reform, Restatement and the Law Commission," p. 247.

14 Lord Kilbrandon, the first chairman, made the observation that the differential staffing showed how much less reform was needed in the Scottish system. "The Scottish Law Commission," 2 *Georgia Law Review* (1968) 193–206.

15 This method was regarded by Lord Scarman, the first English chairman, as a singular contribution to procedure; see Marsh, "Law Reform," p. 278.

16 W. H. Hurlburt, *Law Reform Commissions in the United Kingdom, Australia and Canada* (1986), p. 63. The number does not include proposals for the consolidation of laws or for statute revision.

17 Section 3 (4); see also 3 (1) (f): "to obtain such information as to the legal systems of other countries as appears to the Commissioners likely to facilitate the performance of any of their functions."

18 Stephen Woolman, "The Law Commissions," 1982 *Statute Law Review* 164.

19 L. C. B. Gower, "Reflections on Law Reform," 23 *University of Toronto Law Journal* (1973) 264. Also see Hurlburt, *Law Reform Commissions*, p. 72.

20 The attribution was made by the attorney general in the announcement of 1974; see O'Connor, "Law Reform Commission," p. 15.

21 The English rule was stated in *London Street Tramways Co. v. London County Council* [1898] A.C. 375. The Supreme Court took the new position in *Attorney General v. Ryan's Car Hire Ltd.* [1965] I. R. 642.

22 3 All E.R. 77.

23 Kilbrandon, "Scottish Law Commission," p. 205.

24 Andrew Dewar Gibb, *Law from over the Border* (1950), pp. 19, 57.

25 The effects of migration were of course unpredictable. See Cockburn's complaint that "the transplanted Scotchman must lose his Scots law. Nothing oozes out of a man so fast as law." *Journal* (1874, v. 2, p. 278) cited by Smith, *Studies Critical and Comparative* (1962), p. 124.

26 *Thompson v. Williamson* (1831) 5 E.R. 833.

27 3 MacQ. 266 at 285.

28 *Fleeming v. Howden* 6 M. (HL) 113 at 121; see criticism by Lord Watson in *Heritable Reversionary Co.* (1892) 19 R. (HL) 43.

29 *Camille & Henry Dreyfus* [1956] A. C. 39 at 47.

30 This more accurate definition is explained by W. D. H. Sellar in "A Historical Perspective," in Meston and Sellar, eds., *Scottish Legal Tradition*, pp. 29–30.

31 John W. Cairns, "Institutional Writings in Scotland Reconsidered," 4 *Journal of Legal History* (1983) and reprinted in Kiralfy and MacQueen, *New Perspectives in Scottish Legal History* (1985), pp. 76–117. This is the best overview of the difficult problem of definition and selection of "institutional" writers," those whose works will be taken by judges to be authoritative. Cairns sets the origins in a European context, but his definition is placed in a long view of Scottish legal history which recognizes both an older historical definition and a modern technical usage of the term "institute."

32 1945 *Juridical Review* 151.

33 Pp. 127, 129.

34 Lord Cooper's opinion is printed as an appendix to Meston and Sellar, eds., *Scottish Legal Tradition*, p. 98.

35 D. L. Carey Miller and D. W. Meyers, eds., *Comparative and Historical Essays in Scots Law: A Tribute to Professor Sir Thomas Smith Q.C.*(1992) contains a valuable Foreword by the Rt. Hon. Lord Hope, Lord President of the Court of Session (pp. xi–xiv). See Smith, "English Influences" in *Studies Critical and Comparative*, pp. 116–136; and his contributions to the section on Constitutional Law in *The Laws of Scotland: Stair Memorial Encyclopedia* (1987), v. 5.

36 *Glasgow Corporation v. Central Land Board* (1956) S.C. (HL) 1.

37 Also see T. B. Smith, *British Justice: The Scottish Contribution* (1961).

38 1932 A. C. 562. R. F. V. Heuston, "Donoghue v. Stevenson in Retrospect," 20 *Modern Law Review* (1957)1–23; J. C. Smith and Peter Burns, "Donoghue v. Stevenson—The Not So Golden Anniversary," 46 *Modern Law Review* (1983) 147–163; Alan Rodger, "Mrs Donoghue and Alphenus Varus," 41 *Current Legal Problems* (1988) 1–22; Martin Davies, "The End of the Affair: Duty of Care and Liability Insurance," 9 *Legal Studies* (1989) 67–83; Alan Rodger, "Lord Macmillan's Speech in Donoghue v. Stevenson," 108 *Law Quarterly Review* (1992) 236–259.

39 *Borrowing From Scotland*, pp. 34–35.

40 *Radcliffe v. Ribble Motor Services Ltd.* [1939] A. C. 215.

41 5 Irv. 480.

42 560 P. D. 1254.

43 *Crime and Insanity.* 2 vols. (1968–1973), v. 1, p. 11.

44 *Smith v. Lord Advocate* 25 R. 112 extended to Scotland the concept that "the king can do no wrong."

45 Loren P. Beth, *The Development of Judicial Review in Ireland, 1937–1966* (1967).

46 *Pickin v. British Railways Board* [1974] A. C. 765.

47 Warren Freedman, *Foreign Plaintiffs in Products Liability Actions: The Defense of forum non conveniens* (1988).

48 [1970] A. C. 583.

49 But see the table of "Statutory Reversals of House of Lords Decisions in Scottish Appeals," in Blom-Cooper and Drewry, *Final Appeal,* p. 389.

50 10 & 11 George V c. 5, amended in 1964 (c. 38); this act had some limits: the emergency had to be ratified by Parliament within seven days, and the term of its operation could not exceed one month. The act was invoked in 1921, 1924, and 1926. See Charles Townshend, *Making the Peace* (1993), pp. 85–88.

51 10 & 11 George V c. 31.

52 *R. (O'Brien) v. Military Governor of the North Dublin Union Internment Camp* [1924] 1 I. R. 32; see Gerard Hogan and Clive Walker, *Political Violence and the Law in Ireland* (1989), pp. 16–18, 175–177.

53 855 P.D. 276.

54 John Jackson and Sean Doran, *Judge Without Jury: Diplock Trials in the Adversary System* (1995) is the most complete scholarly assessment.

55 Hogan and Walker, *Political Violence and the Law in Ireland,* p. 109.

56 There was some pressure on this pillar of the common law as the use of jury trial steadily declined, in civil and criminal cases, in the twentieth century. See Spencer, *Jackson's Machinery of Justice,* chapter 32. In the case of *Ward v. James* (1965) it

was held that a jury trial could not be claimed as of right, but only with special permission of the judge. [1965] 2 W.L.R. 455.

57 H. E. L. Phillips, "The Last Years of the Court of Star Chamber, 1630–1641," *Transactions* of the Royal Historical Society, 4th ser. v. 21, p. 103 (1938); John Kenyon, *The Stuart Constitution* (1969), p. 117. John Lilburne was punished for refusing to answer in Star Chamber (1637), and the House of Lords said it was "contrary to the laws of nature and the kingdom for any man to be his own accuser." Geoffrey Robertson, *Freedom, the Individual and the Law* (1993), p. 32.

58 Cmnd. 3301.

59 "There is no question of the erosion of essential national sovereignty." The United Kingdom and the European Communities, Cmnd. 4715 (1971). Lawrence Collins, *European Community Law in the United Kingdom* (1992), p. 22. A good recent study of the relationship is B. S. Markesinis, *The Gradual Convergence: Foreign Ideas, Foreign Influences and English Law on the Eve of the 21st Century* (1994).

60 This power was unsuccessfully challenged in *Blackburn v. Attorney General* [1971] 2 All E.R. 1380.

61 European Communities Act, 1972; the preamble said the act was "to make provision in connection with the enlargement of the European Communities to include the United Kingdom, together with (for certain purposes) the Channel Islands, the Isle of Man and Gibraltar" (section 2–6). A similar act was passed in Ireland, as well as a constitutional amendment (art. 29.4).

62 Both aspects are well served with clearly written guides. For the law in the United Kingdom, see Lawrence Collins, *European Community Law in the United Kingdom*, 4th ed. (1990). For the community and the law within it, see D. Lasok and J. W. Bridge, *Law and Institutions of the European Communities*, 5th ed. (1991).

63 *Bulmer v. Bollinger* [1974] Ch. 401; [1974] 2 All E.R. 1226; and see 1975 2 C.M.L.R. 479.

64 Some tallies have been made. Finbarr Murphy counted nineteen Irish cases in "Community Law and Irish Courts, 1973–1981," 7 *European Law Review* (1982) 331–345. Christine Boch noted only seven references from Scotland to the Court of Justice in "Using EC Law before Scottish Courts," 36 *Journal of the Law Society of Scotland* (1991) 6–10.

65 The first Scottish reference from the High Court of Justiciary was a fishing case: *Geweise and Mehlich v. Mackenzie* , 1984 S.L.T. 449; 1985 S.L.T. [News] 53.

66 *Schorsch Meirer v. Hennin* [1975] 1 All E.R. 1520.

67 See *R. v. Marlborough Street Stipendiary Magistrate ex parte Bouchereau* [1977] 1 W. L. R. 414.

68 *McCarthys Ltd. v. Smith* [1979] 3 All E.R. 325.

69 *R. v. Henn and Darby*, 34/79; see also [1980] 2 All E.R. 166.

70 T. C. Hartley, *Civil Jurisdiction and Judgments* (1984).

71 *Mareva Compania Naviera SA v. International Bulkcarriers SA* [1975] 2 Lloyd's Rep 509; see Collins, *European Community Law*, p. 112.

72 *E.C. Commission v. U.K.* 231/78.

73 *Journal of the Irish Society for European Law* (1978), p. 87; see Finbarr Murphy, "The Irish Legal System," in David Coombes, *Ireland and the European Communities* (1983), p. 41.

74 *Van Duyn v. Home Office* [1974] 1 W. L. R. 1107; 41/74; [1974] E. C. R. 1337 and [1975] 1 C. M. L. R. 1.

75 *A. Bulloch and Co. v. The Distillers Co. Ltd.* [1978] 1 C. M. L. R. 400; W. A. Wilson, *Introductory Essays on Scots Law* 2nd ed. (1984), p. 111.

76 *Garden Cottage Foods v. Milk Marketing Board* [1983] 2 All E.R. 770; [1984] A.C. 130.

77 Law Reform (Miscellaneous Provisions) (Scotland) Act 1990, s. 30; White and Willock, *Scottish Legal System*, p. 242.

78 Courts and Legal Services Act (1990); Law Reform (Scotland) Act (1990); and for Ireland, Solicitors (Amendment) Act (1994) and Courts and Court Officers Act (1995).

Conclusion **Law and the British Isles**

1 "Why the History of English Law Is Not Written," *Collected Papers*, ed. H. A. L. Fisher. 3 v. (1911), v. 1, pp. 480–497. See C. H. S. Fifoot, *Frederic William Maitland: A Life* (1971), and G. R. Elton, *F. W. Maitland* (1985).

2 Geoffrey Robertson, *Freedom, the Individual and the Law* (1993) presents an updated account of Harry Street's landmark work of 1963. The recent effort to obtain a Bill of Rights attests to the absence of such formal legal safeguards.

3 Maitland's edited works included *Records of the Parliament holden at Westminster...1305* (1893) and *Year Books of Edward II* (1903); his major work (with Frederick Pollack) was *The History of English Law before the Time of Edward I*. 2 vols. (1891); his other chief contributions, often originating as lectures, were *Justice and Police* (1885); *Equity and The Forms of Action at Common Law* (1909); *Township and Borough* (1898); and *Roman Canon Law in the Church of England: Six Essays* (1898).

4 Greene, *Peripheries and Center* (1986); Reid, *Constitutional History of the American Revolution* (1986-1993); J. Willard Hurst, *The Growth of American Law* (1950); Morton J. Horwitz, *The Transformation of American Law, 1780–1860* (1977); Hoffer, *Law and People in Colonial America* (1998).

5 An interesting collection of essays on the history of criminal law can be found in Clive Emsley and Louis A. Knafla eds., *Crime History and Histories of Crime* (1996). For the field of civil actions, see Christopher W. Brooks, *Lawyers, Litigation and English Society since 1450* (1998).

6 G. R. Rubin, "Law, Poverty and Imprisonment for Debt, 1869–1914," in G. R. Rubin and David Sugarman, eds. *Law, Economy and Society* (1984), 246–249; also see V. Markham Lester, *Victorian Insolvency: Bankruptcy, Imprisonment for Debt, and Company Winding-up in Nineteenth Century England* (1995), p. 116.

7 Brooks, *Lawyers, Litigation and English Society*, chapter 6.

8 Hooker, *Legal Pluralism*, 1975.

9 Townshend, *Making the Peace*, p. 2.

Selected Bibliography

This list includes secondary works related to English, Scottish, and Irish legal history published over the past forty years. It will serve as a guide for further reading and an aid to beginning research in the fields of legal history which have been discussed here.

Abel, Richard L. *The Legal Profession in England and Wales.* Oxford: Blackwell, 1988.

Abel, Richard L., and P. S. C. Lewis, eds. *Lawyers in Society.* 3 volumes. Berkeley: University of California Press, 1988–1996.

Abel-Smith, Brian, and Robert Stevens. *Lawyers and the Courts: A Sociological Study of the English Legal System, 1750–1965.* London: Heinemann, 1967.

_____ . *In Search of Justice: Society and the Legal System.* London: Allen Lane, 1968.

Allan, T.R.S. *Law, Liberty and Justice: The Legal Foundations of British Constitutionalism.* Oxford: Clarendon Press, 1993.

Allen, Sir Carleton Kemp. *Law in the Making*, 7th ed. Oxford: Clarendon Press, 1964.

_____ . *Law and Orders*, 2nd ed. London: Stevens, 1956.

Anderson, J. Stuart. *Lawyers and the Making of English Land Law, 1832–1940.* Oxford: Clarendon Press, 1992.

Arthurs, H. W. *"Without the Law" Administrative Justice and Legal Pluralism in Nineteenth Century England.* Toronto: University of Toronto Press, 1985.

Atiyah, P. S. *Form and Substance in Anglo-American Law.* Oxford: Clarendon Press, 1987.

_____ . *The Rise and Fall of the Freedom of Contract.* Oxford: Clarendon Press, 1985.

Babington, Anthony. *For the Sake of Example: Capital Courts Martial, 1914–1920.* New York: St. Martin's Press, 1984

Bailey, S. H., and M. J. Gunn. *Smith and Bailey on the Modern English Legal System*, 3rd ed. London: Sweet and Maxwell, 1996.

Baker, J. H. *An Introduction to English Legal History*, 3rd ed. London: Butterworths, 1990.

Baldwin, John, and Michael McConville. *Jury Trials*. Oxford: Clarendon Press, 1979.

Bartlett, Thomas. *The Fall and Rise of the Irish Nation: The Catholic Question, 1690–1830*. Savage, Md.: Barnes & Noble Books, 1992.

Bartrip, P. W. *Workmen's Compensation in Twentieth Century Britain: Law, History and Social Policy*. Aldershot: Gower, 1987.

Bartrip, P. W., and S. B. Burman, *The Wounded Soldiers of Industry: Industrial Compensation Policy, 1833–1897*. Oxford: Oxford University Press, 1983.

Beattie, J. M. *Crime and the Courts in England, 1660-1800*. Princeton: Princeton University Press, 1986.

Beth, Loren P. *The Development of Judicial Review in Ireland, 1937–1966*. Dublin: Institute of Public Administration, 1967.

Birks, Michael. *Gentlemen of the Law*. London: Stevens, 1960.

Blom-Cooper, Louis, and Gavin Drewry. *Final Appeal: A Study of the House of Lords in Its Judicial Capacity*. Oxford: Clarendon Press, 1972.

Bolton, G. C. *The Passing of the Irish Act of Union*. London: Oxford University Press, 1966.

Bonfield, Lloyd. *Marriage Settlements, 1601–1740: The Adoption of the Strict Settlement*, Cambridge Studies in English Legal History. Cambridge: Cambridge University Press, 1983.

Bonner, David. *Emergency Powers in Peacetime*. London: Sweet & Maxwell, 1985.

Brand, Paul. *The Origins of the English Legal Profession*. Oxford: Blackwell, 1992.

Brewer, John and John Styles, eds. *An Ungovernable People: The English and Their Law in the Seventeenth and Eighteenth Centuries*. London: Hutchinson, 1980.

Brewer, John, and Susan Staves, eds. *Early Modern Conceptions of Property*. London: Routledge, 1995.

Bromhead, Peter. *Britain's Developing Constitution*. New York: St. Martin's Press, 1974.

Brooks, Christopher W. *Lawyers, Litigation and English Society since 1450*. London: Hambledon Press, 1998.

_____. *Pettyfoggers and Vipers of the Commonwealth: the "Lower Branch" of the Legal Profession in Early Modern England.* Cambridge: Cambridge University Press, 1986.

Brown, Elizabeth Gaspar. *British Statutes in American Law, 1776–1836.* Ann Arbor: University of Michigan Law School, 1964.

Brownlee, David B. *The Law Courts: The Architecture of George Edmund Street.* Cambridge, Mass.: M. I. T. Press, 1984.

Burgess, Michael. *The British Tradition of Federalism.* London: Leicester University Press, 1995.

Burgess, Robert. *Perpetuities in Scots Law.* Edinburgh: Stair Society, 1979.

Burgess, Robert, and Geoffrey Morse. *Partnership Law and Practice in England and Scotland.* London: Sweet & Maxwell, 1980.

Byrne, Raymond, and J. Paul McCutcheon. *The Irish Legal System,* 3rd ed. Dublin: Butterworths, 1996.

Calvert, Harry. *Constitutional Law in Northern Ireland: A Study in Regional Government.* London: Stevens, 1968.

Cameron, Joy. *Prisons and Punishment in Scotland from the Middle Ages to the Present.* Edinburgh: Canongate, 1983.

Campbell, Colm. *Emergency Law in Ireland, 1918–1925.* Oxford: Clarendon Press, 1994.

Cannadine, David. *The Decline and Fall of the British Aristocracy.* New Haven: Yale University Press, 1990.

_____ . *Lords and Landlords: The Aristocracy and the Towns, 1774–1967.* Leicester: Leicester University Press, 1980.

_____ . *Patricians, Power and Politics in Nineteenth Century Towns.* New York: St. Martin's Press, 1982.

Cantor, Norman. *Imagining the Law: Common Law and the Foundations of the American Legal System.* New York: HarperCollins, 1997.

Cartwright, Timothy J. *Royal Commissions and Departmental Committees in Britain; a Case-Study in Institutional Adaptiveness and Public Participation in Government.* London: Hodder and Stoughton, 1975 .

Casey, James. *Constitutional Law in Ireland,* 2nd ed. London: Sweet & Maxwell, 1992.

Castles, Alex C. *An Australian Legal History*. Sydney: Law Book Co., 1982.

Challinor, Raymond. *A Radical Lawyer in Victorian England: W. P. Roberts and the Struggle for Workers' Rights*. London: I. B. Tauris, 1990.

Chapin, Bradley. *The American Law of Treason: Revolutionary and Early National Origins*. Seattle: University of Washington Press, 1964.

Chester, Daniel N. *The English Administrative System, 1780–1870*. Oxford: Clarendon Press, 1981.

_____ . *The Organization of British Central Government, 1914–1964*, 2nd ed. London: Allen & Unwin, 1968.

Clark, J. C. D. *The Language of Liberty 1660–1832: Political Discourse and Social Dynamics in the Anglo-American World*. Cambridge: Cambridge University Press, 1994.

Clive, Eric M., and J. G. Wilson. *The Law of Husband and Wife*. Edinburgh: W. Green, 1974.

Cocks, Raymond. *The Foundations of the Modern Bar*. London: Sweet & Maxwell, 1983.

Collins, Lawrence A. *European Community Law in the United Kingdom*, 4th ed. London: Butterworths, 1990.

Connolly, S. J. *Religion, Law and Power: The Making of Protestant Ireland, 1660–1760*. Oxford: Clarendon Press, 1992.

Cooke, C. A. *Corporation, Trust and Company: An Essay in Legal History*. Cambridge, Mass: Harvard University Press, 1951.

Cornish, W. R. *Crime and Law in Nineteenth Century Britain*. Dublin: Irish Universities Press, 1978.

_____ . *The Jury*. London: Allen Lane, 1968.

Cornish, W.R., and G. deN. Clark. *Law and Society in England, 1750–1950*. London: Sweet & Maxwell, 1989.

Cosgrove, Richard A. *Our Lady the Common Law: An Anglo-American Legal Community, 1870–1930*. New York: New York University Press, 1987.

_____ . *The Rule of Law: Albert Venn Dicey, Victorian Jurist.* Chapel Hill: University of North Carolina Press, 1980.

Cox, Andrew. *Adversary Politics and Land: The Conflict over Land and Property Policy in Postwar Britain.* Cambridge: Cambridge University Press, 1984.

Cross, Rupert. *Precedent in English Law*, 4th ed. Ed. J. W. Harris. Oxford: Clarendon Press, 1991.

_____ . *Statutory Interpretation.*, 2nd ed. Eds. J. Bell and G. Engle. London: Sweet & Maxwell, 1987.

Crossman, Virginia. *Politics, Law and Order in Nineteenth Century Ireland.* New York: St. Martin's Press, 1996.

Dawson, J. P. *The Oracles of the Law.* Ann Arbor: University of Michigan Law School, 1968.

Delaney, V. T. H. *The Administration of Justice in Ireland*, 3rd ed. Dublin: Institute of Public Administration, 1970.

Dell, Susanne. *Murder into Manslaughter: The Diminished Responsibility Defence in Practice.* Oxford: Oxford University Press, 1984.

Denning, Alfred. *Borrowing from Scotland.* Glasgow: Jackson, Son, 1963.

Dickson, Brice. *The Legal System of Northern Ireland*, 2nd ed. Belfast: SLS Legal Publications, 1989.

Dold, Gilbert W. F. *The Union of South Africa: The Development of Its Laws and Constitution.* London: Stevens, 1955.

Donaldson, A. G. *Some Comparative Aspects of Irish Law.* Durham: Duke University Press, 1957.

Douglas, Roy. *Land, People and Politics: A History of the Land Question in the United Kingdom, 1878–1952.* London: Allison and Busby, 1976.

Drudy, P. J., and Dermot McAleese, eds. *Ireland and the European Community.* Cambridge: Cambridge University Press, 1984.

Duman, Daniel. *The English and Colonial Bars in the Nineteenth Century.* London: Croom Helm, 1983.

_____ . *The Judicial Bench in England, 1727–1875: The Reshaping of a Professional Elite.* London: Royal Historical Society, 1982.

Dummett, Ann, and Andrew Nicol. *Subjects, Citizens, Aliens and Others: Nationality and Immigration Law.* London: Weidenfeld and Nicolson, 1990.

Easton, S. M. *The Right to Silence.* Aldershot: Avebury, 1991

Eltis, David, and James Walvin, eds. *The Abolition of the Atlantic Slave Trade.* Madison: University of Wisconsin Press, 1981.

Elton, G. R. *F. W. Maitland.* New Haven: Yale University Press, 1985.

Emsley, Clive. *Crime and Society in England, 1750–1900.* London: Longman, 1987.

_____ . *The English Police: A Political and Social History.* New York: St. Martin's Press, 1991.

_____ . *Policing and Its Context.* New York: Schocken Books, 1983.

Farmer, J. A. *Tribunals and Government.* London:Weidenfeld and Nicolson, 1974.

Farmer, Lindsay. *Criminal Law, Tradition and Legal Order: Crime and the Genius of Scots Law, 1747 to the Present.* Cambridge: Cambridge University Press, 1997.

Farrar, John H. *Law Reform and the Law Commission.* London: Sweet & Maxwell, 1974.

Feldman, David. *Human Rights and Civil Liberties in England and Wales.* Oxford: Oxford University Press, 1991.

Fifoot, C. H. S. *Frederic William Maitland: A :Life.* Cambridge MA: Harvard University Press, 1971.

_____ . *Judge and Jurist in the Reign of Victoria.* London: Stevens, 1959.

Finn, John E. *Constitutions in Crisis: Political Violence and the Rule of Law.* New York: Oxford University Press, 1991.

Flaherty, David H., ed. *Essays in the History of Early American Law.* Chapel Hill: University of North Carolina Press, 1969.

Foster, Elizabeth Read. *The House of Lords, 1603–1649: Structure, Procedure and the Nature of Its Business.* Chapel Hill: University of North Carolina Press, 1983.

Friedman, Lawrence M., and Harry N. Scheiber, eds. *American Law and the Constitutional Order: Historical Perspectives*. Cambridge, Mass: Harvard University Press, 1988.

Geary, Roger. *Policing Industrial Disputes, 1893–1985*. Cambridge: Cambridge University Press, 1985.

Gibb, Andrew Dewar. *Law from Over the Border: A Short Account of a Strange Jurisdiction*. Edinburgh: W. Green, 1950.

Gledhill, Alan. *The Republic of India: The Development of Its Laws and Constitution*, 2nd ed. London: Stevens, 1964.

Gloag, W. M., and R. C. Henderson. *Introduction to the Law of Scotland*, 8th ed. Edinburgh: Green, 1980.

Gordon, Gerald H. *The Criminal Law of Scotland*, 2nd ed. Edinburgh: W. Green, 1978.

Gordon, William M. *Scottish Land Law*. Edinburgh: W. Green, 1989.

Gow, J. J. *The Mercantile and Industrial Law of Scotland*. Edinburgh: W. Green, 1964.

Grant, John, ed. *Independence and Devolution: The Legal Implications for Scotland*. Edinburgh: W. Green, 1976.

Green, Thomas A. *Twelve Good Men and True: The Criminal Trial Jury in England, 1200–1800*. Princeton: Princeton University Press, 1988.

_____ . *Verdict According to Conscience: Perspectives on the English Criminal Trial Jury, 1200–1800*. Chicago: University of Chicago Press, 1985.

Greene, Jack P. *Peripheries and Center: Constitutional Development in the Extended Polities of the British Empire and the United States, 1607–1788*. Athens: University of Georgia Press, 1986.

Griffith, J. A. G. *The Politics of the Judiciary*. Manchester: Manchester University Press, 1977.

_____ . *Judicial Politics since 1920: A Chronicle*. Oxford: Blackwell, 1993.

Grossman, George S. *Legal Research: Historical Foundations of the Electronic Age*. New York, Oxford: University Press, 1994.

Hall, Kermit C. *The Magic Mirror: Law in American History*. New York: Oxford University Press, 1989.

Hanes, David G. *The First British Workmen's Compensation Act, 1897*. New Haven: Yale University Press, 1968.

Hannay, Robert. *The College of Justice. Essays*. Edinburgh: Scottish Academic Press for the Stair Society, 1990.

Harden, Ian, and Norman Lewis. *The Noble Lie: The British Constitution and the Rule of Law*. London: Hutchinson, 1986.

Harding, A. J. *Public Duties and Public Law*. Oxford: Clarendon Press, 1989.

Harrison, Brian. *Separate Spheres: Opposition to Women's Suffrage, 1867–1928*. London: Croom Helm, 1978.

Hart, James S. *Justice Upon Petition: The House of Lords and the Reformation of Justice, 1621–1675*. London: HarperCollins Academic, 1991.

Hartley, T. C. *Civil Jurisdiction and Judgments*. London: Sweet & Maxwell, 1984.

Hay, Douglas, and Francis Snyder, eds. *Policing and Prosecution in Britain, 1750–1850*. Oxford: Clarendon Press, 1989.

Hepple, B. A. et al. *Labour Law in Great Britain and Ireland to 1978*. London: Sweet & Maxwell, 1981.

Heuston, R. F. V. *Lives of the Lord Chancellors, 1885–1970*. 2 vols. Oxford: Clarendon Press, 1964–1987.

Hewitt, Patricia. *The Abuse of Power: Civil Liberties in the United Kingdom*. Oxford: Martin Robertson, 1982.

Hillyard, Paddy. *Suspect Community: The People's Experience of the Prevention of Terrorism Acts in Britain*. London: Pluto Press, 1993.

Hoffer, Peter Charles. *Law and People in Colonial America*. Rev. ed. Baltimore: Johns Hopkins University Press, 1998.

Hogan, Daire. *The Legal Profession in Ireland, 1789–1922*. Dublin: Incorporated Law Society of Ireland, 1986.

Hogan, Daire, and W. N. Osborough, eds. *Brehons, Serjeants and Attorneys: Studies in the Irish Legal Profession*. Blackrock: Irish Academic Press, 1990.

Hogan, Gerard, and Clive Walker. *Political Violence and the Law in Ireland*. Manchester: Manchester University Press, 1989.

Holdsworth, William S. *A History of English Law*, 7th ed. 16 vols. A. L. Goodhart and H. G. Hanbury eds. London: Methuen, 1956–1966.

Holmes, Geoffrey S. *The Trial of Doctor Sacheverell*. London: Methuen, 1973.

Hooker, M. B. *Legal Pluralism: An Introduction to Colonial and Neo-Colonial Laws* Oxford: Clarendon Press, 1975.

Hoppen, K. Theodore. *Elections, Politics and Society in Ireland, 1832–1885*. Oxford: Clarendon Press, 1984.

Horstman, Allen. *Victorian Divorce*. New York: St. Martin's Press, 1985.

Horwitz, Morton. *The Transformation of American Law, 1780-1860*. Cambridge, MA: Harvard University Press, 1977.

Howell, David. *Land and People in Nineteenth Century Wales*. London: Routledge and Kegan Paul, 1977.

Howell, P. A. *The Judicial Committee of the Privy Council, 1833–1876*. Cambridge: Cambridge University Press, 1979.

Hughes, Hector. *National Sovereignty and Judicial Autonomy in the British Commonwealth of Nations*. London: P. King, 1931.

Hunter, James. *The Making of the Crofting Community*. Edinburgh: Donald, 1976.

Hurlburt, W. H. *Law Reform Commissions in the United Kingdom, Australia and Canada*. Edmonton: Juriliber, 1986.

Hurst, J. Willard. *Growth of American Law: The Law Makers*. Boston: Little, Brown, 1950.

Inglis, Tom. *Moral Monopoly: The Catholic Church in Modern Irish Society*. Dublin: Gill, 1987.

Jackson, John, and Sean Doran. *Judge Without Jury: Diplock Trials in the Adversary System*. Oxford: Clarendon Press, 1995.

Jeffery, Keith, and Peter Hennessy. *States of Emergency: British Governments and Strikebreaking since 1919*. London: Routledge and Kegan Paul, 1983.

Jennings, Sir Ivor. *Constitutional Laws of the Commonwealth*, 2nd ed. Oxford: Clarendon Press, 1952.

Jones, Clyve, ed. *A Pillar of the Constitution: The House of Lords in British Politics, 1603–1784*. Hambledon Press, 1989.

Jowell, Jeffrey, and Dawn Oliver, eds. *The Changing Constitution*, 2nd ed. Oxford: Clarendon Press, 1989.

Keeton, George W., ed. *The United Kingdom: The Development of Its Laws and Constitutions*. 2 vols. London: Stevens, 1955.

_____ . *English Law: The Judicial Contribution*. Newton Abbot: David & Charles, 1974.

Keith, A. B. *The Government of the British Empire*. New York: Macmillan, 1935.

Kelly. J. M. *Fundamental Rights in the Irish Law and Constitution*, 2nd ed. New York: Oceana, 1968.

Kenny, Colum. *King's Inns and the Kingdom of Ireland*. Blackrock: Irish Academic Press, 1992.

_____ . *Tristram Kennedy and the Revival of Irish Legal Training, 1835–1885*. Blackrock: Irish Academic Press, 1996.

Kent, Susan. *Sex and Suffrage in Britain, 1860–1914*. Princeton: Princeton University Press, 1987.

Kiralfy, Albert, and Hector L. MacQueen, eds. *New Perspectives on Scottish Legal History*. London: Frank Cass, 1985.

Kirk, Harry. *Portrait of a Profession: A History of the Solicitors' Profession, 1100 to the Present Day*. London: Oyez, 1976.

Knafla, Louis A. *Law and Politics in Jacobean England*. Cambridge Studies in English Legal History. Cambridge: Cambridge University Press, 1977.

Kostal, R. W. *Law and English Railway Capitalism, 1825–1875*. Oxford: Clarendon Press, 1994.

Kotsonouris, Mary. *Retreat from Revolution: the Dáil Courts, 1920–1924*. Blackrock: Irish Academic Press, 1994.

Lambert, Sheila. *Bills and Acts: Legislative Procedure in Eighteenth-Century England*. Cambridge: Cambridge University Press, 1971.

Langford, Paul. *Public Life and the Propertied Englishman, 1689–1798*. Oxford: Clarendon Press, 1991.

Lasok, Dominik, and J. W. Bridge. *Law and Institutions of the European Communities*, 5th ed. London: Butterworths, 1991.

Lawson, Philip, ed. *Parliament and the Atlantic Empire*. Edinburgh: Edinburgh University Press, 1995.

The Laws of Scotland. Stair Memorial Encyclopedia. 25 vols. The Law Society of Scotland. Edinburgh: Butterworths, 1987–1996.

Lemmings, David. *Gentlemen and Barristers: The Inns of Court and the English Bar, 1680–1730*. Oxford: Clarendon Press, 1990.

Leneman, Leah. *Fit for Heroes? Land Settlement in Scotland after World War I*. Aberdeen: Aberdeen University Press, 1989.

Lester, V. Markham. *Victorian Insolvency: Bankruptcy, Inprisonment for Debt, and Company Winding-up in Nineteenth Century England*. Oxford: Clarendon Press, 1995.

Levack, Brian P. *The Formation of the British State: England, Scotland and the Union, 1603-1707*. Oxford: Clarendon Press, 1987.

Lieberman, David. *The Province of Legislation Determined: Legal Theory in Eighteenth-century Britain*. Cambridge: Cambridge University Press, 1989.

Lobban, Michael. *The Common Law and English Jurisprudence, 1760–1850*. Oxford: Clarendon Press, 1991.

Lutz, Donald S. *The Origins of American Constitutionalism*. Baton Rouge: Louisiana State University Press, 1988.

Lyall, Francis. *Of Presbyters and Kings: Church and State in the Law of Scotland*. Aberdeen: Aberdeen University Press, 1980.

McBride, Lawrence W. *The Greening of Dublin Castle: The Transformation of Bureaucratic and Judicial Personnel in Ireland, 1892–1922*. Washington, DC: Catholic University of America Press, 1991.

McConville, Michael. *Courts, Prosecution and Conviction*. Oxford: Clarendon Press, 1981.

MacGregor, O. R. *Social History and Law Reform*. London: Stevens, 1980.

Macleod, Christine. *Inventing the Industrial Revolution: The English Patent System, 1660–1800*. Cambridge: Cambridge University Press, 1988.

McNair, Arnold Duncan, Baron. *The Legal Effects of War,* 4th ed. Cambridge: Cambridge University Press, 1966.

Malcolm, Joyce Lee. *To Keep and Bear Arms: The Origin of an Anglo-American Right.* Cambridge, MA: Harvard University Press, 1994.

Manchester, A. H. *A Modern Legal History of England and Wales, 1750–1950* . London: Butterworths, 1980.

Markesinis, B. S. ed. *The Gradual Convergence: Foreign Ideas, Foreign Influences and English Law on the Eve of the 21st Century.* Oxford: Clarendon Press, 1994.

Marshall, Enid. *General Principles of Scots Law,* 5th ed. Edinburgh: W. Green, 1991.

Marshall, Rosalind K. *Virgins and Viragos: A History of Women in Scotland From 1080 to 1980.* London: Collins, 1983.

Martin, Ged. *Britain and the Origins of the Canadian Confederation, 1837–1867.* Basingstoke: Macmillan, 1995.

May, Henry John. *The South African Constitution,* 3rd ed. Capetown: Juta, 1955.

Megarry, R. E., and H. W. R. Wade. *The Law of Real Property,* 5th ed. London: Sweet & Maxwell, 1984.

Meston, M. C., W. D. H. Sellar, and Lord Cooper. *The Scottish Legal Tradition,* new ed. Edinburgh: The Saltire Society and the Stair Society, 1991.

Milsom, S. F. C. *Historical Foundations of the Common Law,* 2nd ed. London: Butterworths, 1981.

Mitchell, J. D. B. *Constitutional Law.* Edinburgh: Scottish Universities Law Institute, 1968.

Moran, Clarence G. *The Heralds of the Law.* London: Stevens, 1948.

Morgan, Edmund Sears. *Inventing the People: The Rise of Popular Sovereignty in England and America.* New York: Norton, 1988.

Morgan, Jane. *Conflict and Order: The Police and Labour Disputes in England and Wales, 1900–1939.* Oxford: Clarendon Press, 1987.

Mulholland, R. D. *Introduction to the New Zealand Legal System.* Auckland: Butterworths, 1972.

Nenner, Howard A. *By Colour of Law: Legal Culture and Constitutional Politics in England, 1660–1689.* Chicago: University of Chicago Press, 1977.

New Ireland Forum. *The Legal Systems, North and South.* Dublin: Stationery Office, 1983.

Norton, Mary Beth. *The British-Americans: The Loyalist Exiles in England, 1774–1789.* Boston: Little, Brown, 1972.

Ockrent, Lewis. *Land Rights: An Enquiry into the History of Registration for Publication in Scotland.* London: Hodge, 1942.

Offer, Avner. *Property and Politics, 1870–1914: Landownership, Law, Ideology and Urban Development in England.* Cambridge: Cambridge University Press, 1981.

O'Leary, Cornelius. *The Elimination of Corrupt Practices in British Elections, 1868–1911.* Oxford: Clarendon Press, 1962.

Orth, John V. *Combination and Conspriacy: A Legal History of Trade Unionism, 1721–1906.* Oxford: Clarendon Press, 1991.

Osborough, W. N. *Law and the Emergence of Modern Dublin.* Blackrock: Irish Academic Press, 1996.

Palmer, Stanley H. *Police and Protest in England and Ireland, 1780–1850.* Cambridge: Cambridge University Press, 1988.

Pannick, David. *Judges.* Oxford: Oxford University Press, 1987.

Parry, Clive. *Nationality and Citizenship Laws of the Commonwealth and of the Republic of Ireland.* 2 vols. London: Stevens, 1957.

Paterson, Alan. *The Law Lords.* Toronto: University of Toronto Press, 1982.

Patfield, Fiona, and Robin White eds. *Changing Law.* Leicester: Leicester University Press, 1990.

Pattenden, Rosemary. *English Criminal Appeals, 1844–1994: Appeals Against Conviction and Sentence in England and Wales.* Oxford: Clarendon Press, 1996.

Pawlisch, Hans S. *Sir John Davies and the Conquest of Ireland: A Study in Legal Imperialism.* Cambridge: Cambridge University Press, 1985.

Pencak, William and Wythe W. Holt, Jr., eds. *The Law in America, 1607–1861.* New York: New York Historical Society, 1989.

Phillips, Owen Hood. *Reform of the Constitution*. London: Charles Knight, 1970.

Phillipson, Nicholas T. *The Scottish Whigs and the Reform of the Court of Session, 1785–1830*. Edinburgh: Stair Society, 1990.

Pocock, J. G. A. *The Ancient Constitution and the Feudal Law. A Reissue with a Retrospect*. Cambridge: Cambridge University Press, 1987.

Power, T. P., and Kevin Whelan, eds. *Endurance and Emergence: Catholics in Ireland in the Eighteenth Century*. Dublin: Irish Academic Press, 1990.

Prall, Stuart. *The Agitation for Law Reform during the Puritan Revolution, 1640-1660*. The Hague: Martinus Nijhoff, 1966.

Quinn, Sean E. *Criminal Law in Ireland*, 2nd ed. Killarney: Irish Law Publishing, 1993.

Radzinowicz, Sir Leon. *A History of English Criminal Law and its Administration*.(with Roger Hood). 5 vols. Oxford: Clarendon Press, 1948–1986.

Reid, John Philip. *Constitutional History of the American Revolution*. 4 vols. Madison: University of Wisconsin Press, 1986–1993.

______ . *In a Defiant Stance: The Conditions of Law in Massachusetts Bay, the Irish Comparison, and the Coming of the American Revolution*. University Park: Pennsylvania State University Press, 1977.

Reid, Madeleine. *The Impact of Community Law on the Irish Constitution*. Dublin: Irish Centre for European Law, 1990.

Richardson, H. G., and G. O. Sayles. *Law and Legislation from Aethelberht to Magna Carta*. Edinburgh: University Press, 1966.

Robertson, Geoffrey. *Freedom, the Individual and the Law*. London: Penguin Books, 1993.

Roberts-Wray, Kenneth O. *Commonwealth and Colonial Law*. London: Stevens, 1966.

Robson, William A. *Justice and Administrative Law: A Study of the British Constitution.*, 3rd ed. London: Stevens and Sons, 1951.

Rodes, Robert E. Jr. *Law and Modernization of the Church in England: Charles II to the Welfare State*. South Bend: University of Notre Dame Press, 1991.

Roeber, A. G. *Faithful Magistrates and Republican Lawyers: Creators of Virginia Legal Culture, 1680–1810*. Chapel Hill: University of North Carolina Press, 1981.

Ross, Ian Simpson. *Lord Kames and the Scotland of His Day.* Oxford: Clarendon Press, 1972.

Rubin, Gerry R. *Private Property, Government Requisition and the Constitution, 1914–1927.* London: Hambledon Press, 1994.

_____ . *War, Law and Labour: The Munitions Acts, State Regulation, and the Unions, 1915–1921.* Oxford: Clarendon Press, 1987.

Rubin, Gerry R., and David Sugarman, eds. *Law, Economy and Society: Essays in the History of English Law, 1750–1914.* Abingdon: Professional Books, 1984.

Rudé, George. *Criminal and Victim: Crime and Society in Early Nineteenth Century England.* Oxford: Clarendon Press, 1985.

Sainty, J. C. *The Judges of England, 1272–1990: A List of Judges of the Superior Courts.* London: Selden Society, 1993.

Scarman, Leslie. *Law Reform: The New Pattern.* London: Routledge & Kegan Paul, 1968.

Schwoerer, Lois G. *"No Standing Armies!" The Antiarmy Ideology in Seventeenth Century England.* Baltimore: Johns Hopkins University Press, 1974.

Searle, G. R. *Corruption in British Politics, 1895–1930.* Oxford: Clarendon Press, 1987.

Shanley, Mary L. *Feminism, Marriage and the Law in Victorian England, 1850–1895.* Princeton: Princeton University Press, 1989.

Shapiro, Barbara. *Probability and Certainty in Seventeenth Century England: A Study of the Relationship between Natural Science, Religion, History, Law and Literature.* Princeton: Princeton University Press, 1983.

Shatter, Alan J. *Family Law in the Republic of Ireland.* Portmarnock: Wolfhound Press, 1980.

Shaw, John S. *The Management of Scottish Society, 1707–1764: Power, Nobles,Lawyers, Edinburgh Agents, and English Influences.* Edinburgh: John Donald, 1983.

Simms, J. G. *The Williamite Confiscation in Ireland, 1690–1703.* London: Faber, 1956.

_____ . *William Molyneux of Dublin, 1656–1698.* Dublin: Irish Academic Press, 1982.

Simpson, A.W.B. *A History of the Common Law of Contract: The Rise of Assumpsit.* Oxford: Clarendon Press, 1975.

_____ . *In the Highest Degree Odious: Detention Without Trial in Wartime Britain.* Oxford: Clarendon Press, 1993.

_____ . *An Introduction to the History of the Land Law.* Oxford: Oxford University Press, 1979 .

_____ . *Leading Cases in the Common Law.* Oxford: Clarendon Press, 1995.

Simpson, S. Rowton. *Land Law and Registration.* Cambridge: Cambridge University Press, 1976.

Smith, Annette M. *The Jacobite Estates of the Forty-Five.* Edinburgh: John Donald, 1982.

Smith, Joseph Henry. *Appeals to the Privy Council from the American Plantations.* New York: Columbia University Press, 1950.

Smith, Thomas Broun. *British Justice: The Scottish Contribution.* Edinburgh: W. Green, 1961.

_____ . *The Doctrines of Judicial Precedent in Scots Law.* Edinburgh: W. Green, 1952.

_____ . *A Short Commentary on the Law of Scotland.* Edinburgh: W. Green, 1962.

_____ . *Studies Critical and Comparative.* Edinburgh: W. Green, 1962.

Spencer, J. R. *Jackson's Machinery of Justice,* 8th ed. Cambridge: Cambridge University Press, 1989.

Spring, Eileen. *Law, Land and Family: Aristocratic Inheritance in England, 1300 to 1800.* Chapel Hill: University of North Carolina Press, 1993.

Stanley, George F. G. *A Short History of the Canadian Constitution.* Toronto: Ryerson Press, 1969.

Steele, E. D. *Irish Land and British Politics: Tenant-Right and Nationality, 1865–1870* Cambridge: Cambridge University Press, 1974.

Stetson, Dorothy. *A Woman's Issue: The Politics of Family Law Reform in England.* Westport, CT: Greenwood Press, 1982.

Stevens, Robert. *Law and Politics: The House of Lords as a Judicial Body, 1800–1976.* Chapel Hill: University of North Carolina Press, 1978.

Stone, Lawrence. *Road to Divorce: England, 1530–1987.* Oxford: Oxford University Press, 1990.

Stout, Ronald M. *Administrative Law in Ireland.* Dublin: Institute of Public Administration, 1985.

Strayer, Barry L. *The Canadian Constitution and the Courts: The Function and Scope of Judicial Review*, 3rd ed. Toronto: Butterworths, 1988.

Supperstone, Michael. *Judicial Review.* London: Butterworths, 1992.

Swatland, Andrew. *The House of Lords in the Reign of Charles II.* New York: Cambridge University Press, 1996.

Swinfen, D. B. *Imperial Appeal: The Debate on the Appeal to the Privy Council, 1833–1985.* Manchester: Manchester University Press, 1987.

_____ . *Imperial Control of Colonial Legislation, 1813–1865: A Study of British Policy Toward Colonial Legislative Powers.* Oxford: Clarendon Press, 1970.

Thomas, P. D. G. *British Politics and the Stamp Act Crisis.* Oxford: Clarendon Press, 1975.

_____. *The House of Commons in the Eighteenth Century.* Oxford: Oxford University Press, 1971.

Thompson, Edward P. *Whigs and Hunters: The Origins of the Black Act.* Harmondsworth: Penguin Books, 1990.

Townshend, Charles. *Britain's Civil Wars: Counter-Insurgency in the Twentieth Century.* London: Faber and Faber, 1986.

_____ . *Making the Peace: Public Order and Public Security in Modern Britain.* Oxford: Oxford University Press, 1993.

_____ . *Political Violence in Ireland: Government and Resistance since 1848.* Oxford: Clarendon Press, 1983.

Trakman, Leon E. *The Law Merchant: The Evolution of Commercial Law.* Littleton, CO: Rothman, 1983.

Turberville, A. S. *The House of Lords in the Reign of William III.* Oxford: Clarendon Press, 1913.

Vaughan, William E. *Landlords and Tenants in Mid-Victorian Ireland.* Oxford: Oxford University Press, 1994.

Veall, Donald. *The Popular Movement for Law Reform, 1640-1660.* Oxford: Clarendon Press, 1970.

Vogler, Richard. *Reading the Riot Act: The Magistracy, the Police and the Army in Civil Disorder.* Milton Keynes: Open University Press, 1991.

Walker, David M. *The Law of Contracts and Related Obligations in Scotland,* 3rd ed. Edinburgh: T & T Clark, 1995.

_____ . *The Oxford Companion to Law.* Oxford: Clarendon Press, 1980.

_____. *The Scottish Jurists.* Edinburgh: W. Green 1985.

_____ . *The Scottish Legal System: An Introduction to the Study of Scots Law,* 6th ed. Edinburgh: W. Green, 1992.

Walker, Nigel. *Crime and Insanity in England.* 2 vols. Edinburgh: Edinburgh University Press, 1968–1973.

Wall, Maureen. *The Penal Laws, 1691–1760.* Dundalk: Dublin Historical Association, 1961.

Ward, Alan J. *The Irish Constitutional Tradition: Responsible Government and Modern Ireland, 1782–1992.* Washington, DC: Catholic University of America Press, 1994.

Watson, Alan. *Legal Transplants: An Approach to Comparative Law* Charlottesville: University of Virginia Press, 1974.

_____ . *The Making of the Civil Law.* Cambridge, MA: Harvard University Press, 1981.

_____. *Sources of Law, Legal Change and Ambiguity.* Edinburgh: T. & T. Clark, 1985.

Weston, Corinne C. *English Constitutional Theory and the House of Lords, 1556–1832.* London: Routledge & Kegan Paul, 1965.

Weston, Corinne C., and Janelle R. Greenberg. *Subjects and Sovereigns: The Grand Controversy over Legal Sovereignty in Stuart England* Oxford: University Press, 1980.

Wharam, Alan. *The Treason Trials, 1794*. Leicester: Leicester University Press, 1992.

White, Robin C. A. *The Administration of Justice*, 2nd ed. Oxford: Blackwell, 1991.

White, Robin M., and Ian Willock. *The Scottish Legal System*. Edinburgh: Butterworths, 1993.

Wiener, Frederick B. *Civilians under Military Justice*. Chicago: University of Chicago Press, 1967.

Wight, Martin. *The Development of the Legislative Council, 1606–1945*. London: Faber and Faber, 1946.

Willock, I. D. *The Origins and Development of the Jury in Scotland*. Edinburgh: Stair Society, 1966.

Wilson, W. A. *Introductory Essays on Scots Law*, 2nd ed. Edinburgh: W. Green, 1984.

Windlesham, David, Baron. *Responses to Crime*. 3 vols. Oxford: Clarendon Press, 1987–1996.

Woffinden, Bob. *Miscarriages of Justice*. London: Hodder & Stoughton, 1987.

Wraith, Ronald E., and P. G. Hutchesson. *Administrative Tribunals*. London: Allen & Unwin, 1973.

Wylie, J. C. W. *Irish Land Law*, 2nd ed. Abingdon: Professional Books, 1986.

Index

A

B

D

E

F

G

H

N

O

P

T

U

V

W

Y

Studies in Modern European History

The monographs in this series focus upon aspects of the political, social, economic, cultural, and religious history of Europe from the Renaissance to the present. Emphasis is placed on the states of Western Europe, especially Great Britain, France, Italy, and Germany. While some of the volumes treat internal developments, others deal with movements such as liberalism, socialism, and industrialization, which transcend a particular country.

The series editor is:

Frank J. Coppa
Director, Doctor of Arts Program
in Modern World History
Department of History
St. John's University
Jamaica, New York 11439

To order other books in this series, please contact our Customer Service Department:

(800) 770-LANG (within the U.S.)
(212) 647-7706 (outside the U.S.)
(212) 647-7707 FAX

or browse online by series at:
WWW.PETERLANG.COM

For the avoidance of doubt, input of the whole or any part of this publication into any generative artificial intelligence model, chatbot, program, software or technology is expressly prohibited without the prior written consent of the publisher.